Welcome back to Camden Market!

Megan McGregor

- 12 years old
- sees her dad at the weekend or in the holidays
- has got a half brother, Fergus (3)
- has got a dog, Sir Barks-A-Lot
- likes rugby and animals

Sandeep Chopra

- 12 years old
- family is from India
- parents have got a shop
- has got a sister, Neela (7) and a brother, Pradeep (9)
- likes music and football

Jasmine Bolt

- 12 years old
- her dad's family is from the Bahamas
- has got a brother, Jason (15)
- has got a cat, Bagheera and a guinea pig, Baloo
- likes basketball and taking photos

Ben Hancock

- 13 years old
- has got two sisters, Sarah (14) and Emma (16) and a brother, Steven (17)
- has got two budgies, A and B
- likes drawing and computers

R = *revision* (Wiederholung)

INHALT

R = *revision* (Wiederholung)

Die Angebote in *Camden Market* sind nicht linear abzuarbeiten.
Die Auswahl richtet sich nach den Schwerpunkten des schulinternen Curriculums.

INHALT

Die Angebote in *Camden Market* sind nicht linear abzuarbeiten.
Die Auswahl richtet sich nach den Schwerpunkten des schulinternen Curriculums.

Zusätzliches Online-Material zum Buch kann über die Eingabe des jeweiligen Webcodes auf **www.westermann.de/webcode** abgerufen werden. Dazu zählen folgende Angebote:

- **Medienbildung**: Dieses Symbol zeigt Aufgaben an, in denen Medienkompetenz aufgebaut wird, und es verweist auf passende Arbeitsblätter zum Download (WEB 1). Weitere, vertiefende Übungsblätter zur Medienbildung finden sich unter www.westermann.de/medienbildung.
  Webcode: **WES-149119-001**
- **Grammatik-Videos**: Zu ausgewählten Grammatikthemen gibt es kurze Erklärvideos auf der DVD und online. Hinweise auf diese Videos (14, WEB 7) befinden sich im *Grammar*-Teil.
  Webcode: **WES-149119-002**
- **Portfolio-Fragebögen**: Die Fragebögen aus dem Workbook zur Überprüfung des Lernfortschritts gibt es auch online. Hinweise darauf stehen an der Target Task am Ende eines *Themes* (WEB P1).
  Webcode: **WES-149119-003**

Zu diesem Band gibt es ein passgenaues **Arbeitsbuch Inklusion** als alternatives Angebot zum Schülerbuch.

Aufbau der *Themes*

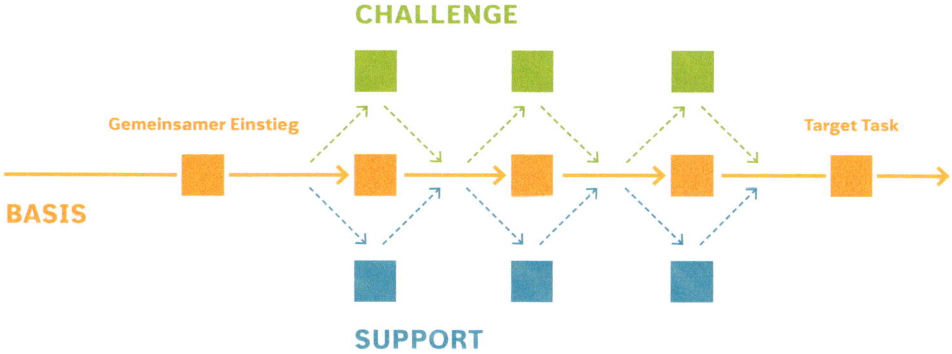

Der Basis-Teil erfüllt die Grundanforderungen für Klasse 6 und ist Start- und Zielpunkt für alle. An geeigneten Stellen können die Schülerinnen und Schüler in den *Support*- bzw. *Challenge*-Teil aussteigen, wo sie parallele und zusätzliche Aufgaben als Unterstützung bzw. als Herausforderung vorfinden. Am Ende jedes Themenkreises schließen alle Schülerinnen und Schüler gemeinsam mit der *Target task* ab.

Symbole

Differenzierungssymbole und -verweise stehen in der **Randspalte**:

1c p. 29

Hierfür gibt es eine einfachere passgenaue Parallelaufgabe im *Support*-Teil.

5c p. 34

Hierfür gibt es eine schwierigere passgenaue Parallelaufgabe im *Challenge*-Teil.

3.1 p. 31

Hierfür gibt es eine zusätzliche unterstützende Aufgabe im *Support*-Teil.

3.1 p. 33

Hierfür gibt es eine zusätzliche herausfordernde Aufgabe im *Challenge*-Teil.

Die Krone kennzeichnet schwierige Texte und Aufgaben im *Challenge*-Teil.

Verweise auf den Anhang stehen in der **Fußzeile**:

Skills Listen | p. 233

Grammar **5** | p. 248

Wordbank Free time | p. 214

Verweise auf andere Materialien stehen **hinter den Aufgabentiteln** bzw. **Aufgabenstellungen**:

L 1.8

6

WB **2** p. 10

Portfolio-Ordner

Das Symbol kennzeichnet Aufgaben zur **Medienbildung**, in denen Medienkompetenzen aufgebaut werden oder zu denen es online vertiefende Arbeitsblätter gibt.

Theme 1

After the holidays

In diesem *Theme* ...

- übst du, über deine Ferien und die Ferien anderer zu berichten.
- lernst du die Landesteile Großbritanniens kennen.
- findest du Unterschiede und Gemeinsamkeiten von britischen und deutschen Schulen heraus.
- stellst du deine Schule vor.

1 Megan's holidays WB 1 + 2 p. 6

a) Look at the pictures. What can you see?

b) Read what Megan says about her holidays. Where did she go?

First Megan went to … and then to …

c) Listen to Megan. What else do you learn about her holidays? L 1.1

Megan and her dad went	some German kids.
It was	to the cinema.
In Spain Megan met	a nice party on the beach.
They had	cold and rainy in London.

2 My holidays WB 3 + 4 p. 7

Talk to a partner about your holidays.

My holidays were great / boring / …

I was in … / I was at home.

The weather was good / bad / …

I/We played …

I/We visited …

What about your holidays?

2: Grammar 5 | p. 246, 4 | p. 245
2: Skills Milling around | p. 238
2: Wordbank Free time | p. 209
Travelling | p. 212

3 Back home WB 5 p. 8

a) Look at the title and the picture. What do you think Jasmine and Sandeep are talking about?

b) Listen and read along. Were you right in a)? L 1.2

Jasmine: Hello Sandeep. How are you?
Sandeep: Oh, hi Jasmine. I'm fine. How was your holiday?
Jasmine: Fantastic!
Sandeep: You went to France, right?
Jasmine: Yeah, first we went to Paris. It's a really beautiful city.
Sandeep: Did you visit the Eiffel Tower?
Jasmine: Yes, of course. We went all the way to the top and had a great view of the city. Look. That's me at the top of the Eiffel Tower.
Sandeep: Cool!
Jasmine: And look at this photo. Me and Jason were on the Atlantic coast.
Sandeep: Oh, it looks really windy there.
Jasmine: Yeah, it was windy and cloudy, but we had fun on the beach. We went swimming and played beach volleyball. Wait a minute, I've got a little present for you. Here you are.
Sandeep: Oh, wow! A mini Eiffel Tower. That's great. Thank you.
Jasmine: You're welcome. So what did you do in your holidays?
Sandeep: Well, I didn't do much. It was often cold and rainy here. So I helped my parents in the shop. And I visited my grandmother and drank tea with her.
Jasmine: Aww, that's nice! What about Megan and Ben? Did you meet them?
Sandeep: I met Ben yesterday. We went to the cinema and watched a really cool film.
Jasmine: Great! Let's phone Megan and Ben. Maybe they're free this afternoon.

3.1 p. 34

3: Skills Listen | p. 228

c) Read the dialogue again. Then look at these sentences. Are they right or wrong? Correct what's wrong.

1. Jasmine and her family went to Paris and then to the Atlantic coast.
2. You can go to the top of the Eiffel Tower.
3. It was cloudy and rainy on the beach.
4. Jasmine has got a present for Sandeep.
5. Sandeep helped his parents and visited his grandparents.
6. He went to the cinema with Megan and Ben.

d) Did YOU buy any souvenirs or presents in your holidays?

No, I didn't.

Yes, I did. I bought **a nice fridge magnet** in **Hamburg**.

4 Weather words

WB 6 p. 9

a) Match the weather words with the pictures.

windy | cold | sunny | rainy | warm | cloudy

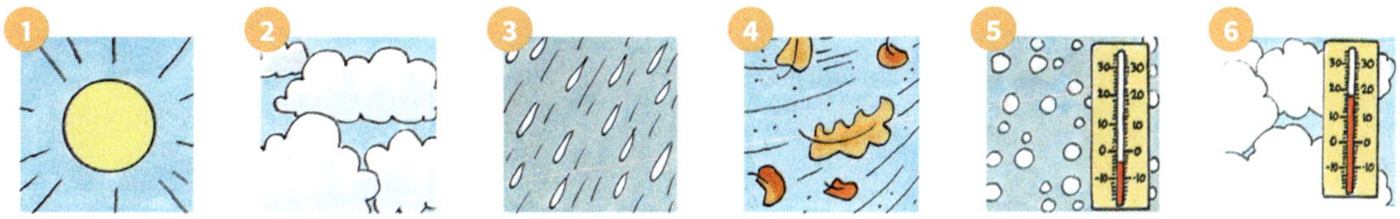

b) What other weather words do you know?

c) What is the weather like today?

It's **warm** and **sunny**.

4.1 p. 26
4.2 p. 26
4.1 p. 34
5 p. 26

5 Language detective

a) Look at the verbs in the box. Find the other forms of these verbs in number 3.

have | be (*2x*) | play | watch | do | help | drink | meet | visit | go

have – had
be – was, ...
play – ...
...

b) Be a language detective.

- Was ist mit den Verben in a) passiert?
- Wann benutzt man die neuen Verbformen?

Tausche dich mit einem Partner / einer Partnerin aus.

4: Wordbank Weather | p. 208
5: Grammar 5 | p. 246, 4 | p. 245

6 p.27

6 Ben's holidays

What did Ben do in his holidays?
Complete the sentences with verbs from the box. There are more verbs than you need.

went | drank | played | did | visited | had | watched | was | met | stayed

1. Ben was in Wales.
…

1

Ben XX in Wales.

2

He XX at a campsite.

3

He XX a castle.

4

He XX to the top of Mount Snowdon.

5

He XX dolphins.

6

He XX minigolf.

6.1 p.27

LAND & LEUTE 1

Die Britischen Inseln

Das Vereinigte Königreich Großbritannien und Nordirland (*United Kingdom of Great Britain and Northern Ireland, UK*) besteht aus England, Schottland (*Scotland*), Wales und Nordirland (*Northern Ireland*). England, Schottland und Wales liegen zusammen auf einer großen Insel (*Great Britain*). Nordirland liegt im Norden der Insel Irland (*Ireland*).
England mit der Hauptstadt London ist der größte Landesteil des Vereinigten Königreiches. Die anderen Landesteile haben auch jeweils eine Hauptstadt.
Viele Waliser sprechen neben Englisch auch Walisisch (*Welsh*). Deshalb sind in Wales auch alle Straßenschilder zweisprachig.

Schaue dir die Karte vorne im Buch an. Welche Gegend würde dich interessieren?
Sieh dir nun den Clip an und finde heraus:

- Wie heißen die Hauptstädte von Schottland, Wales und Nordirland?
- Was ist ein *kilt*?
- Wo wurde die Titanic gebaut?

6: Grammar 5 | p. 246, 4 | p. 245

7 Holidays in Wales
WB 7 p. 9

Learn more about Ben's holidays. Complete the sentences with "was" or "were".

Ben's holidays XX really good. He XX in Wales with his family. The weather XX OK. Some days XX sunny and warm, others XX windy and rainy. They stayed at a campsite in a caravan for one week. There XX lots of other nice families. In the evenings there XX always a big campfire.

7.1 p. 27

8 A postcard
8 p. 28
8 p. 35

a) Look at Ben's postcard. What differences can you find between an English and a German address?

b) Complete the postcard with the verbs in the past.

12th August

Dear Sandeep,
Wales is a cool place.
Yesterday we (visit) a famous castle.
Today we (go) to the top of Mount Snowdon. We (walk) for four hours. Sarah and my dad only (need) one hour because they (take) the Snowdon Mountain Railway.
We (be) really lucky. There (be) no clouds in the sky and we (have) a great view from the top.
Bye for now,
Ben

Sandeep Chopra
87 Camden High Street
London
NW1 0JH

Unregelmäßige Verben haben in der Vergangenheit eine eigene Form, die du lernen musst (siehe S. 334–335):
meet → *met*
take → *took*
...

7: Grammar 5 | p. 246
8: Grammar 5 | p. 246, 4 | p. 245

9 I didn't

a) Listen to the rap.
What did the boy do in the holidays? L 1.3

b) Listen to the rap again and act it out.

c) What do you think? Why did the boy not do the other things?

d) Ask and answer questions with a partner.

Did you **watch films** this summer?

Yes, I did. No, I didn't.

I didn't watch films at the cinema each day,
I didn't go out to the playground to play.

I didn't go swimming or eat ice cream a lot,
I didn't read books in a sunny spot.

I didn't play football or tennis outside,
I didn't have a picnic or go on a bike ride.

I didn't go abroad or to anywhere hot,
now that I think about it I didn't do a lot.

I didn't join a band or become a top drummer,
but man,
I played lots of computer games this summer!

9.1 p. 28

10 Holiday activities WB 8 p. 10

a) What did they do in the holidays (✓)? What didn't they do (✗)? Write about them.

Sarah

✓ go to Wales
✓ meet her friend Karla
✗ play basketball

Sarah went to Wales.
She ...
She didn't ...

Jason

✓ drink lots of lemonade
✓ take some great photos
✗ write any postcards

Sir Barks-A-Lot

✓ walk to the park
✓ play with Bagheera
✗ go to Edinburgh or Spain

Wenn du Sätze mit *didn't* (*did not*) verneinst, steht das Verb dahinter immer im Infinitiv (Grundform):
I didn't go to Spain.

b) What about YOU?

I ...
I ... but I didn't ...

10.1 p. 35

9: Grammar 6 | p. 246, 7 | p. 246
9d: Skills Double circle | p. 238
10: Grammar 6 | p. 246

11 Lynn's holiday diary WB 9 p. 10

11 p. 29
11 p. 36

In the summer holidays Jasmine's friend Lynn from Leeds went to Germany with her parents.

a) Read Lynn's holiday diary. Did she like her holiday in Germany?

Saturday 15th August

Today I arrived in Frankfurt am Main. We needed twelve hours by car to get here. I was so bored!
We are staying with my aunt and her family. They have a small flat in the city centre.
We wanted to go for a walk and see Frankfurt by night, but it started to rain and we had to stay inside.
We sat in the living room and played board games. Not my thing … So after a while I went to the kitchen with my phone and chatted with my friends.
I miss them already … I'm feeling really sad and lonely now.

Sunday 16th August

In the morning it was sunny. We hired bikes and went on a ride along the Main. My cousin came with us. He is thirteen and so nice!
We saw Frankfurt's fantastic skyscrapers.
After the ride we were really hungry. So we went to a restaurant. I had eggs with the famous Frankfurt green sauce. Yummy!
In the afternoon we went to the zoo. There weren't any elephants, but I loved the beautiful tigers.
Now I'm really tired. I wasn't sad today. I was really happy. It was a wonderful day!

b) Put the sentences in the right order.

- **A** Lynn was bored and went to the kitchen.
- **B** After the ride they had something to eat.
- **C** Lynn arrived in Frankfurt on Saturday.
- **D** Then they went to the zoo.
- **E** They stayed inside and played board games.
- **F** On Sunday morning they hired bikes.

c) Look at the diary again. How did Lynn feel …

1. when they went to Frankfurt by car?
2. at the end of their first day in Frankfurt?
3. after the ride along the Main?
4. at the end of their second day?

She felt …

d) Describe a fantastic or a boring day for YOU. What is the weather like? What do you do? How do you feel? Tell your partner.

A fantastic day is warm and … I … and …

A boring day is rainy. I …

…

11d: Wordbank Weather | p. 208
Free time | p. 209
People | p. 210

12 Word groups

a) Find the right titles for these word groups.

1. sad – tired – happy – lonely
2. aunt – cousin – mother – sister
3. play – chat – walk – visit
4. castle – zoo – beach – cinema

activities | places | family | feelings

b) Now find words for these titles: weather | food and drink | animals | …

13 Verbs, verbs, verbs

a) What are the simple past forms of these verbs? You can look at number 11 for help.

chat | be | play | love | need | come | go | have | arrive | sit

chat – chatted
be – …
…

b) Complete the sentences with the simple past forms from a).

1. We XX two days to get to Turkey by car.
2. My best friend XX with us.
3. Every day we XX breakfast in the garden.
4. Then we XX to the beach.
5. In the evening we XX games.
6. My holidays XX fantastic.

14 Choose an activity

You can:

- Make an ABC of holiday words.

A – activities, …
B – beach, …
C – camping, …
…

- Say which language the people speak in the country you went to. Do you know any words in that language? Tell your class.

I went to Spain.
In Spanish, "good morning" is "buenos días" and "hello" is "hola".

- Bring pictures or souvenirs from your holiday into class and talk about them.
"I took this photo in … It shows …"
"I bought this souvenir in … I like it because …"

13: Grammar 5 | p. 246, 4 | p. 245

15 Question time

Look at these questions and think about your answers. Then talk to a partner.

Where did you go on holiday?

I went to Hamburg/Spain/… / I stayed at home.

How did you get there?

I got there by car/ train/plane/…

Where did you stay?

We stayed in a hotel / holiday apartment / at a campsite / with some friends.

What was the weather like?

It was rainy/fantastic/…

What did you do?

I went swimming / visited a museum / played … / …

16 Target task: YOUR holidays

a) Write about your holidays. Look at number 15 for help. Add pictures or postcards, too.
Portfolio-Ordner

b) Ask a partner or your teacher to check your text. Computer programs can check texts, too. Then correct it. WEB 1

c) Present your text to your class. Read it, record it or put it up in the classroom – in a special holiday corner.

My summer holidays

I stayed at home.
The weather was hot and it didn't rain.
I often went swimming and to the skate park with my friends.
I also went on a long bike ride with my dad. That was cool.
In the last week of the holidays my grandmother visited us. I went shopping with her and she bought me a really nice T-shirt.
After that we had lots of ice cream.
My holidays were great.

15: Grammar 5 | p. 246, 7 | p. 246
15: Skills Milling around | p. 238
15: Wordbank Weather | p. 208, Free time | p. 209
Travelling | p. 212
16: Skills Write | p. 235

1 Back to school WB 10 p. 11

a) How many school words do you remember? Make a word web.

b) Now work with a partner and complete your word webs.

1.1 p. 30

c) Then sit together with another pair and compare your word webs.

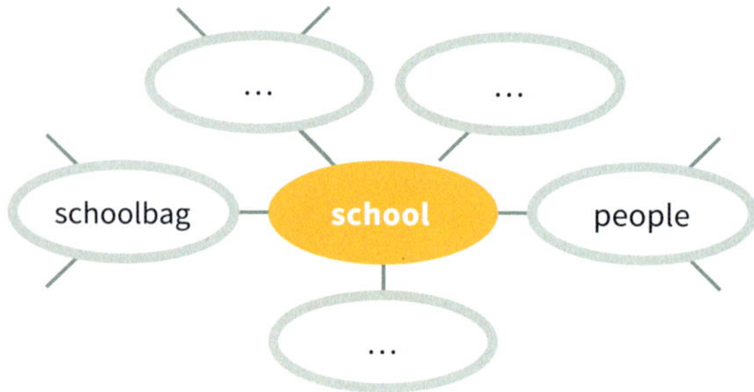

2 School poems

Read the examples. Then write YOUR school poem and present it in class.

SCHOOL
funny classmates
crazy teachers
boring biology
exciting maths
school

Pencils
and folders
and exercise books
my schoolbag is full

LAND & LEUTE ⊙ 2

Schulsystem in Großbritannien

Für britische Kinder beginnt die Schulpflicht an einer Grundschule (*primary school*), wenn sie vier oder fünf Jahre alt sind. Die *primary school* wird sieben Jahre besucht.
Anschließend geht es auf eine weiterführende Schule (*secondary school*). Die meisten Schülerinnen und Schüler besuchen dabei eine staatliche Schule, z. B. eine Gesamtschule (*comprehensive school*). Auch Haverstock ist eine Gesamtschule.
Es gibt in Großbritannien allerdings auch einige Privatschulen (*public schools*) und Internate (*boarding schools*), für die man oft eine Menge Geld bezahlen muss.

Was weißt du über das Schulsystem in Deutschland oder in anderen Ländern? Sieh dir nun den Clip an und finde heraus:
- Kann man in Großbritannien sitzenbleiben?
- Wie ist ein Schuljahr in Großbritannien unterteilt?

1: Skills Think – pair – share | p. 238
1: Wordbank At school | p. 211

3 Haverstock School WB 11 p. 11

a) Look at the information on the website. What is new or interesting to you?

Welcome to Haverstock

Haverstock School in central London is a secondary school with more than 1,000 students.

Library
The school has got a large library. It is open until 4:30 p.m. There is always a librarian to help students find the books they need.

Cafeteria
Friendly staff serve students at morning break and lunchtime. During the morning break you can buy drinks, snacks, sandwiches and fruit in the school cafeteria. At lunchtime there is also a selection of healthy meals with lots of fresh vegetables.

Sports
In the gym students can take part in basketball, indoor cricket, badminton and indoor football. There are also classes in table tennis, dance and wall climbing. There is also an outdoor basketball court.

Clubs and activities
Haverstock School offers many different clubs and activities in the morning, at lunchtime and in the afternoon, for example ICT clubs, games clubs (chess, darts, snooker) and of course many sports clubs.

Uniforms
Students have to wear school uniforms: a grey shirt with the school logo, a dark blue blazer with the school logo and a tie, black trousers (not jeans or tracksuit trousers) or a black skirt (knee length or longer). Students also have to wear black shoes.

Homework
Students use the 'Havafax' which is a personal diary and planner to note down homework and set learning goals.

b) Read the website. Can you guess the meaning of new words?
Look up words you can't guess in your dictionary (pages 289 to 315).

3b: Skills Read | p. 229
Work with words | p. 227

4 p. 30

4 Working with words

a) Put these words in alphabetical order.

library | cafeteria | fruit | vegetables | snack | meal | shirt | logo | trousers | blazer | tie | shoes

b) Match the words from a) with these adjectives:

healthy | fresh | grey | big | green | dark blue | yummy | red | large | black | long | …

a grey shirt, fresh fruit, …

5 p. 31

5 What's different, what's the same?

a) Copy the table. Find the information for the table on the Haverstock website (page 21). Then add information about YOUR school.

	Haverstock School	**our school**
number of students	…	…
uniform	…	…
…	…	…

b) Talk to a partner about what is different and what is the same.

5.1 p. 37

At Haverstock School there is/are …

There is/are … at our school / Haverstock School, too.

We don't have …

…

6 p. 31

6 School sounds

Listen to four dialogues at Haverstock School. Where do they take place? L 1.4

computer room | library | classroom | school kitchen | drama studio | cafeteria | gym

The **first** dialogue takes place in the …

5: Wordbank Clothes | p. 214
Food and drink | p. 215
Free time | p. 209

7 Sound check

Listen to the sentences. Then say them yourself. L 1.5

[uː]

1. We have to wear black shoes at school.
2. Don't bring food into the classroom.

[ʊ]

3. Look, this is my favourite book.
4. He is really good at playing football.

8 Dear students …

Höre dir die Lautsprecher-Durchsage des Schulleiters an.
Beantworte die Fragen von jemandem, der nur wenig Englisch versteht. L 1.6

1. Wie ist das Wetter?
2. Was brauchen die Schülerinnen und Schüler momentan nicht zu tragen?
3. Was müssen sie weiterhin tragen?
4. Was ist bei den Hemden und Blusen zu beachten?
5. Was soll jeden Tag mitgebracht werden?

8.1 p. 38

9 Haverstock School Library WB 12 p. 12

Sieh dir die Informationen zur Schulbücherei an. Beantworte die Fragen von jemandem, der kein Englisch versteht.

Haverstock School Library

Opening times:
Mon – Fri 7:30 a.m. – 4:30 p.m.

Students can use the library for quiet study, reading and borrowing books and using the computers. There are 30 computers and 30 laptops with filtered Internet access. They may not be used for games or chat rooms.
Students may borrow up to three books at a time.

1. Wann hat die Schulbücherei geöffnet?
2. Was kann man in der Schulbücherei machen?
3. Was wird über die Computer und Laptops gesagt?
4. Wie viele Bücher darf man gleichzeitig ausleihen?

Du musst nicht Wort für Wort übersetzen. Wichtiger ist es, den Sinn wiederzugeben.

9.1 p. 38

8: Skills Help out | p. 234
9: Skills Help out | p. 234

10 A new classmate WB 13 p. 12

a) There is a new boy in the kids' class at Haverstock. Sandeep is talking to him. Match the questions and the answers.

1. Hi, I'm Sandeep. What's your name?
2. Where are you from?
3. Where do you live now?
4. Have you got brothers and sisters?
5. What are your hobbies?
6. What sports do you like?
7. What about a game of football after school?

A No, I haven't.
B I like judo, basketball and football, of course.
C That's a good idea!
D Hello, I'm Josh.
E Only five minutes from here, on Eton Road.
F I'm from Cardiff.
G Music, playing video games and lots more.

10b p. 32
b) Think of more questions to ask Josh. Write them down and make up possible answers.

10c p. 39
c) Work with a partner. One of you is a new classmate. Ask each other the questions from a) and b) and answer them.

10.1 p. 32
Then act out your dialogue in class.

11 p. 32
11 p. 39

11 More about Josh WB 14 p. 13

Read about Josh.
Complete the sentences with the correct verbs.

plays | lives | does | has to | likes | is (*2x*) | hates | wears | listens | has got (*2x*) | loves

1. Josh XX from Cardiff in Wales, but he XX in London now.
2. He XX twelve years old and XX dark brown hair and brown eyes.
3. He usually XX jeans and a T-shirt, but at school he XX wear a uniform.
4. Josh XX two guinea pigs. Their names are Mickey and Mouse.
5. He XX the guitar and XX to music a lot.
6. He also XX judo and other sports, but he XX inline skating.
7. Josh XX Chinese food. At the weekend he sometimes XX the cooking.

10: Grammar 2R | p. 242/243, 1R | p. 241
10c: Skills Talk | p. 231
11: Grammar 2R | p. 242

12 This is our school WB 15 p. 13

a) Watch the clip. What can you understand? 3

b) Watch the clip again and find out:
- What places and rooms are there at the school?
- Where does assembly take place?
- What do the students wear for PE?
- What is a tutor room?

c) Watch the clip a third time and check your answers.

13 Target task: YOUR school WB test yourself p. 14 + 15; Portfolio p. 123 / WEB P1

13 p. 33

a) Work in small groups on a presentation about your school.
What do you want to talk about?
Think about and collect information on:
- number of students, teachers, …
- different places and rooms (library, gym, …)
- clubs and activities
- subjects
- …

You can visit the homepage of your school or interview other students, your teacher, the headteacher, …

b) Put your information on a poster, on transparencies or on a computer. Add pictures or photos, too. WEB 2

c) Ask your classmates or your teacher to check your text. Then correct it.

d) Practise your presentation.
Then present your school to your class or other classes or your parents.

e) Ask for and give feedback.

12: Skills Watch a video clip | p. 228
13: Wordbank At school | p. 211
13: Skills Give a talk | p. 232, Talk | p. 231

4.1 The weather

a) Write down the correct weather words.

1. su--y | 2. c--d | 3. win-- | 4. wa-- | 5. cl--dy | 6. r--ny

b) Work with a partner and compare your words.

c) Spell three words from a). Your partner writes them down.

4.2 Today's weather

Listen. What is the weather like in London?
Choose A, B OR C. L 1.7

A It is cold and sunny in London.
B It is cold and windy in London.
C It is cloudy and warm in London.

5 p. 13

5 Language detective

a) Match the verb forms.

have | be (2x) | play | watch | do | help | drink | meet | visit | go

helped | met | watched | was | played | visited | went | had | were | did | drank

have – had
be – was, were
play – ...
...

b) Be a language detective.
- Sieh dir die Sätze an. Was ist mit den Verben hier und in a) passiert?
- Wann benutzt man die neuen Verbformen?

Tausche dich mit einem Partner / einer Partnerin aus.

Today is a sunny day.	→	Last Saturday was a sunny day.
The kids are in the garden.	→	The kids were in the garden.
They usually have lots of fun.	→	They had lots of fun.
They often play football.	→	They played football.

4.1: Wordbank Weather | p. 208
5: Grammar 5 | p. 246, 4 | p. 245

6 Ben's holidays

6 p. 14

What did Ben do in his holidays? Complete the sentences with verbs from the box.

went | played | visited | watched | was | stayed

1. Ben was in Wales.
...

1

Ben XX in Wales.

2

He XX at a campsite.

3

He XX a castle.

4

He XX to the top of Mount Snowdon.

5

He XX dolphins.

6

He XX minigolf.

6.1 Scrambled words

What are these words from number 6? Write them down.

1. pto
2. stcale
3. iimnflog
4. sicamtep
5. phdoisnl

7.1 More about Ben

Complete the sentences with "was" or "were".

1. Ben and his family XX in Wales.
2. The campsite XX very nice.
3. There XX a little shop on the campsite.
4. On the first two days it XX really warm.
5. The children XX happy and went swimming.
6. There XX some other nice kids on the campsite.
7. It XX a fantastic holiday for Ben and his family.

I/he/she/it **was**
you/we/they **were**

6: Grammar **5** | p. 246, **4** | p. 245
7.1: Grammar **5** | p. 246

8 p. 15

8 A postcard

a) Write down your address. Then look at Ben's postcard. What differences can you find between an English and a German address?

b) Find eight verbs in the past in the snake.

c) Complete the postcard with the verbs in the past from b).

12th August

Dear Sandeep,
Wales is a cool place.
Yesterday we (visit) a famous castle.
Today we (go) to the top of Mount Snowdon. We (walk) for four hours.
Sarah and my dad only (need) one hour because they (take) the Snowdon Mountain Railway.
We (be) really lucky. There (be) no clouds in the sky and we (have) a great view from the top.
Bye for now,
Ben

Sandeep Chopra
87 Camden High Street
London
NW1 0JH

Unregelmäßige Verben haben in der Vergangenheit eine eigene Form, die du lernen musst (siehe S. 334–335):
meet → *met*
take → *took*
...

9.1 Yesterday

Ask your partner about yesterday. Take turns.

- ... play a game?
- ... do your homework?
- ... visit a friend?
- ... help your mother?
- ... go to the park?
- ...

Did you **read a book**?

Yes, I did.

No, I didn't.

8: Grammar 5 | p. 246, 4 | p. 245
9.1: Grammar 6 | p. 246, 7 | p. 246

11 Lynn's holiday diary

WB 9 p. 10

11 p. 17

In the summer holidays Jasmine's friend Lynn from Leeds went to Germany with her parents.

a) Read Lynn's holiday diary. Did she like her holiday in Germany?

Saturday 15th August

Today I arrived in Frankfurt am Main. We needed twelve hours by car to get here.
I was so bored!
We are staying with my aunt and her family.
We wanted to go for a walk. But it started to rain and we had to stay inside.
We sat in the living room and played board games. Not my thing …
So I went to the kitchen with my phone and chatted with my friends.
I miss them …
I'm feeling really sad and lonely now.

Sunday 16th August

In the morning it was sunny.
We hired bikes and went on a ride along the Main.
My cousin came with us. He is thirteen and so nice!
We saw Frankfurt's fantastic skyscrapers.
After the ride we were really hungry. So we went to a restaurant.
In the afternoon we went to the zoo. I loved the beautiful tigers.
Now I'm really tired. I was very happy today. It was a wonderful day!

b) Put the sentences in the right order. Start with C.

- **A** Lynn was bored and went to the kitchen.
- **B** After the ride they had something to eat.
- **C** Lynn arrived in Frankfurt on Saturday.
- **D** Then they went to the zoo.
- **E** They stayed inside and played board games.
- **F** On Sunday morning they hired bikes.

c) Look at the diary again. How did Lynn feel …

1. when they went to Frankfurt by car?
2. at the end of their first day in Frankfurt?
3. after the ride along the Main?
4. at the end of their second day?

She felt …

happy	sad
lonely	bored
hungry	…

d) Describe a fantastic or a boring day for YOU. Tell your partner.

A fantastic day is **warm** and **sunny**. I **get up late** and …

A boring day is **rainy**. I have to **do my homework** and …

…

11d: Wordbank Weather | p. 208
Free time | p. 209
People | p. 210

1.1 School subjects

1. history
2. ...

a) Look at the pictures. What school subjects do they stand for?

1

2

3

4

5

6

7

8

b) What other school subjects do you know? Write them down or draw them and let your partner guess.

4 p. 22

4 Working with words

a) Work with a partner. What are the English words for these German words?

What's **Schuhe** in English?

It's **shoes**.

Schuhe | Gemüse | Hemd/Bluse | Krawatte | Frucht/Obst | Essen/Mahlzeit | Abzeichen | Hose | Blazer/Jacke | Bücherei | Snack/Imbiss | Cafeteria/Mensa

library | cafeteria | fruit | vegetables | snack | meal | shirt | logo | trousers | blazer | tie | shoes

Now put the words in alphabetical order.

blazer, cafeteria, ...

b) Match the words from a) with these adjectives:

healthy | fresh | grey | big | green | dark blue | yummy | red | large | black | long | ...

a grey shirt, fresh fruit, ...

1.1: Wordbank At school | p. 211

5 What's different, what's the same?

5 p. 22

a) Copy the table. Find the information for the table on the Haverstock website (page 21). Then add information about YOUR school.

	Haverstock School	**our school**
number of students	…	…
uniform	grey shirt, dark blue blazer, …	…
food in cafeteria	drinks, snacks, …	…
clubs and activities	ICT clubs, …	…
sports	basketball, …	…
…	…	…

b) Talk to a partner about what is different and what is the same.

At Haverstock School there are **lots of clubs and activities**.

There are **lots of clubs and activities** at our school, too.

At Haverstock School there is **a school uniform**.

We don't have **a school uniform**.

…

6 School sounds

6 p. 22

Listen to four dialogues at Haverstock School. Where do they take place? L 1.4

library | classroom | cafeteria | gym

The **first**/**second**/**third**/**fourth** dialogue takes place in the …

5: Wordbank Clothes | p. 214
Food and drink | p. 215
Free time | p. 209

10 A new classmate WB 13 p. 12

10b p. 24 **b)** Write down the correct questions. Then make up possible answers for Josh.

1. pet – Have – got – a – you – ?
2. favourite – What's – football club – your – ?
3. like – you – London – Do – ?
4. old – you – How – are – ?
5. birthday – When – your – is – ?
6. number – phone – your – What's – ?

10.1 Finding words

a) Find the words and write them down.

bro-	ga-	ho-	sp-	min-
id-	cla-	sc-	sis-	mu-

-mes	-orts	-ters	-ssmate	-bbies
-hool	-sic	-thers	-ea	-utes

b) Listen and check your words. L 1.8

11 p. 24

11 More about Josh WB 14 p. 13

Read about Josh.
Pick the correct verb and complete the sentences.

1. Josh **is / lives** from Cardiff in Wales, but he **lives / loves** in London now.
2. He **has got / is** twelve years old and **wears / has got** dark brown hair and brown eyes.
3. He usually **hates / wears** jeans and a T-shirt, but at school he **has to / likes** wear a uniform.
4. Josh **has got / has to** two guinea pigs. Their names are Mickey and Mouse.
5. He **listens to / plays** the guitar and **is / listens** to music a lot.
6. He also **lives / likes** judo and other sports, but he **hates / plays** inline skating.
7. Josh **loves / does** Chinese food. At the weekend he sometimes **has to / does** the cooking.

10: Grammar 1R | p. 241, 2R | p. 242/243
11: Grammar 2R | p. 242

13 Target task: YOUR school

WB **test yourself** p. 14 + 15; **Portfolio** p. 123 / **WEB** P1

13 p. 25

a) Work in small groups on a presentation about your school.
What do you want to talk about?
Think about and collect information on:
- number of students, teachers, …
- different places and rooms (library, gym, …)
- clubs and activities
- subjects
- …

You can visit the home page of your school or interview other students, your teacher, …

b) Put your information on a poster, on transparencies or on a computer. Add pictures or photos, too. **WEB** 2

c) Ask your classmates or your teacher to check your text. Then correct it.

d) Practise your presentation.
Then present your school to your class or other classes or your parents.

This is our presentation about our school.
There are … students and … teachers.
This is a picture of our school. You can see …
We also have a gym. …
Another important place is the …
There are … classrooms. …
Here you can see …
And now we want to give you some more information about …
Thank you for listening.
Have you got any questions?

e) Ask for and give feedback.

Did you like our presentation?

Yes, it was very interesting.

Did you understand everything?

Yes, it was easy to understand. You spoke loudly and clearly.

…

13: **Wordbank** At school | p. 211
13: **Skills** Give a talk | p. 232, Talk | p. 231

3.1 A survey WB 1 + 2 + 3 p. 18, 19

a) Watch the clip and find out: 4
- Who went on holiday in England?
- Who stayed at home?
- Who went abroad?

What else did you understand?

b) Where did YOUR classmates go on holiday?
Do a class survey and ask these three questions:

Did you go on holiday in Germany?

Did you stay at home?

Did you go abroad?

c) Make a bar chart and talk about the results of your survey. WEB 3

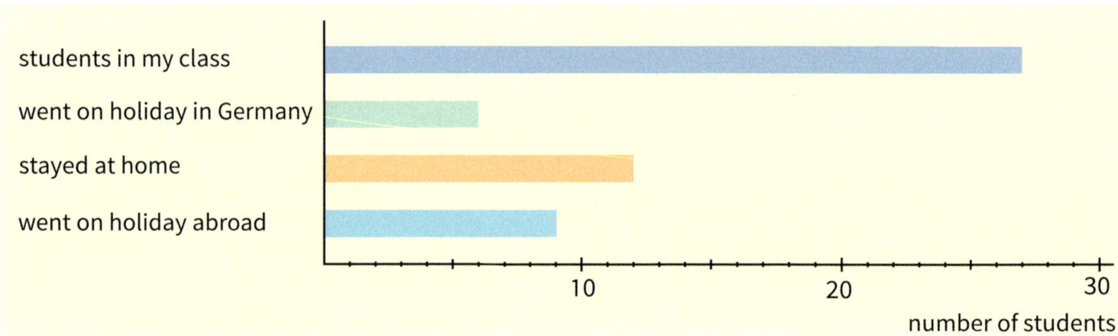

The bar chart shows that six students went …

d) Write about the results of your survey.

Six of my classmates went on holiday in Germany.
Twelve students … …

4.1 A weather forecast WB 4 p. 19

Listen to the weather forecast. What is the weather like in Scotland?
Complete the sentences. L 1.9

It is a XX and XX day in Scotland. In the north there are many XX on the coast and there might be some XX. The XX is coming from the west. Temperatures are between XX and XX degrees Celsius.

8 A postcard

8 p. 15

a) Look at Ben's postcard. What differences can you find between an English and a German address?

b) Complete the postcard with the verbs in the past.

be (*2x*) | need | have | go | take | visit | walk

12th August

Dear Sandeep,
Wales is a cool place.
Yesterday we XX a famous castle.
Today we XX to the top of Mount Snowdon. We XX for four hours.
Sarah and my dad only XX one hour because they XX the Snowdon Mountain Railway.
We XX really lucky. There XX no clouds in the sky and we XX a great view from the top.
Bye for now,
Ben

Sandeep Chopra
87 Camden High Street
London
NW1 0JH

Unregelmäßige Verben haben in der Vergangenheit eine eigene Form, die du lernen musst (siehe S. 334–335):
meet → *met*
take → *took*
…

10.1 A game

Write one thing you did in your holidays on a card.
Play in a group (4-6 students) and show your card.

I played football.

I went to the zoo.

Student 1: "I played football."
Student 2: "I didn't play football, but I went to the zoo."
Student 3: "I didn't go to the zoo, but I visited a museum."
Student 4: "I didn't …"
…

8: Grammar 5 | p. 246, 4 | p. 245
10.1: Grammar 6 | p. 246
10.1: Wordbank Travelling | p. 212

11 p. 17

11 Lynn's holiday diary WB 8 p. 10

In the summer holidays Jasmine's friend Lynn from Leeds went to Germany with her parents.

a) Read Lynn's holiday diary. Did she like her holiday in Germany?

Saturday
15th August

Today I arrived in Frankfurt am Main. We needed twelve hours by car to get here. I sat in the back of the car and was so bored! We are staying with my aunt and her family. They have a small flat in the city centre. After a small snack we wanted to go for a walk and see Frankfurt by night, but it started to rain and we had to stay inside. We sat in the living room and played board games. Not my thing ... but everyone else had fun. So after a while I went to the kitchen with my phone and chatted with my friends. I miss them already ... I wish I could be with them now. I'm feeling really sad and lonely.

Sunday
16th August

In the morning it was sunny and dry. We hired bikes and went on a ride along the Main. My cousin came with us. He is thirteen and so nice! We saw Frankfurt's fantastic skyscrapers. I like it when people call Frankfurt Mainhattan. After the ride we were really hungry. So we went to my aunt's favourite restaurant. I had eggs with the famous Frankfurt green sauce. Yummy! In the afternoon we went to the zoo. There weren't any elephants, but I loved the beautiful tigers. They're just great and I could watch them all day long. Now I'm really tired. I wasn't sad today. I was really happy. It was a wonderful day!

b) Put the sentences in the right order.

A Lynn was bored and went to the kitchen.
B After the ride they had something to eat.
C Lynn arrived in Frankfurt on Saturday.
D Then they went to the zoo.
E They stayed inside and played board games.
F On Sunday morning they hired bikes.

c) Look at the diary again. How did Lynn feel …

1. when they went to Frankfurt by car?
2. at the end of their first day in Frankfurt?
3. after the ride along the Main?
4. at the end of their second day?

She felt …

d) Write a diary entry about a fantastic day or a boring day during your holidays. Think about activities, the weather and your feelings.

11d: Wordbank Weather | p. 208
Free time | p. 209
People | p. 210
11d: Skills Write | p. 235

5.1 An email from Carlos WB 5 p. 20

Megan's class takes part in the eTwinning project 'School days around the world'.

a) Read the email they get from Carlos. What does he like about his school?

From [illegible]
Subject My school

Hello,
I'm Carlos Gómez Flores and I go to school in Mexico City. I'm in the last year of *primaria* or primary school. We go to *primaria* for six years. Then we go to *secundaria* or secondary school for three years. After that we can go to *preparatoria* or high school to get our *bachillerato* (A levels).
School starts at 8 a.m. every morning. I usually have six hours of lessons with a lunch break after three hours. During our break I love playing football with my friends. School usually ends at half past two.
Every Monday morning and on special days we sing the Mexican National Anthem to celebrate Mexico. It's a very long song so we only sing the first verse.
I have to wear a school uniform every day. It has the colours of my school. I usually wear a red polo shirt and black trousers. It's OK, but I prefer wearing my jeans and football shirts.
I don't really like school, but I love English. It's my favourite subject. Half of my school day is in Spanish and the other half is in English, so I can practise speaking English every day.
My other subjects are Spanish, maths, science, history, geography, art and PE.
We get marks from 0 to 10. 10 is the best mark and 0 to 5 are the worst. Every six to eight weeks we get a report.
My favourite time of the year is our summer holidays. We have six weeks of summer holidays and they start in June. The new school year then starts again in August. We also have Christmas and Easter holidays.
What are your school day and year like?
Best wishes,
Carlos

b) What is different and what is the same at YOUR school? Make notes. Then talk to a partner.

c) Write an email to Carlos. Tell him about your school day and year. Also write about what you like and don't like about his school and why. Here is some help: WEB 4

To [illegible]
Subject Re: My school

Dear Carlos,
It's interesting to see what school days and years are like in Mexico.
I go to school in … My school …
I like that your school … I also like … because …
What I don't like about your school is that …
I think …
…

5.1: Skills Read | p. 229
5.1: Skills Write an email | p. 236/237

8.1 Lots of information WB 6 p. 21

a) Listen. What kind of school event is it? L 1.10

registration | school club | assembly

b) Read the students' notes. Then listen again. Which notes are correct?

A

- Havafax and PE clothes!!!
- Mondays: drama club (Oliver), 3:45–5:45
- Thursdays: football (3:20) and skateboarding (4:30)
- Wednesdays: book club in library during morning break
- Friday: Japan evening (5-7)

B

- don't forget: Havafax + PE clothes
- Mondays drama club from 3:45 p.m. to 5:45 p.m.
- football at 3:30 p.m. on Thursdays and skateboarding club at 4:30 p.m.
- book club during lunchtime on Wednesdays
- this Friday from 5 to 7 p.m.: Japan evening (video)

C

- *bring Havafax and PE clothes*
- *drama club on Mondays (3:45–5:45)*
- *Thursdays: football (3:20) and skateboarding (4:30)*
- *book club, Wednesdays at lunchtime*
- *Japan evening, Friday 5-7 p.m.*

9.1 Helping out WB 7 p. 21

Deine Mitschülerin Alisha hat eine englische Austauschschülerin zu Besuch. Sie heißt Layla. Alisha spricht kaum Englisch, Layla kaum Deutsch. Kannst du den beiden helfen?

Layla	You	Alisha
1 When does the library close today? I need some books.	2 Sie möchte wissen, wann …	3 Sie schließt heute um …
	4 …	
5 Where can I get exercise books and folders? Does the school sell them?	6 …	7 Nein, aber …
	8 …	
9 I'd like to join a school club. What clubs are there at this school?	10 …	11 Es gibt …
	12 …	

8.1: Skills Listen | p. 228
9.1: Skills Help out | p. 234

10 A new classmate WB 13 p. 12

c) Work with a partner. Partner B is a new classmate. Act out the dialogue. 10c p. 24

Partner A	Partner B
1 Begrüße B, nenne deinen Namen und frage B nach seinem/ihrem Namen.	2 Begrüße A und beantworte seine/ihre Frage.
3 Befrage B zu folgenden Dingen und beantworte auch seine/ihre Fragen: – Alter – Herkunft – Geschwister – Haustiere – Hobbys – Lieblingsessen / … – …	4 Antworte und befrage auch A zu folgenden Dingen: – Alter – Herkunft – Geschwister – Haustiere – Hobbys – Lieblingsessen / … – …
5 Schlage B eine gemeinsame Aktivität vor: – *Let's …* – *What about …?*	6 Sage, dass du einverstanden bist oder mache einen anderen Vorschlag.

11 More about Josh WB 14 p. 13

11 p. 24

Read about Josh.
Complete the sentences with the verbs from the box in the correct form.

play | live | do | have to | like | be (*2x*) | go | hate | wear | think | listen | have got (*2x*) | love

1. Josh XX from Cardiff in Wales, but he XX in London now.
2. He XX twelve years old and XX dark brown hair and brown eyes.
3. He usually XX jeans and a T-shirt, but at school he XX wear a uniform.
4. Josh XX two guinea pigs. Their names are Mickey and Mouse.
5. He XX the guitar and XX to music a lot.
6. He also XX judo and other sports, but he XX inline skating.
7. Josh XX Chinese food. At the weekend he sometimes XX the cooking.
8. He XX to Haverstock School. He can walk there.
9. He XX that the new school and the teachers are OK.

10: Skills Talk | p. 231
11: Grammar 2R | p. 242

Theme 2

Around London

In diesem *Theme* …

- lernst du viele Londoner Sehenswürdigkeiten kennen.
- erstellst du einen Audioguide zu Sehenswürdigkeiten in deiner Region.
- lernst du, Bilder genau zu beschreiben.
- übst du, Wegbeschreibungen zu geben.
- erfährst du etwas über den Londoner Zoo.
- sprichst und schreibst du über Tiere.

C

B

A

Enjoy a great view from **the London Eye**. On a clear day you can see three airports, 13 football stadiums and 36 bridges.

Shops and stalls, acrobats and musicians – you can find them all at **Covent Garden**. Enjoy an exciting afternoon and watch, watch, watch!

Platform 9 ¾ at **King's Cross Railway Station** is a "must-see" for all Harry Potter fans. That's where Harry caught the train to Hogwarts.

The Queen lives at **Buckingham Palace** when she is in London. Come and watch the Changing of the Guard or even visit this beautiful palace.

1 London

What comes to your mind when you think of London?

I think of …

2 Famous sights WB 1 p. 22

Read about the sights and match them with the pictures.

I think picture **A** is **Buckingham Palace**.

E

D

F

G

H

Hyde Park is the perfect place to relax. Sit on the grass and enjoy the sun. Or go for a boat ride on the Serpentine, a big lake in the middle of Hyde Park.

The Natural History Museum is a perfect museum for kids. Meet the dinosaurs or find out what an earthquake feels like. It's all free.

Tower Bridge is an amazing bridge over the River Thames. Come and watch it open up when large ships pass through.

Big Ben is the clock tower at the Palace of Westminster. Its official name is Elizabeth Tower. Listen to the world-famous chime of Big Ben.

3 London sounds

Imagine you are in London now. Listen to the sounds. Where are you? L 1.11

4 What can you do there? WB 2 p. 22

In Covent Garden In Hyde Park At the Natural History Museum At Buckingham Palace At King's Cross Railway Station	you can	see the Harry Potter platform. learn about dinosaurs. watch the Changing of the Guard. listen to musicians. go for a boat ride.

4.1 p. 56
4.2 p. 56
4.1 p. 64

5 Where to go in London

Look at the London sights on pages 40–41 again. Ask and answer questions with a partner.

Where can you go
- when it is sunny?
- when it is rainy?
- when you have no money?
- when you want to see acrobats?
- when you want to see large ships?
- …

Where can you go when it is sunny?

You can go to Hyde Park.

6 A London vlog WB 3 p. 23

a) Watch the vlog. What do Jack and Emily talk about? 5

b) Which of these sights did they visit?

Tower Bridge | Covent Garden | the Gherkin | Big Ben | the Tower of London | Hyde Park | the London Eye

c) What do you learn about these sights? Match the sentence parts. There is one more ending than you need.

1. Tower Bridge
2. The Tower of London
3. In the Jewel House at the Tower of London
4. The Gherkin
5. It has got 41 floors and

A is London's famous castle.
B is 180 metres tall.
C is 80 metres tall.
D opens up 1000 times every year.
E you can see the Crown Jewels.
F looks like an egg made of glass.

The Tower of London

The Gherkin

d) What are Emily's top three London sights?

6: Skills Watch a video clip | p. 228

7 Odd one out

a) Find the odd one out.

1. park • museum • bridge • history
2. acrobats • dinosaurs • musicians • kids
3. watch • where • what • when
4. airport • lake • stadium • station
5. clean • visit • relax • enjoy
6. amazing • exciting • cold • perfect

b) Write a new "odd one out" for your partner.

7.1 p. 56

8 Sound check WB 4 p. 24

Listen to the sentences. Then say them yourself. L 1.12

[w]

1. Big Ben at the Palace of Westminster is world-famous.
2. What can we watch today?

[v]

3. There are lots of bridges over the River Thames.
4. Let's visit Covent Garden every day.

8.1 p. 64

9 YOUR favourite sights WB 5 p. 24

9 p. 57

a) Make a list of your top three London sights.
Why did you choose them? Tell a partner.

My top three London sights:
1. ...
2.
3.

My top three London sights are **Covent Garden**, **Big Ben** and **the Tower of London**.

I would like to visit **Covent Garden**. There are **acrobats** and **...**

I also want to visit **Big Ben**. It looks **really cool**.

The Tower of London sounds great, too. I like **old castles**.

b) Write about your top three sights.
What can you do there?
Look at pages 40–42 for help.

My day in London
First I want to visit Covent Garden because
I love shopping. I think it is interesting to watch ...
Then ...
After that ...

9.1 p. 65

9a: Skills Milling around | p. 238

LAND & LEUTE ⊙ 6

Unterwegs in London

London ist eine sehr große Stadt. Sie ist mehr als zweimal so groß wie Berlin. Zum Glück gibt es dort ein weit verzweigtes U-Bahnnetz – die *London Underground*, sodass man überall gut und schnell hinkommt. Die Londoner haben ihrer *Underground* einen lustigen Namen gegeben, nämlich *the Tube* (Röhre).
Willst du mehr von London sehen, solltest du unbedingt den Bus nehmen. Die roten *double-deckers* (Doppeldeckerbusse) bieten dir vom Oberdeck eine wunderbare *sightseeing tour* (Stadtrundfahrt).
Weltberühmt, aber natürlich auch wesentlich teurer als Bus oder *Tube*, sind die meist schwarzen *cabs* (Taxis).
Fahrradfahren ist ziemlich gefährlich, denn die Straßen sind extrem voll. Viele der Sehenswürdigkeiten sind aber auch gut zu Fuß zu erreichen.

Welche Verkehrsmittel gibt es in deinem Ort? Welche benutzt du?
Sieh dir nun den Clip an und finde heraus:

- Welches Verkehrsmittel wird für eine Stadtrundfahrt in London empfohlen?
- Welche Sehenswürdigkeiten werden genannt?
- Was erfährst du über das London Eye?

10 On the London Underground WB 6 p. 25

Sieh dir die Informationen in einer Londoner U-Bahn-Station an. Beantworte die Fragen von jemandem, der kein Englisch versteht.

1. Was soll man auf der Rolltreppe alles beachten?
2. Worauf ist bei Kindern zu achten?
3. Was muss man tun, wenn man einen Hund dabei hat?
4. Was ist verboten?

Du kannst viele Informationen auch den Bildern entnehmen.

10.1 p. 57

10.1 p. 65

10: Skills Help out | p. 234

11 A chat

a) Read the chat between Ben and Jasmine. What are their plans? WEB 5

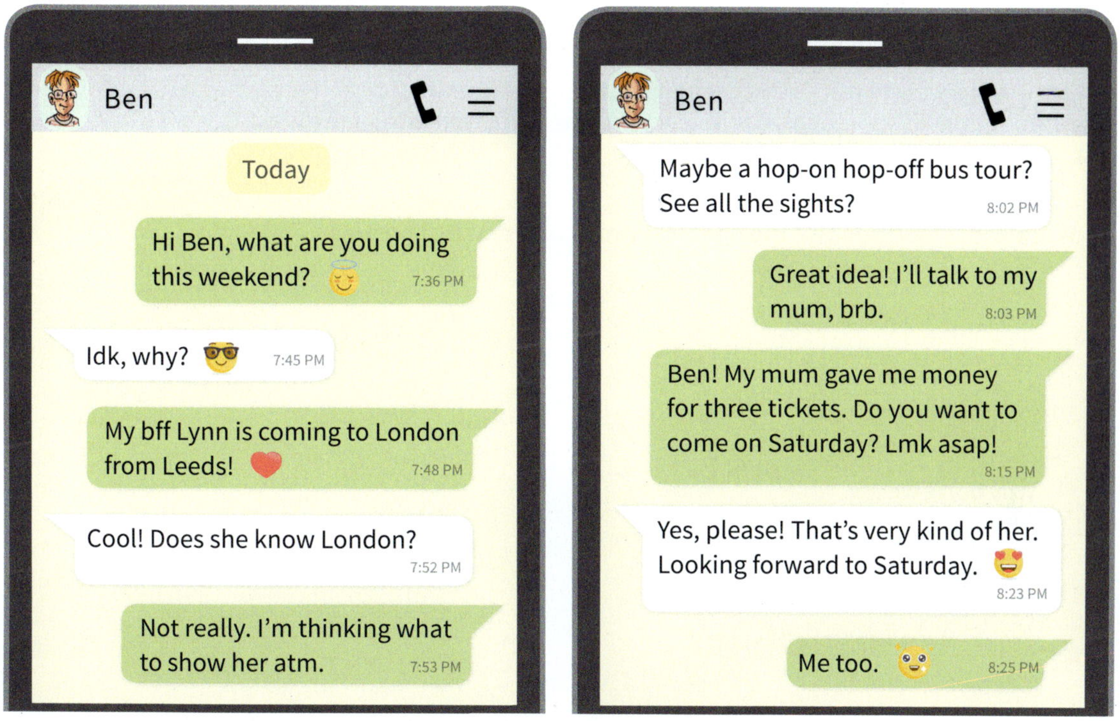

b) What do these text messaging short forms from the chat mean?

1. Idk
2. bff
3. atm
4. brb
5. lmk
6. asap

let me know | as soon as possible | be right back | I don't know | best friend forever | at the moment

What other text messaging short forms do you know?

11.1 p. 58

12 A sightseeing tour WB 7 p. 25

12 p. 58
12 p. 66

a) Listen to the tour guide.
What London sights does he talk about? L 1.13

b) Listen again and answer the questions. L 1.13

1. What is the weather like?
2. What do some Londoners call Buckingham Palace?
3. Where do Jasmine, Lynn and Ben get off?
4. What does Ben want to see?

11: Skills Read | p. 229
12: Skills Listen | p. 228

13 Let's …

a) Match the verbs with the nouns to make chunks.

watch | listen to | visit | go on | enjoy | go to | drink | sit on

a sightseeing tour | the cinema | a museum | the acrobats | tea | the grass | the sun | the musicians

watch the acrobats,
…

b) Work with a partner. Use the chunks from a) and make dialogues.

Let's **watch the acrobats**.

We could …

Why don't we …?

Great idea!

That sounds good.

I don't know.

No, that's boring.

14 Choose an activity

You can:

- Make a crossword with London sights for your classmates.

- Listen to the poem and read along. L 1.14
  Work with a partner or on your own.
  Learn the poem by heart and present it in class.
  Or record it as a rap or …

Let's all go to London, there's so much to do,
for children, for parents, for grandparents, too!

We can sit in Hyde Park and relax in the sun,
go to London Zoo – that's always good fun.

We can visit a palace, the home of the Queen.
We can even go on an earthquake machine!

We can look down on London from up in the sky,
as we go on a trip on the London Eye.

There are galleries and museums
and much more to see,
so why don't you all come to London with me?

- Write quiz cards for your classmates. Look at numbers 2, 4 and 6 for help.

> It crosses the River Thames
> and opens up for large ships.
> What famous sight is it?

- Find out more about one of the London sights.
  Go to the library, search the Internet, … Make notes. WEB 6
  Then give a short talk in class.

14.1 p. 66

15 Target task: An audio guide for YOUR town or city

15 p. 59

a) Work in small groups. Choose an interesting sight in your town or city.
Then collect information on it. You can:
- ask friends, parents, …
- go to the library
- go to the tourist information centre
- search the Internet WEB 6
- …

b) Write about your sight. Use short sentences. Remember: The tourists can't read your text, they can only hear it.

c) Ask your classmates or your teacher to check your text. Then correct it.

d) Practise reading your text. Everyone in your group should read one part of the text.

e) Record your text. Then listen to the recording: Is everything OK? If not, record your text again.
WEB 7

f) Play your audio guide to your class.

g) Ask for and give feedback.

> Hello and welcome to Berlin!
> Our names are … and we are your tour guides.
> Today we are at the Kurfürstendamm.
> It is a very famous shopping street.
> As you can see, it is …
> There are …
> Here are some more facts: …
> Did you know that …?
> Enjoy your visit!

14: Skills Search the Internet | p. 233, Give a talk | p. 232
15: Skills Search the Internet | p. 233, Write | p. 235, Talk | p. 231

1 p. 60

1 Two pictures WB 8 p. 926

a) Look at the two pictures and describe them. What can you see?

In picture A I can see …

In the middle there is/are …

On the left/right there is/are …

At the top/bottom I can see …

b) What are the people doing?

In picture A Jasmine is looking at her phone. The children behind her are …

In picture B Lynn is …

1.1 p. 61

1: Skills Talk about pictures | p. 230
1b: Grammar 3R | p. 244

2 What happened? WB 9 p. 26

a) Get together in groups. Look at the two pictures in number 1 again.
How do Ben, Jasmine and Lynn feel? Why? What do you think happened?

I think **Lynn** feels **worried** because …

I think … wanted to …

…

nervous | happy | bored | sad | hungry | lonely | tired | worried | …

Then choose a member of your group to present your results to the class.

b) Listen and read along. Were you right in a)? L 1.15

A

Ben: Where is Lynn? It's quarter past three already.
Jasmine: I don't know. She wanted to buy some souvenirs at Camden Market and then come right here.
Ben: Yes, I know. But does she know how to get here?
Jasmine: No, she doesn't. But she wanted to follow the directions on her phone.
Ben: So why don't you phone her and ask her where she is?
Jasmine: OK, OK. … That's strange. I can't reach Lynn on her phone.
Ben: Maybe she forgot it at your house.
Jasmine: No, she didn't. She texted me from the market an hour ago.
Ben: Then text her and tell her to hurry up … please.

B

Lynn: Damn! My phone is dead. How do I get to London Zoo now? … I could ask someone. … Excuse me, can you tell me the way to London Zoo, please?
Woman: I'm sorry, I'm not from here.
Lynn: No problem, thanks. … Excuse me, how can I get to London Zoo, please?
Man: Let's see. Ah, OK. We're on Camden High Street now. So …

c) Read the two dialogues again and finish the sentences. 2c p. 67

1. Lynn wanted to buy …
2. She wanted to follow …
3. Jasmine can't …
4. Lynn's phone …
5. The woman is not …
6. The man can tell Lynn …

2a: Skills Buzz groups | p. 239
2: Wordbank People | p. 210

3 The way to London Zoo

a) Look at these phrases and symbols. Then listen to the man telling Lynn the way to London Zoo. Which phrases do you hear? L 1.16

1  turn left

2  turn right

3 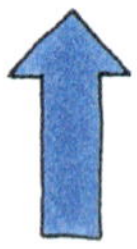 go straight on

4 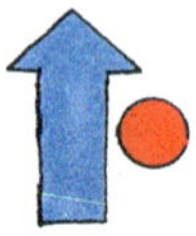 walk past …

5  walk on until you get to …

6 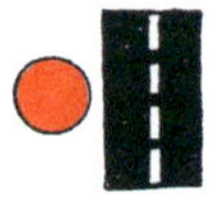 on your left

7  on your right

8  cross the street

b) Now look at the map and listen again. Follow the way with your finger.

Lynn

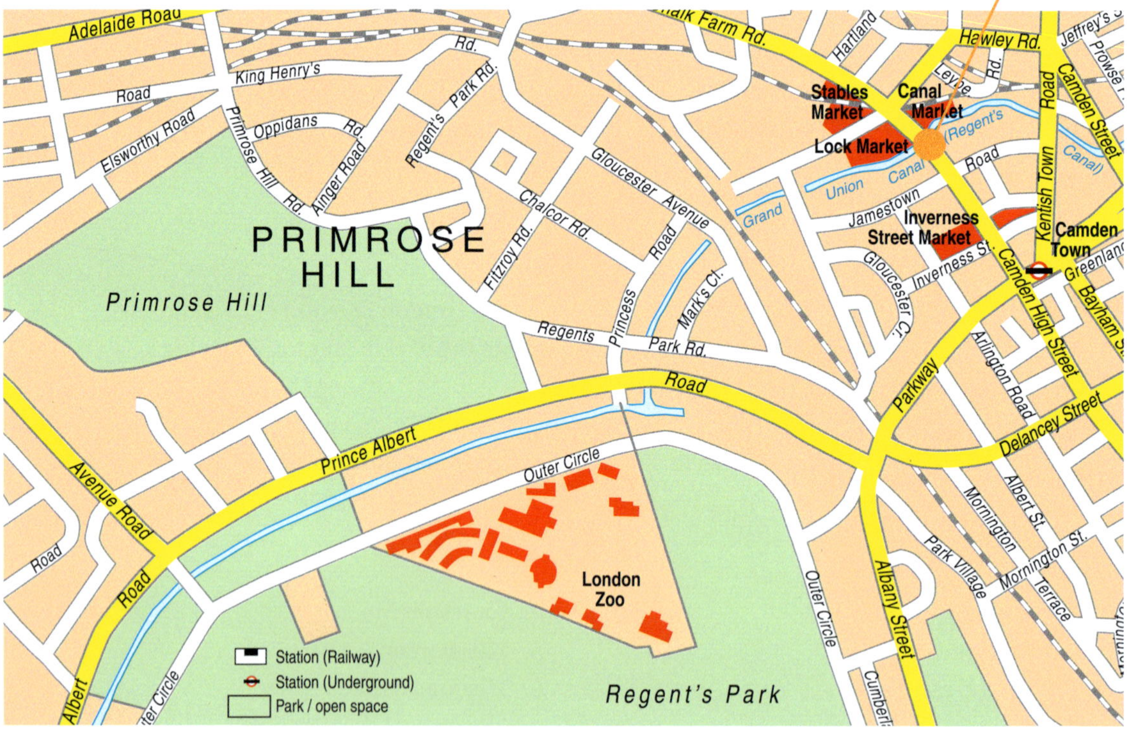

3.1 p. 61
3.2 p. 61

c) Is there another way to London Zoo? Check with an online map. WEB 8

4 Giving directions

WB 10 p. 27

a) Listen to the directions and follow them on the map. Where do you get to? L 1.17

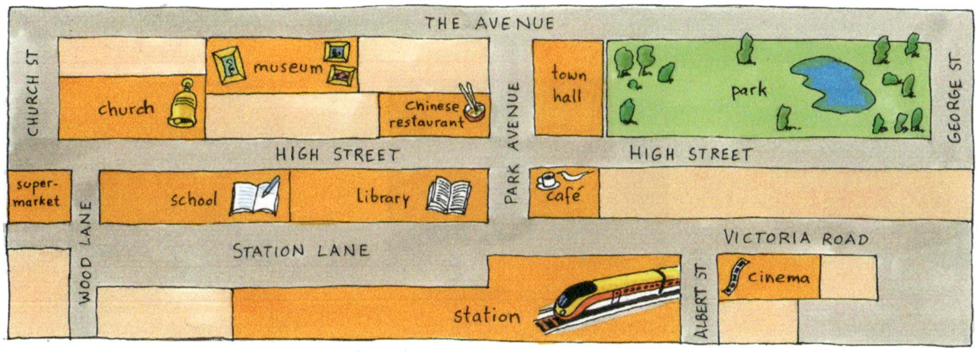

b) Work with a partner. Tell your partner where you are. Then ask him/her for directions.

Excuse me, can you tell me the way to …, please?

5 Together again

WB 11 p. 28

5 p. 67

a) When Lynn arrives at London Zoo, Ben and Jasmine have lots of questions. Match the questions and the answers.

1. Hi Lynn, why didn't you phone us?
2. How did you know how to get here?
3. Were you worried?
4. Did you enjoy shopping at Camden Market?
5. What did you buy?

- A I asked someone and he told me the way.
- B I bought some really nice things. This cap and …
- C Yes, I did. It's so cool there.
- D Sorry, my phone is dead. I forgot to charge it.
- E No, I wasn't. Not really.

b) Work with two partners. Practise the dialogue in a). Then act it out in class.

4: Wordbank Travelling | p. 213
5: Grammar 5 | p. 246, 7 | p. 246
5b: Skills Talk | p. 231

6 Animals at London Zoo

a) Look at the information about different animals.
What information is new for you? What do you find interesting?

HIPPOS

From: Africa
Food: plants, grass
Live: 40–50 years

FROGS

From: all over the world
Food: insects, small animals
Live: 10–20 years

GORILLAS

From: Africa
Food: fruit, leaves, roots
Live: 50 years

GIRAFFES

From: Africa
Food: leaves
Live: 25 years

LIONS

From: Africa, Asia
Food: meat
Live: 14–20 years

TORTOISES

From: Galapagos Islands (South America)
Food: vegetables, grass, leaves
Live: 150 years

6.1 p. 68
6.2 p. 68

b) What else do you know about these animals? Talk in groups.

7 Lunch for the animals

What do these animals eat? Test your partner. You can ask funny questions, too.

giraffes | gorillas | lions | frogs | hippos | tortoises | penguins | snakes | tigers | …

grass | meat | eggs | mice | chocolate | leaves | fish | pizza | insects | apples | carrots | …

Do **hippos** eat **eggs**?

Yes, they do.

No, they don't.

I'm not sure.

I don't think so.

8 Lions

a) Look at these words. Which of them go with lions? Write a list.

cats | predators | Asia | Africa | a zoo | golden or brown fur | large ears | a long tail | a long nose | sharp teeth | two long teeth | a mane | four paws

wild | clever | grey | strong | big | fast | tall | dangerous

jump | swim | eat fruit and grass | eat meat | run

b) Talk about lions.

"Lions live in …" "They have …" "They are …"
"They can be …" "They can …" "They …"

c) Look at the other words in a). Which other animal do they describe?

8.1 p. 62
8.2 p. 62

9 Which animal is it?

Work with a partner. Your partner thinks of an animal. Ask questions to find out about the animal.

Is it big / small / dangerous / …?

Yes, it is. / No, it isn't.

Does it have four legs / a long nose / …?

Yes, it does. / No, it doesn't.

Can it jump / swim / fly / …?

Yes, it can. / No, it can't.

9.1 p. 69

9: Grammar 1R | p. 241, 2R | p. 243
9: Wordbank Animals | p. 216

10 Animals in action

Look at the pictures. What do the animals normally do and what are they doing now?

The gorilla usually eats in its cage, but now it is eating in a restaurant.

1. The gorilla usually (eat) in its cage, but now it (eat) in a restaurant.
2. The penguin normally (swim) in the pool, but at the moment it (play) football.
3. The giraffe usually (drink) water, but today it (drink) cocktails on the beach.
4. The lion normally (sleep) a lot, but now it (fly) to Hawaii.
5. The zebra usually (stay) in its cage, but at the moment it (walk) around London.
6. The hippo normally (relax) in the water, but today it (go) skateboarding.

11 p. 63
11 p. 69

11 A day out

WB 12 + 13 p. 29

a) Read about Gernot the gorilla and his day out. Which London sights did he visit?

I'm Gernot the gorilla and I'm new at London Zoo. Last Monday Zadie the zookeeper left my cage door open. I wanted to see some of London's famous sights so I quickly left my cage.
I didn't want to walk so I took the Tube. There were lots of people and all of them looked at me. Some of them screamed and ran away. I wonder why.
I got off the Tube at Covent Garden and had a look around. I really enjoyed watching the acrobats. Some children wanted to ride on my back, but their parents didn't let them. I think they were scared.

10: Grammar 2R | p. 242, 3R | p. 244
11: Skills Read | p. 229

Next I went for a ride on the London Eye. It was exciting to be so high up and to see so much of London.
Then I went to Buckingham Palace and stood next to one of the guards. Someone took a photo of us. I smiled, but the guard didn't. Maybe he didn't feel so good.
Afterwards I went to Hyde Park. It's really big and has lots of trees. I felt tired and hungry so I sat under a tree and ate some leaves. A friendly woman gave me a banana.
I still felt hungry so I went to a restaurant. A nice man paid for my food. He could see that I was tired so he showed me the way back to the zoo. What a nice man!
When I got back to the zoo, everyone was very happy to see me. I had an exciting day, but I'm glad to be back home with my friends.

b) How did the people around Gernot feel? How did he feel?

c) Two weeks later Gernot had another day out. He went to Tower Bridge and the Natural History Museum. What happened? Write about it.

12 Target task: YOUR animal book

WB **test yourself** p. 30 + 31; **Portfolio** p. 124 / **WEB** P2

a) Each student finds out about a different animal at the zoo and makes one (digital) page for the animal book.

Think about:
- where the animal comes from
- what it looks like
- what it eats
- what is interesting about it
- …

Collect information. You can go to the library, search the Internet, …
Make notes. **WEB** 1 + 2 + 6

b) Use your notes to write a text.

c) Ask your classmates or your teacher to check your text. Then correct it.

d) Put your pages together to make an animal book.

Gorillas

Gorillas come from Africa.
They are big and strong and have dark brown or black fur.
Male gorillas have silver hair on their backs when they get older. They are called silverbacks.
Silverbacks are the leaders of a group of five to thirty gorillas.
Gorillas can live for about 50 years.
They eat fruit, leaves and roots.
Gorillas are very intelligent animals.

11b: Wordbank People | p. 210
11c: Skills Write | p. 235
12: Wordbank Animals | p. 216
12: Skills Search the Internet | p. 233, Write | p. 235

4.1 Things to do

Read about the sights on pages 40–41 again. What can you do there?
Complete the sentences with verbs from the box.

watch | see | enjoy | find | listen to | visit | learn | relax

1. You can XX Buckingham Palace.
2. You can XX in Hyde Park.
3. You can XX the chime of Big Ben.
4. You can XX Tower Bridge open up.
5. You can XX a great view from the London Eye.
6. You can XX about dinosaurs at the Natural History Museum.
7. You can XX Platform 9 ¾ at King's Cross Railway Station.
8. You can XX shops, stalls, acrobats and musicians at Covent Garden.

4.2 Right or wrong?

a) Read these sentences about the sights on pages 40–41. Are they right or wrong?

1. You can see five airports from the London Eye.
2. Harry Potter caught the train to Hogwarts at Platform 9 ¾.
3. You can enjoy an exciting afternoon at Covent Garden.
4. You can go for a boat ride on the Thames in Hyde Park.
5. Tower Bridge opens up for all ships.
6. Big Ben is the clock tower at Buckingham Palace.

b) Work with a partner. Compare your results and correct the wrong sentences.

7.1 Give me five!

Look at pages 40–42 and find …
- five words with "ee": *free*, …
- five words with "ou": …
- five words with "ea": …

Du kannst dir die Schreibweise der englischen Wörter besser einprägen, wenn du die schwierigen Stellen farbig hervorhebst:
clear, *out*, …

7.1: Skills Work with words | p. 226

9 YOUR favourite sights WB 5 p. 24

9 p. 43

a) Make a list of your top three London sights.
Why did you choose them? Tell a partner.

My top three London sights:
1. ...
2.
3.

My top three London sights are Covent Garden, Big Ben and the Tower of London.

I also want to visit Big Ben. It looks really cool / amazing / beautiful / exciting.

I would like to visit Covent Garden. There are acrobats, musicians and shops.

The Tower of London sounds great, too. I like old castles.

b) Write about your top three sights. What can you do there?
Look at pages 40–42 for help.

My day in London
First I want to visit Covent Garden because I love shopping. I think it is interesting to watch the acrobats and the musicians.
Then I want to see Big Ben. It looks really cool and I want to listen to the world-famous chime.
After that I want to go to the Tower of London because I like old castles. I think it is fun to look at the beautiful Crown Jewels.

10.1 Can you help?

Sieh dir die Informationen in einer Londoner U-Bahn-Station an.
Beantworte die Fragen von jemandem, der kein Englisch versteht.

1. Warum ist dort ein Pfeil abgebildet?

2. Warum sind dort Hände zu sehen?

10.1: Skills Help out | p. 234

11.1 Who is it?

Read the chat in number 11 (page 45) again. Ask and answer questions with a partner.

1. Who is chatting with Ben?
2. Who is from Leeds?
3. Who has the idea to go on a bus tour?
4. Who gave the money for the tickets?
5. Who is coming to London?
6. Who is looking forward to Saturday?
7. Who says "Great idea!"?

Ben | Jasmine | Lynn | Jasmine's mum

It's **Jasmine**.

12 p.45

12 A sightseeing tour WB 7 p. 25

a) Listen to the tour guide.
What London sights does he talk about? L 1.13

Buckingham Palace | Hyde Park | London Zoo | the Palace of Westminster | the London Eye | Big Ben | Covent Garden | the River Thames | the Gherkin | Tower Bridge | the Tower of London

b) Listen again and answer the questions. L 1.13

1. What is the weather like?
   a) not bad for a London tour
   b) sunny and really hot
   c) perfect for a London tour

2. What do some Londoners call Buckingham Palace?
   a) Palace of Westminster
   b) Buck House
   c) Buck Palace

3. Where do Jasmine, Lynn and Ben get off?
   a) at Tower Bridge
   b) at Elizabeth Tower
   c) at the Tower of London

4. What does Ben want to see?
   a) the ravens
   b) the Crown Jewels
   c) the ravens and the Crown Jewels

12: Skills Listen | p. 228

15 Target task: An audio guide for YOUR town or city 15 p.47

a) Work in small groups. Choose an interesting sight in your town or city.
Then collect information on it. You can:
- ask friends, parents, …
- go to the library
- go to the tourist information centre
- search the Internet WEB 6
- …

b) Write about your sight. Use short sentences.
Remember: The tourists can't read your text, they can only hear it.

Hello and welcome to Berlin!
Our names are Jana, Selim, Luca and Tarik and we are your tour guides.
Today we are at the Kurfürstendamm.
It is a very famous shopping street.
As you can see, it is full of shops. Some of them are very expensive.
There are lots of houses, hotels, cafés and restaurants, too.
Here are some more facts: The Kurfürstendamm is 3.5 km long and there are lots of trees.
Did you know that people often call it Ku'damm?
Enjoy your visit!

c) Ask your classmates or your teacher to check your text. Then correct it.

d) Practise reading your text. Everyone in your group should read one part of the text.

e) Record your text. Then listen to the recording:
Is everything OK? If not, record your text again. WEB 7

f) Play your audio guide to your class.

g) Ask for and give feedback.

Did you like our audio guide?

Yes, it was fun and very interesting.

Did you understand everything?

Yes, it was easy to understand.
You spoke loudly and clearly.

…

15: Skills Search the Internet | p.233, Write | p.235, Talk | p.231

1 p. 48

1 Two pictures

WB 8 p. 26

a) Look at the two pictures and describe them. What can you see?

In picture A I can see …

In the middle there is/are …

On the left/right there is/are …

At the top/bottom I can see …

b) What are the people doing?

In picture A Jasmine is looking at her phone. The children behind her are …

In picture B Lynn is talking to a man. The young man next to her is …

is selling balloons | are buying tickets | is talking on the phone | are eating ice cream | …

1: Skills Talk about pictures | p. 230
1b: Grammar 3R | p. 244

1.1 What is happening?

Look at the picture. Write down what the people are doing.

play | walk | sit | ride | read | eat | talk

1. Two kids are playing with their phones.
2. …

1. Two kids XX with their phones.
2. A woman XX to a man.
3. A girl XX her dog.
4. A woman XX an apple.
5. A man XX his bike.
6. Two men XX on a bench.
7. A girl XX a book.

3.1 Go straight on

Work with a partner. Play the game in class.

Go straight on.

Stop!

Turn right.

Turn left.

3.2 Directions

Match the symbols and the phrases. Write them down.

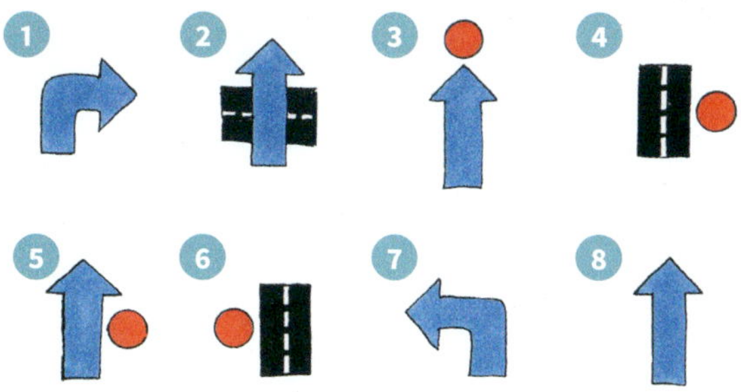

cross the street | on your left | turn right | go straight on | walk past … | walk on until you get to … | on your right | turn left

1. turn right
2. …

1.1: Grammar 3R | p. 244
3.1: Wordbank Travelling | p. 213
3.2: Wordbank Travelling | p. 213

8.1 Describing animals

a) Work with a partner. Talk about the lion's body.

leg | head | tail | fur |
ear | mane | paw | back

Number **one** is the lion's **back**.

b) Choose an animal and draw it. Then label its body parts.

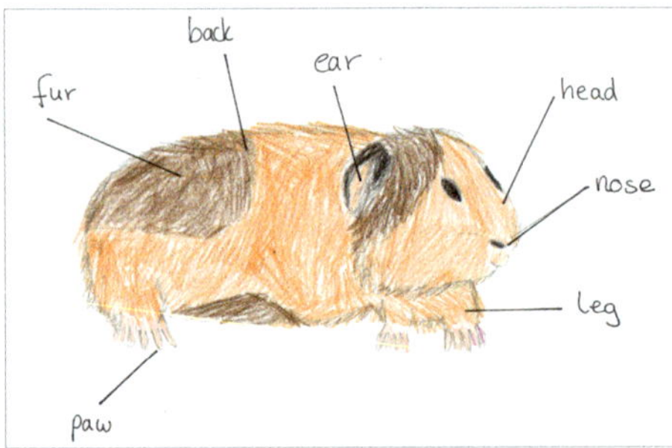

c) Describe your animal from b). You can use these adjectives:

small | big | short | long | slim | strong | grey | brown | …

The guinea pig has four short legs and …
It has …
…

8.2 Rhyming pairs

a) Find the rhyming pairs.

zoo | wild | nose | ear |
strong | meat | walk |
think | park | fur

talk | here | bark | feet |
child | wrong | pink |
shoe | her | goes

zoo – shoe
…

b) Listen and check your pairs. L 1.18

8.1: Wordbank Animals | p. 216

11 A day out WB 12 + 13 p. 29

11 p. 54

a) Read about Gernot the gorilla and his day out. Which London sights did he visit?

I'm Gernot the gorilla and I'm new at London Zoo. Last Monday I wanted to see some of London's famous sights so I went on a day out.
First I took the Tube to Covent Garden. There were lots of people on the Tube and all of them looked at me.
I really enjoyed watching the acrobats at Covent Garden. Some children wanted to ride on my back, but their parents didn't let them. I think they were scared.
Next I went for a ride on the London Eye. It was very exciting. Then I went to Buckingham Palace. Someone took a photo of me and one of the guards. I smiled, but the guard didn't. Maybe he didn't feel so good.
I felt tired and hungry so I went to Hyde Park and sat under a tree. I ate some leaves, and a friendly woman gave me a banana.
I still felt hungry so I went to a restaurant. A nice man paid for my food. Then he showed me the way back to the zoo. What a nice man!
When I got back, everyone was very happy to see me. I had an exciting day, but I'm glad to be back home with my friends.

b) Put the pictures in the right order.

c) How did the people around Gernot feel? How did he feel?

11: Skills Read | p. 229
11c: Wordbank People | p. 210

4.1 More London sights WB 1 p. 34

a) Look at the tips for sightseeing in London on pages 40–41. Read them again and collect adjectives and phrases from the texts that make a place sound interesting.

enjoy an exciting afternoon
come and watch ...
...

b) Choose one of the sights below and look at the information. Use adjectives and phrases from a) to write a short text about them. Present it to the class.

Westminster Abbey
- large and famous church
- William and Kate got married here
- many kings and queens are buried here

Harrods
- biggest department store in Europe
- sells everything
- 35,000 people visit every day

Arsenal museum
- in the stadium in North London
- see shirts, caps, medals from former players
- do a tour of the stadium

8.1 Sights and sounds

a) What are these sights in London? Write them down.

1. Come to [ˌbɪg ˈben] with me.
2. Let's relax in [ˌhaɪd ˈpaːk].
3. We could go to [ˌkɒvənt ˈgaːdn].
4. I would enjoy a ride on the [ˌlʌndən‿ˈaɪ].
5. Let's have a look at the beautiful [ˌbʌkɪŋəm ˈpæləs].
6. We could visit [ˌtaʊə ˈbrɪdʒ].
7. Why don't we go to the [ˌtaʊər‿əv ˈlʌndən] afterwards?

b) Listen and check. L 1.19

9.1 My home town WB 2 + 3 p. 35

a) Look at the photo.
What can you say about the building?
Do you know its name and where it is?

b) Listen to Kaan talking about his city.
What did you understand? L 1.20

c) Listen again and find out:
- What does Kaan like about his city?
- What doesn't he like?
- What sights does he mention?

Take notes.

d) Compare your notes with a partner.

e) Prepare a short talk about YOUR town or city. Present it to the class.

10.1 Madame Tussauds

Sieh dir die Informationen aus dem Internet zu einer weiteren Londoner Attraktion an. Beantworte die Fragen von jemandem, der kein Englisch versteht.

Search

Madame Tussauds
Marylebone Road, London NW1 5LR

Visit this top tourist attraction with more than 250 lifelike wax figures, all designed with great detail.
Meet the British Royal Family and drink tea with the Queen, say hello to sports legends and world leaders and come face to face with stars and superheroes.
You are welcome to touch the figures and take photos with them.
There is something new to discover every month.

Open daily from 10 a.m. – 4 p.m.
(The opening times can vary. Please check Madame Tussaud's official website for more information.)
Children under the age of 16 must be accompanied by a paying adult of 18+ years.

Buy tickets on our website by following this link: **TICKETS**

1. Was gibt es dort zu sehen?
2. Was kann man dort machen?
3. Was ist bei den Öffnungszeiten zu beachten?
4. Was wird über Kinder unter 16 gesagt?

9.1e: Skills Give a talk | p. 232
10.1: Skills Help out | p. 234

12 p. 45

12 A sightseeing tour WB 7 p. 25

a) Listen to the tour guide.
What London sights does he talk about? L 1.13

b) Listen again and answer the questions. L 1.13

1. What is the weather like?
2. What do some Londoners call Buckingham Palace?
3. Where do Jasmine, Lynn and Ben get off?
4. What does Ben want to see?
5. What is there inside Buckingham Palace?
6. Why does the tour guide say "perfect timing"?
7. What does he say about the ravens?

14.1 A special building

a) Read about a special building in London. What do you find interesting?

The Shard

Paris has the Eiffel Tower, New York has the Empire State Building and London has The Shard – a tall and very special landmark for a beautiful and special city.

The Shard is 309.6 metres high, which makes it the tallest building in Western Europe. Before The Shard was opened in July 2012, the tallest building was a tower in Frankfurt.
The building looks a bit like a pyramid that is covered entirely in glass. This is the reason for its name: "shard".
The design of the building is environmentally friendly: 95% of construction materials used were recycled.
There are 72 floors that can be used for offices, shops, restaurants, a 5-star hotel and luxury flats. And from the top floor you can enjoy a spectacular 360° view. You can see all the famous sights from there. On a sunny day you can see for 64 kilometres.

b) Make a fact file about The Shard.

c) Tell your class about The Shard.

12: Skills Listen | p. 228
14.1: Skills Read | p. 229

2 What happened? WB 9 p. 26

c) Read the two dialogues on page 49 again and answer the questions in complete sentences. 2 p. 49

1. What did Lynn want to buy?
2. How did she want to get to London Zoo?
3. What is Jasmine's problem?
4. What is wrong with Lynn's phone?
5. Why can't the woman tell her the way to London Zoo?
6. Who can tell Lynn the way?

5 Together again WB 11 p. 28

5 p. 51

a) When Lynn arrives at London Zoo, Ben and Jasmine have lots of questions. Write down the correct questions. Then match them with the answers.

1. Hi Lynn, – didn't – us – you – why – phone – ?
2. get – did – here – know – how – you – how to – ?
3. you – worried – were – ?
4. enjoy – Market – did – Camden – shopping – you – at – ?
5. buy – you – did – what – ?

A I asked someone and he told me the way.
B I bought some really nice things. This cap and …
C Yes, I did. It's so cool there.
D Sorry, my phone is dead. I forgot to charge it.
E No, I wasn't. Not really.

b) Can you think of two more questions to ask Lynn? Write them down and make up possible answers.

c) Work with two partners. Practise the dialogue in a) and include your questions from b). Then act it out in class.

5: Grammar 5 | p. 246, 7 | p. 246
5c: Skills Talk | p. 231

6.1 Working at a zoo

WB 4 p. 36

a) Read the sentences. Then listen to Sam, a zookeeper at London Zoo. Which sentences are correct? L 1.21

1. Sam says that he has the best job in London.
2. He says that people are lovely and friendly.
3. He says that animals are so much nicer than people.
4. He says that penguins are his favourite animals.
5. He says that his colleagues always come to say hello.

b) Listen again. Which colleagues does Sam talk about? What jobs do they do?

Mary | Simon | Pete | Sonja | Mrs Miller | Mr Perkins

ice cream seller | vet | gardener | zoo director

1. ... is the ...

c) Would YOU like to work at a zoo? Why? / Why not? What would you like to do there? Write about it.

6.2 What does he say?

a) Tell someone what Sam the zookeeper says about his colleagues.

1. "I have some nice colleagues." → He says that he has some nice colleagues.

1. I have some nice colleagues.
2. I'm helping Sonja to learn English.
3. Pete begins work very early.
4. My favourite colleague is Mary.
5. Mr Perkins talks to me every day.

b) Be a language detective. Look at your sentences with a partner. What changes when you turn direct speech into reported speech?

6.1: Skills Listen | p. 228
6.1a: Grammar 15 | p. 257
6.2: Grammar 15 | p. 257

9.1 An animal quiz WB 5 p. 37

a) What are the animals?

1. It is small with grey, white or brown fur. It has got a tail. It can run fast. It doesn't like cats.
2. It is long and thin with little black eyes. It doesn't have legs or fur. People often hate it.
3. It is tall and yellow with brown spots. It has got a long neck. It can run very fast.

b) Now make a quiz for your partner.

11 A day out WB 12 + 13 p. 29

11 p. 54

a) Read about Gernot the gorilla and his day out. Which London sights did he visit?

I'm Gernot the gorilla and I'm new at London Zoo. Last Monday Zadie the zookeeper left my cage door open. I was bored and wanted to see some of London's famous sights so I quickly left my cage. London is very big and I didn't feel like walking so I decided to take the Tube. There were lots of people and all of them looked at me. Some of them even screamed and ran away. I wonder why.
I got off the Tube at Covent Garden and had a look around. I really enjoyed watching the acrobats. I showed them some of my tricks, but I don't think they liked them. Some children wanted to ride on my back, but their parents didn't let them. I think they were scared. People are strange!
Next I walked across a bridge and went for a ride on the London Eye. It was exciting to be so high up and to see so much of London.
Then I went to Buckingham Palace and stood next to one of the guards. Someone took a photo of us. I smiled, but the guard didn't. Maybe he didn't feel so good.
Afterwards I went to Hyde Park. It's really big and has lots of trees. I felt tired and hungry so I sat under a tree and ate some leaves. They didn't taste very good. A friendly woman gave me a banana. It tasted great.
I still felt hungry so I went to a nice restaurant and had a lovely salad. When I couldn't pay for it, the waiter got angry with me. A man at the next table got up and paid for my food. He could see that I was tired so he showed me the way back to the zoo. What a nice man!
When I got back to the zoo, everyone was very happy to see me. I told them about my exciting day. I had a fantastic time, but I'm glad to be back home with my friends now.

b) How did the people around Gernot feel? How did he feel?

c) Think of another zoo animal. Write about its day out in London or Berlin or …

9.1: Wordbank Animals | p. 216
11: Skills Read | p. 229
11b: Wordbank People | p. 210
11c: Skills Write | p. 235

Camden Chronicle

Learn English the Camden way

Good to know ...

Waliser, Schotten und Nordiren sind sehr stolz auf ihre Herkunft. Sie mögen es deshalb nicht besonders, wenn man sie als Engländer bezeichnet. Wenn du dir also nicht sicher bist, aus welchem Teil des Vereinigten Königreiches jemand kommt, dann bezeichne ihn oder sie als Brite bzw. Britin (*British*).

"Yech...I hate when they put that sauce on."

A poem

It's the end of summer.
No more playing all day, having fun.
No more lazy days in the hot, hot sun.
It's the end of summer.
No more ice cream and jumping in the pool.
Instead it's time to go back to boring school.
Back to homework and getting up early
every day.
No more sleeping in and having your friends
over to stay.
Summer, we will miss you.
And all the great times, too!

Non-uniform day

At most schools in Great Britain students have to wear a school uniform. However, many schools have a non-uniform day once a year or several times a year. On non-uniform days students are allowed to come to school in their normal clothes. Sometimes students also wear funny costumes on non-uniform day. The schools often use this day to collect money for charity.

Good to know ...

In Großbritannien herrscht Linksverkehr. Touristen sehen oft automatisch in die falsche Richtung. Als Warnung steht in London daher meist Look right auf den Straßen eines Fußgängerübergangs.

A limerick

There was a young woman from Riga,
who smiled as she rode on a tiger.
They came back from the ride,
with the woman inside,
and the smile on the face of the tiger.

London Zoo

Did you know that you can spend the night at London Zoo? You sleep in a private lodge inside the Land of the Lions exhibit and wake to the sound of lions, monkeys, parrots and flamingos. You also go on three exclusive tours when the zoo is closed to everyone else! The tours are at sunset, after dark and in the early morning.

Tongue twisters

Ten tiny tigers take
twelve tomatoes
to town.

Seven sweet
snakes sang some
stupid songs.

Five fat frogs find funny
French fish.

Theme 3

Dreams

In diesem *Theme* ...

- lernst du, über die Zukunft und deine Zukunftsträume zu sprechen.
- berichtest du über Berufe und Berufswünsche.
- erzählst du von deinen Vorbildern und Helden.
- beschäftigst du dich mit einer britischen Heldin.

1 Kitchen talk

a) Look at the picture and describe it. What can you see? What are the people doing?

b) Listen and read along. L 1.22
What is Sarah's star sign?
What is YOUR star sign?
Look at page 96 for help.

1a: Skills Talk about pictures | p. 230

2 Horoscopes WB 1 p. 38

a) What does Sarah think about horoscopes?

b) Do YOU read horoscopes? Do you believe in them?

Yes, I do. They're often true.

No, never. I don't believe in them.

I always read my horoscope. It's fun.

No, I don't. They're stupid.

…

3 Talking on the phone WB 2 + 3 p. 38

a) Listen to Ben and Megan. Does Megan want to know what her horoscope says? L 1.23

b) Now read the dialogue. What is Megan's lucky colour? What does she say about it?

Ben: Hi Megan.
Megan: Hi Ben. What are you doing?
Ben: I'm looking at the horoscopes in my mum's magazine.
Megan: Ah, OK.
Ben: I'm sure you want to listen to your horoscope. Please say yes.
Megan: Why not? Go ahead.
Ben: That's great. So, what star sign are you?
Megan: Gemini.
Ben: Let's see. Ah, here it is. Your horoscope says: Your lucky colour this month is pink. Wear it on the 15th and something wonderful will happen.
Megan: Ha ha! I don't like pink and I won't wear it.
Ben: But you could wear pink just for one day, on the 15th and see what happens.
Megan: I'll think about it. What does your horoscope say?
Ben: It says: You worry about the future. Just listen to your heart. It will tell you what to do.
Megan: Is it true, Ben? Do you worry about the future?

Ben: No, I don't. I'm sure I'll get a good job. I think I'll work with computers or draw comics.
Megan: Sounds good. I love animals so I think I'll be a vet.
Ben: Cool!
Megan: Will you marry someone? And will you have children?
Ben: Maybe I'll marry a nice woman. But I hope I won't have four kids like my parents. What about you?
Megan: I won't marry anyone. But I'll always have a dog and great friends like you.
Ben: Aww, that's nice!

3: Grammar 8 | p. 247

4 Ideas about the future

Look at number 3 again. What do Megan and Ben say about their future?

get a good job | have four kids | be a vet | …

I will …

I won't …

I will …

I won't …

4.1 p. 88
4.1 p. 96

5 When I'm 25 WB 4 p. 39

5 p. 88

a) Look at Sandeep and Jasmine. Write down what they think about their future.

Sandeep: I think I will …
I won't …

Jasmine: I think I will …
I won't …

b) Now write about YOUR ideas about the future and draw them.

6 Language detective

Be a language detective:
- Finde in Aufgabe 3 alle Sätze mit *will*, *won't* und *-'ll*.
- Warum benutzen Ben und Megan diese Formen?
- Wie sagt man die Sätze auf Deutsch?
  Kannst du sie auch in einer anderen Sprache ausdrücken? Vergleiche.

Die Kurzform von *will* lautet *-'ll*. Auch die Verneinung *will not* hat eine Kurzform: *won't*.

4: Grammar 8 | p. 247
5: Grammar 8 | p. 247
6: Grammar 8 | p. 247

7 A fortune-telling game

WB 5 p. 40

a) Think of eight different fortunes and write them down in a list. Here are some ideas.

b) Make a paper fortune-teller and play this game.

1. You will have a good job.
2. You will be a pop star.
3. You won't be famous but you will have many friends.
4. ...

Tell me your favourite number and I'll tell you your fortune.

Two.

You will be a pop star.

I like that idea. / That's wrong. I can't sing. / I don't know.

8 p. 89

8 A horoscope

Sieh dir das Horoskop aus einer Jugendzeitschrift an. Was steht darin? Berichte jemandem, der kein Englisch versteht.

Aquarius

20 January – 18 February

Lucky number: 7
Lucky colour: green

This is the perfect month for new ideas. Get into action and your days will be really exciting.
Also look at the faces of the people around you. Do you see any sad people?
You are just the right person for them to talk to. It will help them a lot and it will make you happy, too.

8.1 p. 96

9 Sound check

Listen to the sentences. Then say them yourself. L 1.24

[g]

1. She will get a good job.
2. Don't forget your magazine.

[dʒ]

3. Don't put oranges in the budgies' cage.
4. Are you a real Gemini? Find out on this page.

7: Grammar 8 | p. 247
8: Skills Help out | p. 234

10 Jobs

WB 6 + 7 + 8 p. 40, 41

a) Look at the photos. What do these people do?

A vet takes care of ill animals.

bus driver

bricklayer

vet

shop assistant

design computer games | build houses | take care of ill people | drive buses | sell things | help people in trouble and catch criminals | take care of ill animals | cut and style people's hair | fly planes | repair cars |

police officer

hairdresser

video game designer

pilot

mechanic

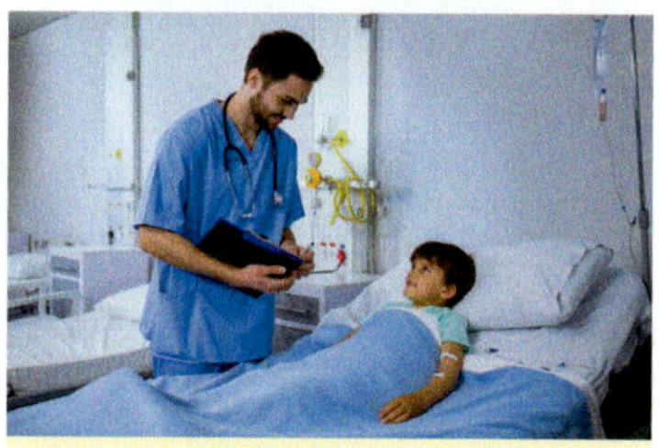
nurse

b) Which jobs in a) do you find interesting?

I think **mechanic** is an interesting job.

c) | What job would YOU like to have? What is it in English?
Then walk around the classroom and ask your classmates about their future jobs.

| 10c p. 96

What will you be when you grow up?

I think I'll be a **nurse**.

Perhaps I'll be a …

10.1 p. 89
10.2 p. 90

11 What are their jobs?

Name the people's jobs.

1. Who helps you when you want to buy something in a shop?
2. Who washes and cuts your hair?
3. Who looks after you when you are in a hospital?
4. Who helps your family with their car?
5. Who drives lots of children to school every day?
6. Who uses his or her hands and tools to build things?
7. Who often wears a uniform and catches criminals?
8. Who takes care of your pet when it is ill?
9. Who flies you on holiday to far away places?
10. Who creates games on the computer?

11.1 p. 90

12 p. 97

12 Our dream jobs

a) Watch the clip. What are these jobs in German? 7

chef | photographer | baker | vet | zoologist | pilot | racing driver | singer | actress

b) Watch the clip again. Who wants to have which job?

Maria | George | Rosa | Joe | Zoe | Lewis | Eran |

Maria wants to be a / an …

c) What else did you understand?

13 p. 90
13 p. 97

13 Josh in Japan WB 9 p. 42

a) Listen to Josh. What does he talk about? L 1.25

b) Listen again and take notes. Then write about Josh.

Wenn du Notizen machst, schreibst du keine vollständigen Sätze auf. Lasse Wörter aus, die unwichtig sind.

Josh thinks he'll be …
He'll play …
He'll go …
He'll try …
He'll have …
He'll do …
His kids will …
…

14 Will I be happy?

What will your future be like? Write down some questions. Then ask your partner. Take turns.

Will I	be live in have meet fly to work as …	a big city? famous? my dream partner? a car? a mechanic? New York? …

Yes, you will.

No, you won't.

If you're lucky.

I can't tell you.

14.1 p. 91
14.1 p. 97

15 What will happen? WB 10 p. 42

Think about the questions and take notes. Then ask and answer the questions with a partner.

1. Where will you live when you are 25?
2. What car will you have?
3. Who will you marry?
4. How many children will you have?
5. What will you buy when you have your first job?
6. What will you do on this day in five years?

…

I think Perhaps / Maybe I hope I'm sure …	I'll … I won't …

15.1 p. 91
15.1 p. 98

16 Target task: YOUR future

a) I Make a poster or a digital page about your future in 20 years. Portfolio-Ordner
Think about:
- what you will be
- what you will do or have
- where you will live
- what the world will be like
- …

WEB 2

b) Ask your classmates or your teacher to check your text. Then correct it.

c) Present your poster or your digital page to your class.

I 16a p. 91

14: Grammar 8c | p. 247
14: Wordbank Jobs | p. 217
15: Grammar 8c | p. 247
16: Skills Write | p. 235

1 p. 92

1 All kinds of heroes WB 11 p. 43

1a p. 99

a) Read the blog entries. Who are the children's heroes?

Search

Victor
Today in our English lesson we talked about Grace Darling. In 1838 there was a terrible storm in the north of England. Together with her father Grace went out to sea in a boat and rescued nine people from a shipwreck. Grace was very brave. She risked her life to help others. So for me she is a real hero. Who is your hero?

Megan
My hero is my dog. His name is Sir Barks-A-Lot and he is always friendly. When I come home from school, he is so happy to see me. I can tell him about all my problems. He listens and makes me feel much better.

Sandeep
I'm a big football fan. So my heroes are usually football players. There are lots of great players but my favourite player at the moment is Dele Alli. He can run really fast, he is clever and he scores fantastic goals.

Ben
I think my hero is my sister Sarah. She is in a wheelchair because she can't walk. Sometimes she is sad about it but most of the time she is happy. Sarah is really good at playing wheelchair basketball. And she loves helping other people.

Jasmine
My hero is Jane Goodall. In the 1960s she went to Africa and studied chimpanzees. She found out that they eat meat and work together in groups. Jane works hard to protect animals and our planet. There are also other people who do that. So they are my heroes, too.

b) Why are they the children's heroes? Take notes in a table.

Grace Darling	...	...	...	...
rescued nine people, ...	...	...	...	...

c) Who is YOUR hero or favourite person? Why? Tell your partner about him/her.

"My hero / favourite person is ..." "He/She lives in ..." "He/She is ..."
"He/She can ..." "I like him/her because he/she ..."

1.1 p. 100

1: Skills Read | p. 229

2 YOUR hero or favourite person WB 12 p. 43

2 p. 93

a) Copy the table. Then fill in the words from the box.
Can you find more words for your table? Look at number 1b) for help.

What is a hero / favourite person like?	What does a hero / favourite person do?
cool, …	works hard, …

cool | funny | works hard | goes on adventures | interesting | sings well | …

b) Write a blog entry about your hero or favourite person. WEB 9

Search

My favourite person is my cousin Vito. He lives in Bremen. He is funny and he can cook really well. I like him because he always has lots of good ideas.

3 My favourite person

a) Listen to the song and sing along. L 1.26

You're clever, you're cool,
You're my favourite person.

You're funny, you make me laugh,
You're my favourite person.

You tell great stories, you know so much,
You're my favourite person.

You do crazy things, you dance so well,
You're my favourite person.

You're always there for me, you never let me down,
You're my favourite person.

b) Write one or two more verses for the song. Portfolio-Ordner

2: Wordbank People | p. 210

4 Grace Darling WB 13 p. 44

a) Read the story.

Grace Darling, her parents and her brothers and sisters lived in the Longstone Lighthouse on the Farne Islands. Mr Darling was the lighthouse keeper.

On 7 September 1838 there was a terrible storm.

Grace and her father brought the survivors safely to the lighthouse. Mrs Darling and her daughters cooked soup and made tea for everyone.

b) Put the sentences in the right order.

4b p. 93

- A They rowed quickly to the shipwreck.
- B Grace could see a shipwreck from her window.
- C Grace and her father brought the survivors safely to the lighthouse.
- D In September 1838 there was a terrible storm.
- E The survivors got in the boat carefully.
- F She and her father went out to sea in a boat.

4.1 p. 100

LAND & LEUTE 8

Grace Darling

Grace Darling wurde am 24. November 1815 in Bamburgh im Nordosten Englands geboren. Ihr Vater war Leuchtturmwärter auf den Farne-Inseln. Als am 7. September 1838 der Raddampfer SS Forfarshire bei einem schweren Unwetter verunglückte, retteten Grace und ihr Vater neun der ca. 60 Passagiere. Weitere neun Passagiere hatten sich zuvor schon mit einem Rettungsboot in Sicherheit bringen können.
Grace wurde nach der Rettungsaktion als Heldin gefeiert. Sie erhielt einen persönlichen Brief von Queen Victoria und eine Belohnung in Höhe von 50 Pfund. Es gab Postkarten, Pralinenschachteln und Teller zu kaufen, auf denen Grace abgebildet war.
Grace Darling starb am 20. Oktober 1842 im Alter von nur 26 Jahren an Tuberkulose.

Sieh dir nun den Clip an und finde heraus:
- Welche Medaille erhielten Grace und ihr Vater?
- Worum wurde Grace von ihren Bewunderern gebeten?
- Was wurde zu Ehren von Grace errichtet?

4: Grammar 9 | p. 248

5 What are the words? WB 14 p. 44

a) Write the words. You can look at number 4 for help.

1. r – – → **row**
2. p – – r
3. s – v –
4. k – – per
5. res – – e
6. ca – – ful
7. s – – vivor
8. ship – – eck
9. li – – thouse

b) Complete the sentences with words from a).

1. He is the keeper of the XX.
2. She can see a XX.
3. They XX the boat.
4. They want to XX the survivors.
5. They have to be XX.
6. They XX nine lives.

6 p. 94
6 p. 101

6 Grace's story

What did Grace Darling tell her brothers afterwards?
Put the sentences in the correct order.

1. my window – I – a shipwreck – This morning – saw – from – .
2. could – survivors – see – I – also – some – .
3. poor – needed to – the – We – rescue – people – .
4. went out – Father and I – our – to sea – in – boat – .
5. quickly – rowed – the shipwreck – We – very – to – .
6. helped – the boat – Father – to get in – the survivors – .
7. We – the people – brought – to the lighthouse – safely – .
8. and – made – our sisters – for everyone – Mother – tea and soup – .
9. very happy – I'm – saved – we – that – so many lives – .

7 Sound check

a) Copy the words. Then listen. Which letters can't you hear? Circle them. L 1.27

island | window | lighthouse | shipwreck | row | daughter | write | talk | listen

b) Listen again and say the words.

8 A dramatic reading

a) Listen to Grace and her parents. How do they talk? L 1.28

Grace Mrs Darling Mr Darling	talks speaks	happily. quickly. loudly. sadly. worriedly.

b) Look at these sentences. Say each sentence in many different ways.

Where are my children?

We need to rescue the survivors!

Help me, please!

You saved my life.

Here is some soup for you.

c) In groups of six practise reading Grace's story (number 4).
You need a narrator, Grace, her father, her mother and two survivors (a man and a woman).

Lies dir den Text zu deiner Rolle mehrmals mit leiser Stimme durch. Schaue dir jeden Satz einzeln an und präge ihn dir ein. Wie fühlt sich die Person gerade? Betone die Sätze entsprechend.

9 Do this carefully

a) What are the adverbs of these adjectives?

happy – happily	sad – …
quiet – …	safe – …
easy – …	

Adverbien der Art und Weise bildest du, indem du an das Adjektiv die Endung *-ly* anhängst.

Einige Adverbien haben jedoch Sonderformen (siehe S. 248).

b) The adverbs of *fast*, *hard* and *good* are special.
Can you find them in numbers 1 and 2 (pages 80 – 81)?

c) Be a language detective.
Wann benutzt man Adverbien?
Tausche dich mit einem Partner / einer Partnerin aus.

8: Skills Dramatic reading | p. 239
8: Grammar 9 | p. 248
9: Grammar 9 | p. 248

10 You can do this easily

a) Find ten adverbs in the snake.

b) Find the adjectives for the adverbs and write them down.

10.1 p. 94

loudly – loud, ...

11 p. 94
11 p. 101

11 How are they doing things?

a) Read the sentences and complete them with an adverb.

carefully | dangerously | fast | beautifully | hard | loudly

1. The man is driving XX.
2. The girl is running XX.
3. The boy is working XX.
4. The old man is walking XX.
5. The dog is barking XX.
6. The woman is singing XX.

b) Think of more (crazy) sentences.

Bagheera is dancing happily.
My friend and I are ...
...

12 Brave or bravely? WB 15 p. 45

Pick the right word (adjective or adverb) to complete the sentences.

1. Grace Darling was a very **brave / bravely** young woman.
2. On a **cold / coldly** and stormy morning she saw a shipwreck.
3. Grace and her father wanted to rescue the survivors **quick / quickly**.
4. Mrs Darling told them to be **careful / carefully**.
5. She also told them to come back **safe / safely**.
6. She waited in the lighthouse **nervous / nervously**.
7. When Grace and her father came back, Mrs Darling was very **happy / happily**.

12.1 p. 101

10: Grammar 9 | p. 248
11: Grammar 9 | p. 248
12: Grammar 9 | p. 248

13 Choose an activity WB 16 p. 45

13 p. 95

You can:

- Look at all the information you have about Grace Darling. Make a quiz for your classmates.

  1. Grace Darling lived in ...
  2. She had ... brothers and ... sisters.
  3. ...
  ...

- Be Grace Darling and tell your story to the class.

  Hello everyone, my name is Grace Darling.
  I'm 22 years old and …
  Last week there was a terrible storm. …

- Work with a partner. One of you is Grace Darling, the other one is the interviewer. Think about questions to ask Grace. Then practise the interview. Act out the interview or record it and play it to the class. WEB 7

  Excuse me, can I ask you some questions, please?

  Yes, of course.

- Present another hero. What do you know about him or her? Go to the library or search the Internet for more information. Make notes. Then give a short talk in class. WEB 6

14 Target task: YOUR audio play WB test yourself p. 46 + 47; Portfolio p. 125 / WEB P3

a) Work in groups and act out Grace's story from number 4.
You will need:
- a narrator
- people to play the characters
- people to make the right noises
- …

b) Record your play. Then listen to the recording: Is everything OK? If not, record your play again. WEB 7

c) Present your audio play to the class.

d) Ask for and give feedback.

13: Skills Search the Internet | p. 233,
Give a talk | p. 232
14: Skills Talk | p. 231

4.1 Megan and Ben

Complete the sentences with “will” or “won’t”.

1. Ben is sure he **will / won’t** get a good job.
2. He hopes he **will / won’t** have four kids.
3. Megan is sure she **will / won’t** marry anyone.
4. She hopes she **will / won’t** be a vet.
5. She is sure she **will / won’t** always have a dog and great friends.
6. Ben hopes Megan **will / won’t** wear pink on the 15th.
7. Megan is sure she **will / won’t** wear pink on the 15th.

5 p. 75

5 When I’m 25 WB 4 p. 39

a) Look at Sandeep and Jasmine. Write down what they think about their future.

marry a nice man and have two children | work in my parents’ shop | play professional basketball | have any children | have a fast car | play the guitar in a band

Sandeep: I think I will ...
I won’t ...

Jasmine: I think I will ...
I won’t ...

b) Now write about YOUR ideas about the future and draw them.

I think I will ...
I won’t ...

4.1: Grammar 8 | p. 247
5: Grammar 8 | p. 247

8 A horoscope

8 p. 76

Sieh dir das Horoskop aus einer Jugendzeitschrift an. Beantworte die Fragen von jemandem, der nur wenig Englisch versteht.

Aquarius

20 January – 18 February

Lucky number: 7
Lucky colour: green

This is the perfect month for new ideas. Get into action and your days will be really exciting.
Also look at the faces of the people around you. Do you see any sad people?
You are just the right person for them to talk to. It will help them a lot and it will make you happy, too.

1. Um welches Sternzeichen geht es hier?
2. Warum steht dort eine 7?
3. Wofür ist das der perfekte Monat?
4. Was soll man sich anschauen? Und warum?

10.1 Which job is it?

a) Work with a partner. What are the English words for these German words?

What's **Polizeibeamter/Polizeibeamtin** in English?

It's **police officer**.

Polizeibeamter/Polizeibeamtin | Mechaniker/in | Friseur/in | Pilot/in | Verkäufer/in | Krankenschwester/Krankenpfleger | Tierarzt/Tierärztin | Busfahrer/in | Videospielentwickler/in | Maurer/in

b) Play a guessing game with your partner. Mime and guess the jobs in a).

What's my job?

Are you a bricklayer?

That's right/wrong.

8: Skills Help out | p. 234
10.1: Wordbank Jobs | p. 217

10.2 What do they do?

Put the sentences in the correct order.

1. drives – bus driver – buses – A – .
2. planes – A – flies – pilot – .
3. cars – repairs – mechanic – A – .
4. bricklayer – houses – A – builds – .
5. sells – A – things – shop assistant – .
6. A – computer – video game designer – games – designs – .
7. trouble – helps – A – in – police officer – people – .

11.1 Maybe you'll be a ...

Match the sentences.

1 I enjoy cutting hair.
2 I want to build things with my hands.
3 I love animals.
4 I'd like to take care of ill people.
5 I enjoy repairing cars.
6 I want to sell things.
7 I'd like to help people in trouble.

A You'll be a mechanic.
B I think you'll be a police officer.
C Perhaps you'll be a hairdresser.
D You'll be a shop assistant.
E Maybe you'll be a vet.
F I think you'll be a bricklayer.
G Perhaps you'll be a nurse.

13 p. 78

13 Josh in Japan WB 9 p. 42

a) Listen to Josh. What does he talk about? L 1.25

b) Listen again. What do you learn about Josh?

Josh thinks he'll be	lots of sport to keep fit.
He'll play	all the different food.
He'll go	with him in their school holidays.
He'll try	rock music.
He'll have	a guitar player in a band.
He'll do	on tour around the world.
His kids will come	ten or more guitars.

11.1: Grammar 8 | p. 247
13: Grammar 8 | p. 247

14.1 Yes or no?

Look at these questions. Answer them with "Yes, I will." or "No, I won't."

1. Will you marry when you are 16?
2. Will you have a car when you are 18?
3. Will you live with your parents when you are 20?
4. Will you live in Germany when you are 25?
5. Will you have lots of money when you are 30?
6. Will you be your own boss when you are 35?

15.1 What will be?

a) Complete the questions with the right question words.

who | what (*2x*) | how many (*2x*) | where

1. XX will you do next Saturday?
2. XX children will you have?
3. XX will you live in ten years?
4. XX car will you have?
5. XX will you marry?
6. XX pets will you have?

b) Write down your answers.

I think Perhaps / Maybe I hope I'm sure	I'll … I won't …

16 Target task: YOUR future

a) Make a poster or a digital page about your future in 20 years. Portfolio-Ordner
Think about:
- what you will be
  (I will be a mechanic / a nurse / …)
- what you will do or have
  (I will play hockey / have a dog / …)
- where you will live
  (I will live in a big house / in London / …)
- what the world will be like
  (People won't eat animals;
  There will be more parks; …)
- …

WEB 2

16 p. 79

1 p. 80

1 All kinds of heroes WB 11 p. 43

a) Read the blog entries. Who are the children's heroes?

Victor's hero is …

Search

Victor
Today in our English lesson we talked about Grace Darling. In 1838 there was a terrible storm in the north of England. Grace and her father went out to sea in a boat and rescued nine people from a shipwreck. Grace was very brave. For me she is a real hero. Who is your hero?

Megan
My hero is my dog. His name is Sir Barks-A-Lot and he is always friendly. When I come home from school, he is so happy to see me. I can tell him about all my problems. He listens and makes me feel much better.

Sandeep
I'm a big football fan. There are lots of great players but my favourite player at the moment is Dele Alli. He can run really fast, he is clever and he scores fantastic goals.

Ben
I think my hero is my sister Sarah. She is in a wheelchair because she can't walk. She is really good at playing wheelchair basketball. And she loves helping other people.

Jasmine
My hero is Jane Goodall. In the 1960s she went to Africa and studied chimpanzees. She found out that they eat meat and work together in groups. Jane works hard to protect animals and our planet.

b) Why are they the children's heroes?
Take notes in a table.

Grace Darling	Sir Barks-A-Lot	…	…	…
rescued nine people, very brave	always friendly, …	…	…	…

1: Skills Read | p. 229

c) Who is YOUR hero or favourite person? Why? Tell your partner about him/her.

My hero / favourite person is …

He/She lives in **Mainz**.

He/She is **friendly** and **clever**.

He/She can **play the guitar**.

I like him/her because he/she **listens to my problems**.

2 YOUR hero or favourite person WB 12 p. 43

| 2 p. 81

a) Copy the table. Then fill in the words from the box.
Can you find more words for your table? Look at number 1b) for help.

What is a hero / favourite person like?	What does a hero / favourite person do?
cool, …	works hard, …

cool | funny | works hard | good-looking | goes on adventures | interesting | sings well | nice | writes great books | …

b) Write a blog entry about your hero or favourite person. WEB 9

Search

My favourite person is **my cousin Vito**. **He** lives in **Bremen**. **He** is **funny** and **he** can **cook really well**. I like **him** because **he always has lots of good ideas**.

4 Grace Darling WB 13 p. 44

b) Complete the sentences with words from the box.

| 4b p. 83

survivors | boat | storm | lighthouse | shipwreck | window

1. In September 1838 there was a terrible XX.
2. Grace could see a shipwreck from her XX.
3. She and her father went out to sea in a XX.
4. They rowed quickly to the XX.
5. The XX got in the boat carefully.
6. Grace and her father brought the survivors safely to the XX.

2: Wordbank People | p. 210

6 p. 84

6 Grace's story

What did Grace Darling tell her brothers afterwards?
Put the sentences in the correct order.

1. from my window – I saw – a shipwreck – This morning – .
2. some survivors – also see – I could – .
3. needed to – the poor people – We – rescue – .
4. went out – Father and I – in our boat – to sea – .
5. very quickly – rowed – to the shipwreck – We – .
6. helped the survivors – the boat – Father – to get in – .
7. We – the people – brought – safely to the lighthouse – .
8. made – for everyone – Mother and our sisters – tea and soup – .
9. very happy – I'm – we saved – that – so many lives – .

10.1 What's missing?

Write down the missing adjectives and adverbs.

1. dangerous – …	2. … – safely	3. careful – …	4. … – terribly
5. fast – …	6. … – well	7. hungry – …	8. … – hard

11 p. 86

11 How are they doing things?

a) Look at the six pictures. Then complete the sentences with an adverb from the box.

carefully | dangerously | fast | beautifully | hard | loudly

1. The man is driving XX.

2. The girl is running XX.

3. The boy is working XX.

10.1: Grammar 9 | p. 248
11: Grammar 9 | p. 248

4. The old man is walking XX.

5. The dog is barking XX.

6. The woman is singing XX.

b) Write more (crazy) sentences.

Bagheera Sandeep My friend and I A and B …	is are	dancing flying eating sleeping …	happily. quietly. well. terribly. …

13 Choose an activity WB 16 p. 45

13 p. 87

You can:

- Look at all the information you have about Grace Darling. Make a quiz for your classmates.

1. Grace Darling lived in …
2. She had … brothers and … sisters.
3. Her father was …
4. On … 1838 there was a terrible storm.

…

- Be Grace Darling and tell your story to the class. Look at number 6 (page 94) for help.

Hello everyone, my name is Grace Darling.
I'm 22 years old and …
Last week there was a terrible storm. …

- Work with a partner. Make up an interview with Grace Darling. Practise the interview and act it out. Or record it and play it to the class. WEB 7

Excuse me, can I ask you some questions, please?

Yes, of course.

When did you see the shipwreck? – Why didn't your brothers rescue the survivors? – What did your mother say when you went out to the sea? – How did you feel in the boat? – …

13: Grammar 7 | p. 246

4.1 Emma's horoscope WB 1 p. 50

a) Listen to Ben and his sister Emma. Find out. L 1.29
- What is Emma's star sign?
- What does she think about horoscopes?

b) Listen again. What are Emma's and Ben's ideas about the future? Take notes.

	Emma	Ben
ideas about the future	– will help … …	– will … …

c) Compare your notes with a partner.

8.1 A horoscope for a friend WB 2 + 3 p. 50, 51

Write a horoscope for a friend. Look at the horoscope in number 8 (page 76) and the horoscopes on page 200 for help.

10 Jobs WB 6 + 7 + 8 p. 40, 41

10 p. 77 **c)** Walk around the classroom and ask your classmates about their future jobs. Take notes.

What will you be when you grow up?

I think I'll be a **nurse**.

Perhaps I'll be a …

Think of a way to present your results in class.

12 Our dream jobs

12 p. 78

a) Watch the clip. What are these jobs in German? 7

vet | pilot | actress | photographer | racing driver | zoologist | singer | chef | baker

b) Watch the clip again. Who wants to have which job?

Maria | George | Rosa | Joe | Zoe | Lewis | Eran |

Maria wants to be a / an …

c) Why are the children interested in these jobs?

d) Which of the jobs in a) would YOU like to have? Why?

13 Josh in Japan WB 9 p. 42

13 p. 78

a) Listen to Josh. What does he talk about? L 1.25

b) Listen again and take notes. Then write about Josh.

Josh thinks he'll be … He'll play … He'll …

14.1 A guessing game

Play a guessing game with a partner or in a group.
One of you thinks of a future job. The others ask questions to guess the job.

Will you work with people/animals/…?
Will you work in an office / a shop / …?
Will you use tools / a computer / …?
Will you wear a uniform / special clothes?
Will you …?
Will you be a …?

Yes, I will. / No, I won't.

14.1: Wordbank Jobs | p. 217

15.1 The year 3030 WB 4 p. 51

a) What do you think life will be like in the year 3030? Talk to a partner.

b) Read about Callum and his trip to the year 3030. What do you learn from the text?

It was a Sunday morning and Callum was still in bed. He looked out of his window and couldn't believe his eyes. The trees were gone, the cars were gone and all the houses looked very strange. They were huge, made of shiny metal and had funny shapes. Callum quickly got dressed and went outside. The streets were completely empty. Callum started walking and looked at the strange houses. Suddenly he saw a small spaceship slowly turn onto his street. But before he could take a good look, someone pulled him behind a house. Callum tried to scream but a blond boy held his mouth shut. Callum looked into the faces of a group of children and teenagers. They wore dirty clothes and had simple weapons in their hands. The tallest kid was a red-haired girl.
"Are you crazy? The robots almost saw you!" she said.
"The robots?! What robots?" Callum asked.
The red-haired girl looked at him and said: "What robots!? Are you joking? Do you really not know!? Well, many, many years ago humans had really good lives. Robots did everything for them. They cooked, cleaned, did the shopping, just everything! But about 50 years ago the robots started a war – and now they rule the world."
"Wow, that's crazy!" Callum said. "And where are all the humans now?"
"Well, most of them work as slaves for the robots," the red-haired girl said. "Some of us live in secret camps and fight back. But the robots try to find and catch us. So now you know why it's dangerous out here. OK, let's get back to the camp. Follow us!"
And the kids started running down dark alleys and small side streets. Callum followed them.
"We're almost there. Keep going", the blond boy told him.
Suddenly a huge robot stepped into their path. The kids started running in different directions to get away from it, but Callum tripped and fell. The robot walked towards him. When Callum looked up, the robot's huge hand tried to grab him. Callum screamed ... and woke up. He looked around and was back in his bed. He laughed happily. It had all been a crazy dream!

c) Read again and answer the questions in complete sentences.

1. Why couldn't Callum believe his eyes?
2. What turned onto his street?
3. Who told Callum about the robots?
4. What happened to the humans?
5. What did the huge robot do?
6. Why did Callum feel happy in the end?

d) Imagine YOU are in the year 3030. What can you see there? Who do you meet? What else do you experience? Write about it.

1 All kinds of heroes

WB 11 p. 43

a) Read the blog entries. Who are the children's heroes?

1a p. 80

Victor
Today in our English lesson we talked about Grace Darling. In 1838 there was a terrible storm in the north of England. Together with her father 22-year-old Grace went out to sea in a rowing boat and rescued nine people from a shipwreck. Grace was very brave. She risked her life to help others. So for me she is a real hero. Who is your hero?

Megan
It might sound funny but my hero is my dog. His name is Sir Barks-A-Lot and he is always friendly. During the day he is on his own. When I come home from school at quarter to five, he is so happy to see me. I can tell him about all my problems. He listens and makes me feel much better.

Sandeep
I'm a big football fan. So my heroes are usually football players. There are lots of great players all over the world but my favourite player at the moment is midfielder Dele Alli. He can run really fast, he is clever and he scores fantastic goals. Dele started playing for England when he was only 19 years old.

Ben
I think my hero is my sister Sarah. She is in a wheelchair because she can't walk. Sometimes she is sad about it but most of the time she is happy and doesn't complain. Sarah is really good at playing wheelchair basketball. And she loves helping other people, for example me. Then it is like having two mothers at home.

Jasmine
My hero is Jane Goodall. In the 1960s she went to Africa and studied chimpanzees. She was the first person to study wild chimps. She found out that they eat meat and work together in groups. Jane fights for the rights of apes and works hard to protect animals and our planet. There are also other people who do that. So they are my heroes, too.

1: Skills Read | p. 229

1.1 An interview with Sarah WB 5 p. 52

a) Listen to an interview with Sarah for the school magazine. What is Sarah talking about? L 1.30

her favourite pop star | her favourite film star | her favourite sportsperson

b) Listen again.
- What do you learn about Sarah's favourite person? Take notes.
- What do you find interesting? Why? Talk to a partner.

4.1 Royal National Lifeboat Institution WB 6 p. 52

Sieh dir die Informationen zur *Royal National Lifeboat Institution* an. Beantworte die Fragen von jemandem, der kein Englisch versteht.

The Royal National Lifeboat Institution (RNLI) was founded in 1824.

It has 238 lifeboat stations and operates 444 lifeboats.

The RNLI rescues people who are in trouble at sea. Lifeboat crews and lifeguards risk their lives to save others in the face of great danger – just as Grace Darling and her father did in 1838.

The RNLI provides – on call – a 24-hour search and rescue service.
It operates around the coasts of the United Kingdom, the Republic of Ireland, the Channel Islands and the Isle of Man.

The RNLI has saved more than 144,000 lives since 1824.

1. Was macht diese Organisation?
2. Wann wurde sie gegründet?
3. Wo ist sie tätig?
4. Welche Erfolge kann sie verzeichnen?

4.1: Skills Help out | p. 234

6 Grace's story

6 p. 84

What did Grace Darling tell her brothers afterwards?
Look at the story in number 4 again and write keywords for the pictures.
storm, morning, saw shipwreck from window, …
Then use the keywords to write Grace's story.

Let me tell you what happened after the terrible storm.
This morning I saw ...
Then ...
After that ...
Later ...
Finally ...

11 How are they doing things?

11 p. 86

a) Make adverbs from these adjectives.
Then read the sentences and complete them with an adverb.

careful | dangerous | fast | beautiful | hard | loud

1. The man is driving XX.
2. The girl is running XX.
3. The boy is working XX.
4. The old man is walking XX.
5. The dog is barking XX.
6. The woman is singing XX.

b) Think of more (crazy) sentences.

Bagheera is dancing happily.
My friend and I are ...
...

12.1 Mr Darling

WB 7 p. 53

Pick the right word (adjective or adverb) to complete the sentences.

1. Mr Darling looked at the sea **nervous / nervously**.
2. It was very stormy and he knew that **terrible / terribly** things could happen in this weather.
3. Very early on 7 September the storm wrecked the **beautiful / beautifully** SS Forfarshire.
4. His daughter Grace could see some survivors and wanted to help them **quick / quickly**.
5. Mr Darling needed time to think **clear / clearly** and decide what to do.
6. His sons weren't at home and the sea was very **rough / roughly**.
7. Finally he took his **brave / bravely** daughter with him to rescue the survivors.

6: Skills Write | p. 235
11: Grammar 9 | p. 248
12.1: Grammar 9 | p. 248

1 A spooky school trip

a) Listen to the story and read along. L 1.31

It was a cold and stormy autumn evening, and the windows of the big, old castle creaked in the wind. Sam and his classmates were on a school trip. Late in the evening Sam and his friends, Luke and Amy, were in Sam and Luke's room. The only light in the room came from the full moon outside. The friends were quietly telling each other spooky stories about angry ghosts and werewolves. Suddenly Sam noticed that Amy was missing.
"Where's Amy?" he asked.
"I don't know, she was here a minute ago," answered Luke.

The friends went to Amy's room, but she wasn't there. They couldn't find her anywhere. Then the boys noticed that the back door of the castle was open. A cold wind blew in from the dark forest outside. The friends looked at each other with big eyes.
Sam gulped nervously and said: "I think she's in the forest. Let's find her before the teachers notice she's missing."
Luke looked scared. "Shouldn't we ask one of the teachers for help?"
But Sam answered: "No, let's try and find her on our own. I don't want her to get in trouble for leaving the castle at night."

So the boys got their torches and quickly left through the back door. They could see some footprints in the soft ground and followed them into the forest. After a while there were no more footprints and soon they were lost. Then suddenly there was a noise in the bushes.
"What was that?" whispered Luke with panic in his voice.
"I don't know, maybe an animal!?" said Sam nervously.

Suddenly a huge wolf jumped out of the bushes and ran towards the boys. They screamed, turned around and started running. After a few steps, Sam fell over a big branch and dropped his torch. When he turned around, he looked straight into the big red eyes of the wolf. Without thinking, Sam picked up the big branch and hit the wolf in the face. The wolf yelped in pain and after a moment ran back into the woods.

Sam lay on the cold forest ground, breathing hard. He quietly called Luke's name. After a minute or two, he saw the light of Luke's torch coming towards him. The friends were glad that they were both OK. The big wolf was gone, but they still couldn't find their way back.

About twenty minutes later, they heard some noise and were relieved when they saw it was the castle's caretaker Mr McClement and their teachers, Mrs Muir and Mr Davis.
"What were you boys thinking? It's not safe to be out in the forest in the middle of the night! Let's get you back to your room. We'll talk about this in the morning," said Mrs Muir.
Before they started walking back, Sam asked: "Where's Amy? We tried to find her, but then there was a big wolf with red eyes …"
"What are you talking about? There are no wolves in this forest," said Mr McClement.
"And Amy is in her room. We checked everyone's rooms when we noticed that you two were missing," said Mr Davis.
Sam and Luke looked at each other and gulped. How was that possible? They were happy that Amy was back and couldn't wait to talk to her in the morning.

The next day, they went over to Amy's breakfast table to check if she was OK. Amy turned around to look at them – and Sam's heart nearly stopped: She had a big bruise on her face exactly where Sam had hit the wolf!

b) The story has six parts. Choose a good heading for each part.

Lost in the forest | The caretaker and the teachers | Angry ghosts | Looking for Amy | Amy's face | Lost in the castle | Telling stories | The wolf

c) Talk about the story.

The story is about …

At the beginning the friends …

In the second/third/… part …

At the end …

I think the story is …

I think the ending is …

2 How to make a story interesting

a) Look at these two texts. What is different?

① It was an autumn evening, and the windows of the castle creaked in the wind. The only light in the room came from the moon outside. The friends were telling each other stories about ghosts and werewolves.

② It was a cold and stormy autumn evening, and the windows of the big, old castle creaked in the wind. The only light in the room came from the full moon outside. The friends were quietly telling each other spooky stories about angry ghosts and werewolves.

b) Which words make the second text more interesting? Write them down. What kind of words are these?

c) Which words describe these people or things? Collect ideas.

my friend: scared | clever | funny | …

ghost: white | angry | strange | …

house: spooky | cold | empty | …

weather: rainy | dark | grey | …

d) Read the beginning of this story and make it more interesting.
Write an ending to the story, too.
These words can help you:

big | old | black | dark | spooky | cold | bright | old | warm | interesting | loud | strange | slowly | carefully | …

There was a house in a forest. It was night but there was a light at the window. A woman was sitting by the fire in the living room. She was reading a book. Suddenly the light went out. There was a noise. The woman went to the door, opened it and …

3 A different ending

a) Read the last part of the story "A spooky school trip" in number 1 again. Think of a different ending. Collect ideas with a partner and make notes.

b) Now write YOUR ending. Portfolio-Ordner

c) Read your ending to the class.

3+: Skills Write | p. 235

4+ YOUR story

Make up a story. You can look at the pictures for ideas. Portfolio-Ordner

PLAN IT

- Collect ideas first and make notes, for example:

WHO?	WHERE?	WHEN?	WHAT?
– I	– old castle	– last weekend	– weather
– two friends	– dark tower	– two years ago	– noises
– ghosts	– ...	– ...	– lights
– ...			– ...

DO IT

- Write your story.
  Your story needs a beginning, a middle and an end.
  Here is an example of a beginning:

> Last weekend Julian and Lana got lost on a hiking trip. It was late and the weather was ... Suddenly ...

- Use adjectives and adverbs to make your story interesting.
- Use *time words* and *linking words*.
  Time words help to show when something happened.
  Linking words help you to connect ideas and sentences.
- Think of a good title, too.

time words (when?)
last weekend/… | first | then | at … o'clock | in the morning/… | before | after (that) | finally | …

linking words (connect sentences)
and | because | so | but | …

CHECK IT

- Is the English OK?
- Is your story interesting enough for others to read or listen to?
- Swap stories with a partner and give each other feedback on your texts.
- Edit your text.

PRESENT IT

- Show your story to the class. Read it, record it or put it up in the classroom.

4+: Skills Write | p. 235, Talk | p. 231

Theme 4

Celebrations

In diesem *Theme* ...

- berichtest du über Feste und Feiern.
- erfährst du etwas über traditionelle Feste und über Feste anderer Kulturen in Großbritannien.
- sprichst du über Pläne und Vorhaben in der Zukunft.
- lernst du, Gegenstände und Personen zu vergleichen.

B

A

C

D

1 Lots of festivals WB 1 p. 54

a) Look at the pictures of different festivals and talk about them.

In picture A I can see ...

There is/are ...

...

b) Match the pictures with the correct names. Which pictures were easy to match?

Halloween | Eid | Christmas | Mother's Day | Hanukkah | Chinese New Year | Easter | New Year's Eve

I think picture A is ...

4

E

F

G

H

c) What other festivals do you know? What festivals do YOU celebrate?

> I celebrate …

d) Look at the pictures again and listen to five dialogues.
What are the people celebrating? L 1.32

> In dialogue 1 the people are celebrating …

What else did you understand?

2 Festival activities
WB 2 p. 54

What do you know about these festivals? Match the sentence parts.

1. For Halloween
2. At Easter
3. On New Year's Eve
4. On Mother's Day
5. During Eid
6. On Chinese New Year
7. During Hanukkah
8. For Christmas

A people often have parties and set off fireworks.
B Jews light a new candle on the Menorah every evening.
C people decorate pumpkins and wear scary costumes.
D Muslims celebrate the end of Ramadan.
E people often give each other chocolate eggs as presents.
F children thank their mums.
G people usually decorate a tree at home and give each other presents.
H children get red envelopes from their family and friends with good-luck money for the New Year.

2.1 p. 122
2.1 p. 130
2.2 p. 130

3 Favourite festivals

a) What is YOUR favourite festival? Think about it and make notes. Then talk about it with a partner.

What's your favourite festival?

When is it?

How do you celebrate it?

We I ...	usually often sometimes ...	go to / have a party. have a big meal. eat ... and drink ... visit friends. decorate our house. go to church. set off fireworks. go to bed early/late. wear special clothes. ...

b) Form a double circle in class and tell each other about your favourite festivals.

My favourite festival is ...

It's in ... We usually ...

3.1 p. 122
3.1 p. 131
3.2 p. 131

3: Wordbank Celebrations | p. 218
3: Skills Double Circle | p. 238

LAND & LEUTE ▶ 9

Traditionelle Feste in Großbritannien

Die meisten Briten feiern Ostern (*Easter*) und Weihnachten (*Christmas*). Es gibt in Großbritannien auch einen Muttertag (*Mother's Day*), der jedoch nicht wie bei uns im Mai, sondern im März stattfindet. Auch der Valentinstag (*Valentine's Day*) am 14. Februar wird in Großbritannien etwas anders begangen als bei uns. Man schenkt sich nicht nur Blumen oder Pralinen, sondern verschickt auch Karten, und zwar ohne seinen Namen zu nennen.
Ein beliebtes Fest im Herbst ist *Halloween*. Es entstand vor über eintausend Jahren in der Keltenzeit auf den Britischen Inseln. Heute gehen die Kinder verkleidet von Haus zu Haus. Sie fordern mit „Süßem oder Saurem" (*trick or treat)* die Bewohner auf, ihnen Süßigkeiten zu geben.
In den meisten Gegenden Großbritanniens wird am 31. Dezember Silvester so gefeiert, wie ihr es auch aus Deutschland kennt, allerdings wird auf der Straße nur selten Feuerwerk gezündet. Um Mitternacht singen viele Menschen das traditionelle Lied *Auld Lang Syne*. Dabei stehen sie im Kreis und halten sich an den Händen. Da in Großbritannien Menschen aus aller Welt leben, werden dort auch noch andere Neujahrsfeste gefeiert.

Welche anderen Neujahrsfeste kennst du? Wie feierst du Neujahr?

Sieh dir nun den Clip an und finde heraus:
- Wann wird in Großbritannien Weihnachten gefeiert?
- Was befindet sich in den *Christmas stockings* und *Christmas crackers*?
- Was singen Affen an Weihnachten?

4 Sound check

a) Listen to the words and repeat them. L 1.33

b) Which words are spoken like <u>ce</u>lebrate (<u>O</u>oo)? Which words are spoken like ad<u>ven</u>ture (o<u>O</u>o)? Make two lists.

festival | decorate | musician | together | beautiful | exciting | fantastic | family | tomorrow | envelope

Ooo	oOo
celebrate	adventure
…	…

c) Listen again and check your lists.

5 It's Diwali time WB 3 p. 55

Sandeep and his family are Hindus. Their favourite festival is Diwali.

a) Listen to the dialogue. Where does London's big Diwali festival take place? L 1.34

b) Now read the dialogue. What do you learn about Diwali?

Neela: Guess what's coming up soon?

Pradeep: Oh Neela, we all know. It's Diwali.

Neela: Exactly! I'm really looking forward to it. This year I'm going to wear my most beautiful sari, the purple one.

Mrs Chopra: And I'm going to wear my new green sari. Oh, I can't wait to decorate our house with fresh flowers.

Mr Chopra: We need lots of candles, too. I'm going to buy new ones next week and put them in the windows.

Sandeep: I'd like to invite my friend Josh to our house. Is that OK? I don't think he knows much about Diwali.

Mrs Chopra: No problem. I hope he likes our traditional Indian food and sweets.

Sandeep: I'm pretty sure about that. And he'll love our firework display.

Mr Chopra: Brilliant! He could also come with us to the Diwali festival on Trafalgar Square. There's going to be live music and fantastic singing and dancing.

Pradeep: But it's best in the evening. Trafalgar Square looks great when all the buildings shine in different colours.

Sandeep: Yeah, you're right. I'm going to call Josh and ask him. Let's see if he's ready for Diwali.

5c p. 122 **c)** Who is going to do what?

Mr Chopra Sandeep Neela and Mrs Chopra	is are	going to	wear … buy … call … put …

5: Grammar 10 | p. 249

6 Facts about Diwali WB 4 p. 55

6 p. 123

a) Listen to the dialogue. What does Josh say to Sandeep about Diwali? L 1.35

b) Read the sentences. Then listen again. Are they right or wrong? Correct what's wrong.

1. Diwali is the Hindu festival of lights.
2. Hindus celebrate for seven days.
3. First they clean their houses and decorate them.
4. Then they meet their family and friends.
5. They give them presents and money.
6. People hope that Lakshmi comes to their house.
7. She is the goddess of money and light.

7 Plans for Diwali WB 5 p. 56

The Chopras are looking forward to Diwali. Look at the pictures and write about their plans.

wear their best clothes | decorate his room | make Diwali cards for family and friends | give their children presents and sweets | buy fireworks | cook traditional food

1. Neela is going to ...
2. Mr Chopra and Pradeep are going to ...
...

1

2

3

4

5

6

7.1 p. 123

7.1 p. 131

7: Grammar 10 | p. 249

I8 p. 124

8 What are their plans?

What are the Chopras going to do? What aren't they going to do?

Sandeep The Chopras	is isn't are aren't	going to	wear a sari. give Josh some sweets, too. decorate their windows with balloons. celebrate Diwali with Megan and Ben. wear his best shirt and trousers. set off fireworks.

9 Plans for the weekend WB 6 p. 56

a) What can you do at the weekend? Make notes.

go to a party, meet friends in town,
play ..., ...

b) Walk around the classroom and ask your classmates about their plans.
Look at your notes from a) for help.

Are you going to **go to a party** this weekend?

Yes, I am.

No, I'm not.

9.1 p. 132

c) Write about your plans for a perfect weekend.
What are you going to do?

My plans for a perfect weekend
On Friday evening I'm going to ... Then ...
On Saturday morning I'm going to ...
After that ... ...

10 Choose an activity

You can:

- Make a calendar for your classroom with all the special days and festivals that you and your classmates celebrate.
- Make an ABC of festival or celebration words.

A – activities, ...
B – big meals, ...
C – celebrate, ...
...

- Show pictures of a family celebration and talk about them.
  "This is a picture of ... Here you can see ... We're dancing and ..."

8: Grammar 10b | p. 249
9: Grammar 10c | p. 249
10: Wordbank Celebrations | p. 218

11 Lena's email WB 7 p. 57

11 p. 124
11 p. 132

Sandeep's class takes part in the eTwinning project 'Festivals around the world'.

a) Read the email they get from Lena. What does she get during Hanukkah?

From [illegible]
Subject Festivals

Hello everyone,
My name is Lena and I'm from Poland. My family and I are Jewish.
My favourite festival is Hanukkah. It's the Jewish festival of lights. It's at the end of November or the beginning of December and it lasts eight days.
During Hanukkah my grandparents come to our house every evening. Right after sunset we light a new candle on the Menorah. It looks beautiful! We say blessings and pay respect to God.
Afterwards we play games and sing traditional Jewish songs. I also get small presents each night and chocolate coins.
During Hanukkah we eat latkes. They are pancakes made from potatoes and fried in oil. We eat them with apple sauce or sour cream. They are delicious. We often have jam doughnuts, too.
This year we're going to decorate the living room with some really nice Hanukkah garlands. I can't wait to celebrate Hanukkah.
What is your favourite festival?
Bye for now,
Lena

b) Read the email again and find out:
- What kind of festival is Hanukkah?
- When is it?
- What does Lena's family do during Hanukkah?
- What do they eat?

11.1 p. 125

12 Target task: YOUR favourite festival

12 p. 125

a) Write an email to an English-speaking partner class and tell them about your favourite festival.
Think about:
- when the festival takes place
- why you celebrate it
- what you need
- what you do
- what you wear
- what you eat and drink
- …

Look at numbers 3 and 11 for help. WEB 4 Portfolio-Ordner

b) Ask your classmates or your teacher to check your email. Then correct it.

c) Collect all your emails and send them to your partner class.

11: Skills Read | p. 229
12: Skills Write | p. 235, Write an email | p. 236/237
12: Wordbank Celebrations | p. 218

I1 p. 126

1 A brilliant idea WB 8 p. 58

a) Listen to the phone call. Who is talking? L 1.36

b) Listen again.
- What is the problem?
- What is the plan?
- Where and when are they going to meet?

2 Let's get started WB 9 p. 58

a) Look at the picture. Where are the kids? What do you think they are doing?

b) Listen and read along. What do the kids need for the party? What is on their shopping list? L 1.37

Megan: So what do we need for the surprise party?
Sarah: I guess we need lots of sweets. And crisps, of course. At least five packets.
Sandeep: Wait a second. I'll write it down for us.
Megan: Thanks. We should buy some sausages, too.
Sir Barks-A-Lot: Woof woof!
Megan: No, you can't be hungry, good boy.
Sarah: Ha ha! We could also make some vegetable sticks. So we need a few carrots, a cucumber and some red or yellow peppers.
Sandeep: Ugh, that sounds too healthy.
Megan: But it's good for you, Sandeep. And if you like, you can also eat salad. My mum is going to make one for us.
Sarah: That's great. Do we need any muffins for the party?
Megan: Sure. But we don't need to buy any because Jasmine is going to bring her extra yummy chocolate muffins.
Sandeep: Sounds good. What about water and lemonade? I think we need at least six bottles of each.
Sarah: You're right. And we should buy some decorations.
Megan: I guess we don't need to buy any. We've got loads of balloons and garlands in our party box. Let's have a look.

c) What else do the kids need for a good party? Talk in groups.

3 What do they want to buy?

Look at number 2 again and complete the sentences.

carrots | muffins | packets of crisps | bottles of water and lemonade | cucumber | decorations | sausages | peppers

1. The kids want to buy at least five XX.
2. They want to buy some XX, too. Sir Barks-A-Lot likes them a lot.
3. They also need a few XX, a XX and some XX.
4. They don't have to buy any XX. Jasmine wants to make them.
5. They want to buy some XX but they don't need any coffee or tea.
6. What about XX? They don't have to buy any. Megan has got loads of balloons and garlands.

3.1 p. 126

4 What's in the party box?

WB 10 p. 59

Talk about what you can see in Megan's party box. Use **some** or **any**.

sweets | balloons | games | pizza | presents | party hats | crisps | garlands | candles | cake

Megan has got some …
but she hasn't got any …

There are … in the party box.

There isn't/aren't …
in the party box.

4.1 p. 126
4.1 p. 133

5 Sound check

Listen to the sentences. Then say them yourself. L 1.38

[æ]

1. Thank you for the delicious salad.
2. We need a packet of carrots.

[eɪ]

3. He wants to make a nice cake.
4. Let's buy some lemonade and decorations.

4: Grammar 12a | p. 252

6 p. 127

6 A recipe for a party salad

WB 11 + 12 p. 59, 60

Sieh dir das Rezept an. Welche Zutaten braucht man dafür? Welche Arbeitsschritte sind nötig? Berichte jemandem, der kein Englisch versteht.

Für dieses Rezept braucht man …

Zuerst muss man … Danach …

Party Salad

500 g pasta (penne or fusilli)
1 yellow pepper
1 zucchini
1 red onion
200 g cherry tomatoes
120 g black olives
5 tablespoons olive oil
3 tablespoons vinegar
1 teaspoon black pepper
1 teaspoon salt

1. Cook the pasta in boiling salted water until it is ready to eat. Pour away the water.
2. Wash the vegetables. Cut the yellow pepper and the zucchini into small pieces.
3. Cut the tomatoes in half.
4. Peel the onion and cut it into small pieces.
5. Put the pasta and all the vegetables into a large bowl. Then mix everything with a large spoon.
6. Take a cup and mix the olive oil, the vinegar, the black pepper and the salt.
7. Pour the dressing over the pasta and vegetables. Then mix again.

Enjoy!

7 p. 128

7 How much?

WB 13 p. 60

Work with a partner. Look at the recipe in number 6 again. Ask and answer questions.

How much **olive oil** do we need for the salad?

We need **five tablespoons**.

How many **yellow peppers** do we need?

We need **one**.

How much benutzt du mit <u>nicht zählbaren</u> Nomen (z. B. *water*, *oil*, *salt*, *time*, *money*, …).
How many benutzt du mit <u>zählbaren</u> Nomen (z. B. *eggs*, *tomatoes*, *olives*, *books*, *phones*, …).

7.1 p. 128

6: Skills Help out | p. 234
7: Grammar 12b | p. 253

8 Looking for a present WB 14 p. 61

a) What do you think: What would be a good present for Ben?

b) Listen to the dialogue. What present do Jasmine and Sandeep choose for Ben? L 1.39

c) Now read the dialogue. What ideas for presents have Jasmine and Sandeep got? Are they similar to your ideas in a)?

Jasmine: This is a great shop. We'll definitely find a good present for Ben.
Sandeep: Yeah, let's have a look around.
Jasmine: Here is some hair gel. Hm, smells good.
Sandeep: Let me see. No, I think this hair gel here smells better. But I don't know if Ben wants any hair gel. Ah, here are some caps. This green one is cool.
Jasmine: I think this blue cap is cooler than the green one. And that black one is definitely the coolest. But is a cap a good present for Ben?
Sandeep: Probably not. We could buy him a voucher. Then he could choose a nice present himself.
Jasmine: Well, a voucher is OK. But isn't it much nicer to get Ben a real present?

15 minutes later …

Sandeep: I'm sure we've found the best present for Ben, much better than a voucher and cheaper than one of the caps.
Jasmine: You're right. Ben loves good pens for drawing. Should we get some chocolate for him, too?
Sandeep: Yeah, why not? Or jelly beans. They're just as yummy as chocolate.
Jasmine: You really have a sweet tooth. But let's pay for the pens first. We can buy some sweets later.
Shop assistant: Hello. That's £6.50, please.
Jasmine: Here you are.
Shop assistant: Thank you. And here's your change. Have a nice day!
Jasmine and **Sandeep:** Thanks. Bye!

8.1 p. 133
8.2 p. 134

8a: Skills Think – pair – share | p. 238
8c: Grammar 11a | p. 250

9 Presents

a) What are these presents? You can look at number 8 for help.

1. You wear it on your head.
2. You can write and draw with them.
3. It is usually brown and delicious.
4. You can buy something nice with it.
5. You style your hair with it.
6. They are bad for your teeth.

b) Write a quiz for your partner. Describe three more presents for a friend.

10 What's nicer? WB 15 p. 61

a) Work with a partner. Compare the presents Jasmine and Sandeep looked at in the shop.

I think the cap is as cool as the sunglasses.

But I think the cap is cheaper than the sunglasses.

I think	the cap the sunglasses the voucher the scarf …	is are	nicer than cooler than prettier than cheaper than better than as nice as as cool as as pretty as as good as as yummy as	the …

b) What do you think is the best / the coolest / the nicest / ... present?

11 Language detective

a) Be a language detective. Mit Adjektiven kannst du Dinge und Menschen vergleichen. Schreibe die Adjektive von Aufgabe 10 wie folgt auf. Welche Regeln kannst du finden?

- nice – nicer – the nicest
- …

b) Wie kannst du ausdrücken, dass Dinge gleich sind?

9: Wordbank Things | p. 219
10: Grammar 11a | p. 250
11: Grammar 11a | p. 250

12 A poem

a) Listen to the poem and read along. L 1.40

It's my birthday – it's the best day of the year!
I opened all my presents when my friends were here.
Fancy sunglasses and a really pretty scarf.
A nice poster and an even nicer phone case.
The funniest comic book and a little chocolate, too.
They are the greatest presents, they are really cool.

b) Change lines 3–5 to write one more verse for the poem. Portfolio-Ordner

13 Good, better, best

a) Put the adjectives in alphabetical order.

funny | big | small | short | clever | hot | tall | good | strong | happy

b) Add the comparative and superlative forms.

big, bigger, the biggest
...

Aufgepasst:
Bei manchen Adjektiven ändert sich die Schreibweise, wenn du sie steigerst (siehe S. 250).

c) Compare your results with a partner.

13.1 p. 129

14 I'm as strong as you!

Use the adjectives from number 13 and write comparisons with **than** or **as ... as**.
You can write funny comparisons, too.

Robin Hood is as clever as Tarzan.
My feet are bigger than Onur's feet.
...

14.1 p. 129

13: Grammar 11a | p. 250
14: Grammar 11a | p. 250

15 Different people

Look at the picture and compare the friends.

short | tall | funny | big | long | cool | nice | …

Sandeep is taller than Lynn.
Josh is the tallest.
Ben's hair is as short as …
…

16 Birthday songs

a) Listen to the song and sing along. L 1.41

b) What other birthday songs do you know in English? Or do you know any birthday songs in other languages? Present them to the class.

c) Make a class recording with all your birthday songs.

For he's a jolly good fellow,
for he's a jolly good fellow,
for he's a jolly good fellow,
and so say all of us,
and so say all of us,
and so say all of us,
For he's a jolly good fellow,
for he's a jolly good fellow,
for he's a jolly good fellow,
and so say all of us!

17 Celebrating your birthday

a) Watch the clip. How do these people like to celebrate their birthday?
Take notes. 10

Tom | Abigail | Joe | Vicky | George | Ken | Rosa | Jessica

b) Whose birthday celebration do you like best? Why?

c) Interview your friends and family about how they celebrate their birthday. Make a video and show it to the class. WEB 10

17.1 p. 134
17.2 p. 135

15: Grammar 11a | p. 250
17: Skills Watch a video clip | p. 228

18 The surprise party

a) Look at the pictures. Then listen and put them in the right order. L 1.42

1

2

3

4

5

6

b) ❙ Ben's friend David couldn't come to the party.
The next day Ben told him about his special birthday.
What did he say?

❙ 18b p. 129

> You knew about Sarah and Megan's plan, right? Well, I didn't. So yesterday Sarah and I went to Megan's house. We wanted to watch a film in the living room. When I opened the door, …

c) What would YOU do to surprise someone on his or her birthday?

19 Target task: YOUR party

WB **test yourself** p. 62 + 63; **Portfolio** p. 126 / **WEB** P4

a) Work in groups and plan a party in your class. Collect ideas. Think about:
- party theme
- decorations
- things you need
- party food and drink
- games and activities
- music
- …

b) Present your ideas in class.

c) Choose the best ideas and decide who brings or does what. Then have a great party.

> So kannst du Ideen äußern und diskutieren:
> *I think we need …*
> *We could/ should …*
> *Let's …*
> *What about …?*
> *Why don't we …?*
>
> *That's a great idea.*
> *That sounds good.*
> *I don't know.*
> *I think … is better.*

2.1 Festivals

Complete the sentences with words from the box.

celebrate | decorate | set off | eggs | costumes | chocolate | envelopes | candles

1. For Christmas people usually buy a tree and XX it.
2. On Halloween people enjoy wearing scary XX.
3. During Hanukkah Jews light the XX on the Menorah.
4. On Mother's Day children often give their mums cards and XX.
5. During Eid Muslims XX the end of Ramadan.
6. On Chinese New Year children get red XX with good-luck money.
7. On New Year's Eve people often XX fireworks.
8. On Easter people often eat chocolate XX.

3.1 Odd one out

a) Find the odd one out.

1. Easter • Eid • Christmas • Chinese
2. house • church • fireworks • school
3. decorate • visit • pumpkin • celebrate
4. people • presents • children • friends
5. new • have • special • scary
6. late • often • usually • always

Manchmal passt das gesuchte Wort inhaltlich nicht in die Reihe. Manchmal gehört das gesuchte Wort zu einer anderen Wortart (Nomen, Verb, Adverb, Adjektiv).

b) Write a new "odd one out" for your partner.

5 It's Diwali time WB 3 p. 55

5 p. 110 **c)** Who is going to do what in Sandeep's family (page 110)?

Mr Chopra Sandeep Neela and Mrs Chopra	is are	going to	wear saris. buy candles. call his friend Josh. put candles in the windows.

5: Grammar 10 | p. 249

6 Facts about Diwali WB 4 p. 55

6 p. 111

a) Listen to the dialogue. What does Josh say to Sandeep about Diwali? (Four sentences are correct.) L 1.35

A I can bring some candles, too. | B Five days is a long time. | C I like Indian food. | D I sometimes cook Indian food at home. | E A firework display sounds like fun. | F I'm going to wear my best shirt. | G I'm looking forward to Diwali.

b) Read the sentences. Then listen again. Pick the correct sentence ending.

1. Diwali is the Hindu festival of **lights / candles**.
2. Hindus celebrate for **seven days / five days**.
3. First they clean their **houses and decorate them / windows and decorate them**.
4. Then they meet their **family and friends / best friends**.
5. They give them **presents and money / presents and sweets**.
6. People hope that Lakshmi **comes to their house / has a great time**.
7. She is the goddess of **money and light / money and good luck**.

7.1 Plans for a party

Jasmine and her family are going to have a New Year's Eve party at their house. Look at the pictures and write about their plans.

buy food and drinks | wear her new skirt | invite their family and friends | decorate the house | make pizza | play good music

1. Jasmine and her father are going to ...
2. Jason is going to ...
...

1 

2 

3 

4 

5 

6 

7.1: Grammar 10 | p. 249

8 p. 112

8 What are their plans?

What are the Chopras going to do? What aren't they going to do?

Sandeep The Chopras	is isn't are aren't	going to	wear a sari. give Josh some sweets, too. decorate their windows with balloons. set off fireworks. celebrate Diwali with Megan and Ben. wear his best shirt and trousers.

11 p. 113

11 Lena's email

WB 7 p. 57

Sandeep's class takes part in the eTwinning project 'Festivals around the world'.

a) Read the email they get from Lena. What does she get during Hanukkah?

From [illegible]
Subject Festivals

Hello everyone,
My name is Lena and I'm from Poland.
My favourite festival is Hanukkah. It's the Jewish festival of lights.
It's at the end of November or the beginning of December and it lasts eight days.
During Hanukkah my grandparents come to our house every evening. Then we light a new candle on the Menorah. It looks beautiful! We say blessings and pay respect to God.
Afterwards we play games and sing traditional Jewish songs.
I also get small presents and chocolate coins.
During Hanukkah we eat latkes. They are pancakes made from potatoes. They are delicious.
We often have jam doughnuts, too.
What is your favourite festival?
Bye for now,
Lena

8: Grammar 10c | p. 249

b) Read the email again and find out:
- What kind of festival is Hanukkah?
- When is it?
- What does Lena's family do during Hanukkah?
- What do they eat?

11.1 What are the words?

Find the words in number 11 and write them down.

1. a country
2. two months
3. a number
4. something that gives light
5. a brown sweet
6. another word for yummy

12 Target task: YOUR favourite festival

12 p. 113

a) Write an email to an English-speaking partner class and tell them about your favourite festival. Think about:
- when the festival takes place
- why you celebrate it
- what you need
- what you do
- what you wear
- what you eat and drink
- …

Look at numbers 3 (page 108) and 11 (page 113/124) for help. WEB 4 Portfolio-Ordner

To [illegible]
Subject Festivals

Hello everyone,
My name is … and I'm from …
My favourite festival is …
It's in …
We celebrate it because …
On/During … we …
We also …
I/We usually wear …
We always/often eat … and drink …
…
What is your favourite festival?
Bye for now,
…

Beginne deine E-Mail mit *Hello everyone, Dear partner class, Hi, …*

Fange die erste Zeile nach der Begrüßung mit einem Großbuchstaben an.

So kannst du deine E-Mail beenden: *Bye for now, Best wishes, All the best, …*

b) Ask your classmates or your teacher to check your email. Then correct it.

c) Collect all your emails and send them to your partner class.

12: Skills Write | p. 235,
Write an email | p. 236/237

1 p. 114

1 A brilliant idea WB 8 p. 58

a) Listen to the phone call. Who is talking? L 1.36

b) Listen again.
- What is the problem?
  a) Ben has problems with his parents.
  b) Ben doesn't want to celebrate his birthday.
- What is the plan?
  a) The friends want to organise a surprise party for Ben.
  b) The friends want to talk to Ben's parents.
- Where and when are they going to meet?
  a) They are going to meet at Ben's house on Saturday.
  b) They are going to meet at Megan's house the next day.

3.1 What did they buy?

Look at the pictures. What did the friends buy for the party?

bottle(s) of | box(es) of | packet(s) of

sweets | water | sausages | orange juice | crisps | lemonade | vegetables

The friends bought six packets of ...,
...

4.1 What's on the table?

Write about what you can see on the breakfast table. Use **some** or **any**.

There is some tea but there isn't any milk.
There are some cornflakes but there aren't any ...

milk | coffee | toast | cornflakes | jam | tea | orange juice | eggs | sausages | honey | ...

4.1: Grammar 12a | p. 252

6 A recipe for a party salad WB 11 + 12 p. 59, 60

6 p. 116

a) Sieh dir das Rezept an.
Welche Zutaten braucht man dafür?

b) Ordne die Arbeitsschritte den Bildern zu.

c) Berichte nun jemandem, der kein Englisch versteht, wie man diesen Salat zubereitet.

Für dieses Rezept braucht man …

Zuerst muss man … Danach …

Sind dir einige Wörter in der Zutatenliste nicht bekannt? Dann überlege, ob du ähnliche Wörter aus deiner Muttersprache kennst.
Das Wort *pepper* hat übrigens zwei Bedeutungen. Welche sind das?

Party Salad

500 g pasta (penne or fusilli)	1 red onion	5 tablespoons olive oil
1 yellow pepper	200 g cherry tomatoes	3 tablespoons vinegar
1 zucchini	120 g black olives	1 teaspoon black pepper
		1 teaspoon salt

1. Cook the pasta in boiling salted water until it is ready to eat. Pour away the water.
2. Wash the vegetables. Cut the yellow pepper and the zucchini into small pieces.
3. Cut the tomatoes in half.
4. Peel the onion and cut it into small pieces.
5. Put the pasta and all the vegetables into a large bowl. Then mix everything with a large spoon.
6. Take a cup and mix the olive oil, the vinegar, the black pepper and the salt.
7. Pour the dressing over the pasta and vegetables. Then mix again.

Enjoy!

A

B

C

D

E

F

G

7 p. 116

7 How much? WB 13 p. 60

Work with a partner. Look at the recipe in number 6 again. Ask and answer questions.

How much **olive oil** do we need for the salad?

We need **five tablespoons**.

olive oil | salt | vinegar | black pepper | pasta

How much benutzt du mit nicht zählbaren Nomen (z. B. *water, oil, salt, time, money, …*). *How many* benutzt du mit zählbaren Nomen (z. B. *eggs, tomatoes, olives, books, phones, …*).

How many **yellow peppers** do we need?

We need **one**.

yellow peppers | olives | cherry tomatoes | onions | zucchinis

7.1 Much or many?

a) Complete the questions with "much" or "many".

1. How **many** / **much** apples can you eat in one day?
2. How **many** / **much** water do you drink in one day?
3. How **many** / **much** toast do you have for breakfast?
4. How **many** / **much** books did you read in your holidays?
5. How **many** / **much** sweatshirts are there in your wardrobe?
6. How **many** / **much** money do you have in your schoolbag?
7. How **many** / **much** time do you need for your homework every day?
8. How **many** / **much** cousins do you have?

b) Ask and answer the questions with a partner.

How many apples can you eat in one day?

Maybe four.

7: Grammar 12b | p. 253
7.1: Grammar 12b | p. 253

13.1 Chocolate is sweeter

a) Write comparisons.

sweet → fruit – chocolate – marshmallows
tall → gorillas – elephants – giraffes

small → guinea pigs – mice – butterflies
fast → cars – trains – planes

Fruit is sweet. Chocolate is sweeter. Marshmallows are the sweetest.
...

b) Can you find more examples?

14.1 Different or the same?

Write comparisons with **than** or **as ... as**.

The white car is dirtier than the yellow car.
Maths is ...
...

dirty

good

cheap

yummy

tall

nice

18 The surprise party

b) Ben's friend David couldn't come to the party.
The next day Ben told him about his special birthday.
What did he say?

I saw ... | sang "Happy Birthday" |
gave me their presents | I got ... |
we ate ... and drank ... | we danced |
took lots of photos | it was ... | ...

You knew about Sarah and Megan's plan, right? Well, I didn't. So yesterday Sarah and I went to Megan's house. We wanted to watch a film in the living room. When I opened the door, ...

18b p. 121

13.1: Grammar 11a | p. 250
14.1: Grammar 11a | p. 250

2.1 St Patrick's Day

a) Andrew from Ireland is talking about St Patrick's Day, an important Irish festival.
Listen to the radio interview.
Take notes on these questions: L 1.43
- When is St Patrick's Day?
- What happens on St Patrick's Day?
- What are Andrew's plans?

Then check your notes with a partner.

b) Who was St Patrick? Find out more about him and tell your class. WEB 6

2.2 Christmas WB 1 p. 67

a) Read Jasmine's text for the Haverstock school project "Christmas celebrations".
What do you like about her Christmas? What don't you like?

Christmas Jasmine Bolt, year 8

About a week before Christmas we buy a Christmas tree. We put it up in our living room and decorate it. We also write Christmas cards and send them to friends and relatives. We hang the cards we get on our living room door or put them on the mantelpiece. The 24th December, Christmas Eve, is a normal working day. In the evening we put mince pies for Father Christmas and some carrots for his reindeer in front of the chimney. We also put presents under the Christmas tree and hang stockings from the mantelpiece. When Father Christmas comes down the chimney at night, he puts the presents for the children in the stockings. On Christmas Day, the 25th December, my brother Jason and I open our presents in the morning. There is always a big family meal, it's usually turkey for lunch. Everyone gets a Christmas cracker that you pull open with your neighbour. In our crackers there are some small plastic toys and a paper crown. Then everyone wears the paper crown on their head – it looks really funny. We play lots of silly games and have a great time. The 26th December is also a holiday. It is called Boxing Day because in the past rich people gave poor people boxes of food. On this day we always have the leftovers from the Christmas meal, go for a walk and visit relatives.

b) Read the text again and write down what is similar and different to Christmas in Germany.
What could you tell Jasmine about how people celebrate Christmas in Germany?

similar	different
a Christmas tree	presents on the 25th December
…	…

3.1 A festival dialogue

Work with a partner and act out the dialogue.

Partner A	Partner B
1 Frage B, was sein/ihr Lieblingsfest ist.	2 Antworte A.
3 Frage B, warum es sein/ihr Lieblingsfest ist.	4 Erläutere den Grund. Erkläre dabei auch, was du normalerweise an dem Fest machst, mit wem du feierst, was du trägst und was du isst und trinkst. Frage dann A, was sein/ihr Lieblingsfest ist.
5 Antworte B.	6 Frage A, warum es sein/ihr Lieblingsfest ist.
7 Erläutere den Grund. Erkläre dabei auch, was du normalerweise an dem Fest machst, mit wem du feierst, was du trägst und was du isst und trinkst.	8 Sage, dass sich das nach einem tollen Fest anhört.

3.2 A carnival poster

Sieh dir das Poster an. Beantworte die Fragen von jemandem, der wenig Deutsch versteht.

1. Where is the carnival party?
2. Should I wear a costume?
3. What will happen at the party?
4. How much money should I take with me?

7.1 Different plans

a) What are these people's plans? What do you think they are going to do?

1. Liam: "I'm so hungry."
2. Annie: "My jeans are too short."
3. Selim: "I can't find my phone."
4. Layla: "It's Halloween tomorrow."
5. Samuel: "Rap is my favourite music."

1. I think Liam is going to ...
...

b) Compare your ideas with a partner.

3.2: Skills Help out | p. 234
7.1: Grammar 10b | p. 249

9.1 What are you going to do?

Put the questions in the correct order and write them down.
Then ask and answer the questions with a partner.

1. are – after school today – to do – what – going – you – ?
2. going – this evening – what – you – to eat – are – ?
3. to bed tonight – going – are – to go – when – you – ?
4. to meet – who – at the weekend – you – going – are – ?
5. are – going – you – your next birthday – how – to celebrate – ?

11 p. 113

11 Lena's email WB 7 p. 57

Sandeep's class takes part in the eTwinning project 'Festivals around the world'.

a) Read the email they get from Lena. What does she get during Hanukkah?

From [illegible]
Subject Festivals

Hello everyone,
My name is Lena and I'm from Poland. My family and I are Jewish.
My favourite festival is Hanukkah. It's the Jewish festival of lights and it's celebrated all over the world. Hanukkah is at the end of November or the beginning of December and it lasts eight days.
During Hanukkah my grandparents come to our house every evening. Right after sunset we light a new candle on the Menorah. We say blessings as a way of paying respect to God.
To light the candles we use the Shamash. This candle is usually in the middle of the Menorah and set higher than the other eight candles. We place the Menorah near our living room window so that everyone passing by can see it. It looks beautiful!
Afterwards we play games and sing traditional Jewish songs. I also get small presents each night and chocolate coins.
During Hanukkah we eat latkes. They are pancakes made from potatoes and fried in oil. We eat them with apple sauce or sour cream. They are delicious. We often have jam doughnuts, too.
This year we're going to decorate the living room with some really nice Hanukkah garlands. They are blue, white and silver because these are the traditional Hanukkah colours.
I can't wait to celebrate Hanukkah. What is your favourite festival?
Bye for now,
Lena

b) Read the email again and find out:

- What kind of festival is Hanukkah?
- When is it?
- What does Lena's family do during Hanukkah?
- What is the Shamash?
- What does Lena's family eat?
- What colour are the garlands? Why?

9.1: Grammar 10c | p. 249

4.1 A party checklist WB 2 p. 68

Josh is planning a party at his house and is writing a checklist.
Read his thoughts and copy them into your exercise book. Fill in **some** and **any**.

First of all I need XX cool music. Do I have XX good dance music on my phone? I need to check that. Maybe Sandeep can bring his guitar. Then we could play XX cool songs for our friends. I'll ask him. I should get XX fun games, too … for those who love playing games. And I need XX balloons to decorate the house. Do I need XX garlands, too? I don't know. But I definitely need XX sweets and lots of crisps. Yummy! What about drinks? We've always got water but we haven't got XX lemonade or orange juice. Party punch would be nice, too. I think I have to get XX exotic fruit juices for it. Let's see if I can find a good recipe on the Internet.

8.1 Don't repeat it, please WB 3 p. 68

a) Look at these sentences from Theme 4. What can you write instead of "one" or "ones"?

I think this blue cap is cooler than the green one.

This year I'm going to wear my most beautiful sari, the purple one.

We need lots of candles, too. I'm going to buy new ones next week.

Im Deutschen kannst du das Nomen einfach weglassen, wenn du es nicht wiederholen möchtest. Im Englischen ist das nicht möglich. Du musst die Stützwörter *one* oder *ones* benutzen.

b) Replace the marked word in each sentence with "one" or "ones".

1. This is a great book, much better than the book we read in our German lesson.
2. This computer is faster than the computer we use at school.
3. Our flat has three bedrooms. My sister and I sleep in the two smallest bedrooms.
4. I'm going to sell my phone and buy a new phone.
5. This bus is more comfortable than the bus we usually take.
6. Where are my sneakers? They are the black sneakers I bought last week.

4.1: Grammar 12a | p. 252
8.1: Grammar 16 | p. 257

8.2 Which ones?

a) Copy the sentences and complete them with "one" or "ones".

1. Here are some peppers. The red XX look good.
2. We also need a cucumber. I'll take this XX here.
3. What about tomatoes? There are red XX and yellow XX.
4. We need some carrots, too. Shall I take a small packet or a large XX?
5. Don't forget the crisps. Take the cheap XX. They're really good.
6. I'll also buy a garland. I think this green XX looks nice.

b) Mark the words "one" or "ones" and the words they stand for in your sentences. Draw a line between the words.

1. Here are some peppers. The red ones look good.
2. ...

17.1 Party games

a) Read about these two party games. Which game would you like to play? Say why.

Bed sheet ping-pong
(from the USA)

You need a ping-pong ball and a bed sheet. Split the group into teams or play as individuals. The players stand and hold the bed sheet at opposite ends. The ping-pong ball is put in the middle of the bed sheet. The aim is to get the ping-pong ball to fall off the other team's side. You do this by raising or lowering the bed sheet. The first team to score ten points is the winner.

Lion and mouse tag
(from South Africa)

Stand in a circle. Two players are in the circle. Both wear blindfolds. One of them is the lion and the other is the mouse. The lion tries to catch the mouse. When the lion roars, the mouse must squeak. When the lion catches the mouse, the game stops. The mouse then becomes the lion and a new player becomes the next mouse. Then the game continues.

b) What games do YOU enjoy playing at parties? Choose one and write down the rules.

c) Explain YOUR game or one of the games above to your class. Then play the game.

8.2: Grammar 16 | p. 257

17.2 Birthdays around the world WB 4+5 p. 69

An international teen magazine wanted to know how its readers celebrate their birthdays. Lots of readers sent emails.

a) Here are some of the emails. Which countries are they from?

Mexico Russia Australia China India

I think the first email is from …

1

From

Subject: Birthdays around the world

We get new clothes for presents. We usually get up at six o'clock and then we go to the temple. We always wear our colourful new birthday clothes. In the afternoon our family eats a birthday meal: a delicious curry and a sweet rice pudding.

2

My birthday is in December. I often go to the beach with my friends. We go surfing or swimming. I usually get my presents then. Or we have a barbecue in the garden and play fun games. Young children often eat "fairy bread" at their birthday parties. "Fairy bread" is white bread with hundreds of colourful sprinkles on it. It's yummy!

3

From

Subject: Birthdays around the world

In my country we usually don't have birthday parties with cakes and presents because it is not a tradition to celebrate birthdays. In fact, some people don't celebrate their birthdays until they turn 60! But we often eat long noodles on our birthdays – long noodles for a long life!

4

I usually invite lots of friends and have a big party. There is always a piñata with lots of sweets and other nice things in it. And I have to eat birthday cake without using my hands – it's messy but very funny for everyone!

5

From

Subject: Birthdays around the world

When we have our birthdays, we get small presents at school. Teachers often give students flowers, pencils or books. After school we usually have a birthday party at home. We play a game where prizes hang down from a rope. Each guest can cut down a prize and take it home.

b) Read the emails again. Which birthday party do you like best? Say why.

c) Write about how you celebrate YOUR birthday. Think about: Portfolio-Ordner
food – activities – presents – guests – …

17.2c: Wordbank Celebrations | p. 218
17.2c: Skills Write | p. 235

Theme 5

Dos and don'ts

In diesem *Theme* ...

- beschäftigst du dich mit Regeln daheim und in der Schule.
- berichtest du, was du tun musst und was du (nicht) tun darfst.
- stellst du Vergleiche an.
- erfährst du mehr über Schuluniformen in Großbritannien.
- äußerst du deine Meinung zu Schuluniformen und Regeln.

1 Problems WB 1 p. 70

a) Look at the pictures. What are the problems between the children and their parents?

The father in picture 1 doesn't like ...

The girl ...

...

b) Listen to four dialogues. Which dialogue goes with which picture? L 1.44

The first dialogue goes with picture ...

The second ...

...

c) How do you think the children and their parents feel?

The girl in picture 1 is …

Her father is …

…

worried | sad | angry | scared | lonely | nervous | bored | happy | frustrated | …

d) Can you think of more problems between parents and children? What are they? Talk in groups.

1c: Wordbank People | p. 210

2 Megan and her mum WB 2 p. 70

a) Megan has lots of questions. What are her mum's answers?

1. Mum, can I wear these jeans for Grandma's birthday?
2. May I watch the film at ten o'clock tomorrow night?
3. Can I go to Sandeep's house first and study for the maths test later?
4. Mum, please can I go shopping on Oxford Street after school?
5. Can I have these trainers? They're really cool.
6. May I go to the youth club with Jasmine?

A. No, you can't. You have to study for the maths test before you leave.
B. No, not after school. You can go shopping on Saturday afternoon.
C. OK, but you have to be back by eight o'clock.
D. No, you can't. They're too expensive.
E. No, you can't. It's a horror film and it's too late.
F. Sorry, not the ones with all those holes.

b) Work with a partner and act out the dialogues. You can make your own dialogue, too.

3 p. 152
3 p. 160

3 Talking to Dad WB 3 p. 71

a) Listen to Megan and her dad.
What problems do they talk about? L 1.45

friends | music | clothes | homework | going out | make-up | pets | money

b) Listen again and finish the sentences.

1. Megan's grandmother doesn't like …
2. Megan's mum wants her mother to …
3. Megan's dad thinks the trainers are …
4. He says that Megan could get them for …
5. Or she could pay for …
6. Megan's dad wants to …

4 A chat WB 4 p. 71

a) Read the chat between Jasmine and Sandeep. What is Jasmine angry about?

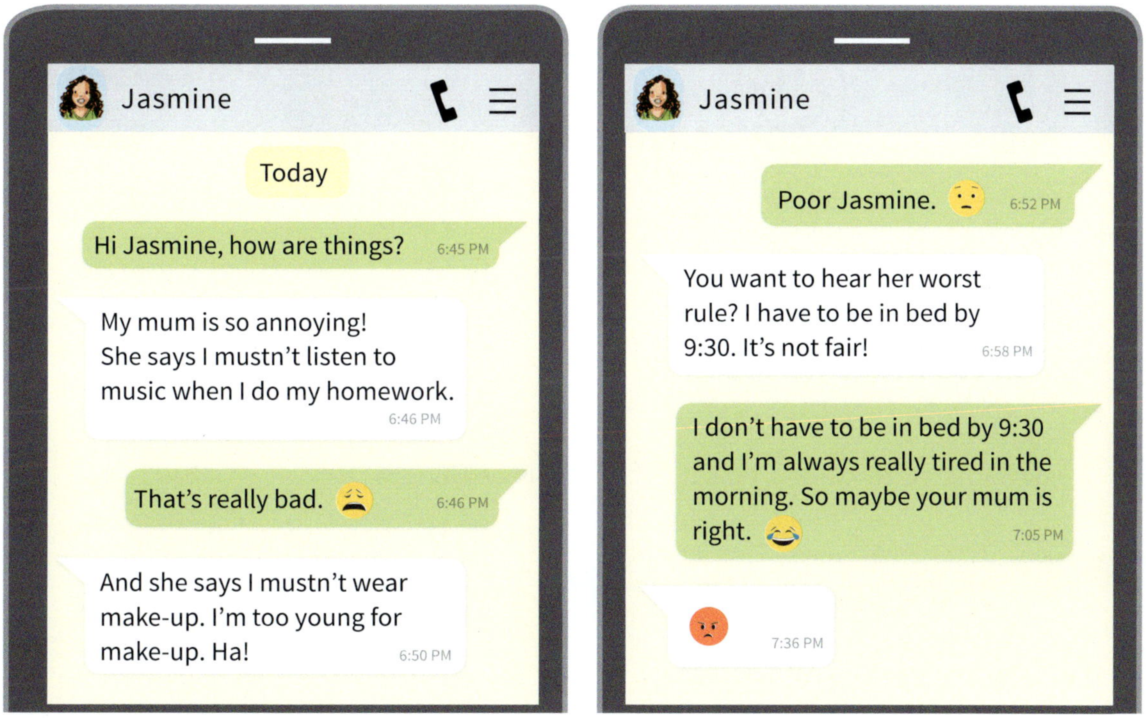

b) Do you understand Jasmine? Do you understand her mother? Say why.

4b p. 152
4.1 p. 160
4.2 p. 161

5 Solving a problem WB 5 p. 72

a) Watch the clip without sound. Look at the people. How do they feel? 11

First … | Then … | At the end …

b) Turn on the sound and watch the clip again. What is the problem?

A The girl didn't clean the kitchen after cooking and wants her father to do it for her.
B The girl didn't clean the kitchen after cooking because she didn't know how to do it.
C The girl didn't clean the kitchen after cooking and has no time to do it now.

c) How do they solve the problem?

4: Grammar 13 | p. 254/255
5: Skills Watch a video clip | p. 228
5: Wordbank People | p. 210

6 YOUR rules at home WB 6 p. 72

a) Work in a group. Talk about your rules at home.

I must … / I have to …	I don't have to …	I mustn't …	I can …	I can't …

use my phone at mealtimes. | wear what I want when I go to school. | do my homework before I can … | be in bed by … o'clock. | have a pet. | wear make-up. | take out the rubbish. | eat sweets before dinner. | …

6.1 p. 152
6.2 p. 153
6.1 p. 161
6.2 p. 162

b) Now write about your rules at home.

7 Rules for Ben

a) Read what Ben's parents say. Then write down the rules for Ben.

Be home by 8:30 p.m.!
No feet on the table!
Tidy your room!

No more pets! A and B are enough.
It's 10 p.m. Bed time!

Ben	has to mustn't	have any more pets. tidy his room. go to bed at 10 p.m. put his feet on the table. be home by 8:30 p.m.

Mustn't klingt wie im Deutschen „muss nicht", heißt aber „nicht dürfen".

7.1 p. 153
7.2 p. 153

b) Can you think of more rules for Ben? Write them down.

6: Grammar 13 | p. 254/255
7: Grammar 13 | p. 254/255

8 Rules for Bagheera WB 7 p. 73

a) What are Jasmine's rules for her cat?

can | has to | mustn't

1. Bagheera (+) sleep all day.
2. She (x) bring home any mice.
3. She (+) play with Sir Barks-A-Lot.
4. She (!!!) drink enough water every day.
5. She (!!!) stay away from the fridge.
6. She (x) steal Jasmine's lunch from the kitchen table.

b) Do YOU have a pet? What are your rules for it? Tell your class.

9 Strange parents

9 p. 154
9 p. 162

a) Read Victor's blog entry. Why can't he stand his mother and her boyfriend?

Search

I can't stand my mother and her boyfriend, Rémy – at least not at the moment. It's always "Do this, don't do that!" They have too many rules. And they're really strange, too. Rémy usually does the cooking at the weekend and he loves talking about healthy food. Today at lunch he said that salad is more delicious than a hamburger. He must be crazy. I'm a huge fan of hamburgers so for me nothing is better than a hamburger! And all this stuff they say about school. They think that German is more important than PE. Can you believe it? They want to send me to Germany in the school holidays. I'd rather play football with my friends. But there's even more. Rémy thinks maths is the most interesting subject at school. Ha! Do you have such strange parents, too?

b) What do YOU think? What is the most delicious food? What is the most interesting subject?

c) Are your parents strange, too? Talk to a partner.

8: Grammar 13 | p. 254/255

10 YOUR opinion WB 8 p. 73

a) What do you like? What don't you like? Make top three lists. Look at the pictures and adjectives for some ideas.

difficult | delicious | boring | beautiful | expensive | exciting | dangerous | famous | important | interesting | wonderful | …

difficult subjects
1. German
2. …
3. …

delicious food
1. pizza
2. …
3. …

clothes

singers/bands

sports

books/comics

films / TV series

b) Work with a partner. Discuss your top three lists and compare them.

I think German is the most difficult subject. What about you?

I don't agree. I think maths is more difficult than German.

I think pizza is the most delicious food. What about you?

I agree.

Mehrsilbige Adjektive werden mit *more* und *most* gesteigert. Das Adjektiv bleibt unverändert.
difficult / …
more difficult / …
the most difficult / …

10.1 p. 154
10.2 p. 155

11 The most interesting

Think about the last two or three weeks. What was …

- the most interesting film / TV series you saw?
- your biggest problem?
- your nicest day?
- your most boring day?
- the most fantastic surprise you had?
- your funniest moment?
- your most delicious meal?
- …?

Make notes. Then talk about them with a partner.

11.1 p. 155

10b: Grammar 11b | p. 251
11: Grammar 11 | p. 250/251

12 Choose an activity

You can:

- Make a poster with rules for your family or your pet or …
  Portfolio-Ordner

- Draw or make signs for rules at home that are important to you.
  Then tell your class about them. Portfolio-Ordner

- Write a chat in which two friends talk about problems at home.
  You can look at number 4 for help. Portfolio-Ordner

13 Target task: YOUR role play

a) Work with a partner or in groups. Think about a problem between children and their parents. 13a p. 155
How can you solve the problem?

b) Make notes on your ideas, then write a dialogue.

c) Ask other classmates or your teacher to check your dialogue. Then correct it.

d) Learn your role. Then practise the dialogue with your partner(s). Try to express your feelings.
Think about clothes and other things you need for your role play, too.

e) Present your play to the class. Then ask your class for feedback.

I think your dialogue was fantastic/funny/OK/…

I liked your solution.

I couldn't hear everything.

Why didn't you …?

13: Skills Talk | p. 231

1 Haverstock school rules WB 9 + 10 p. 74

a) Read the school rules. Then look at the pictures. Which rules are the students breaking?

> The student in picture A is breaking rule number …

Who is not breaking a rule?

A

B

C

D

HAVERSTOCK SCHOOL RULES

1. Be polite and show respect for other students and the teachers.
2. School starts at 8:50 a.m. Students who are late must report to the deputy head.
3. Students must not run in the school building.
4. Students must wear the correct school uniform.
5. Students are not allowed to leave the school grounds at break or at lunchtime.
6. Eat and drink in the right place and at the right time.
7. Students are not allowed to chew chewing gum at school.
8. Students are not allowed to use mobile phones at school.
9. Students must wear sports kit for PE.
10. This is your school, so look after it. Separate your litter (paper, plastic, …) and put it in the correct bins.

b) Read the school rules again and answer the questions.

1. Ken's alarm clock didn't work. He arrives at school at 9 a.m. What does he have to do?
2. Nasaar wants to wear her new miniskirt at school. Is she allowed to wear it?
3. Mark has PE today. What does he have to wear?
4. Hila wants to throw her litter away. What does she have to do?
5. Tim wants to call a friend on his mobile phone at lunch. Why can't he do that?
6. Rosie wants to go home for lunch. Is she allowed to do that?

1.1 p. 156

2 Dear students …

Höre dir die Lautsprecher-Durchsage des Schulleiters an.
Beantworte die Fragen von jemandem, der nur wenig Englisch versteht. L 1.46

1. Was wird von den Schülerinnen und Schülern allgemein erwartet?
2. Was sollen sie vor Stundenbeginn machen?
3. Wie sollen sie sich in den Pausen verhalten?

3 Sound check

Listen to the sentences. Then say them yourself. L 1.47

[aɪ]

1. She arrives at school at the right time.
2. Be polite and don't use your mobile phone.

[aʊ]

3. They are not allowed to leave the school grounds.
4. Next to our house is a field with some cows.

4 Rules at YOUR school WB 11 p. 75

4 p. 156
4 p. 163

a) Work in small groups. Think of the rules at your school or in your class and write them down.

1. We must …
2. We must not …
…

b) What do you think about the rules? Are they OK or not OK? Give reasons. Then discuss in your groups.

I think rule number … is important/OK/stupid/… because … What about you?

I don't agree. I think …

I agree.

…

4.1 p. 163
4.2 p. 164

2: Skills Help out | p. 234
4: Grammar 13 | p. 254/255

5 School cafeteria rules

Sieh dir die Mensa-Regeln der Haverstock Schule an. Berichte jemandem, der kein Englisch versteht.

Man muss/soll …

Man darf nicht/soll nicht …

Cafeteria Rules

- *Enter and exit the cafeteria quietly.*
- *Be polite to the cafeteria staff.*
- *Choose a seat and don't run around.*
- *Only eat food from your own lunch.*
- *Eat the vegetables, they are not just for decoration.*
- *Talk quietly.*
- *Keep your table and eating area clean.*

6 What to wear? WB 12 p. 76

a) What do YOU and your friends wear when you go to school?

I We	always usually often sometimes never	wear	a shirt. a pullover/sweatshirt. jeans/trousers. a skirt/dress. trainers/boots. a jacket. …

b) What must the students at Haverstock School wear?

grey shirt with the school logo | black trousers | black shoes | dark blue pullover with the school logo | black skirt | dark blue blazer with the school logo | tie

Girls must wear …
Boys must wear …
Students must also wear …

5: Skills Help out | p. 234
6: Wordbank Clothes | p. 214

c) What do you think about the clothes students wear at school?

I think it's	better worse cheaper more expensive nicer more boring …	to wear	jeans a uniform skirts ties …	at school.

6.1 p. 157
6.2 p. 157

7 Give me five!

Look at pages 144–147 and find …

- five words with "ea".
- five words that end with "y".
- five words to do with lunchtime.
- five places.

LAND & LEUTE 12

Schuluniformen

An vielen britischen Schulen tragen Schülerinnen und Schüler eine Schuluniform. Für Mädchen ist das oft ein dunkler Rock und eine Bluse mit Schulkrawatte. Jungen tragen in der Regel eine dunkle Hose und ein helles Hemd mit Krawatte. Auch die Schuhe sind vorgeschrieben.
Die Schülerinnen und Schüler dürfen normalerweise keine Sportschuhe tragen.
An den meisten Schulen kommen Pullover und Blazer mit dem Abzeichen der Schule hinzu. So kann auf dem Schulweg jeder sofort erkennen, zu welcher Schule man gehört. Es gibt auch keinen Streit über die „richtige" Jeans- oder Sportschuhmarke oder das coolste Sweatshirt.

Welche Vor- und Nachteile einer Schuluniform fallen dir noch ein? Gibt es an deiner Schule Schulkleidung? Wenn nicht, wie könnte sie aussehen?

Sieh dir nun den Clip an und finde heraus:
- Was tragen die Schülerinnen und Schüler vom Midhurst Rother College?
- Wie finden sie ihre Schuluniform? Was gefällt ihnen, was nicht?
- Welches Problem hat Fergus mit seinem Blazer?

6c: Grammar 11 | p. 250/251

8 For or against?

a) Read what these students say about their school uniforms. Do they like them?

Hannah (15) from Bristol

I think my school uniform is ugly and horrible. I hate wearing it. I would love to go to school in clothes that look nice on me.

Joel (13) from Milton Keynes

I think my school uniform is cool and I'm proud to wear it. It just makes me feel good. We're going to have a new logo on our pullover soon. It's going to be better and even smarter.

b) Listen to Will and find out: L 1.48
- What does he think about his school uniform?
- What does it look like?

c) Now have a vote in your class.

Hands up:
Who is for/against school uniforms?

… students are for school uniforms.

… students are against school uniforms.

8.1 p. 165

9 A uniform for YOUR school

a) What could a uniform at your school look like? Draw it or make a collage. Then label it.
Portfolio-Ordner

b) Put up all your designs in the classroom and present them.

c) Put a smiley on the design you like most.

5f: Wordbank Clothes | p. 214

10 What is happening?

a) Work with a partner. Look at the pictures and talk about them.
You can use the phrases in the box.

> In picture A
> a group of girls is …

a strong boy is attacking a younger student |
someone is sending a student a threatening text message |
a girl is calling a classmate names |
a group of girls is saying bad things about another girl |
a group of boys is ignoring a classmate |
two boys are taking a classmate's phone

A

B

C

D

E

F

b) What you can see in the pictures above is called bullying.
Read the six statements and match them with the pictures.

Bullying is when …

1. classmates ignore you.
2. other children call you names.
3. a stronger boy or girl attacks you.
4. people say bad things about you.
5. people take money or things from you.
6. someone sends you a threatening text message.

c) Can you think of more types of bullying?

10.1 p. 158

11 Jack's story WB 13 p. 77

a) Read the article from a school magazine. What happened to Jack?

There is something you can do!

Jack lived with his mum and two older sisters. The family didn't have much money so Jack couldn't buy many of the things that other kids had. His mum worked a lot. Jack was often alone and didn't have many friends.

The kids from his school often made fun of Jack because he wore a second-hand school uniform and old trainers. That made him sad. One day some of his classmates held their noses when Jack walked past and everyone laughed. Jack felt embarrassed and quickly walked away.

Then Jack started getting horrible text messages that said things like "You stink!" or "Where did you get those ugly trainers?" Someone even posted a picture of Jack online and people wrote horrible comments under it.

Jack started feeling really bad about himself. He got angry at his mum because she couldn't buy him expensive clothes and trainers. He didn't talk much anymore and stopped spending time with his friends. He was scared to go to school. Jack didn't know what to do and was too afraid to ask anyone for help.

Jack now usually spent his breaks alone. One day an older girl asked him if he was OK. Jack started to cry and the girl took him to one of the teachers, Mrs Ahmed. Mrs Ahmed asked Jack lots of questions until Jack finally told her what was wrong.

Mrs Ahmed told Jack not to worry. She spoke to his mum and then to his classmates. She told them that bullying was never OK and that you get into big trouble for sending horrible text messages and posting pictures of someone online.

Things started to slowly get better for Jack. His friends spent more time with him and made sure he wasn't alone at school and during the breaks. Jack also started seeing the school counsellor. Talking to him made Jack feel better about himself and he got some important tips. Sometimes he is still scared, but he now knows how to get help and how to help himself.

++ Take action now! — Say 'no' to bullies! — Don't look away! — Don't be afraid of them! — Don't be afraid to tell someone! ++

11b p. 158 **b)** Look at the article again.
Why did Jack feel sad/embarrassed/angry/scared?

> Jack felt **sad** because …

11c p. 158 **c)** Tell the story from Jack's point of view. You can start like this:

The students from my school often made fun of me because …
One day …   Then … …

11.1 p. 159
11.2 p. 159

12 Bullying: no chance!

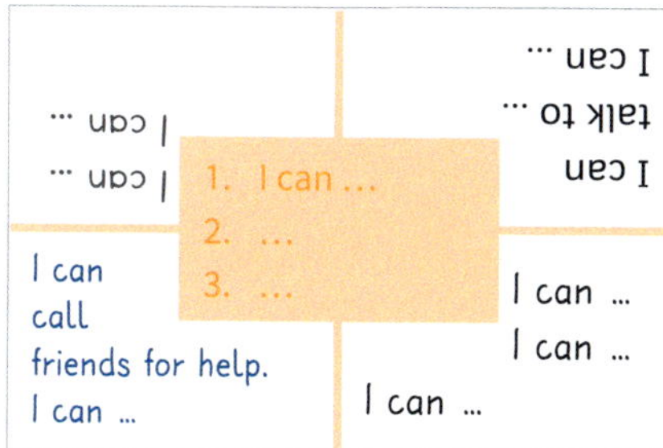

a) What can you do when someone bullies you?
Work in groups of four and make a placemat.

b) Talk about your ideas. Then agree on the three most important ideas and write them down in the middle of the placemat.

c) Compare your placemat results in class.

d) *Childline* offers help to children and young people in the UK.
Read the tips from *Childline*'s website. What do you think about them?
Are they similar to your ideas?

Search

How to beat bullying – top tips

- Don't ignore bullying. It won't go away on its own.
- Tell someone – for example a teacher, your parents or a friend.
- Remember: It's not your fault.
- Stay away from the bullies.
- Stay with a group when you don't feel safe.
- Don't fight back. You could get into trouble.

Contact *Childline* for free on 0800 1111.

12.1 p. 165

13 Target task: Rules for YOUR class

WB **test yourself** p. 78 + 79;
Portfolio p. 127 / **WEB** P5

a) Work in groups. Look through Theme 5 again and collect ideas for good and important classroom rules.
Think about some rules for your teachers and some anti-bullying rules, too.

b) Discuss your ideas in class. Rank your ideas and agree on ten important rules.

c) Design a poster and put it up in your classroom.

12: Skills Placemat | p. 239

3 p. 138

3 Talking to Dad

WB 3 p. 71

a) Listen to Megan and her dad.
What problems do they talk about? L 1.45

music | clothes | homework | going out | money

b) Listen again. Then pick the correct sentence ending.

1. Megan's grandmother doesn't like **jeans with holes / jeans**.
2. Megan's mum wants her mother to **have a good time / wear jeans without holes**.
3. Megan's dad thinks the trainers are **too expensive / not really cool**.
4. He says that Megan could get them for **Christmas / her birthday**.
5. Or she could pay for **part of the trainers / the next trainers**.
6. Megan's dad wants to **talk to Megan's mum / come to the birthday party**.

4 A chat

WB 4 p. 71

4b p. 139

b) Do you understand Jasmine?
Do you understand her mother? Say why.

Yes, I do. …

- Music helps you concentrate on your homework.
- Jasmine is old enough to wear make-up.
- 9:30 is too early to go to bed.
- …

No, I don't. …

- You can't concentrate on your homework when you listen to music.
- Jasmine is only 12 years old and too young to wear make-up.
- If Jasmine goes to bed late, she will be tired the next morning.
- …

6.1 What does it mean?

Match the English and the German phrases.

1. you must / you have to (!!!)
2. you don't have to (☺)
3. you mustn't (⊗)
4. you can (+)
5. you can't (−)

- A du kannst, du darfst
- B du musst
- C du kannst nicht, du darfst nicht
- D du darfst nicht
- E du musst nicht

6.1: Grammar 13 | p. 254/255

6.2 All those rules

What are the rules for Jason?
Write them down.

1. You (+) go to the youth club today.
2. But you (!!!) be home at 9 o'clock.
3. You (!!!) do your homework first.
4. You (X) forget to feed Bagheera and Baloo.
5. You (☺) tidy your room today.
6. I'm sorry but you (–) have this new pullover. It's too expensive.

7.1 Opposites

a) Match the opposites.

before | early | cheap | yesterday | best | can | right | must

tomorrow | wrong | can't | late | expensive | don't have to | after | worst

before – after
early – ...

b) Listen and check the pairs. L 1.49

7.2 Things to do

a) Match the verbs with the nouns.

wear | watch | study for | go to | use | wear | take out | tidy

a test | the youth club | the rubbish | the phone | your room | jeans | some make-up | a film

wear jeans,
...

b) Complete the sentences with your chunks from a).

1. Dad, can I XX tonight? There's always good music.
2. May I XX? All the girls in my class do that.
3. Mum, can I XX to Uncle Tom's birthday? They look really cool.
4. Please XX before your friends visit you this afternoon.
5. And XX from the kitchen, too. Thanks!
6. You and your friends may XX in the living room. Have fun!

6.2: Grammar 13 | p. 254/255

9 p. 141

9 Strange parents

a) Read Victor's blog entry. Why can't he stand his mother and her boyfriend?

I can't stand my mother and her boyfriend, Rémy. It's always "Do this, don't do that!" They have too many rules. And they're really strange, too. Rémy loves talking about healthy food. Today at lunch he said that salad is more delicious than a hamburger. He must be crazy. Nothing is better than a hamburger! And all this stuff they say about school. They think that German is more important than PE. Can you believe it? And Rémy thinks maths is the most interesting subject at school. Ha! Do you have such strange parents, too?

b) What do YOU think? What is the most delicious food? What is the most interesting subject?

c) Are your parents strange, too? Talk to a partner.

Yes, my parents are sometimes strange. They …

Yes, my mum/dad is sometimes strange. He/she …

…

10.1 Three forms

a) Write down the three forms of these adjectives.

delicious | beautiful | expensive | exciting | dangerous | famous

delicious – more delicious – the most delicious

…

b) What are the three forms in German? Ask a partner. Take turns.

What are the three forms of **delicious** in German?

lecker – leckerer – am leckersten

That's right/wrong.

10.1: Grammar 11b | p. 251

10.2 What do you think?

What is more delicious/expensive/…?

1. chocolate – jelly beans (delicious)
2. dog – horse (expensive)
3. car – lion (dangerous)
4. skateboarding – playing video games (exciting)
5. Big Ben – the London Eye (beautiful)
6. the Queen – James Bond (famous)

1. I think jelly beans are more delicious than chocolate.
2. …
…

11.1 What does Nele think?

a) What does Nele think about her school subjects?

1. Maths is more difficult than history.
2. Music is better than …
…

1. maths / difficult / history
2. music / good / drama
3. English / important / RE
4. art / easy / German
5. geography / boring / science
6. PE / cool / ICT

b) Compare your results with a partner.

13 Target task: YOUR role play

13 p. 143

a) Work with a partner or in groups. Think about a problem between children and their parents. How can you solve the problem? Here are some ideas:

Problem	Possible solution
A Child uses the phone too often.	**A** Child puts the phone in the living room during homework. Child uses an app to limit his/her time on the phone.
B Child doesn't like the food for dinner.	**B** Child and parents plan the meals together. Child helps with the cooking.
C Child doesn't do his/her homework.	**C** Parents talk to the child to find out: Is the homework too difficult? Does the child need help with it? Does the child have enough time for it?
D Child's room is a mess.	**D** Child chooses a day to tidy the room, for example every Friday. Parents show child how to make the bed or vacuum the floors. They help child to sort out things he/she doesn't need anymore.
…	…

10.2: Grammar 11b | p. 251
11.1: Grammar 11 | p. 250/251

1.1 Don't …

What do the teachers say? Match the sentence parts and write them down.

1 Don't run
2 Don't chew
3 Don't use
4 Don't throw
5 Don't leave
6 Don't eat

A litter on the floor.
B the school grounds at lunchtime.
C in the classroom.
D your mobile phone.
E in the school building.
F chewing gum.

4 p. 145

4 Rules at YOUR school WB 11 p. 75

a) Work in small groups. Think of the rules at your school or in your class and write them down. Here are some ideas:

eat and drink in the classroom | be polite and show respect for other students | wear a cap in the classroom | chew chewing gum at school | wear a school uniform | leave the school grounds at break or lunchtime | skate on school grounds | listen to music | bring your pet to school | …

1. We must …
2. We must not …
…

b) What do you think about the rules? Are they OK or not OK? Give reasons. Then discuss in your groups.

I think rule number … is important because **we have to understand the teacher**. What about you?

I don't agree. I think …

I think rule number … is OK because **skating on school grounds can be dangerous**. What about you?

I agree.

I think rule number … is stupid because **chewing gum helps you concentrate**. What about you?

4: Grammar 13 | p. 254/255

6.1 Different clothes

Look at the pictures.
What does Charlie wear for school?
What does he usually wear in his free time?

T-shirt | trainers | grey shirt | jacket | black shoes | jeans | dark blue blazer | black trousers | tie

For school Charlie always wears ...

In his free time Charlie usually wears ...

6.2 Let's compare

a) Look at the adjectives in the box. Write down their three forms.

small | boring | cheap | difficult | interesting | easy | expensive | good | delicious | clever | bad

small – smaller – the smallest
boring – more boring – the most boring
...

b) Check your results with a partner. Then quiz your partner. Take turns.

What are the three forms of **small**?

small – smaller – the smallest

That's right/wrong.

c) Write what you think.

1. school uniforms – normal clothes (good)
2. our school – Haverstock School (small)
3. a meal at the cafeteria – a meal at home (delicious)
4. students – teachers (clever)
5. a shirt – a T-shirt (expensive)
6. music – biology (interesting)

1. I think normal clothes are better than school uniforms.
2. ...
...

6.1: Wordbank Clothes | p. 214
6.2: Grammar 11 | p. 250/251

10.1 Bullying

Look at the pictures from number 10 again. Write about what the people are doing.

A girl	is sending	bad things about another girl.
A strong boy	is saying	a classmate names.
Someone	is attacking	a classmate's phone.
Two boys	is ignoring	a threatening text message.
A group of girls	are taking	a younger student.
A group of boys	is calling	a classmate.

11 Jack's story

WB 13 p. 77

11b p. 150 **b)** Look at the article (p. 150) again. Why did Jack feel sad/embarrassed/angry/scared?

1. Jack felt sad
2. He felt embarrassed
3. He felt angry
4. He felt scared

- A because he got some terrible text messages.
- B because the other kids often made fun of him.
- C because his mum couldn't buy him expensive clothes and trainers.
- D because some of his classmates held their noses when he walked past.

11c p. 150 **c)** Tell the story from Jack's point of view. You can start like this:

The students from my school often made fun of me because
I wore …
One day some of my classmates …
I felt embarrassed and …
Then …
…
One day an older girl …
Mrs Ahmed …
…
Sometimes I still feel …

Du kannst dich eng am Artikel auf Seite 150 entlang hangeln. Du kannst aber auch freier erzählen, was Jack erlebt hat. Achte auf die richtige zeitliche Abfolge der Ereignisse. Beschreibe auch Jacks Gefühle.

11.1 Feelings

a) Find ten adjectives in the snake.

b) Which two adjectives don't fit?

c) How do YOU feel in these situations? Use the adjectives from a).

1. I feel XX when I do well in a test.
2. I feel XX when I walk past a big dog.
3. When I forget my homework, I feel XX.
4. I feel XX when other kids ignore me.
5. When I can't meet my friends, I feel XX.
6. I feel XX when other people say bad things about me.

11.2 What happened?

Put the sentences in the right order to tell Jack's story. Start with E.

Jack wore ...

...

- **A** Jack also got horrible text messages.
- **B** One day an older girl asked him if he was OK.
- **C** Mrs Ahmed talked to Jack, his mum and his classmates.
- **D** He was scared to go to school.
- **E** Jack wore a second-hand school uniform and old trainers.
- **F** It helped him to feel better.
- **G** But he was too afraid to ask anyone for help.
- **H** She took him to Mrs Ahmed.
- **I** Jack started seeing the school counsellor, too.
- **J** That's why the kids from his school often made fun of him.

11.1: Wordbank People | p. 210

3 p. 138

3 Talking to Dad WB 3 p. 71

a) Listen to Megan and her dad.
What problems do they talk about? L 1.45

b) Listen again and answer the questions.

1. What doesn't Megan's grandmother like?
2. What does Megan's mum want her mother to have?
3. What does Megan's dad think about the trainers?
4. When could Megan get the trainers?
5. What else does Megan's dad suggest?
6. What does Megan's dad want to do?

4.1 Jasmine's diary WB 1 + 2 p. 82

a) Do YOU write a diary? When and why do you write it? Talk to a partner.

b) Read Jasmine's diary entry. How does she feel?

Wednesday, 7th April

I'm still angry. If I can't wear make-up, I'll phone Grandma and tell her about my problem. Grandma is cool. She loves fashion and wears lots of make-up herself. Maybe she can talk to Mum and tell her that nothing is wrong with wearing make-up when you're 12 years old.
I should also talk to Dad about Mum's other annoying rules. He is often more relaxed than Mum. If he understands me, he will try to convince Mum that listening to music helps you concentrate on your homework.
If I have children one day, I won't tell them what to wear or when to go to bed. I'm sure about that. If they want to wear make-up, I won't say a word. And if they want to stay up till 11 p.m., they will be free to do so. And if I earn enough money, I'll buy them really good loudspeakers for their rooms and then they can listen to music all day long. Everyone will be happy and there won't be any arguing or fighting.
Thank you diary. I'm feeling so much better now.

c) Read again and find out:
- What does Jasmine say about her grandma and her dad?
- What are Jasmine's plans?

4.1: Grammar 17 | p. 258

4.2 What if? WB 3 p. 83

a) Look at number 4.1 again and match the sentence parts.

1 If Jasmine can't wear make-up,
2 If Mr Bolt understands his daughter,
3 If Jasmine has children one day,
4 If her children want to wear make-up,
5 If Jasmine earns enough money,

A she won't tell them what to wear or when to go to bed.
B she will buy them really good loudspeakers.
C she will phone her grandma.
D he will talk to his wife.
E she won't say a word.

b) What will or won't YOU do if this happens to you?

1. If I can't wear my favourite clothes to my friend's party, I will/won't …
2. If I have children one day, …
3. If I earn enough money, …

6.1 The room WB 4 p. 83

a) Look at the pictures. What can you see? Talk to a partner.

1

2

3

4

b) Imagine YOU are the girl or the mother. Tell her story. Make notes first. Portfolio-Ordner
You can start like this: *My room is always a mess but I like it. … Yesterday when I was at school, …*
or: *My daughter's room is always a mess. I just hate it. … Yesterday when she was at school, …*
Then read your story to the class.

c) What do you think? What could the girl and her mother do to solve the problem?

4.2: Grammar 17 | p. 258
6.1b: Skills Write | p. 235

6.2 Helping out

Nassim hat einen englischen Austauschschüler zu Besuch. Er heißt Morris.
Nassim spricht kaum Englisch, Morris kaum Deutsch. Kannst du den beiden helfen?

Morris	You	Nassim
1 What are the rules at your home?	2 Er möchte wissen, welche …	3 Ich muss jeden Tag mein Bett machen und die Hausaufgaben erledigen.
	4 …	
5 I have to do that, too. Can you use your phone all day long?	6 Er sagt, dass …	7 Nein, ich darf mein Handy während der Hausaufgaben nicht benutzen. Wie ist das bei dir?
	8 …	
9 I have to put my phone in the living room at 8 p.m. Can you wear what you like to school?	10 …	11 Ja, die Sachen müssen aber sauber sein. Meine Mutter mag es auch nicht, wenn ich eine Trainingshose in der Schule trage.
	12 …	

9 p. 141

9 Strange parents

a) Read Victor's blog entry. Why can't he stand his mother and her boyfriend?

I can't stand my mother and her boyfriend, Rémy – at least not at the moment. It's always "Do this, don't do that!" They have too many silly rules.
And they're really strange, too. Rémy usually does the cooking at the weekend and he loves talking about healthy food. I can't hear it anymore. Today at lunch he said that salad is more delicious than a hamburger. He must be crazy. I'm a huge fan of hamburgers so for me nothing is better than a juicy hamburger with lots of beef, cheese, tomato and onion!
And all this stuff they say about school. They think that German is more important than PE. Can you believe it? They want to send me to a language school in Germany in the school holidays to improve my German. I'd rather play football with my friends. But there's even more. Rémy thinks maths is the most interesting subject at school. What nonsense!
Do you have such strange parents, too?

b) What do YOU think? What is the most delicious food? What is the most interesting subject?

c) Are your parents strange, too? Talk to a partner. Then write an answer to Victor.

4 Rules at YOUR school WB 11 p. 75

4 p. 145

a) Work in small groups. Think of the rules at your school or in your class and write them down.

1. We must ...
2. We must not ...
...

b) Now write about the rules at your school.

We can wear our own clothes, We can skate to school, We can bring our own lunch to school, We can bring our phones, ...	but we	have to ... must ... must not ... are not allowed to ... ...

c) What do you think about the rules at your school? Are they OK or not OK? Give reasons. Then discuss in your groups.

I think rule number ... is important/OK/stupid/... because ... What about you?

I don't agree. I think ...

I agree.

...

4.1 Our and their school rules

a) Look at number 1 (p. 144) again with a partner. Compare your school rules with the Haverstock school rules.

The students at Haverstock are not allowed to ... but we can ...

We have to ... but the students at Haverstock don't have to ...

They must ...

...

b) Now write about what is different and what is the same.

4: Grammar 13 | p. 254/255
4.1: Grammar 13 | p. 254/255

4.2 An email from Josh WB 5 p. 84

a) Alex is Josh's friend from Berlin. Read Josh's email to him about classroom rules at Haverstock. How many rules does Josh mention?

To

Subject Classroom rules

Dear Alex,

Thanks so much for your email! It was great to read about your school.

You asked me about classroom rules at Haverstock. There are lots of rules. First of all, we are not allowed to put our bags and blazers on the tables. That is OK because the desks are small. Then we are not allowed to eat or drink. Only water is allowed. We are not allowed to chew chewing gum in the classroom. I don't really understand that because chewing gum helps me to concentrate. Sometimes I do chew chewing gum and then my teacher says: "Josh, chewing gum is against the classroom rules. Please take out your chewing gum and put it in the bin. This is your first warning." If you get three warnings, the teacher sends you to a special room where you spend the rest of the school day. With the help of a social worker you think about your behaviour in class. You also have to do school work. That's pretty tough!

At Haverstock we must wear the correct school uniform, of course. I don't really like the strange trousers. I wish I could wear regular clothes like you in Berlin. But I'm glad we don't need to wear those ugly green pullovers we had in primary school.

In the lessons we must listen to the teachers and do what they tell us to do. If we want to say something, we must put our hands up. That is OK and I guess it's the same at your school. Oh, and I nearly forgot: We are not allowed to use swearwords. What a silly rule!

What classroom rules are there at your school?

Hope to hear from you soon.

All the best,
Josh

b) Read the email again and complete the sentences.

Josh and his classmates are allowed to …
They must …
They are not allowed to …
They don't need to …

c) What does Josh think about the rules?

d) Imagine YOU are Alex. Write an email to Josh and answer the following questions: WEB 4

- What do you think about the rules at Haverstock?
- What are the rules at your school?
- What happens if you break a rule?
- What do you think about the rules at your school?

4.2d: Skills Write | p. 235,
Write an email | p. 236/237

8.1 Uniform or no uniform? WB 6 p. 85

a) Here are some arguments for and against wearing a school uniform. Sort them in a table. Can you think of more arguments?

You see no differences between rich and poor kids.

They can be expensive for parents to buy.

It makes us feel that we belong together.

It's easy to decide what to wear in the morning.

People like to look different and individual.

SCHOOL UNIFORMS

for	against
...	...

b) Have a discussion in class.
You need three groups:
- Group one speaks for school uniforms.
- Group two speaks against school uniforms.
- Group three listens to the arguments and can take notes.

c) At the end of the discussion group three decides: Which group had the best arguments?

12.1 Calling *Childline* WB 7 p. 85

a) Trisha and Jasper call *Childline* about their problems with bullying. Listen to the two kids. Take notes on these questions: L 1.50
- Why does Trisha/Jasper call *Childline*?
- What do other kids do to them?
- What does Trisha's mother / Jasper's friend say?

b) What could Trisha, Jasper and their friends do against bullying? Talk to a partner. Then write down some tips.

I think Trisha could …

Jasper should …

12.1a: Skills Listen | p. 228

Theme 6

Let's go!

In diesem *Theme* ...

- sprichst du über Aktivitäten am Wochenende.
- lernst du, ein Gespräch beim Arzt zu führen.
- schreibst du über dein Lieblingsfernsehprogramm oder deine Lieblingsserie.
- lernst du eine weitere Region Großbritanniens kennen.
- stellst du deine Ferienpläne vor.

1 Weekend plans WB 1 p. 86

a) What are you going to do at the weekend? Talk to your classmates. Take notes.

What are you going to do this weekend?

I'm going to **sleep over at a friend's house**.

read ... | listen to ... | visit ... | meet ... | play ... | go to ... | ...

b) Tell the class one interesting thing about someone in your class.

I learned that **Alia** is going to ...

6

2 A weekend in Camden WB 2 p. 86

a) Ben is ill. He has a bad cold.
Listen to him and read along. What were his plans for the weekend? L 2.1

b) Read again. What do you learn about these people? 2b p. 182

Megan Jasmine and Jason Their mum Ben	has have	gone been taken used …	ill for three days. with them. to Edinburgh. lots of tissues. Sir Barks-A-Lot with her. to a concert. …

2.1 p. 190
2.2 p. 191

3 Visiting a friend WB 3 p. 87

a) Listen to the dialogue. Who visits Ben? What does Ben get? L 2.2

b) Now practise reading the dialogue with a partner. Try to express the boys' feelings.

Sandeep: Hi mate, how are you?
Ben: Still bad. My mum wants to take me to the doctor tomorrow.
Sandeep: I'm sorry, mate. But maybe I can cheer you up. Here's some fruit from our shop. My parents want you to get well soon.
Ben: That's very kind. Please say thank you to them.
Sandeep: And here's something else for you.
Ben: What is it? Homework? Have I missed much at school?
Sandeep: No, it's not. And no, you haven't missed much. So have a look.
Ben: Oh, it's a card. Is it from you?
Sandeep: No, it isn't.
Ben: It's from Megan and Jasmine. How sweet of them.
Sandeep: So what does the card say?
Ben: It says "Cheer up, Ben! We miss you a lot. Love from Megan and Jasmine".
Sandeep: I hope I'll get a card like that next time I'm ill.
Ben: Sure. Jasmine will send you loads of cards.
Sandeep: Ha ha!

c) What else could you do to cheer up a friend who is ill? Talk in groups.

4 What are the words?

a) What are these words from number 3?

1. d – – tor	3. ch – – r	5. tomorr – –	7. we – –
2. k – – d	4. l – – e	6. ca – –	8. fr – – t

b) Complete the text with words from a).

Ben is still ill and has to go to the XX tomorrow. Sandeep visits Ben and brings him XX and a XX. He wants to XX up his friend. That is very XX of him.

c) Turn other words from number 3 into "strange words" like in a). Then test your partner.

5 Already done?

5 p. 182

a) Find the three verb forms that go together. Write them down.

take | wrote | went | **drink** | taken | eaten | **go** | drunk | written | **put** | gone | put | **write** | drank | ate | **eat** | put | took

1. take – took – taken
2. ...

Für die neue Zeitform, das *present perfect*, brauchst du die dritte Verbform. Unregelmäßige Verben haben eigene Formen, die du lernen musst (siehe S. 334–335).

b) It is 5:30 p.m. Ben thinks about his day. What has he already done? What hasn't he done yet? Look at the verb forms in a) for help.

Ben has already taken his medicine.
He hasn't ... yet.
...

- take his medicine ✓
- go to the doctor
- eat fruit
- drink lots of tea and water ✓
- write to Megan and Jasmine ✓
- put his tissues in the bin

5.1 p. 183
5.2 p. 183

6 Poor Ellie

WB 4 + 5 p. 87, 88

a) Watch the clip. What is wrong with Ellie? 13

b) What do Ellie's family and friends do to cheer her up?

c) Did you like the clip?
Talk about it with a partner.

Did you like the clip?

Yes, I did. / No, I didn't.
I thought it was funny/cool/boring/...
What about you?

I agree / don't agree.
I thought the story was ...
I liked / didn't like ... because ...

5: Grammar 14 | p. 255/256
6: Skills Watch a video clip | p. 228

7 At the doctor's
WB 6 p. 88

a) Listen and read along. What are these words in English? Find them in the dialogue. L 2.3

Kopfschmerzen | Halsschmerzen | Fieber | Hals | entzündet | wehtun | gurgeln

Doctor Clarke: Hello Ben. What's wrong with you?
Ben: Hello Doctor Clarke. I don't feel very well. I have a headache and a sore throat.
Doctor Clarke: Let me see. Well, you don't have a temperature. Now open your mouth, please. OK, your throat is sore. Does it hurt a lot?
Ben: Yes, it does.
Doctor Clarke: Oh dear. It's best to gargle with salt water. Your mum will show you how to do it. And drink lots of warm tea.
Ben: OK, I will.
Doctor Clarke: You can go to school again in two days.
Ben's mum: Thank you, Doctor Clarke.
Doctor Clarke: You're welcome. Goodbye!
Ben and his mum: Goodbye!

b) What does Doctor Clarke tell Ben to do? What else could Ben do? Do you have any tips? Talk to your partner.

7.1 p. 184
7.2 p. 184

c) Look at these phrases. Who says them – the patient or the doctor?

7.1 p. 192

I've hurt my leg/arm. | How are you today? | How did that happen? | It hurts a lot / a little. | Stay at home today / for a week. | Take this medicine / these tablets. | I fell off my bike / a chair. | Let's have a look.

8 p. 184
8 p. 192

8 What's the problem?
WB 7 p. 89

a) Listen to this dialogue at the doctor's. Who is the patient? L 2.4

b) Listen again and take notes to answer the questions.
1. What is wrong with the patient?
2. What happened?
3. What does the doctor tell the patient to do?
4. What do you learn about the doctor?

7: Wordbank Body and health | p. 220

9 Sound check

Listen to the sentences. Then say them yourself. L 2.5

[ə]

1. Ben has a headache and a sore throat.
2. He gargles with salt water to get better again.

Dieser Laut heißt Schwa.
Er kommt häufig in unbetonten Silben vor.

10 What has changed?

10 p. 185

a) Look at the pictures of Ben's room. Find the differences.

1

2

b) What has changed in picture number 2? Use these verbs:

make | put | clean | tidy | put away | open | ...

Ben has made his bed.
He ...

11 Choose an activity

You can:

- Make a get well card for someone who is ill. Write a nice message.

  Get well soon. | I hope you will ... | We miss you a lot. | You haven't missed much at school. | Cheer up! | ...

- Draw two pictures with differences. Look at number 10 for ideas. Write down some verbs, too. Then let your classmates say what has changed.
- Work with a partner and write your own dialogue at the doctor's. You can look at numbers 7 and 8 for help. Then act out your dialogue in class.

10: Grammar 14 | p. 255/256
11: Wordbank Body and health | p. 220

12 What to watch? WB 8 p. 89

a) When Ben is ill, he can watch a lot of programmes. There are many different programmes. Match the words with the pictures.

a soap opera | a talk show | a film | a talent show | a quiz show | a sports programme | the news | a cartoon

Picture … is **a soap opera**.

1

2

3

4

5

6

7

8

b) Work with a partner. What kind of programmes do/don't YOU like? Why? WEB 11

I like … but I don't like …

I think … is more interesting/boring than …

I often/sometimes/never watch … because …

I (don't) agree. I think …

13 Watching TV

Lies dir Bens Blogeintrag über seine Fernsehgewohnheiten durch.
Beantworte die Fragen von jemandem, der kaum Englisch versteht.

Ben

I usually watch TV when I'm ill or when I have nothing else to do. Sometimes my whole family sits in front of the telly at the weekend. That's always fun. My favourite TV programme is Ackley Bridge. It's on Channel 4 and it's a kind of soap. It's about the students and teachers at a school in the north of England. The students are from British and Pakistani families. You learn about the problems and friendships between them and about a lot more. I like watching Ackley Bridge because it's exciting and serious but also very funny.

13.1 p. 192

1. Wann schaut Ben fern?
2. Was bedeutet *telly*?
3. Wo kann man Bens Lieblingssendung sehen?
4. Worum geht es in der Sendung?

LAND & LEUTE ▷ 14

Fernsehen in Großbritannien
Wie bei uns gibt es auch in Großbritannien ein großes Angebot an nationalen und privaten Fernsehsendern. Dazu gehören die beiden werbefreien Sender *BBC1* und *BBC2* der britischen Rundfunkgesellschaft, der *British Broadcasting Corporation*.
Die *BBC* sendet viele beliebte Programme. Manche von ihnen laufen schon seit vielen Jahren.
Mit Begeisterung sehen sich Jugendliche in Großbritannien Castingshows an, die auf verschiedenen Sendern gezeigt werden. Aber auch in Großbritannien schauen immer mehr junge Leute Filme und Serien auf ihrem Mobiltelefon, Laptop oder Tablet und nicht auf dem Fernsehgerät.

Welche Geräte nutzt du, um dir Filme oder Serien anzuschauen?

Sieh dir nun den Clip an und finde heraus:
- Was zahlt man in Großbritannien, um verschiedene Fernsehprogramme zu empfangen?
- Welche beliebte Seifenoper läuft schon seit 1985 auf *BBC1*?
- Welches spezielle Angebot hat die *BBC* für Kinder?

14 Target task: YOUR favourite programme or series

a) ❙ Write about your favourite programme or series. Portfolio-Ordner ❙ 14a p. 185
Look at numbers 12 and 13 for help and ideas.
Think about:
- what kind of programme / series it is
- what channel it is on / how you watch it
- when it is (day and time) / when you watch it
- what it is about / what happens
- why you like it
- …

WEB 11

b) Ask a partner or your teacher to check your text. Then correct it. WEB 1

c) Present your text to your class:
Read it, record it or put it up in the classroom. WEB 7

My favourite programme

My favourite programme is "Wer wird Millionär". It is a quiz show.
It is on RTL every Monday at 8:15 p.m. and sometimes on Fridays at the same time.
I usually watch it with my sister in the living room.
In the quiz show people have to answer questions. If they can answer all of them correctly, they win a million euros.
I like "Wer wird Millionär" because it is always exciting and you learn a lot, too.

14: Skills Write | p. 235

1 Have you ever …? WB 9 p. 90

a) Listen to the song and sing along. L 2.6

Have you ever been to Paris?
Have you ever been to Rome?
Have you ever been to London?
No, I've just been here at home.

Have you ever met a stunt man?
Have you ever met the Queen?
Have you ever met a T. Rex?
No, I've just seen them on screen.

Have you ever eaten snails?
Have you ever eaten snake?
Have you ever eaten frogs' legs?
No, I've just had too much cake.

Have you ever done a backflip?
Have you ever done things wrong?
Have you ever done a marathon?
No, I've just done a song and the last line got too long.

b) How many questions in the song can YOU answer with "yes"?

c) Walk around the classroom and interview your classmates.
Who can answer with "yes" the most often?

1.1 p. 186

Have you ever been to Paris?

Yes, I have.

No, I haven't.

Have you ever …

2 Choose an activity

You can:

- Work with a partner or in groups. Practise the song in number 1 and present it in class. You can also record it.
- Work with a partner and make up (silly) questions with "Have you ever …?" Then interview each other. Act out the interview in class or record it and play it to the class.
- Write more verses for the song in number 1 and present them. L 2.7 You can use these verbs:

see | play | watch | listen to | find | buy | …

Have you ever …?
Have you ever …?
Have you ever …?
No, I've just …

1: Grammar 14b | p. 256
1c: Skills Milling around | p. 238
2: Grammar 14b | p. 256

3 Holiday plans WB 10 p. 90

a) The friends are in Megan's garden. Listen to them. What are they planning to do in their holidays? L 2.8

b) Listen again and find out:
- Who has never been to Cornwall?
- Who wants to eat ice cream every day?
- Who is looking forward to the sea?
- Who is interested in visiting a castle?

What else did you understand?

4 Our trips

Work in small groups and talk about your trips.

Have you ever been to Cornwall/ Scotland/Turkey/Poland/…?

Yes, I have.

What was it like?

It was great/boring/…

Have you ever been to an adventure camp / a sports camp?

No, I haven't but I've been to …

5 More questions

5 p. 186

a) Put the questions in the correct order and answer them.

1. Have – done – already – your homework – you – ?
2. ever – had – Have – a bad cold – you – ?
3. you – your room – tidied – already – Have – ?
4. a film star – Have – ever – you – met – ?
5. your pet – you – fed – Have – already – ?
6. been – Have – ever – you – to a concert – ?

1. Have you already done your homework?
2. Have you ever …?

b) Be a language detective.
- Wie würdest du *ever* und *already* in den Fragen oben übersetzen?
- *Ever* und *already* sind Signalwörter für das *present perfect*. Wo stehen diese Signalwörter in Fragen im *present perfect*?

4: Grammar 14 | p. 255/256
5: Grammar 14 | p. 255/256

6 p. 187
6 p. 193

6 Holidays in Cornwall WB 11 + 12 p. 91

a) Read the brochures. Can you guess the meaning of new words?
Look up words you can't guess in your dictionary (pages 289 to 315).

Cornish Adventure Camp
for young people from 8 to 16

There is never a boring moment at the Cornish Adventure Camp in the beautiful town of **Newquay**.

Newquay has some of the best beaches in the UK. We do lots of fun activities at the beach, like bodyboarding and surfing. We also go on a treasure hunt to explore Newquay.

What's more, you can come with us to Blue Reef Newquay. It's an amazing aquarium with an underwater tunnel.

And last but not least we visit the magical birthplace of King Arthur – Tintagel Castle.

So don't miss out!
Spend your holidays at the
Cornish Adventure Camp!

ADVENTURE CAMP PENZANCE

There's lots to do …

- Penzance has fantastic beaches where you can try all kinds of water sports, like surfing, sailing and kayaking.
- You can also go mountain biking or horse riding with us along the beautiful coast.
- Every evening there are more activities, for example a Friday night disco plus karaoke and quiz nights.

… and lots to see …

Come with us to the lovely island of St Michael's Mount and explore the amazing castle. And join us on our tour to Land's End, Britain's most south-westerly point.

Are you between 10 and 18 years old? Then come to Penzance and have fun at the Adventure Camp Penzance.

b) What do you learn about Cornwall from the brochures?

There is/are …

You can …

c) Copy the table and fill in the information from the brochures.

	Cornish Adventure Camp	**Adventure Camp Penzance**
where?	…	…
activities?	…	…
age?	…	…
anything special?	…	…

6.1 p. 194

d) Which adventure camp would YOU like to go to? Why?

I'd like to go to … because …

7 So much to do

Look at the two brochures again and complete the sentences.

visit | go | try | spend | come | explore

1. You can XX your holidays at an adventure camp.
2. You can go on a treasure hunt to XX a new place.
3. You can XX all kinds of water sports.
4. You can XX mountain biking or horse riding along the beautiful coast.
5. You can XX one of Cornwall's great castles.
6. You can XX to Cornwall and have lots of fun.

8 What do they need?

a) Look at the pictures. What do the children need for their trip to Cornwall? Why?

I think they need … because …

sweets

some money

a mobile phone

sunglasses

swimwear

a book

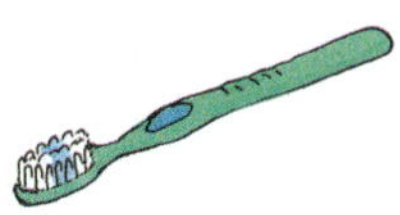
a toothbrush

a torch

b) What would YOU pack for a summer holiday?

I would pack …

c) Read these descriptions. What are the things? Look at a) for help.

A You use it when you want to see in the dark.

B It is made of metal or paper.

C You can eat them and they are yummy.

D You need it to go swimming in the sea.

d) | Describe three more things from number a). Then quiz your partner. | 8d p. 187

8d: Wordbank Things | p. 219

9 On the beach in Cornwall WB 13 p. 92

a) Look at the title and the pictures. What do you think happens in the story?

b) Listen and read along. L 2.9

It was a beautiful and hot summer's day in Newquay. The four friends were on the beach with the other children from their adventure camp. Laura and Justin, two of their supervisors, taught them how to bodyboard. The campers had to learn the movements on land first.

Laura: Very good, Jasmine, just lean over to the left a bit more. That's it, Jasmine, great.
Justin: Perfect, Megan and Sandeep. Ben, you have to move up on your board a bit. And lift your upper body. Look at Megan – do it just like her.
Ben: But my body hurts from all those steps at Tintagel Castle yesterday! I can't even lift my little finger!
Megan: Oh, come on, Ben, it's not that hard. Just try it!

Ben looked bored and unhappy, but tried to move on his bodyboard like Megan.

Soon it was time to take the boards to the water. The campers laughed as they jumped into the waves and tried to stay on their boards. They had great fun. All of them but Ben! He stood at the edge of the water and looked unsure.

Sandeep: This is so much fun. Wow, Megan, you are really good at this.
Megan: Thank you, it's so cool!
Jasmine: Oh, there's a big wave, let's go and catch it.

After the big wave, Sandeep noticed that Ben was missing.

Sandeep: Where is Ben? I can't see him anywhere!
Jasmine: Oh dear, I hope he didn't get knocked over by that big wave!
Megan: You know Ben, he's probably back on the beach. I don't think he likes bodyboarding.

The friends went back to the beach and started looking for Ben, but they couldn't see him anywhere. They called his name, they asked the other campers and people on the beach, but no one knew where he was. After a while they started to get really worried. Then Jasmine saw something at the bottom of a cliff.

Jasmine: Isn't that Ben and his green cap over there?
Sandeep: Yeah, that could be him.

The friends ran over to the cliff and sure enough, it was Ben. He was sitting on his bodyboard with his sketchbook and was drawing a picture.

Megan: What are you doing? We were worried about you!

Ben was very surprised to see his friends.

Ben: Oh, hi, guys! Sorry, but I just didn't feel like bodyboarding. My legs are still tired from our trip to Tintagel Castle yesterday. So I decided to sit down and draw a picture of you on your bodyboards.

The friends looked at the picture and laughed.

Jasmine: Oh Ben, you're so lazy! It's a lovely picture though …

c) Read the story again. Then look at these sentences. Are they right or wrong? Correct what's wrong.

1. The campers were on the beach with their bodyboards.
2. Then they took their boards to the water and jumped into the waves.
3. After a big wave Sandeep was missing.
4. The friends were worried and looked for him.
5. Then they noticed him at the edge of the water.
6. He didn't feel like bodyboarding and took a photo of the friends.

9.1 p. 188
9.2 p. 188

d) Would YOU like to try bodyboarding? Or would you rather sit on the beach and draw a picture? Say why.

I'd like to … because …

9.1 p. 194

10 p. 188
10 p. 195

10 A holiday dialogue WB 14 p. 93

a) Read the dialogue. Then practise reading it with a partner.

Felix: Hi, I'm Felix. What's your name?
Sandeep: Hi, my name is Sandeep. Where are you from?
Felix: I'm from Stuttgart in Germany. What about you?
Sandeep: I'm from London. Is this your first time in Cornwall?
Felix: Yes, it is. I think it's great here.
Sandeep: I think so, too. Why don't we play some beach volleyball?
Felix: Yeah, good idea.
Sandeep: I need to put on a shirt and a cap first. I'll be right back.
Felix: No problem. See you.
Sandeep: See you.

b) Make up a different holiday dialogue with a partner and present it in class.

11 A postcard from Cornwall

a) Read Megan's postcard. Does she like her holiday in Cornwall?

9th July

Dear Mum,
Hi from Newquay!
On our first day we went on a treasure hunt and got to know Newquay. It's a really nice place.
Yesterday we visited Tintagel Castle.
I didn't see King Arthur but it was fun anyway.
Today we went bodyboarding at the beach.
It was fantastic! Only Ben doesn't like all the sports activities. Well, you know him.
The weather is great – sunny and windy most of the time.
Say hello to Sir Barks-A-Lot!
Love,
Megan

Mrs
Helen McGregor
49 Hartland Road
London
NW1 8DB

b) Read again and find out:

- What did Megan and her friends visit?
- What did they do?
- What was the weather like?
- What else do you learn from the postcard?

c) ▎YOU are Ben. Write a postcard to your family. Tell them what you think about your holiday in Cornwall, what you did, …

9th July

Dear all,

…

The Hancock Family
25 Clarence Way
London
NW1 8RJ

▎11c p. 189

11.1 p. 195

12 Target task: YOUR holiday plans

WB **test yourself** p. 94 + 95; **Portfolio** p. 128 / **WEB** P6

a) Work with a partner or in small groups on a presentation about a place you would like to go on holiday.
Think about:
- where you would like to go
- how long you want to stay there

Collect information on:
- how you can get there (by train/plane/…)
- what you can do there
- what is special about the place
- where you can stay
- what you should take with you
- …

You can interview your family, go to the library or a travel agency, search the Internet, … **WEB** 6

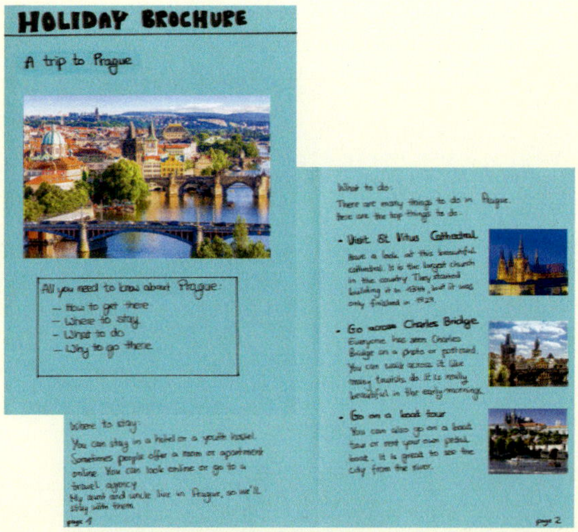

b) Put your information on a poster, a brochure, on transparencies or on a computer. Add pictures or photos, too. **WEB** 2

c) Ask your classmates or your teacher to check your text. Then correct it.

d) ▎Practise your presentation. Then present your holiday plans to your class.

▎12d p. 189

e) Ask for and give feedback.

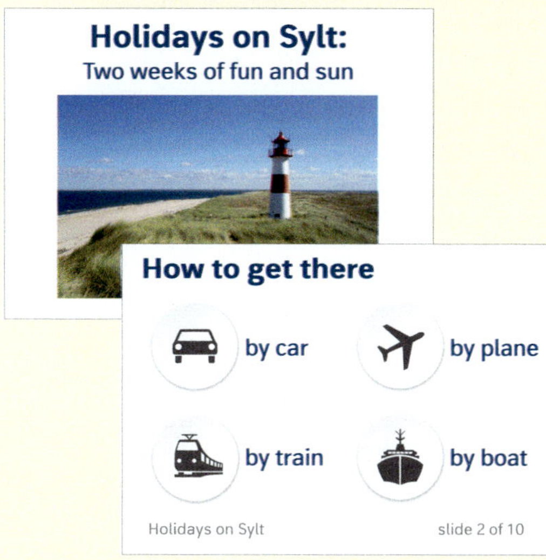

11c: Skills Write a postcard | p. 237
12: Wordbank Travelling | p. 212/213
12: Skills Search the Internet | p. 233
Give a talk | p. 232

2 A weekend in Camden WB 2 p. 86

2b p. 167 **b)** Read again. What do you learn about these people?

Megan Jasmine and Jason Their mum Ben	has have	gone to a concert. gone to Edinburgh. been ill for three days. gone with them. taken Sir Barks-A-Lot with her. used lots of tissues. played with his phone. watched TV.

5 p. 169

5 Already done?

a) Put the three verb forms in the right order. Write them down.

taken – take – took | wrote – written – write | go – gone – went | drunk – drink – drank | ate – eaten – eat | put – put – put

1. take – took – taken
2. …

Für die neue Zeitform, das *present perfect*, brauchst du die dritte Verbform. Unregelmäßige Verben haben eigene Formen, die du lernen musst (siehe S. 334–335).

b) It is 5:30 p.m. Ben thinks about his day.
What has he already done? What hasn't he done yet?
Look at the verb forms in a) for help.

Ben has already taken his medicine.
He hasn't gone to the doctor yet.
He hasn't … yet.
He has already …
He has already …
He hasn't … yet.

- take his medicine ✓
- go to the doctor
- eat fruit
- drink lots of tea and water ✓
- write to Megan and Jasmine ✓
- put his tissues in the bin

2: Grammar 14 | p. 255/256
5: Grammar 14 | p. 255/256

5.1 Sorry, I can't!

Work with a partner and make dialogues.

Would you like to **watch a film** with me?

Sorry, I can't! I haven't **eaten dinner** yet.

watch a film | go skateboarding | play basketball | go to the cinema | eat a pizza | …

emptied the dishwasher | done my homework | eaten dinner | fed my pet | tidied my room | …

5.2 Jobs done!

What have the kids already done?
You can look at the box for help.

1. Josh has already done his homework.
2. Megan and Jasmine have already …

…

write – has/have written
buy – has/have bought
help – has/have helped
do – has/have done
clean – has/have cleaned
make – has/have made

1 
do his homework

2 
write a card for Ben

3 
make her bed

4 
help their mum with the shopping

5 
clean the bathroom

6 
buy new pens for school

5.1: Grammar 14 | p. 255/256
5.2: Grammar 14 | p. 255/256

7.1 What's wrong with Ben?

Look at number 7 (p. 170) again and complete the sentences.

sore | hurts | gargle | throat | temperature | sore throat | headache

1. Ben's head XX. He has a XX.
2. His head doesn't feel hot. He doesn't have a XX.
3. But his XX hurts. It is XX.
4. It is best to drink lots of warm tea when you have a XX.
5. Or you can XX with salt water.

7.2 Doctor and patient

a) What does the doctor say? What does the patient answer? Match the sentences.

doctor	patient
1 Good morning. How are you today?	A Ouch, it hurts a lot!
2 What's wrong?	B I will. Thank you, doctor.
3 Let's have a look.	C The street was wet and I fell off my bike.
4 Your leg is sore. How did that happen?	D Goodbye!
5 Oh dear. I'll put some cream on your leg. And please come again tomorrow.	E I've hurt my leg.
6 You're welcome. Goodbye!	F Good morning, doctor. I don't feel very well.

b) Read the dialogue with a partner.

8 p. 170

8 What's the problem? WB 7 p. 89

a) Listen to this dialogue at the doctor's. Who is the patient? L 2.4

Jasmine | Jasmine's mother | Jasmine's cat

b) Listen again and answer the questions.

1. What is wrong with the patient?
   a) Her hand hurts.
   b) Her head hurts.
2. What happened?
   a) She tripped over her cat and fell.
   b) It was dark outside and she fell.
3. What does the doctor tell the patient to do?
   a) Use this cream and come again tomorrow.
   b) Use this cream and come again if it doesn't get better.
4. What do you learn about the doctor?
   a) He doesn't have a cat.
   b) He likes cats a lot.

10 What has changed?

10 p. 171

a) Look at the pictures of Ben's room. Find the differences.
"In picture 1 Ben's room is untidy but in picture 2 it is ..."
"In picture 1 there are ... on the floor. In picture 2 they are ..."
"In picture 1 I can see ... in Ben's room. I can't see any ... in picture 2." "..."

1

2

b) What has changed in picture number 2? Use these verbs:

make | put | clean | tidy | put away | open | ...

Ben has made his bed.
He has cleaned ...
He has ...

14 Target task: YOUR favourite programme or series

a) Write about your favourite programme or series. WEB 11 Portfolio-Ordner
Look at numbers 12 and 13 for help and ideas.
Think about:

14a p. 173

- what kind of programme / series it is
- what channel it is on / how you watch it
- when it is (day and time) / when you watch it
- what it is about / what happens
- why you like it
- ...

My favourite programme	series
My favourite programme is "Wer wird Millionär".	series "..."
It is a quiz show. It is on RTL every Monday at	soap opera / fantasy drama / ...
8:15 p.m. and sometimes on Fridays at the same time.	I watch it on my computer / ...
I usually watch it with my sister in the living room.	with my best friend / ... in my room
In the quiz show people have to answer	series young people dance and sing.
questions. If they can answer all of them correctly,	They want to ... / The series is about ...
they win a million euros.	
I like "Wer wird Millionär" because it is always	"..." the story is funny/cool/...
exciting and you learn a lot, too.	the music is really good ...

10: Grammar 14 | p. 255/256

1.1 Tell me …

a) Write down questions with "Have you ever …?". Use the words from the boxes.

play | make | buy | visit | see | meet | eat

a lion | a star | tennis | a cake | sushi | Florida | butter

1. Have you ever played tennis?
2. Have you ever made …?

…

b) Ask and answer the questions with a partner. Take turns.

Have you ever **played tennis**?

Yes, I have.

No, I haven't.

5 p. 175

5 More questions

a) Put the questions in the correct order and answer them.

1. Have you – done – already – your homework – ?
2. ever – had – Have you – a bad cold – ?
3. your room – tidied – already – Have you – ?
4. a film star – Have you – ever – met – ?
5. your pet – fed – Have you – already – ?
6. been – Have you – ever – to a concert – ?

1. Have you already done your homework?
2. Have you ever had …?

b) Be a language detective.

- Wie würdest du *ever* und *already* in den Fragen oben übersetzen?

jemals | immer | schon | noch | bereits | …

- *Ever* und *already* sind Signalwörter für das *present perfect*. Wo stehen diese Signalwörter in Fragen im *present perfect*?

Sie stehen …

a) hinter *have* oder *has*.
b) vor der dritten Verbform (*past participle*).
c) am Anfang der Frage.

1.1: Grammar 14b | p. 256
5: Grammar 14b | p. 256

6 Holidays in Cornwall WB 11 + 12 p. 91

b) What do you learn about Cornwall from the brochures on page 176? 6b p. 176

There is **an aquarium in Newquay**.

There are **great beaches**.

You can **go surfing**.

c) Copy the table and fill in the information from the brochures.

	Cornish Adventure Camp	Adventure Camp Cornwall
where?	Newquay	…
activities?	…	water sports: …, …
age?	8 to 16	…
anything special?	…	Land's End, …

d) Which adventure camp would YOU like to go to? Why?

I'd like to go to **the Adventure Camp Cornwall** because **I want to visit Land's End**.

8 What do they need?

d) Describe three more things. Then quiz your partner. 8d p. 177

a book

a mobile phone

a toothbrush

sunglasses

You can use these phrases:

You use it/them when you want to …

You need it/them to …

You can … it/them and it is / they are …

It is / They are made of …

Mehr Hilfen zur Beschreibung von Gegenständen findest du hinten im Buch auf der Seite 219.

8: Wordbank Things | p. 219

9.1 Finding words

Copy the table. Then look at number 9 again (pages 178–179) and find more words for the table.

places	people	things you can do (verbs)	what people/things are like (adjectives)
beach …	friends …	learn …	beautiful …

10 to 15 words: Look again! 16 to 25 words: Good! more than 25 words: Great!

9.2 Ben on the beach

Use words from your table in number 9.1 (or the story on pages 178–179) to complete the text.

It was a XX day in Newquay. The XX were on the XX to learn bodyboarding. They took their boards and XX into the waves. Only Ben didn't XX this sport. He sat down at the bottom of a XX and started drawing. Jasmine said Ben was XX but she thought the picture was XX.

10 p. 180

10 A holiday dialogue WB 14 p. 93

a) Read the dialogue. Then practise reading it with a partner.

Felix: Hi, I'm **Felix**. What's your name?
Sandeep: Hi, my name is **Sandeep**. Where are you from?
Felix: I'm from **Stuttgart** in **Germany**. What about you?
Sandeep: I'm from **London**. Is this your first time in **Cornwall**?
Felix: Yes, it is. I think it's **great** here.
Sandeep: I think so, too. Why don't we **play some beach volleyball**?
Felix: Yeah, good idea.
Sandeep: I need to **put on a shirt and a cap** first. I'll be right back.
Felix: No problem. See you.
Sandeep: See you.

b) Work with a partner. Find YOUR words for the blue words and make up a holiday dialogue. Present it in class.

Here are some ideas:

go swimming | buy an ice cream | go skateboarding | …
put on my swimwear | get some money | get my skateboard | …

11 A postcard from Cornwall

c) YOU are Ben. Write a postcard to your family. Tell them what you think about your holiday in Cornwall, what you did, … 11c p. 181

9th July

Dear all,
Hi from …!
It's … here.
On our first day we …
…
Yesterday we …
…
Today we went bodyboarding at the beach. It was … I …
…
The weather is …
…
See you soon,
Ben

The Hancock Family
25 Clarence Way
London
NW1 8RJ

12 Target task: YOUR holiday plans

WB test yourself p. 94 + 95;
Portfolio p. 128 / WEB P6

d) Practise your presentation.
Then present your holiday plans to your class. 12d p. 181

We are now going to present our holiday plans to you.
We would like to go to … Here are some pictures.
We want to stay there for … days/weeks/months.
We can get to … by train/plane/car/bike/ …
In … you can go swimming in the sea / go cycling / eat in a nice restaurant / …
There are lots of great sights, for example …
Look at this picture. It shows …
Here you can see …
There is the most beautiful beach / …
You can get the best ice cream / … there.
We want to stay in a hotel / holiday apartment / at a campsite / …
We would take these things with us: our swimwear, sunglasses, some games, …
Thank you for listening.
Have you got any questions?

11: Skills Write | p. 235,
Write a postcard | p. 237

2.1 The backstage report WB 1 p. 98

a) A few days after the Wild Gang concert there was an interview with Jasmine and Jason for the school magazine. Read the article and find out: Why were Jasmine and Jason allowed to go backstage? What could they do there?

Backstage with the WILD GANG

Everyone at our school has probably heard of the Wild Gang but very few have had the chance to meet the band. Last Saturday Haverstock students Jasmine and Jason Bolt went to see the Wild Gang live and also met the famous band before the concert. They were allowed to go backstage after Jasmine won a contest on the band's home page.

Jasmine and Jason arrived at the concert hall at about five o'clock and a lot of people were already waiting outside. The lucky fans made their way through the crowd and showed their backstage passes at the door. A young woman then took them through the backstage rooms.

The band was practising their new hit song when Jasmine and Jason walked into the room. "It was amazing! I'll never forget it," said Jasmine. The members of the band then talked to the two fans. "At first I didn't know what to say because I was so excited," laughed Jason. "They asked about our favourite songs and our hobbies, and it turned out that lead singer Rick and I both like playing hockey."

The band members gave both fans caps with the band's name and also wrote autographs on Jasmine's T-shirt. She thought it was great and was laughing the whole time. When asked what she will do with the T-shirt, Jasmine answered: "I'll never wash this T-shirt again!"

Jasmine and Jason were still talking to the band when reporters suddenly came into the room. "It was crazy," explained Jason. "The reporters were asking questions and running around until the manager finally shouted 'time's up!'. Then the band had to go for make-up. They were getting ready for the concert so the manager had time to show the fans the tour bus. Jason really liked the bus. "It's so cool, not like a normal bus. It's a living room with a big TV screen and a great sound system."

Jasmine and Jason then got another surprise: The band invited them to stand at the front and watch the show. Jasmine was very excited. "When the band came on stage, everyone was screaming. I was screaming, too. What an incredible feeling!"

The concert was fantastic and everyone had a lot of fun. The band came back on stage three times. "Everyone was still cheering when they came back the third time," said Jason. "We didn't want it to end, we had a great time!"

b) Read the article again and complete the sentences.

1. When Jasmine and Jason arrived at five o'clock, …
2. When they walked into the room, …
3. When the band wrote their autographs on Jasmine's T-shirt, …
4. When reporters suddenly came into the room, …
5. When the manager showed them the tour bus, …
6. When the band came on stage, …
7. When the band came back the third time, …

1. When Jasmine and Jason arrived at five o'clock, a lot of people were already waiting outside.
2. …

c) Who is YOUR favourite singer or band? Have you ever been to a concert by them? Talk to a partner.

2.2 What were they doing? WB 2 + 3 p. 98, 99

a) Look at the pictures. What were the people doing?

1. Ben was watching TV when the phone rang.
2. Megan and Fergus were …

1 
Ben (watch TV) when the phone rang.

2 
Megan and Fergus (do a puzzle) when Sir Barks-A-Lot came into the room.

3 
Sandeep (walk home) when it started to rain.

4 

Neela (ride her bike) when a police officer stopped her.

5 
Jasmine and Jason (make pizza) when their mum got home.

6 
Sarah (listen to music) when the lights went out.

b) Be a language detective. Look at your sentences from a). When do you use the past progressive (<u>was/were</u> watch<u>ing</u>)? When do you use the simple past (rang, came, …)? Talk about the rule with a partner.

2.1: Grammar 18 | p. 258/259
2.2: Grammar 18 | p. 258/259

7.1 Different patients

a) Look at the patients. What's wrong with them?

a headache | a toothache | a bad cold | a stomach ache | a broken arm

1. Patient number 1 has a bad cold.
2. ...

b) YOU are the doctor. What should the patients do / not do to get better?

Patient number 1: Stay in bed. ... Don't go to school. ...
...

8 p. 170

8 What's the problem? WB 7 p. 89

a) Listen to this dialogue at the doctor's. Who is the patient? L 2.4

b) Listen again and take notes to answer the questions.

1. What is wrong with the patient?
2. What happened?
3. What does the doctor tell the patient to do?
4. What do you learn about the doctor?
5. What was wrong with the patient last year?
6. What happened to the cat?
7. How does the doctor know that nothing is broken?

13.1 A German blog entry

Sieh dir den Blogeintrag an. Beantworte die Fragen von jemandem, der wenig Deutsch versteht.

Lara

Ich gucke manchmal nach der Schule fern, wenn ich müde bin oder mir langweilig ist. Am Wochenende sehe ich mir gerne spannende Filme oder Castingshows an. Dann sitze ich mit meiner Mutter vor dem Fernseher und wir essen dabei Chips oder Popcorn. Oft schaue ich mir aber auch Filme oder Videos auf dem Handy an. Dann habe ich zwar nur ein kleines Bild, aber ich kann dabei auf meinem Bett liegen und habe meine Ruhe. Mein Bruder guckt am liebsten amerikanische Serien auf seinem Computer. Auf Serien stehe ich überhaupt nicht.

1. When does Lara watch TV?
2. What does she like watching?
3. What does she say about her phone?
4. What does her brother enjoy watching?

6 Holidays in Cornwall WB 11 + 12 p. 91

6 p. 176

a) Read the two brochures on page 176 and the one below. Can you guess the meaning of new words? Look up words you can't guess in your dictionary (pages 289 to 315).

Are you between 10 and 15 years old and looking for a real summer adventure? Then spend your holidays at our camp in the beautiful Cornish village of **Mevagissey**.

Mevagissey Summer Camp

We'll explore the harbour and go on a boat trip around the bay. We'll also visit the museum where you can learn about life in the village over the years.

Are you interested in sports? Then come with us to the many sandy beaches near Mevagissey where you can try stand up paddleboarding, kayaking and surfing. We'll also walk along some fantastic clifftop paths and look out to sea.

Have you heard of the Lost Gardens of Heligan? Join us on our tour of these beautiful gardens and the exotic outdoor jungle.

Mevagissey Summer Camp is waiting for you!

b) What do you learn about Cornwall from the brochures?

There is/are …

You can …

…

c) Copy the table and fill in the information from the brochures.

	Cornish Adventure Camp	Adventure Camp Penzance	Mevagissey Summer Camp
where?	…	…	…
activities?	…	…	…
age?	…	…	…
anything special?	…	…	…

d) Which adventure camp would YOU like to go to? Why?

I'd like to go to … because …

I like/enjoy … That's why I'd like to …

6.1 Tintagel Castle WB 4 + 5 p. 100

Sieh dir die Informationen zum Tintagel Castle an. Beantworte die Fragen von jemandem, der kein Englisch versteht.

A magical day out at
Tintagel Castle

Tintagel Castle is located on one of the UK's most spectacular stretches of coastline. Imagine what life was like at Tintagel as you enter the breathtaking ruins of the 13th century castle through a wooden door. Discover the legend of King Arthur and learn about the history of the castle. Look down onto the wild Atlantic Ocean and relax on the beautiful beach below the castle.

Mar – Sept: 10 a.m. – 6 p.m.
Oct: 10 a.m. – 5 p.m.
Nov – Feb: 10 a.m. – 4 p.m. (Sat & Sun only)

Adults: £9.50 Students / Over 60s: £8.60
Children aged 5-17: £5.70

Tintagel Castle, Castle Road, Tintagel PL34 0HE

1. Wo befindet sich die Burg?
2. Was kann ich dort sehen und erleben?
3. Wann kann ich die Burg besichtigen?
4. Was muss ich als 72-Jähriger bezahlen?

9.1 Jasmine's holiday diary WB 6 p. 101

Imagine YOU are Jasmine.
Write a diary entry about your day on the beach in Cornwall. Describe what happened and how you and your friends felt.

Tuesday, 9th July

Today the weather was ...
We went to ...
Laura and Justin taught us ...
First ...
Then ...
After that ...
Suddenly ...
Later ...
Finally ...
...

6.1: Skills Help out | p. 234
9.1: Skills Write | p. 235
9.1: Wordbank People | p. 210

10 A holiday dialogue WB 14 p. 93

10 p. 180

a) Read the dialogue. Then practise reading it with a partner.

Felix: Hi, I'm Felix. What's your name?
Sandeep: Hi, my name is Sandeep. Where are you from?
Felix: I'm from Stuttgart in Germany. What about you?
Sandeep: I'm from London. Is this the first time you've been to Cornwall?
Felix: Yes, it is. What about you?
Sandeep: It's my first time, too. Do you like it here?
Felix: Yeah, I think it's great.
Sandeep: I think so, too. By the way, your English is really good.
Felix: Thanks. Do you learn German at school?
Sandeep: No, I don't. But maybe you could teach me some German words.
Felix: Klar, kann ich machen. Äh, sure.
Sandeep: That's great! Why don't we play some beach volleyball?
Felix: Yeah, good idea.
Sandeep: I need to put on a shirt and a cap first. I'll be right back.
Felix: No problem. I'll get the ball. See you.
Sandeep: See you.

b) Make up a different holiday dialogue with a partner and present it in class.

11.1 A phone call WB 7 p. 101

a) Listen to the phone call. What do you learn about Sandeep's mum? How does she feel? L 2.10

b) Listen again and take notes on these questions:
- What is the difference between bodyboarding and surfing?
- What does Sandeep say about the supervisors?
- What does he tell his mum about the food?
- What are the children going to do the next day?

c) Tell someone who hasn't listened to the phone call what it is about. Use your notes from b).

11.1: Skills Listen | p. 228

Camden Chronicle

Learn English the Camden way

Good to know ...

Die Briten sind bekannt für ihre Höflichkeit und Rücksichtnahme. Die Wörter *please* und *thank you* werden für deutsche Ohren auffällig oft gebraucht. So ist es auch selbstverständlich, dass Menschen sich höflich begrüßen. Wenn man jemanden versehentlich anstößt, entschuldigt man sich mit *I'm sorry*. Drängeleien sind nicht üblich. Die Briten stellen sich geduldig in eine Schlange (*queue*) im Supermarkt, am Postschalter oder wenn sie auf den Bus warten.

A rap

You know who they are,
you know what they do.
There's no way to ignore them,
they might bully you, too.

You should tell your friends,
parents and teachers, too,
about the bullies at school
before they bully you.

So let's get together,
come on, let's make some noise.
Don't let them bully you.
Stand up, let's hear your voice.

Funny school rules

- At many schools in Great Britain teachers are not allowed to use red pens to mark students' tests.
- At a school in Nottinghamshire (England) students are not allowed to raise their hands when they want to answer their teachers' questions.
- At schools in China students are allowed to sleep for 30 minutes during the school day.
- Students in Tokyo (Japan) are not allowed to change their hair colour. The schools want all their students to look the same – from the school uniform to their hair!

Good to know ...

Wie in Deutschland ist Fernsehen auch in Großbritannien eine beliebte Freizeitbeschäftigung. Die Briten haben viele verschiedene Bezeichnungen für den Fernseher, z. B. *telly* (als liebevolle Kurzform von *television*), *box* (Kiste), *small screen* (kleiner Bildschirm – der Gegensatz dazu ist der *big screen* im Kino) oder auch *goggle-box* (Glotze).

A time-saving postcard

Dear Jasmine,

Greetings from Greece!

The weather is
☑ great. ☐ terrible.

The food is
☑ delicious. ☐ awful.

The people are
☑ friendly. ☐ unfriendly.

I can't wait to
☑ come back next summer!
☐ go home soon!

Bye! Lynn

Jasmine Bolt
51 Hartland Road
London
NW1 8DB
United Kingdom

Some jokes

Patient: Doctor, when I press my finger here, it hurts. And it hurts when I press it here and here and here ...
Doctor: You've got a broken finger!

Patient: Doctor, Doctor, I think I need glasses!
Man: I think you're right. This is a restaurant!

Your year

Your year with Camden Market 6 is over.
What was ...

- your favourite Theme?
- your favourite page?
- your favourite photo or picture?
- your favourite story?

A The legend of Gelert L 2.11

There is a Welsh[1] legend[2] about a Prince of Wales and his big black dog.

Long, long ago there was a Prince of Wales called Llewellyn. He and his beautiful wife[3], Merfanwi Goldenhair, loved each other and were very happy. Merfanwi laughed, "Soon we'll have a child." It was a boy and the prince and the princess were very happy. Then Merfanwi became very ill.
She kissed her son and looked at Llewellyn for the last time.
"Goodbye, my love. Look after our son."
She died[4] and Llewellyn was heartbroken[5].

One morning Llewellyn and his men and their dogs went hunting[6]. The prince took his baby son with him. In the evening they camped near a river. The next morning was cold and wet, so Llewellyn left[7] his son in the tent[8] with Gelert, his favourite dog.
"Look after my son, old friend. We'll be back in the afternoon."
When Llewellyn and his men came back, Gelert didn't run out to meet them. Something was wrong! Llewellyn ran into his tent. The baby's bed and blanket[9] were on the ground[10] and there was blood[11] on them. There was blood everywhere! The men behind Llewellyn shouted: "Gelert went crazy[12] and killed your son!"

Llewellyn was very angry and he killed Gelert with his spear[13]. And then the baby cried[14]. It was under the blanket. There was a big wolf next to it. It was dead[15]. The blood wasn't from the baby, it was from the wolf and from Gelert.
"Gelert killed the wolf! I made a mistake[16] and killed my best friend!"
Llewellyn was happy about his son but sad about Gelert. He felt ashamed[17]. He and his men collected stones[18] from the river and made a big grave[19] for Gelert.

The grave is still there. In Welsh it's called Beddgelert – Gelert's grave.

There is also a Welsh village[20] called Beddgelert.
Find out more about it on the Internet.

[1]Welsh – *walisisch*; [2]legend – *Sage, Legende*; [3]wife – *Ehefrau*; [4]die – *sterben*; [5]heartbroken – *todunglücklich*; [6]hunt – *jagen*; [7]leave – *hier: lassen*; [8]tent – *Zelt*; [9]blanket – *Decke*; [10]ground – *(Erd)boden*; [11]blood – *Blut*; [12]go crazy – *durchdrehen*; [13]spear – *Speer*; [14]cry – *weinen; schreien*; [15]dead – *tot*; [16]mistake – *Fehler*; [17]feel ashamed – *sich schämen*; [18]stone – *Stein*; [19]grave – *Grab*; [20]village – *Dorf*

B Country life or city life?

Hi, my name is Adam and I'm 13 years old. I live in the countryside[1] in a small village[2] called Gilberdyke in the north of England. I live in a big house with my mum and my little sister, Abby.
Every morning I take the bus to school at about 8:10 a.m. It usually takes about 20 minutes to get there. After school I often meet my friends in the small park. That's the only good place to meet in my village. In summer we like to go for long bike rides around the villages nearby. Having a bike is very useful[3] in my village because there aren't many buses. But there is also a train station. You can take a train to big cities like Hull or York. But the trains stop running quite early, at around 7 p.m. That's why my mum has a car. Every Friday after school, my mum, Abby and I go to Hull in the car to do our weekly grocery[4] shopping at the big supermarket there.
Sometimes at the weekend we take the train to York. That takes about 40 minutes. Then we can go shopping for things like new clothes and games. In our village we only have a small shop, a pharmacy[5], a post office and a butcher's[6].
Oh, I forgot to mention our small dog, Lola. We have a nice, big garden and Lola loves playing in it. Sometimes we go for long walks with her in the fields nearby.
So that's my life in the countryside. I can't imagine living in a busy city. That would be too stressful for me!

Hey! I'm Hannah. I'm 13 years old and I live in London. I live in a flat with my mum and dad. I really want a dog, but our flat is quite small and we don't have a garden.
To get to school I take the Tube. It usually takes about 15 minutes to get there. After school I often hang out with my friends. Sometimes we go to the nearby park to play Frisbee. At the weekend I often take the Tube into the city to meet my friends there. If we have enough pocket money[7], we do something exciting like go to the cinema, go to a café or go shopping. There is lots to do in London! We avoid[8] places that are full of tourists though[9], like Southbank. It is easy to lose each other[10] at places like that.
We live opposite[11] a big supermarket. We usually buy things when we need them. So we don't go once a week to buy lots of things, but we go three or four times a week to buy a few things.
We don't have a car because we don't need one. We have the Tube, lots of buses, and a supermarket right across the road.
Life is great in a big city like London. I don't think I would enjoy living in the countryside – it would be so boring!

What is similar[12] about living in the countryside and living in a big city? What is different?

What do you think? Is life better in the countryside or in a big city? Why?

[1]in the countryside – *auf dem Land*; [2]village – *Dorf*; [3]useful – *nützlich*; [4]grocery – *Lebensmittel-*; [5]pharmacy – *Apotheke*; [6]butcher's – *Fleischerei, Metzgerei*; [7]pocket money – *Taschengeld*; [8]avoid – *(ver)meiden*; [9]though – *aber, allerdings*; [10]lose each other – *sich verlieren*; [11]opposite – *gegenüber*; [12]similar – *ähnlich*

C Horoscopes

Aries
21 March – 19 April
Work really hard at work or school this month. You will be very happy with the result[1].

Lucky number: **5**
Lucky colour: **red**
Friends with: **Virgo**

Taurus
20 April – 20 May
Something strange will happen on a Thursday this month, but you'll enjoy it!

Lucky number: **2**
Lucky colour: **yellow**
Friends with: **Scorpio**

Gemini
21 May – 20 June
Wear your lucky colour on the 15th and something wonderful will happen.

Lucky number: **11**
Lucky colour: **pink**
Friends with: **Libra**

Cancer
21 June – 22 July
Spend lots of time with your friends and you will get a big surprise.

Lucky number: **9**
Lucky colour: **grey**
Friends with: **Pisces**

Leo
23 July – 22 August
You will make a lot of people happy and you will do lots of travelling, too.

Lucky number: **6**
Lucky colour: **orange**
Friends with: **Sagittarius**

Virgo
23 August – 22 Sept.
Turn off[2] the TV or computer and go outside. You will meet someone new!

Lucky number: **1**
Lucky colour: **brown**
Friends with: **Aries**

Libra
23 Sept. – 22 Oct.
You worry about the future. Just listen to your heart. It will tell you what to do.

Lucky number: **10**
Lucky colour: **white**
Friends with: **Gemini**

Scorpio
23 Oct. – 21 Nov.
Be nice to someone you don't know this month and something amazing will happen.

Lucky number: **12**
Lucky colour: **black**
Friends with: **Taurus**

Sagittarius
22 Nov. – 21 Dec.
It will be a difficult month. Don't forget to ask your friends and family for help.

Lucky number: **4**
Lucky colour: **purple**
Friends with: **Leo**

Capricorn
22 Dec. – 19 Jan.
Make sure[3] you think before you speak or you will lose[4] a friend this month.

Lucky number: **8**
Lucky colour: **gold**
Friends with: **Aquarius**

Aquarius
20 Jan. – 18 Feb.
Life is boring at the moment. Do lots of sport and something exciting will happen.

Lucky number: **3**
Lucky colour: **blue**
Friends with: **Capricorn**

Pisces
19 Feb. – 20 March
Go on a trip with someone in your family. It will be unusual[5], but you will have lots of fun!

Lucky number: **7**
Lucky colour: **silver**
Friends with: **Cancer**

What do you think of YOUR horoscope? Would you like to be a different star sign? Why?

Write a horoscope for a friend or for someone in your family. You can decorate it, too.

[1]result – *Ergebnis*; [2]turn off – *ausmachen*; [3]make sure – *darauf achten*; [4]lose – *verlieren*; [5]unusual – *ungewöhnlich*

D Are you fit and healthy?

Do the test and find out.

1. Do you have breakfast before school?

▲ Sometimes.
● No, never.
■ Yes, every day.

2. Walk up and down[1] 20 stairs[2] quickly. Are you out of breath[3]?

■ No, I'm not. That's easy.
● Yes, I am!
▲ Just a little.

3. How often do you laugh every day?

■ Very often.
▲ Often.
● Sometimes.

4. A friend wants to go to the sports centre with you. What do you do?

▲ You stay at home and play video games.
■ You go with him/her. Sport is great.
● You think it's a joke[4].

5. Which meal would you choose for lunch?

● A sausage with chips[5].
▲ Chicken with potatoes and carrots.
■ A salad.

6. What do you drink?

▲ Sometimes water, sometimes sweet drinks.
● Only sweet drinks.
■ Mostly[6] water.

7. How much time do you spend[7] on your mobile phone every day?

● More than 3 hours.
■ Less[8] than an hour.
▲ 1 to 3 hours.

You have answered mostly …

■ Fantastic! You're fit and healthy. Keep up[9] the good work!

▲ Not bad! You're quite[10] fit and healthy but you can do better.

● Oh dear![11] Put your mobile phone away, eat an apple and go outside.

[1]up and down – *auf und ab*; [2]stair – *(Treppen)stufe*; [3]out of breath – *außer Atem*; [4]joke – *Witz*; [5]chips – *Pommes frites*; [6]mostly – *hauptsächlich*; *meistens;* [7]spend – *verbringen*; [8]less – *weniger*; [9]keep up sth – *etw fortführen*; [10]quite – *ziemlich*; [11]Oh dear! – *Du meine Güte!*

E Guy Fawkes and the Gunpowder Plot[1]

Read about Guy Fawkes and another British festival.

Guy Fawkes was born[2] in the English town of York in 1570. His parents and father's family were Protestants[3]. Some of his mother's family were Catholics[4]. When Guy was eight years old, his father died[5]. His mother went on to marry a Catholic man. At the age of 16, Guy decided to become[6] a Catholic, too. But life for Catholics in England was difficult at the time.

When Guy was older, he joined the military[7]. In 1591 he went to mainland Europe. He fought for Catholic Spain against the Protestant Dutch[8] Republic and later against France.

Back in England in 1605, Guy met with 12 other Catholic men. They planned to kill[9] the Protestant King James I. They also wanted to kidnap his daughter, Princess Elizabeth, and make her the Catholic Queen.

The group managed[10] to get into the cellar[11] under the Houses of Parliament[12] in London. They put 36 barrels[13] of gunpowder in it to blow up[14] King James I and everyone else in the English Parliament.

Guy's job was to look after the gunpowder. His final and most important job was to light the fuse[15] and then escape[16] across the Thames. At the same time another group would kidnap Princess Elizabeth.

But the group's plan for the Gunpowder Plot didn't work because someone sent a warning letter[17] to a man in parliament. The man showed the letter to the king who ordered[18] his men to search[19] the cellars.

[1]gunpowder plot – *Schießpulver-Verschwörung*; [2]born – *geboren*; [3]Protestant– *Protestant/in*; [4]Catholic – *Katholik/in*; [5]die – *sterben*; [6]become – *werden*; [7]military – *Militär*; [8]Dutch – *niederländisch*; [9]kill – *töten*; [10]manage – *es schaffen*; [11]cellar – *Keller*; [12]Houses of Parliament – *Sitz des britischen Parlaments*; [13]barrel – *Fass*; [14]blow up – *in die Luft sprengen*; [15]fuse – *Zündschnur*; [16]escape – *flüchten, entkommen*; [17]warning letter – *Warnbrief*; [18]order – *befehlen*; [19]search – *durchsuchen*

During the early hours of 5th November 1605 they found Guy in the cellar and arrested[20] him. They also found the gunpowder. The king's men took Guy to the Tower of London. They questioned and tortured[21] him for several days until he told them everything. Guy and the other men from his group were killed.

The king and the people in parliament were happy. They asked the people in England to celebrate the day with bonfires[22]. Since then[23] it has been a tradition to celebrate Guy Fawkes Day every year. This is also called Bonfire Night.

Today lots of people in Britain set off fireworks in their gardens on Guy Fawkes Day. There are bonfires, too. Young people especially have fun making a "guy[24]" from old clothes, newspapers[25] and a mask[26] and putting him on the bonfire.

People often sing songs that usually start with the famous words:
"Remember[27], remember, the fifth of November – Gunpowder, treason[28] and plot".

Read the text again and complete the sentences.

1. Guy Fawkes was born in XX in XX.
2. When he was 16 years old, he decided to become a XX.
3. A few years later, Guy joined the XX and fought for XX.
4. In 1605 he met with XX in XX.
5. They planned to kill XX and kidnap his XX.
6. The group put XX into the cellar under XX.
7. But the plan didn't work because someone sent a XX to a man in parliament.
8. The king's men found Guy in XX and XX him.
9. Guy and the other men from his group were XX.
10. Lots of people in Britain celebrate Guy Fawkes Day with XX and XX.

[20]arrest – *festnehmen*; [21]torture – *foltern*; [22]bonfire – *(Freuden)feuer*; [23]since then – *seitdem*; [24]guy – *Kerl, Mann*; [25]newspaper – *Zeitung*; [26]mask – *Maske*; [27]remember – *sich erinnern (an), (an etw) denken*; [28]treason – *Verrat*

F Horrid Henry's Birthday Party

Read these four parts from the story "Horrid[1] Henry's Birthday Party" by Francesca Simon.

What do you think about Henry?

I like / don't like Henry because …

I think he is nice/ friendly/funny/ not so nice/OK/… because …

Henry's birthday arrived at last[2].
"Happy birthday, Henry!" said Peter.
"Where are my presents?" said Henry.
Dad pointed. Horrid Henry attacked the pile[3].
Mum and Dad had given him[4] a first encyclopedia[5], scrabble, a fountain pen[6], a hand-knitted cardigan[7], a globe[8] and three sets of vests and pants[9].
"Oh," said Henry. He pushed the dreadful presents aside[10].

Ding Dong.
It was the first guest, Sour[11] Susan. She held a large present.
Henry snatched the package[12].
It was a pad of paper[13] and some felt tips.
"How lovely," said Mum. "What do you say, Henry?"
"I've already got that," said Henry.
"Don't be horrid, Henry," said Mum.

[1]horrid – *entsetzlich, grauenhaft*; [2]at last – *endlich*; [3]attacked the pile – *stürzte sich auf den Haufen*; [4]had given him – *hatten ihm geschenkt*; [5]encyclopedia – *Lexikon*; [6]fountain pen – *Füller*; [7]hand-knitted cardigan – *selbstgestrickte Strickjacke*; [8]globe – *Globus*; [9]three sets of vests and pants – *drei Unterwäsche-Sets*; [10]pushed the dreadful presents aside – *schob die schrecklichen Geschenke zur Seite*; [11]sour – *sauer, griesgrämig*; [12]snatched the package – *schnappte das Paket*; [13]pad of paper – *Papierblock*

Rude[14] Ralph was the last to arrive.
He handed Henry a long rectangular[15] package wrapped in newspaper[16].
It was a Super Soaker 2000 water blaster[17].
"Oh," said Mum.
"Put it away," said Dad.
"Thank you, Ralph," beamed[18] Henry. "Just[19] what I wanted."

Then Henry had a wonderful, spectacular idea.
He got up and sneaked out of the room[20]. [...]
There was a noise outside. Then Henry burst[21] into the kitchen, Super Soaker in hand.

What do you think of the story?

I think it's funny because ...

It's OK, but ...

I don't like it because ...

The ending of the story is missing. What do you think happens next?
Write down what Henry and the other people do.
You can draw a picture, too.
Here is some help:

I think Henry plays with the Super Soaker and then ...
Rude Ralph ... His other friends ...
His parents ...

[14]rude – *unverschämt, unhöflich*; [15]rectangular – *rechteckig*; [16]wrapped in newspaper – *in Zeitung eingepackt*; [17]water blaster – *große Wasserpistole*; [18]beamed – *strahlte*; [19]just – *hier: genau*; [20]sneaked out of the room – *schlich aus dem Zimmer*; [21]burst – *platzte*

G A common illness: the cold

1. How do we catch a cold?

People can catch colds at any time during the year, even in summer. Sometimes it is not clear why you caught a cold. But it is actually very simple.

When you have a cold, you sneeze and cough. You also blow your nose a lot. This produces small droplets in the air. The cold virus can spread to other people through the small droplets.

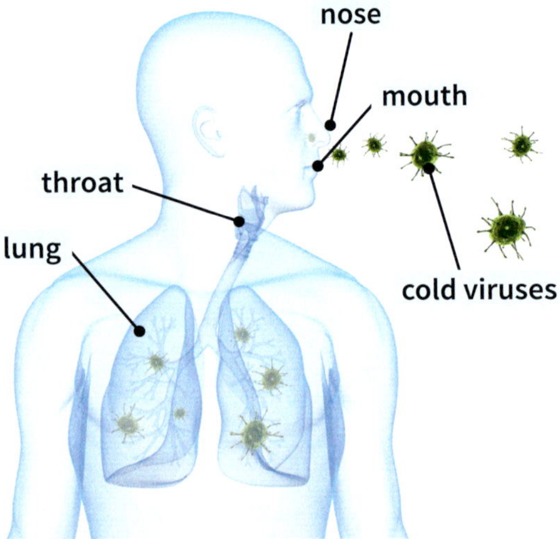

These words can help you to understand the texts:
common illness – *häufige Krankheit*
catch a cold – *sich erkälten*
during – *während*
sneeze – *niesen*
cough – *husten*
blow one's nose – *sich die Nase putzen*
droplet – *Tröpfchen*
spread – *sich ausbreiten/verbreiten*
breathe in – *einatmen*
survive – *überleben*
contagious – *ansteckend*
infect – *infizieren, anstecken*
immediately – *sofort*

If a healthy person breathes in these droplets directly, then they will maybe catch a cold, too.

Cold viruses can survive on objects for up to two days. So if you sneeze on an object such as a toy, door handle or table, then the virus will stay there for up to two days. If a healthy person touches the object and then touches his or her nose, eyes or mouth, then there is a chance that they will get ill.

However, there is not a 100% chance you will get ill. People are most contagious during the first two or three days of having a cold. Usually, a cold is no longer contagious after the first week.

People with a cold can infect other people before they know that they are ill themselves. When you catch a cold, you do not show symptoms immediately. However, you are still contagious and can infect other people.

Match the sentence parts.

1. You sneeze and cough
2. The cold virus spreads
3. Cold viruses can live on
4. During the first few days of a cold,
5. You can still infect people

A through small droplets in the air.
B objects for up to two days.
C even if you are not showing any symptoms yourself.
D when you have a cold.
E people are very contagious.

What do YOU do when you have a cold to make yourself feel better?
Talk to a partner.

I usually stay in bed and …
What about you?

These words can help you to understand the texts:

avoid – *vermeiden*
cover – *bedecken, zudecken*
especially – *vor allem*
surface – *(Ober)fläche*
utensil – *Gerät, Gegenstand*
towel – *Handtuch*
further – *weiter*
bedding – *Bettwäsche*
advice – *Rat(schlag)*

2. How to stop spreading a cold

It is not nice when you have a cold. You should try to avoid infecting others when you are ill. Here are some tips:

1. When you cough or sneeze, cover your mouth with a tissue. Throw the tissue in the bin after you use it.
2. Wash your hands often with water and soap. You should do this especially after you cough or sneeze.
3. Clean any objects or surfaces that you sneeze or cough near.
4. If you need to cough or sneeze, turn away from other people.
5. Don't share cups, utensils or towels with other people.
6. Stay at home if you are ill. Then you can't infect other people and the virus will not spread further.
7. Throw away your old toothbrush when you are feeling better.
8. Wash all your bedding when you are feeling better.

What advice would you give to a healthy person to stop them catching a cold?
You can make a flyer. Present your ideas in class.

stay away from … | don't share … | clean … | eat … | …

A Weather WB A p. 102

What's the weather like today?

It's really bad/nice/wonderful.

It's cold/warm/ hot/wet/…

It is

hot | warm | cold

sun | sunny

What a lovely day! There are no clouds in the sky.

What can we do on a sunny day?

We can go swimming.

snow | snowy

rain | rainy

What was the weather like in London?

It was a bit windy and it rained a lot.

cloud | cloudy

wind | windy

B Free time

WB B p. 102

Activities

meet (my) friends | chat with (my) friends | read books/magazines | listen to music | play the guitar / an instrument | dance | play video games / board games | watch TV / a film | go to the cinema | collect stickers / football cards / … | go shopping | be in / join a club | …

watch TV

listen to music

read a book

go shopping

dance

play the guitar

meet friends

play video games

go to the cinema

play board games

Sports

play table tennis/basketball/football/… | do judo/gymnastics | go swimming/skateboarding/dancing/… | ride a bike/horse | …

play basketball

play football

do judo

go swimming

What do you do in your free time?

I meet my friends.

What can we do this afternoon?

Let's play basketball.

What are you going to do this weekend?

I'm going to go to the cinema.

C People WB C p. 103

family members	other people
• mother – father (parents) • daughter – son • sister – brother • grandmother – grandfather (grandparents) • aunt – uncle • cousin – cousin • relative • …	• woman – man • girl – boy • child, teenager • (best) friend – classmate • girlfriend – boyfriend • neighbour • …

Describing people

positive	neutral	negative
funny | nice | friendly | interesting | good-looking | beautiful | pretty | strong | brave | polite | clever | …	small | large | tall | slim | big | long | short | blond | dark | old | young | rich | poor | careful | slow | fast | ill | quiet | …	angry | strange | ugly | terrible | horrible | silly | stupid | crazy | boring | …

My friend Eric is small and really clever. His hair is dark. I like him because he's funny and always friendly.

Feelings

positive	negative
happy | good | great | wonderful | glad | fantastic | proud | …	bad | bored | lonely | nervous | unhappy | worried | scared | angry | embarrassed | afraid | upset | tired | frustrated | sad | …

I like …
I love …
I enjoy …
I don't like …
I can't stand …
I hate …

I'm feeling great!

I'm really nervous.

D At school WB D p. 104

In the classroom

window | bookcase | door | (interactive) whiteboard | calendar | map | poster | paper | desk | book | chair | schoolbag | bin | computer | classroom rules | …

People and places at school

teacher | student | classmate | secretary | headteacher | school building | classroom | cafeteria | sports ground | (sports) hall | gym | playground | library | office | locker | …

Timetables and subjects

lesson | break | lunchtime | homework | English | German | French | ICT (information and communication technology) | maths | science | biology | geography | drama | music | history | art | RE (religious education) | PE (physical education) | …

Things in a schoolbag

I go to Haverstock School.

I have to wear a school uniform.

I'm in the photo club.
Are you in a school club?

I'm very good at biology.
It's my favourite subject.
I also enjoy PE and art.

Today I must study for the maths test.

E Travelling WB E p. 104

Countries

Germany | Spain | France | Italy | Greece | Turkey | Russia | Poland | Great Britain | the USA | Australia | Mexico | …

Where did you go on holiday?

I stayed at home.

I went to Spain.

Places and buildings

city | town | street | road | shop | market | restaurant | school | library | playground | sports centre | sports ground | skate park | swimming pool | cinema | park | zoo | lake | river | skyscraper | house | flat | room | hotel | holiday apartment | campsite | beach | the sea | church | castle | palace | museum | tower | bridge | airport | railway station | football stadium | …

Where did you stay?

At a campsite in a caravan.

With my grandparents.

Holiday activities

take photos of famous sights | go to the park/beach/… | visit a museum/castle/… | have a barbecue | eat ice cream | go shopping/swimming/… | hire a bike | go on a bike ride | relax in the sun | enjoy the weather | meet new people | write postcards | buy souvenirs | …

What did you do?

I went to the zoo.

I visited a museum.

Getting around

by bus/train/car/bike/plane/boat/ship/… |
take the bus/train/car/… |
walk/drive/fly to …

How did you get to Berlin?

We went there by train.

I went on holiday by plane. I flew to Turkey.

Giving directions

walk past

cross the street

on the/your left

on the/your right

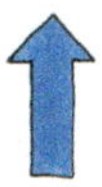
go straight on

walk on until you get to …

turn left

turn right

Excuse me, can you tell me the way to …, please?

Excuse me, how can I get to …, please?

Thanks for your help.

Walk past the church and then turn left.

Turn right at the next corner.

Go straight on. It's next to the cinema.

Talking about places/sights

On your left/right you can see … | In front of you there is/are … | Take a look at … |
You can go inside and see … | … is the oldest/tallest/… | … is famous because … |
My favourite place in town is …

F Clothes WB F p. 106

Clothes (free time)

hat | cap | sunglasses | scarf | gloves | jacket | pullover | shirt | sweatshirt | T-shirt | trousers | jeans | shorts | dress | skirt | socks | boots | shoes | trainers | …

School uniform

shirt | pullover | sweatshirt | trousers | skirt | blazer | tie | school logo | shoes | …

I wear a uniform at school. But at the weekend I wear jeans and trainers.

Where's my new dress?

In your wardrobe.

Hurry up and get dressed!

Put your shoes on, please.

G Food and drink WB G p. 107

Breakfast

butter | jam | marmalade | honey | sausage | baked beans | egg | bacon | salami | cheese | bread (roll) | sandwich | yoghurt | muesli | cornflakes | toast | …

jam

baked beans

sausage

Lunch and dinner

pizza | pasta | burger | beans | chicken | vegetables | potatoes | peppers | tomatoes | cucumber | onions | carrots | salad | rice | meat | bread (roll) | cheese | sandwich | soup | …

vegetables

meat

sandwich

Fruit and snacks

sandwich | apple | banana | orange | yoghurt | cake | chocolate | ice cream | pancake | crisps | …

a packet of crisps

Drinks

Hot drinks	Cold drinks
– tea	– milk
– coffee	– lemonade
– hot chocolate	– milkshake
– …	– orange juice
	– water
	– …

a bottle of water

a cup of tea

a glass of orange juice

lay the table | do the cooking | cook a meal | wash the vegetables | cut the tomatoes in half | make breakfast | have lunch | eat in a cafeteria | go to a restaurant | have a picnic | …

For the table

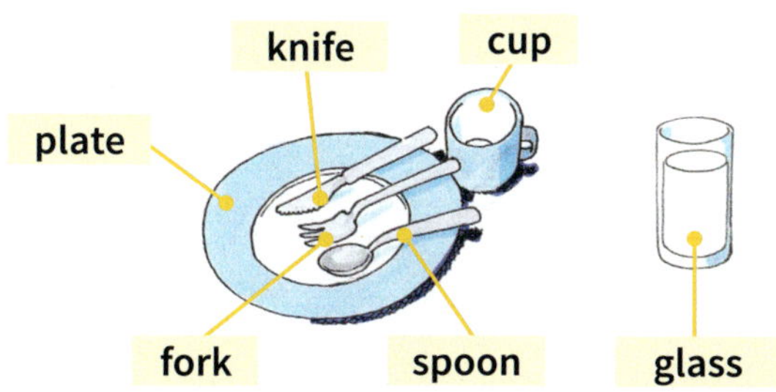

For cooking

Enjoy your meal!

salt and pepper

oil and vinegar

onions

H Animals WB H p. 108

Farm animals

cow | chicken | duck | goat |
sheep | horse | pony | pig | …

Wild animals

elephant | fish | giraffe | kangaroo | lion |
tiger | monkey | gorilla | butterfly | frog |
snake | hippo | penguin | tortoise | …

kangaroo

monkey

snake

hippo

tortoise

penguin

Pets

budgie | parrot | dog | cat |
mouse | guinea pig | hamster | …

parrot

budgie

guinea pig

Looking after a pet

feed it | clean the cage | play with it |
talk to it | walk the dog | …

My favourite animal is the kangaroo.
It has got strong legs and a long tail.
It is beautiful and can jump.

Animals can …	Animals eat/drink …	Animals are …	Animals live/sleep in a …
– swim	– fruit	– clean	– farm
– run	– vegetables	– cute	– cage
– catch	– meat	– sweet	– basket
– fly	– grass	– friendly	– terrarium
– eat/drink	– cat/dog/fish food	– funny	– zoo
– do tricks	– water	– fast	– jungle
– bite	– milk	– dangerous	– forest
– bark	– plants	– strong	– …
– jump	– leaves	– clever	
– …	– insects	– …	
	– …		

I Jobs WB I p. 109

jobs	what you do
bricklayer	build houses
bus driver	drive buses
doctor	take care of ill people
farmer	work on a farm; feed farm animals
football player	play football in a team; score goals
hairdresser	wash, cut and style people's hair
mechanic	repair cars
nurse	take care of ill people
pilot	fly planes
police officer	catch criminals; keep people and the streets safe; help people in trouble
secretary	make phone calls; prepare/write letters
shop assistant	work in a shop; help customers; sell things
teacher	teach at school
vet	take care of ill animals
video game designer	design computer games

I think I'll work as a secretary.

Perhaps I'll be a pilot. Then I'll make lots of money.

I'd like to work with my hands / with people / …

I hope I won't have a boring job.

mechanic

hairdresser

shop assistant

pilot

Jobs at home

make the/your bed | tidy the/your room | take out the rubbish | vacuum the floors | do the shopping | do the cooking | make breakfast | lay the table | empty the dishwasher | clean the kitchen/bathroom | …

I usually make my bed.

I sometimes clean the bathroom.

J Celebrations WB J p. 110

Celebrations and festivals

New Year's Eve | Halloween | Eid | Christmas | Hanukkah | Easter | Valentine's Day | birthday | carnival | Mother's Day | Diwali | St Patrick's Day | Chinese New Year | …

Presents

a scarf | a card | a phone case | flowers | sweets | a cake with candles | a book | a voucher | a poster | a game | a nice surprise | …

Activities

go to / have a party | have a big meal | cook a special meal | make a cake | visit friends | celebrate with family and friends | give/get presents | write invitations | send cards | decorate the house | go to bed early/late | set off fireworks | watch the fireworks | have a great time | make/wear a costume | wear special/traditional clothes | go to church / the mosque[1] / the synagogue / … | look for Easter eggs | dance to music | play games | sing songs | light a candle | …

presents

sweets

flowers

cake with candles

book

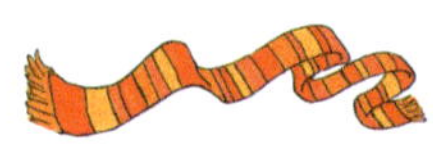
scarf

cards

My favourite festival is Easter. It is in March or April. We look for eggs on Easter Sunday. Afterwards we always have a big family breakfast.

Happy birthday!

birthday

Happy New Year!

New Year's Eve

Merry Christmas!

Christmas

[1]mosque – *Moschee*

K Things WB K p. 111

Things are …

round
oval
square
rectangular
long
short
yellow
green
…

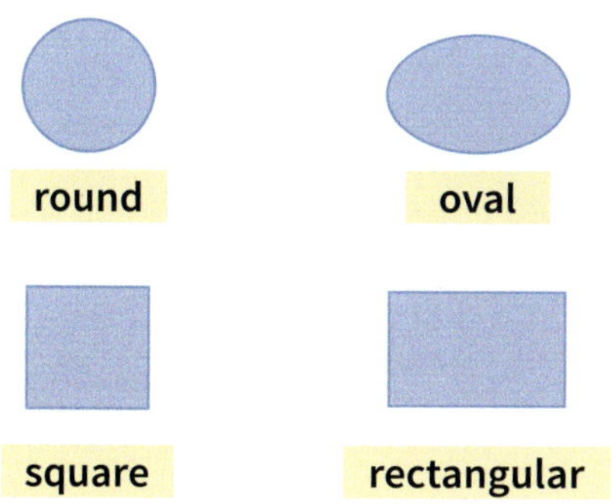

Things are made of …

plastic
paper
metal
glass
wood (*Holz*)
rubber (*Gummi*)
…

Describing things

It is usually … and made of …

You use it when you want to …

You can … it and it is …

You can … with it.

You need it to …

It is about 14 cm long and rectangular.
It is made of metal and plastic.
You can buy it in different colours.
You use it when you want to talk to your friends.

L Body and health WB L p. 112

The body

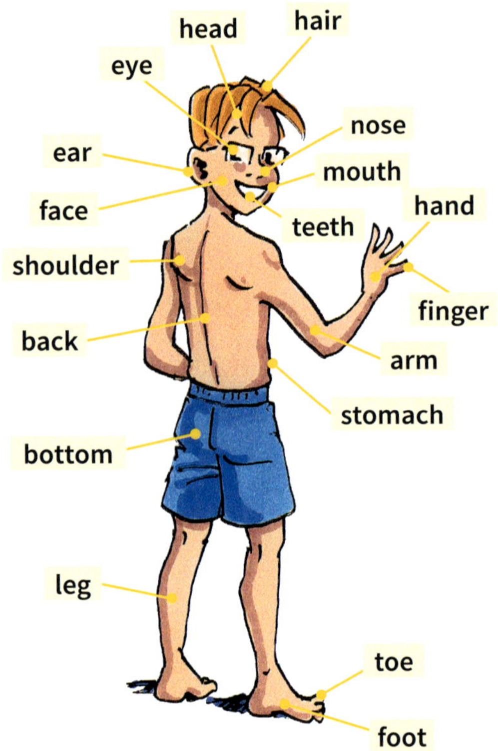

one foot | two feet
one tooth | two teeth

Health problems

be ill | have a temperature | your nose keeps running | you don't feel very well | have a bad cold | have a sore throat | have a broken arm/leg/... | have a headache | have a toothache | have a stomach ache | ...

Things to do to get better

go to the doctor | take medicine | drink lots of tea and water | gargle with salt water | stay at home / in bed | eat fruit and vegetables | ...

Get well soon!

Cheer up!

At the doctor's

What the doctor says	What the patient says
What's the problem? / What's wrong with you?	I don't feel very well.
How did that happen?	I have a headache and a sore throat.
Let me see. / Let's have a look.	I have a bad cold.
Open your mouth, please.	I've hurt my arm/leg.
Does it hurt?	I can't move my finger.
It's best to drink lots of warm tea.	It hurts a lot.
You have to stay in bed.	I fell off my bike / a chair.
Take this medicine / these tablets.	...
Get well soon!	
...	

M Time WB M p. 113

What time is it, please?

It's quarter to three.

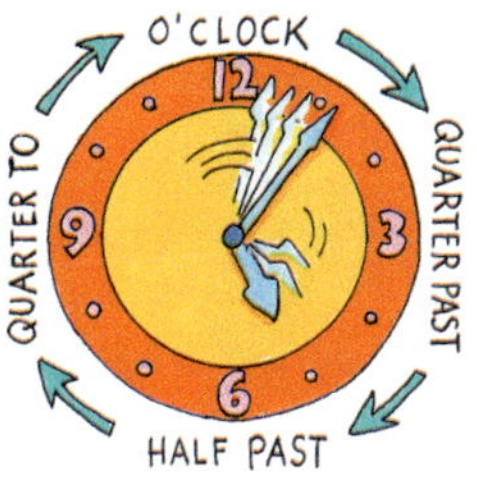

What time do you go to bed?

I go to bed at half past eight.

When do you get up on Sundays?

I get up at ten o'clock.

seven oh five
five past seven

seven fifteen
quarter past seven

seven twenty
twenty past seven

seven thirty
half past seven

seven forty-five
quarter to eight

seven fifty
ten to eight

Days of the week

Monday	Tuesday	Wednesday
Thursday	Friday	Saturday
Sunday		

Months of the year

January	February	March
April	May	June
July	August	September
October	November	December

When?

in the morning/afternoon/evening | at the weekend | on Monday | last Tuesday | (three days) ago | before | first | then | after (that) | afterwards | later | today | yesterday | last year | next week | at the moment | now | every day | …

When is your birthday?

My birthday is on the fourth of April.

Häufig verwendete Arbeitsanweisungen in diesem Buch

Act out the dialogue.	Spielt den Dialog vor.
Answer the questions.	Beantworte die Fragen.
Ask a partner / your classmates.	Frage eine/n Partner/in / deine Klassenkameraden.
Ask for and give feedback.	Bitte um Feedback und gib selbst Feedback.
Be a language detective.	Sei ein/e Sprachendetektiv/in.
Check your text/answers.	Überprüfe deinen Text / deine Antworten.
Choose an activity.	Wähle eine Aktivität aus.
Collect ideas/information.	Sammele Ideen/Informationen.
Compare your answers with a partner.	Vergleiche deine Antworten mit denen eines Partners / einer Partnerin.
Complete the sentences.	Vervollständige die Sätze.
Copy the sentences.	Schreibe die Sätze ab.
Correct the wrong words/sentences.	Verbessere die falschen Wörter/Sätze.
Describe the picture.	Beschreibe das Bild.
Discuss your ideas in class.	Diskutiert eure Ideen in der Klasse.
Draw a picture of …	Zeichne ein Bild von …
Fill in …	Trage … ein.
Find out: …	Finde heraus: …
Find the words.	Finde die Wörter.
Finish the sentences.	Vervollständige die Sätze.
Imagine you are …	Stelle dir vor, du bist …
Interview your classmates.	Befrage deine Klassenkameraden.
Label your picture / the body parts.	Beschrifte dein Bild / die Körperteile.
Listen again.	Höre noch einmal zu.
Listen and read along.	Höre zu und lies mit.
Listen to the dialogue / phone call.	Höre dir den Dialog/Telefonanruf an.
Look at the photos/pictures.	Sieh dir die Fotos/Bilder an.
Make a fact file / poster / word web.	Erstelle einen Steckbrief / ein Poster/ ein Wortnetz.
Make up more questions.	Denke dir mehr Fragen aus.
Match the sentences / words.	Ordne die Sätze/Wörter einander zu.
Mime and guess.	Stellt es pantomimisch dar und ratet.
Pick the correct word.	Suche das richtige Wort aus.
Play a guessing game.	Spielt ein Ratespiel.
Practise your presentation / the dialogue.	Übe deine Präsentation / den Dialog.
Present your results/text.	Stelle deine Ergebnisse / deinen Text vor.
Put the words in alphabetical order.	Ordne die Wörter in alphabetischer Reihenfolge.

Read about …	Lies über …
Read the blog entry / dialogue.	Lies den Blogeintrag / Dialog.
Read the text out loud.	Lies den Text laut vor.
Record your text.	Nimm deinen Text auf.
Right or wrong?	Richtig oder falsch?
Show it to a partner.	Zeige es einem Partner / einer Partnerin.
Sing along.	Singe mit.
Spell your name / the words.	Buchstabiere deinen Namen / die Wörter.
Take notes.	Mache dir Notizen.
Take turns.	Wechselt euch ab.
Talk about …	Sprich/Sprecht über …
Talk to your partner.	Sprich mit deinem Partner / deiner Partnerin.
Tell your class about …	Erzähle deiner Klasse über …
Think about …	Denke über … nach.
Think of more questions/arguments.	Überlege dir weitere Fragen/Argumente.
Walk around the classroom.	Geht im Klassenzimmer umher.
Watch the clip.	Sieh dir den (Film-)Clip an.
What are the words?	Wie heißen die Wörter?
What can you see / understand?	Was kannst du sehen/verstehen?
What do you learn about …?	Was erfährst du über …?
What else do you know?	Was weißt du noch?
Work in groups.	Arbeitet in Gruppen.
Write a dialogue/poem.	Schreibe einen Dialog / ein Gedicht.
Write about …	Schreibe über …
Write down the answers/questions.	Schreibe die Antworten/Fragen auf.

Wenn man ankommt oder geht

Good morning.	Guten Morgen.
Sorry, I'm late.	Tut mir leid, dass ich zu spät komme.
Sorry, I don't have my exercise book with me.	Tut mir leid, ich habe mein Heft nicht dabei.
Sorry, I don't have my homework with me.	Tut mir leid, ich habe meine Hausaufgaben nicht dabei.
What's our homework?	Was haben wir als Hausaufgabe auf?
See you tomorrow.	Bis morgen.

Wenn es ein Problem gibt

What's the matter with you?	Was ist mit dir los?
I'm fine. / I feel sick.	Mir geht's gut. / Mir ist schlecht.
I've got a headache.	Ich habe Kopfschmerzen.
Can I open the window, please?	Kann ich bitte das Fenster öffnen?
Can I go to the toilet, please?	Kann ich bitte zur Toilette gehen?

Wenn man Hilfe braucht

Can you help me, please?	Können Sie / Kannst du mir bitte helfen?
I've got a question.	Ich habe eine Frage.
I don't understand this.	Ich verstehe das hier nicht.
How can I do this exercise?	Wie mache ich diese Aufgabe?
What's ... in English / German?	Was heißt ... auf Englisch / Deutsch?
What does ... mean?	Was bedeutet ... ?
Can you write it on the board, please?	Können Sie / Kannst du das bitte an die Tafel schreiben?
Can you say it again, please?	Können Sie / Kannst du das bitte noch einmal sagen?
Sorry, I don't know.	Tut mir leid, das weiß ich nicht.
What page, please?	Auf welcher Seite bitte?

Wenn man zusammen arbeitet oder spielt

Whose turn is it?	Wer ist dran?
I (don't) like this story.	Diese Geschichte gefällt mir (nicht).
I think it's good/interesting/funny.	Ich finde ... gut/interessant/komisch.
I think it's terrible/boring/sad.	Ich finde ... schrecklich/langweilig/traurig.
Do you want to work with me?	Möchtest du mit mir arbeiten?

Wenn man mit dem Computer arbeitet

What's your email address?	Was ist deine E-Mail-Adresse?
You can click on this link.	Du kannst auf diesen Link klicken.
Can I print it out / download it?	Kann ich das ausdrucken/herunterladen?
I've saved it.	Ich habe es abgespeichert.
My computer has crashed.	Mein Computer ist abgestürzt.

Was die Lehrerin oder der Lehrer sagt

Open your books at page …	Öffnet eure Bücher auf Seite …
Turn to page …	Blättert zu Seite …
Look at line …	Seht euch Zeile … an.
Read the text on page …	Lies/Lest den Text auf Seite …
Work in pairs.	Arbeitet zu zweit.
Work in groups of four/five/…	Arbeitet zu viert/fünft/…
Sit in a circle.	Bildet einen Sitzkreis.
Listen to the CD/…	Hör/Hört die CD/… an.
Write about …	Schreibe/Schreibt über …
Talk about …	Sprich/Sprecht über …
Ask questions about …	Stelle/Stellt Fragen zu …
Answer the question, please.	Beantworte/Beantwortet bitte die Frage.
Match the sentences.	Ordne/Ordnet die Sätze zu.
Who wants to read the text?	Wer möchte den Text vorlesen?
Write down the answers.	Schreibe/Schreibt die Antworten auf.
Act out the dialogue.	Spiel/Spielt den Dialog vor.
Change roles.	Tauscht die Rollen.
Make your own dialogue.	Entwirf/Entwerft selbst ein Gespräch.
Come to the board, please.	Komm/Kommt bitte zur Tafel.
Collect the exercise books, please.	Sammle/Sammelt bitte die Hefte ein.
Do this exercise at home, please.	Mach/Macht diese Aufgabe bitte zu Hause.
Please be quiet.	Sei/Seid bitte ruhig.
Please sit down.	Setz dich / Setzt euch bitte.
Please speak up.	Sprich/Sprecht bitte lauter.
You can do better.	Du kannst das besser.
Try again.	Versuch es noch einmal.
Well done.	Gut gemacht.

A How to work with words

- Führe deinen Vokabelordner, dein Vokabelheft oder deine Karteikarten aus Klasse 5 weiter.
- Übe die Vokabeln immer nur fünf bis zehn Minuten, aber dafür regelmäßig.
- Wichtig ist, dass du auch übst, die Wörter richtig zu schreiben.
- Zu zweit macht Vokabellernen mehr Spaß. Fragt euch gegenseitig ab. Ihr könnt auch selbst Lückentexte, Kreuzwort- oder Buchstabenrätsel für den Partner / die Partnerin erstellen.
- Weitere Tipps zum Vokabellernen findest du in der Wortliste ab Seite 263.

So kannst du Wörter notieren und besser behalten

- Sammle Wörter, die zu einem Oberbegriff passen, in einer Tabelle. Du kannst auch ein Wortnetz (*word web*) zu einem Thema anlegen.

SCHOOL		
people	**places**	**subjects**
classmates teachers ...	library cafeteria ...	maths music ...

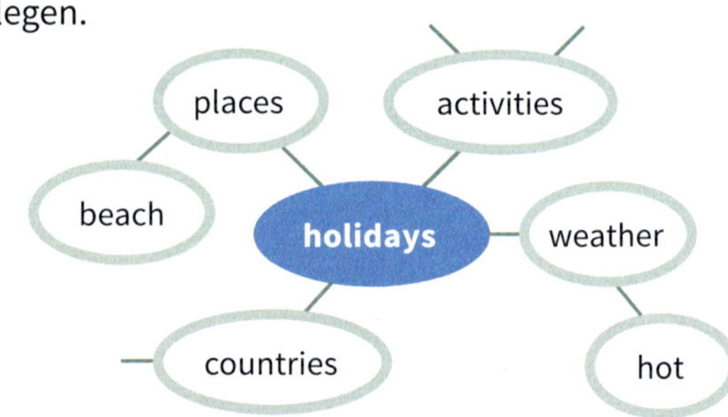

- Sammle Gegensatzpaare und schreibe sie auf.

great ↔ *terrible*   *cold* ↔ *warm*

- Viele Wörter werden ähnlich gebildet. Notiere dir diese Wörter zusammen auf einem Zettel oder einer Karteikarte.

happy → unhappy
friendly → unfriendly

rain → rainy
fun → funny

play → player
drive → driver

- Bilde Sätze mit den Wörtern, die du dir merken willst. Sie können auch lustig sein oder sich reimen.

There was no rain in sunny Spain.

- Manche englischen Wörter sind besonders schwierig zu schreiben. Du kannst dir die Schreibweise besser einprägen, wenn du die schwierigen Stellen farbig hervorhebst oder wenn du die Wörter sortierst.

beautiful, tower, night, ...

ea: weather, beach, already, ...

ou: cloudy, hour, outside, ...

So arbeitest du mit einem Wörterbuch

Inzwischen weißt du ja, dass du Wörter in deinem *dictionary* (Wörterbuch) ab Seite 289 nachschlagen kannst.
Manchmal suchst du aber vielleicht auch ein Wort, das nicht im *dictionary* steht. Dann kannst du ein zweisprachiges Wörterbuch benutzen. Das geht so:

- Schlage das Wort im Wörterbuch nach. Sieh dabei gut hin: Die Wörter sind alphabetisch geordnet. Du musst nicht nur auf den ersten Buchstaben achten, sondern auch auf den zweiten oder sogar dritten.

- Zu vielen Wörtern gibt es mehrere Informationen:

Die Lautschrift zeigt dir, wie man das Wort ausspricht.

Die Abkürzung zeigt dir an, um welche Wortart es sich handelt.
Das Wort *tie* kann sowohl ein Nomen (*n* = *noun*) als auch ein Verb (*v* = *verb*) sein.

Hier findest du die verschiedenen deutschen Bedeutungen von *tie*. Was bedeutet *tie* in den folgenden Sätzen?
My little brother can't tie his shoes.
I think it's cool to wear a tie.

tie [taɪ] *n*
1. Krawatte, Schlips
2. Band, Schnur
3. Last, Belastung
4. Unentschieden; *end in a tie*: unentschieden ausgehen

tie [taɪ] *v*
1. binden (*Krawatte usw.*)
2. verschnüren (*Paket usw.*)
3. fesseln (*Gefangenen*)
4. *be tied to*: (eng) verbunden sein mit
5. *tie for second place*: (*Sport usw.*) gemeinsam den zweiten Platz belegen

Es gibt auch Wörterbücher im Internet, sogenannte Online-Wörterbücher. Dort kannst du dir die Wörter oftmals auch anhören.

B How to listen

1. Vor dem Hören

- Wie lautet die Überschrift des Hörtextes? Welche Hinweise gibt sie dir?
- Gibt es Bilder zum Text? Was ist zu sehen?
- Überlege: Worum könnte es wohl gehen? Was weißt du schon über das Thema?

2. Beim Hören

- Höre dir den Hörtext einmal ganz an. Versuche herauszufinden:

Who?	Where?	When?	What?
Wer spricht? Um wen geht es?	Wo findet das Gespräch / die Geschichte statt?	Wann findet das Gespräch / die Geschichte statt?	Was wird besprochen? Was passiert?

- Achte auch auf Geräusche und darauf, wie die Personen sprechen.
- Lies dir die Höraufgabe im Buch genau durch. Was sollst du herausfinden? Höre dir das Gespräch oder die Geschichte ein weiteres Mal an.

3. Zu guter Letzt

- Vergleicht eure Ergebnisse. Was habt ihr herausgefunden?

C How to watch a video clip

WEB 12

1. Bevor du dir einen Videoclip anschaust

- Wie lautet der Titel des Videoclips? Welche Hinweise gibt er dir?
- Gibt es Bilder zu dem Videoclip? Was ist zu sehen?
- Worum könnte es wohl gehen? Stelle Vermutungen an.

2. Sieh genau hin

- Schau dir den Videoclip an und konzentriere dich zunächst auf das, was du siehst.

Who?	Where?	When?	What?
Wer ist zu sehen? Um wen geht es?	Wo findet das Geschehen statt?	Wann findet das Geschehen statt?	Um was geht es? Was passiert?

- Beim zweiten Anschauen konzentrierst du dich stärker auf das, was du hörst. Kannst du jetzt schon mehr verstehen? Schau dir auch an, wie die Personen im Film aussehen und wie sie sich verhalten. Achte auf ihren Gesichtsausdruck und ihre Gesten. Wie fühlen sie sich?
- Lies dir die Aufgabe zu dem Videoclip im Buch genau durch. Was sollst du herausfinden? Sieh dir den Videoclip nun ein weiteres Mal an.

3. Zu guter Letzt

- Tauscht euch untereinander aus. Was habt ihr herausgefunden?

D How to read

Es gibt viele Tricks, die dir helfen, einen englischen Text leichter zu verstehen. Probiere doch einmal die folgenden Tipps beim Lesen aus:

1. Was verrät das Bild? Worum könnte es in der Geschichte gehen?

2. Was erfährst du aus der Überschrift?

3. Überfliege den Text erst einmal. Versuche herauszufinden, worum es geht. Was passiert? Wer ist beteiligt? Dafür brauchst du nicht jedes Wort zu verstehen.

4. Lies den Text noch einmal gründlich. Mit den *wh*-Fragen kannst du die wichtigsten Informationen herausbekommen: Who? Where? When? What? Mach dir Notizen. Auf Kopien oder in deinen eigenen Büchern kannst du auch wichtige Textstellen markieren.

The orienteering trip

Last summer a group of twenty boys went camping and orienteering in Scotland for two days. They had small tents and sleeping bags in their rucksacks. Every pair had a map, a compass, food and drink and warm pullovers and trousers.

Jim and Kevin were partners. The two boys walked and walked and talked and laughed about lots of things. But they didn't look at their maps and they didn't look at their watches.
It got dark and foggy. They looked for the others but couldn't find them, so they put up their tent, ate some chocolate and told ghost stories.
Suddenly there were strange noises. And then a big dark thing came to their tent. It opened the tent and said, "Ah, it's you two! The others are all here, too. But they're still putting up their tents, so you're the winners. Congratulations!"
It was the guide, John. Jim and Kevin were at the campsite!

So kannst du die Bedeutung eines Wortes ohne Wörterbuch herausfinden:

- Oft kennst du ein deutsches Wort, das ganz ähnlich aussieht, z.B. *orienteering* oder *congratulations*.
- Überlege, ob du ein englisches Wort aus der gleichen Wortfamilie, also einen „Verwandten", kennst, z. B. *sleep – sleeping bag*.
- Häufig kannst du die Bedeutung eines unbekannten Wortes aus dem Satzzusammenhang erschließen. Dabei helfen dir die Wörter, die vor oder nach dem unbekannten Wort stehen. Was könnten die Wörter *tent* und *guide* in der Geschichte oben bedeuten?

E How to talk about pictures

Um ein Bild oder Foto zu beschreiben, gehst du am besten so vor:

1. Fange allgemein an

Sage erst einmal, was du auf dem Bild oder Foto allgemein siehst.
In the picture I can see a street with lots of people.

2. Wähle eine bestimmte Reihenfolge

Sage nun, wen oder was du siehst und wo sich die Personen, Tiere und Gegenstände befinden. Dabei macht es Sinn, eine bestimmte Reihenfolge zu wählen: von links nach rechts oder von oben nach unten.
In the middle / On the left / On the right I can see …
At the top there is …
At the bottom there are …

3. Werde nun genauer

Benutze Präpositionen wie *in, on, in front of, behind, next to, between, over* oder *under*, um genauer zu beschreiben, wo sich eine Person, ein Tier oder ein Gegenstand befindet.
There is a girl with a dog in front of the black car.
There are two motorbikes in the street.
The bird is next to the woman with the green dress and the cat.

4. Beschreibe, was passiert

Beschreibe, was die abgebildeten Personen oder Tiere tun. Benutze dazu das *present progressive*.
The boy with the pizza in the middle is crossing the street.
The man with the pink T-shirt at the top is taking a picture.
The woman on the right is waving at the girl on the motorbike.

F How to talk

Im Englischunterricht arbeitest du oft mit einem Partner oder in einer Gruppe zusammen. Hier findest du dazu einige nützliche Redewendungen und Tipps:

Wenn du mit jemandem zusammenarbeitest

- *Can I be …?*
- *Whose turn is it? – It's your turn.*
- *Sorry, have you finished? Can I say something now?*
- *Can you explain that, please?*
- *Can you say it again, please?*

Wenn du einen Vorschlag machen möchtest

- *Let's do it like this.*
- *You/We could write something different here.*
- *Why don't you/we change this?*

Wenn du Rückmeldung/Feedback geben möchtest

- Nenne zuerst immer die Dinge, die dir gut gefallen haben:
  I really liked your … because …
  Your story/dialogue/… is fantastic/funny/really interesting/…
  Your presentation was easy to understand.
  You spoke loudly and clearly.
  Your poster looks attractive.
  The pictures go well with the texts.
- Dann kannst du Verbesserungsvorschläge machen. Bleibe dabei stets höflich:
  Use more adjectives/linking words/… to make your text more interesting.
  Why don't you use …? It would make the story/dialogue/… more exciting/…
  I would use a different word here. What about …?
  Maybe next time you could use more pictures on your poster. I would also add …
  I couldn't hear everything. Please try to speak more loudly and clearly next time.
- Wenn dir ein Wort mal nicht einfällt, kannst du es umschreiben. Du kannst aber auch deine Hände zu Hilfe nehmen.

Sprich Englisch, sooft du kannst!
- Höre dir die *Camden Market*-CD an und lies die Texte laut mit. Versuche, die Aussprache der Sprecher nachzuahmen. Du kannst auch englische Lieder mitsingen.
- Lies einen Text aus dem Buch laut vor oder sprich Englisch und nimm dich auf. Dann kannst du dich selbst anhören und überprüfen, wie dein Englisch klingt.
- Sprich Englisch mit jemandem, der ebenfalls Englisch sprechen kann.

G How to give a talk

Wenn du Arbeitsergebnisse präsentieren möchtest oder einen Vortrag halten willst, können dir folgende Tipps dabei helfen:

1. Bevor du etwas vorträgst

- Überlege: Was möchtest du zu deinem Thema sagen? Wie viel Zeit hast du für deinen Vortrag?
- Sammle deine Gedanken und schreibe sie in Stichpunkten auf, z. B. in einem *word web* oder auf Karteikarten.
- Entscheide, in welcher Reihenfolge du die Dinge sagen und wie du anfangen möchtest.
- Fertige ein Poster oder eine Folie an, um deinen Vortrag anschaulich zu machen. Du kannst aber auch eine Computer-Präsentation gestalten.
- Übe deinen Vortrag vor dem Spiegel, vor Freunden oder deiner Familie – oder nimm deinen Vortrag zur Probe auf, z. B. mit deinem Handy. Hast du flüssig gesprochen? Kannst du alle Wörter richtig aussprechen?

So sieht ein gelungenes Vortrags-Poster aus:
- ansprechende Überschrift
- interessante Informationen
- verständliche Sätze, aber: nicht zu viel Text
- große Bilder und Schrift: → Jeder im Raum muss sie sehen und lesen können.
- saubere Schrift
- Bilder mit Bildunterschriften

2. Bei deinem Vortrag

- Sprich langsam und deutlich.
- Sieh deine Zuhörer an, wenn du sprichst.
- Versuche, frei zu sprechen. Du kannst die wichtigsten Punkte von deinen Notizen oder deinem Poster / deiner Folie ablesen.
- Zeige deinen Zuhörern auf deinem Poster oder deiner Folie, worüber du gerade sprichst.

3. Nützliche Redewendungen

Zu Beginn deines Vortrags:	*Hello, everyone.*
	My talk is about … / I'd like to talk about …
Im Hauptteil:	*On my poster you can see …*
	Look at this picture. It shows …
	Another thing I want to tell you about is …
Wenn du mal den Faden verlierst:	*Just a moment, please. / Wait a second.*
Zum Schluss:	*Thank you for listening. Have you got any questions?*

H How to search the Internet WEB 6

Hier erfährst du, wie du im Internet zu einem Thema recherchieren kannst.

1. Benutze eine Suchmaschine

- Gute Suchbegriffe erleichtern dir die Suche im Internet. Versuche, möglichst genau zu formulieren, wonach du suchst – und zwar auf Englisch.
- Gib die Suchbegriffe in eine Suchmaschine ein.
- Es kann sein, dass die Suchmaschine eine riesige Anzahl Treffer anzeigt. Oft genügt es aber, sich die ersten 10 bis 20 Suchergebnisse anzuschauen und Werbeangebote von echten Seiten zu unterscheiden.

2. Suche auf englischsprachigen Seiten

- Bei den Einstellungen der meisten Suchmaschinen kannst du Englisch als Sprache wählen. Suche deshalb am besten gleich auf englischsprachigen Seiten.
- Die Übertragung von deutschen Texten mit elektronischen Übersetzungshilfen ins Englische führt oft zu fehlerhaften und unverständlichen Ergebnissen.

3. Halte nützliche Informationen fest

- Überfliege erst einmal die Seiten, die dir interessant erscheinen. Dafür brauchst du nicht jedes Wort zu verstehen.
- Wenn du interessante Webseiten gefunden hast, kannst du dir Notizen zu den Inhalten machen.
- Denke daran, dir auch das Datum der Recherche aufzuschreiben und die Quelle zu sichern. So weißt du später noch, wo du die Informationen gefunden hast.
- Wenn du Textausschnitte für deinen eigenen Text unverändert übernimmst, musst du diese als Zitat kenntlich machen und die Quelle (die Internetadresse) angeben.

4. Sei kritisch

- Informationen, die du im Internet findest, müssen nicht immer richtig sein. Sei deshalb kritisch und überprüfe die Informationen noch einmal auf anderen Seiten oder in einem Lexikon.

Nutze Internetlexika!

- Das Internetlexikon Wikipedia gibt es in vielen Sprachen. Die meisten Einträge hat die englische Version.
- Es gibt auch eine einfachere Fassung in *simple English*. Sie ist für viele Recherchen ein guter Ausgangspunkt.

I How to help out

Du kannst anderen Menschen helfen, die kaum Deutsch oder Englisch verstehen. Hier erfährst du, wie das funktioniert:

1. Gib den Sinn wieder

Stell dir vor, du bist mit einer englischen Austauschschülerin und einem deutschen Freund unterwegs. Sie spricht kaum Deutsch, er kaum Englisch. Du musst jetzt nicht Wort für Wort übersetzen. Wichtiger ist es, den Sinn wiederzugeben. Das kannst du auch in deinen eigenen Worten machen.

2. Bilde kurze Sätze

Bilde einfache, kurze Sätze, wenn du den Sinn wiedergibst.

3. Umschreibe Wörter

Wenn dir ein wichtiges Wort nicht einfällt, kannst du es umschreiben.

- Versuche es mit einem Wort, das dieselbe oder eine ähnliche Bedeutung hat: „winzig" = *very small*
- Versuche es mit dem Gegenteil: „kompliziert" = *not easy*
- Umschreibe es mit einem Satz: „Mütze" = *You wear it on your head.*
- Umschreibe es mithilfe von Ober- oder Unterbegriffen: „Wir brauchen Salat und Pilze." = *We need some vegetables.* / „Besteck" = *forks, knives and spoons*

J How to write

Wenn du Texte schreibst, gehst du am besten Schritt für Schritt vor:

1. Plane deinen Text

- Überlege: Was für einen Text willst du schreiben – einen Text über dich, eine E-Mail, ein Gedicht, eine Geschichte?
- Sammle Ideen und Wörter zum Thema deines Textes in einem *word web* oder einer Liste.
- Überlege dir eine sinnvolle Reihenfolge. Was schreibst du zuerst, was folgt darauf, was kann am Ende stehen?

2. Schreibe den Text

- Schreibe erst einmal in kurzen, einfachen Sätzen einen ersten Entwurf.
- Sieh dir auch Texte zu deinem Thema im Buch an. Du kannst sie als Muster benutzen. Übernimm nützliche Satzanfänge und Ausdrücke und ersetze die Wörter, die nicht zu dir oder zum Thema passen.
- Achte darauf, dass dein Text eine Einleitung, einen Mittelteil und einen Schluss hat.
- Fange deine Sätze unterschiedlich an:
  Megan loves animals. Megan has a dog. → Megan loves animals. She has a dog.
- Verbinde deine Ideen und Sätze mit *linking words* wie *and*, *but*, *or*, *so*, *because*:
  Megan often goes to Edinburgh. Her dad lives there. → Megan often goes to Edinburgh because her dad lives there.
- Benutze *time words*, um zu sagen, wann etwas geschieht, z. B. *in the morning*, *then*, *later*, *yesterday*:
  I went shopping. I met some friends. → Yesterday I went shopping. Later I met some friends.
- Adjektive und Adverbien machen deinen Text interessanter.
  Suddenly a man opened the door and looked at us. → Suddenly a tall man opened the door and looked at us angrily.
- Überlege dir eine passende Überschrift.

3. Überarbeite deinen Text

✓ Hast du alles richtig geschrieben? Schlage schwierige Wörter im *English-German dictionary* ab Seite 316 nach.

✓ Bist du bei der Grammatik unsicher? Schau im *Grammar*-Teil ab Seite 240 nach.

✓ Tauscht eure Texte untereinander aus. Markiert mit einem Bleistift im fremden Text, was euch gefällt, was unverständlich ist, was noch ergänzt und was verbessert werden sollte.
Diese Symbole kannst du dafür verwenden:

++	*(This is good!)*
??	*(I don't understand this.)*
~~	*(I don't think this English is correct.)*

✓ Wenn du deinen Text fertig hast, schreibe ihn ins Reine.
Das kannst du auch mithilfe eines Textverarbeitungsprogramms am Computer machen.

4. Präsentiere deinen Text

- Du kannst deinen Text vorlesen, aufnehmen, aushängen oder in einem *class book* veröffentlichen. Sammle deine besten Texte in deinem Portfolio-Ordner.

K How to write an email WEB 4

Trage in das obere Feld die E-Mail-Adresse des Empfängers ein. In der unteren Zeile (*Subject*) nennst du kurz und knapp das Thema deiner E-Mail.

Beginne deine E-Mail an einen Freund oder eine Freundin mit *Dear …*, *Hi …*, oder *Hello …*,

Fange die erste Zeile mit einem Großbuchstaben an.

Worüber möchtest du im Mittelteil schreiben? Vielleicht darüber, was du am Wochenende erlebt hast? Dann benutze die Vergangenheit (*simple past*): *I went, I played, …* Denke auch an *linking words* und *time words* (siehe *How to write* auf Seite 235).

Am Ende deiner E-Mail kannst du deinem Freund oder deiner Freundin Fragen stellen. Du kannst ihn oder sie auch bitten, dir zurückzuschreiben.

To xxxxxxxxxxxxxxx

Subject Last weekend

Dear Helen,

How are you?

I'm fine. I had a great weekend. On Friday after school my friend Jasmine came to my house. We made pizza and watched a funny film on TV.

On Saturday the weather was warm and sunny. So my parents made some sandwiches and we all went swimming. The water was still cold but I liked it.

On Sunday I stayed in bed until 12:30 p.m.
I listened to my favourite music and finished a book. In the afternoon I met some friends in the park. We played basketball and had a lot of fun.

What did you do last weekend? What was the weather like?

Please write back soon.

All the best,

Ella

So kannst du deine E-Mail beenden:
Best wishes, Love, Lots of love, Yours, All the best, Bye for now, …

- Einen **Brief** schreibst du ganz ähnlich wie eine E-Mail.
- Denke daran, in die rechte obere Ecke der ersten Seite deine Adresse (ohne deinen Namen) zu schreiben.
- Das Datum folgt unter der Adresse auf der rechten Seite.

Waldschmidtstraße 39
60316 Frankfurt
Germany

22nd May 20..

Dear Helen,
How are you?
...

Sieh dir deine E-Mail oder deinen Brief noch einmal genau an:

- ✓ Hast du alles richtig geschrieben?
- ✓ Hast du die richtige Zeitform verwendet?
- ✓ Hast du *linking words* und *time words* verwendet?
- ✓ Hast du Adjektive und Adverbien benutzt, um deinen Text interessanter zu machen?
- ✓ Ist dein Ton höflich und freundlich?

L How to write a postcard

Beginne deine Postkarte mit *Dear …, Hi …, Hello …, …*

Schreibe das Datum auf die Postkarte.

Fange die erste Zeile mit einem Großbuchstaben an. Sage, wo du bist.

Schreibe im Mittelteil über Dinge, die du gemacht und gesehen hast. Was gefällt dir? Was ist besonders?

Beende deine Postkarte mit *Yours, Love, Best wishes, See you soon, …*

Schreibe den Namen und die Adresse auf die rechte Seite.

9th July 20..

Hi James,
I'm in Italy now. It's really nice here.
The weather is hot and sunny and we can go swimming in the sea.
The food is delicious, too. I love Italian ice cream!
Yesterday we visited Rome. It's a cool city with lots of sights and beautiful buildings.
But the beach is the best. Today I played beach volleyball with some nice girls from Croatia. It was great fun!
See you soon,
Oliver

James Green
10 Canons Way
Bristol
BS1 5LF
England

Sieh dir deine Postkarte noch einmal genau an. Überprüfe anhand der Fragen oben auf der Seite, ob du alles Wichtige bedacht hast.

M How to work with others

Think – pair – share

Um etwas zu einem Thema herauszufinden, kannst du in drei Schritten vorgehen:

1. *Think:* Sammle deine Gedanken und Ideen und mache dir Notizen.
2. *Pair:* Tausche dich mit einem Partner / einer Partnerin aus. Ergänze neue Ideen in deiner Liste.
3. *Share:* Teilt dann eure Gedanken und Ideen mit einem anderen Paar oder der gesamten Klasse.

Double circle

Dies ist eine Arbeitsform, bei der du die Ideen und Gedanken von vielen verschiedenen Leuten in deiner Klasse erfährst.

1. Bildet in der Klasse zwei Kreise: einen Innenkreis und einen Außenkreis.
2. Diejenigen von euch, die sich gegenüberstehen, unterhalten sich über ein vorher bestimmtes Thema.
3. Wenn dein Lehrer / deine Lehrerin ein Zeichen gibt, dreht ihr euch in den beiden Kreisen in entgegengesetzte Richtungen weiter.
   Nun sprecht ihr mit jemand anderem über das Thema.

Milling around

Mit der Methode *milling around* (auf Deutsch: umherlaufen) kannst du dich mit deinen Klassenkameraden zu einem Thema austauschen.

1. Gehe mit deiner Aufgabe und einem Stift durch die Klasse, ohne dass du dabei sprichst.
2. Wenn dein Lehrer / deine Lehrerin ein Zeichen gibt, sprich mit der Person, vor der du gerade stehst. Tauscht euch über die Aufgabe aus und notiert die Ergebnisse.
3. Beim nächsten Zeichen gehst du weiter.

Buzz groups

Bei dieser Arbeitsform sprecht ihr alle mit leiser Stimme, damit sich die verschiedenen Gruppen nicht gegenseitig stören. *Buzz* heißt summen oder brummen und beschreibt den Geräuschpegel, der dabei im Raum entsteht.

1. Bildet *buzz groups* mit drei bis fünf Gruppenmitgliedern. Sprecht über das vorgegebene Thema. Ein Gruppenmitglied macht Notizen.
2. Wählt einen Sprecher / eine Sprecherin, der/die die Ergebnisse eurer *buzz group* in der Klasse vorstellt.

Dramatic reading

Um einen Text mit verschiedenen Rollen lebendig vorzutragen, bietet sich *dramatic reading* an:

1. Lies den Text zu deiner Rolle mit leiser Stimme mehrmals durch.
2. Schaue dir jeden Satz einzeln an und präge ihn dir ein. Sieh dann hoch und sprich den Satz nach. Schaue deine Gruppenmitglieder dabei an. Arbeite den ganzen Text auf diese Weise durch.
3. Überlege, wie sich die Person gerade fühlt, deren Rolle du liest. Ist sie verärgert, fröhlich, …? Versuche, die Sätze entsprechend zu lesen und zu betonen.

Placemat

Auf einer *placemat* (auf Deutsch: Tischvorlage, Platzdeckchen) sammelst du mit deinen Gruppenmitgliedern zu einem Thema gleichzeitig Ideen.

1. Jede/r von euch macht auf einem Teil eines großen Bogens Papier Notizen.
2. Anschließend dreht ihr die *placemat* so lange, bis jede/r alle Beiträge gelesen hat.
3. Einigt euch dann in der Gruppe auf die wichtigsten Punkte und notiert sie in der Mitte des Blattes.
4. Schließlich stellt ein Gruppenmitglied das Ergebnis in der Klasse vor.

Dies ist der Grammatikteil von *Camden Market*, in dem die englische Sprache genauer unter die Lupe genommen wird. Wenn vorne im Buch in der Fußzeile zum Beispiel Grammar 4 | p. 245 steht, kannst du hier unter Nummer 4 die passenden grammatischen Regeln nachschlagen.
Das „R“ hinter manchen Nummern steht für *revision* (Wiederholung). So gekennzeichnete Regeln kennst du bereits aus dem letzten Jahr.

Auf dieser Seite findest du die grammatischen Begriffe auf Englisch und auf Deutsch.

Grammatische Fachbegriffe (Grammatical terms)

Englisch		Deutsch	Beispiel
adjective	9, 11	Adjektiv (Eigenschaftswort)	loud, happy, slow, …
adverb of manner	9	Adverb der Art und Weise	loudly, happily, slowly
comparison		Vergleich	
comparative	11	Komparativ (1. Steigerungsform)	Anne is taller than Tom. The skirt is more expensive than the shirt.
superlative	11	Superlativ (2. Steigerungsform)	Stan is the oldest boy. Sue is the most intelligent girl.
conditional clause	17	Bedingungssatz	If it rains, I will stay at home.
direct speech	15	Direkte Rede	Megan: “I play rugby.”
going to-future	10	Futur (Zukunft) mit *going to*	She's going to buy a book.
will-future	8	Futur (Zukunft) mit *will*	I'm sure he will be a pop star.
infinitive	4, 6	Infinitiv (Grundform des Verbs)	walk, read, go, …
modal verb	13	Modalverb	can, must, may, …
negation	2R, 6	Verneinung	I don't like tea.
noun	12, 16	Nomen (Hauptwort, Substantiv)	song, ball, car, dog, …
past participle	14	Partizip Perfekt	eaten, gone, started, …
past progressive	18	Verlaufsform der Vergangenheit	Emma was playing a game.
present perfect	14	Perfekt	He has cleaned the kitchen.
present progressive	3R	Verlaufsform der Gegenwart	It's raining.
prop word	16	Stützwort	one, ones
question	1R	Frage	Where are you from?
reported speech	15	Indirekte Rede	Megan says (that) she plays rugby.
simple past	4–7	einfache Vergangenheit	He played tennis yesterday.
simple present	2R	einfache Gegenwart	He often plays tennis.
statement	2R, 4	Aussage(satz)	I like tea.
verb		Verb (Tätigkeitswort)	
regular/irregular	1R, 4	regelmäßig/unregelmäßig	play, watch, … / go, feel, …

Zu einigen Grammatikthemen gibt es wieder kurze Erklärvideos. Wenn du den Webcode **WES-149119-002** auf **https://www.westermann.de/webcode** eingibst und auf den Link bei Download 13 klickst, erhältst du z. B. das passende Video zum Verb *be* (WEB 13).

1R Das Verb *be* (The verb *be*) 15, WEB 13

Die verschiedenen Formen von ***be*** (***am***, ***are***, ***is***) gibt es als Kurzformen und als Langformen.
Die **Kurzformen** verwendet man meistens beim Sprechen und in persönlichen Briefen, E-Mails, Kurznachrichten oder Chats.
Die **Langformen** verwendet man eher beim offiziellen Schreiben.

	Langform	Kurzform		
Singular	I **am**	I**'m**		*Ich bin …*
	You **are**	You**'re**		*Du bist / Sie sind …*
	He **is**	He**'s**		*Er ist …*
	She **is**	She**'s**	from Camden.	*Sie ist …*
	It **is**	It**'s**		*Es ist …*
Plural	We **are**	We**'re**		*Wir sind …*
	You **are**	You**'re**		*Ihr seid / Sie sind …*
	They **are**	They**'re**		*Sie sind …*

Die Formen von *be* kannst du verneinen, indem du ***not*** einfügst:

	Langform	Kurzform		
Singular	I **am not**	I**'m not**		*Ich bin nicht …*
	You **are not**	You **aren't**		*Du bist nicht / Sie sind nicht …*
	He/She/It **is not**	He/She/It **isn't**	ten.	*Er/Sie/Es ist nicht …*
Plural	We **are not**	We **aren't**		*Wir sind nicht …*
	You **are not**	You **aren't**		*Ihr seid nicht / Sie sind nicht …*
	They **are not**	They **aren't**		*Sie sind nicht …*

Entscheidungsfragen und Kurzantworten mit *be* bildest du so:

	Entscheidungsfragen		Kurzantworten +	–
Singular	**Am I**		**Yes, you are.**	**No, you aren't.**
	Are you		**Yes, I am.**	**No, I'm not.**
	Is he/she/it	late?	**Yes, he/she/it is.**	**No, he/she/it isn't.**
Plural	**Are we**		**Yes, you are.**	**No, you aren't.**
	Are you		**Yes, we are.**	**No, we aren't.**
	Are they		**Yes, they are.**	**No, they aren't.**

Bei Fragen mit Fragewörtern steht das Fragewort immer am Satzanfang:

Fragen mit Fragewörtern
What is your favourite music?
Where are my pens?
Who is Jason?

Who?	Wer?
What?	Was?
When?	Wann?
Where?	Wo?
Why?	Warum?
How?	Wie?

2R Die einfache Gegenwart (The simple present)

16, WEB 14

Das *simple present* verwendest du, um über Gewohnheiten zu sprechen oder über Dinge, die allgemein gültig sind.

a) *Simple present*: Aussagen

	simple present: Aussagen		
Singular	I often	play	basketball.
	You	play	tennis on Mondays.
	He never	plays	handball.
	She	plays	the guitar.
	It always	plays	with other dogs.
Plural	We	play	football every day.
	You sometimes	play	hockey.
	They	play	games at the weekend.

Signalwörter
every day
always, often, sometimes, never, usually
on Mondays/...
in the morning/...
...

Bei ***he***, ***she*** und ***it*** hängst du an das Verb ein ***-s*** an.

Wenn das Verb auf *-ss*, *-sh*, *-ch* oder *-x* endet, hängst du bei *he*, *she*, *it* ein ***-es*** an:

He wash**es** his face in the morning. — *Er wäscht sich morgens das Gesicht.*
Lily sometimes watch**es** TV. — *Lily sieht manchmal fern.*

Auch an die Verben *do* und *go* hängst du bei *he, she, it* ein ***-es*** an.
Achte auf die unterschiedliche Aussprache:

Sam do**es** [dʌz] his homework in the evening. — *Sam macht abends seine Hausaufgaben.*
Jasmine go**es** [gəʊz] to school in London. — *Jasmine geht in London zur Schule.*

Bei Verben, die auf *-y* enden (z. B. *tidy* und *empty*), gilt:
Steht ein Konsonant (Mitlaut) vor dem *-y*, so wird das *-y* zu ***-ies***:

Kenan often tid**ies** his room. — *Kenan räumt oft sein Zimmer auf.*
She never empt**ies** the dishwasher. — *Sie räumt nie den Geschirrspüler aus.*

b) *Simple present*: Verneinung

Sätze im *simple present* kannst du mit *don't (= do not)* verneinen.
Bei *he*, *she*, *it* (also in der 3. Person Singular) verwendest du *doesn't (= does not).*

	***simple present:* Verneinung**			
Singular	I	**don't**		*Ich spiele nicht …*
	You	**don't**		*Du spielst nicht … / Sie spielen nicht …*
	He/She/It	**doesn't**	play football.	*Er/Sie/Es spielt nicht …*
Plural	We	**don't**		*Wir spielen nicht …*
	You	**don't**		*Ihr spielt nicht … / Sie spielen nicht …*
	They	**don't**		*Sie spielen nicht …*

Ben **doesn't** like eating cornflakes every day.

Bei der Verneinung von Sätzen mit *be*, *can* oder *have got* brauchst du *don't* oder *doesn't* nicht:
She isn't from Camden.
I haven't got a computer.
He can't play tennis.

c) *Simple present*: Entscheidungsfragen und Kurzantworten

Fragen, auf die man mit „Ja" oder „Nein" antworten kann, bildest du im *simple present* so:

	***simple present:* Entscheidungsfragen**	**Kurzantworten** +	–
Singular	**Do** I **eat** sweets?	**Yes, you do.**	**No, you don't.**
	Do you **play** hockey?	**Yes, I do.**	**No, I don't.**
	Does he/she/it **like** cats?	**Yes, he/she/it does.**	**No, he/she/it doesn't.**
Plural	**Do** we **talk** a lot?	**Yes, you do.**	**No, you don't.**
	Do you **live** in London?	**Yes, we do.**	**No, we don't.**
	Do they **go** to Haverstock School?	**Yes, they do.**	**No, they don't.**

d) *Simple present*: Fragen mit Fragewörtern

Bei Fragen mit Fragewörtern steht das Fragewort immer am Satzanfang:

***simple present:* Fragen mit Fragewörtern**

Where do you **play** football?
What do you **do** on Fridays?
Why does Joe **like** London?
How do you **write** 'juice'?

***Who**, who, who* – **wer** bist du?
***Where**, where, where* – **wo** kommst du her?

3R Die Verlaufsform der Gegenwart (The present progressive)

17, WEB 15

a) *Present progressive*: Aussagen und Verneinung

Signalwörter
now, right now, at the moment, ...

Mit dem *present progressive* kannst du ausdrücken, was jemand gerade tut oder was gerade passiert:

	***present progressive:* Aussagen**	
Singular	I **am watching** TV now.	*Ich sehe jetzt fern.*
	You **are writing** an email.	*Du schreibst (gerade) eine E-Mail.*
	He **is sitting** on the sofa.	*Er sitzt (gerade) auf dem Sofa.*
	She **is drinking** orange juice.	*Sie trinkt (gerade) Orangensaft.*
	Oh no, it **is raining** again!	*Oh nein, es regnet schon wieder!*
Plural	We **are eating** pizza at the moment.	*Wir essen im Moment Pizza.*
	You **are playing** football.	*Ihr spielt (gerade) Fußball.*
	Listen, they **are singing** a song.	*Hör mal, sie singen (gerade) ein Lied.*

So bildest du das ***present progressive***:
am, **are**, **is** + **Verb** + **-ing**
*She **is drinking** orange juice.*

Endet das Verb auf **-*e***, dann fällt das **-*e*** in der Verlaufsform weg:
write → writing *dance → dancing*

Endet das Verb auf einen kurzen betonten Vokal (Selbstlaut) + Konsonant (Mitlaut), wird der Konsonant verdoppelt:
sit → sitting *run → running*

Für die **Verneinung** fügst du ***not*** hinter *am, are, is* ein. Hier wird oft die Kurzform verwendet.

I **am not** watching TV.	I**'m not** watching TV.
Paul **is not** sitting on the sofa.	Paul **isn't** sitting on the sofa.
They **are not** singing.	They **aren't** singing.

b) *Present progressive*: Fragen

Entscheidungsfragen bildest du, indem du *am, are, is* an den Satzanfang stellst.
Die Kurzantworten sind wie beim Verb *be* (Grammar 1R).
Bei **Fragen mit Fragewörtern** stellst du das Fragewort an den Satzanfang.

Are you **doing** your homework?	**Yes, I am.** / **No, I'm not.**
Is Megan **helping** her dad?	**Yes, she is.** / **No, she isn't.**
What are you **doing**?	I'm writing an email.
Where is he **going**?	He's going to the swimming pool.

4 Die einfache Vergangenheit: Aussagen (The simple past: Statements)

18, WEB 16

Das *simple past* verwendest du, um über Dinge zu sprechen, die in der Vergangenheit passiert und vorbei sind.

Signalwörter
yesterday
last Monday/...
last week/year/...
two days/... ago
...

I **had** a great weekend.
On Saturday I **visited** my best friend and yesterday I **went** to the cinema.

a) Regelmäßige Verben (Regular verbs)

Die meisten Verben sind regelmäßig. Das *simple past* bildest du, indem du die Endung ***-ed*** an das Verb (Infinitiv) anhängst:

look → *look**ed***   *watch* → *watch**ed***

Yesterday I **played** basketball.	*Gestern habe ich Basketball gespielt.*
Sandeep **helped** in the shop.	*Sandeep hat im Laden geholfen.*
Last week we **visited** my aunt.	*Letzte Woche haben wir meine Tante besucht.*

Achtung Schreibweise:
Endet das Verb auf **-e**, dann wird nur ***-d*** angehängt:

*lik**e*** → *lik**ed***   *arriv**e*** → *arriv**ed***

Endet das Verb auf einen kurzen betonten Vokal + Konsonant, wird der Konsonant verdoppelt:

*sto**p*** → *sto**pp**ed*   *cha**t*** → *cha**tt**ed*

Endet das Verb auf Konsonant + ***-y***, dann lautet die Endung im *simple past* ***-ied***:

*tid**y*** → *tid**ied***   *worr**y*** → *worr**ied***

b) Unregelmäßige Verben (Irregular verbs)

Eine Liste der unregelmäßigen Verben, die in diesem Buch vorkommen, findest du auf Seite 334–335.

Die unregelmäßigen Verben haben im *simple past* eine eigene Form, die du lernen musst:

Verb (Infinitiv)	*simple past*	
have	**had**	Mia **had** a great weekend.
go	**went**	She **went** to a fun park.
feel	**felt**	She and her family **felt** really happy.
do	**did**	They **did** lots of interesting things together.
...	...	

5 Die einfache Vergangenheit von *be* ▶ 19, WEB 17
(The simple past of *be*)

Be hat als einziges englisches Verb zwei Formen im *simple past*: ***was*** und ***were***.
I/he/she/it ***was*** – *you/we/they* ***were***

***simple past* von *be*: Aussagen**

I **was** very hungry after school.	*Ich war …*
They **were** in London yesterday.	*Sie waren …*

***simple past* von *be*: Verneinung**

It **wasn't** cold yesterday.	*Es war gestern nicht kalt.*
We **weren't** at the party.	*Wir waren nicht auf der Party.*

***simple past* von *be*: Fragen**

Was Megan at home?	**Yes, she was.** / **No, she wasn't.**
Were they at the cinema?	**Yes, they were.** / **No, they weren't.**
Where was Tim yesterday?	He was at home.
When were you in bed?	I was in bed at 10 p.m.

6 Die einfache Vergangenheit: Verneinung
(The simple past: Negation)

Sätze im *simple past* kannst du mit ***didn't (did not)*** verneinen.
Didn't ist in allen Personen gleich. Das Verb selbst steht dabei immer im Infinitiv.

***simple past*: bejahter Satz**	***simple past*: verneinter Satz**
Jasmine **talked** to Lynn yesterday.	Jasmine **didn't talk** to Lynn yesterday.
I **went** to London last year.	I **didn't go** to London last year.

7 Die einfache Vergangenheit: Fragen
(The simple past: Questions)

Bei Fragen im *simple past* steht ***did*** am Satzanfang bzw. ein Fragewort.
Did ist in allen Personen gleich. Das Verb selbst bleibt im Infinitiv.

***simple past*: Fragen**

Did you **ride** your bike?	**Yes, I did.** / **No, I didn't.**
Did he **buy** a new football?	**Yes, he did.** / **No, he didn't.**
Where did she **go**?	She went to Berlin.
What did they **do** yesterday?	They played table tennis.

Fragen mit *was* oder *were* stellst du ohne *did* (Grammar 5).

8 Die Zukunft mit *will* (The *will*-future) 20, WEB 18

Mit dem *will-future* kannst du über die Zukunft sprechen. Du kannst damit Vermutungen und Vorhersagen äußern sowie Hoffnungen und Wünsche ausdrücken.

a) *Will-future*: Aussagen

Das *will-future* bildest du mit ***will*** und dem Infinitiv des Verbs.
Die Kurzform von *will* heißt ***'ll***. *Will* ist für alle Personen gleich.

will-future: **Aussagen**	
I think our class **will** win the match.	*Ich denke, unsere Klasse wird das Spiel gewinnen.*
I hope I**'ll** be a pilot.	*Ich hoffe, dass ich Pilot werde.*
I'm sure Anna **will** like London.	*Ich bin mir sicher, dass Anna London mögen wird.*
You**'ll** have a great time.	*Du wirst / Ihr werdet eine tolle Zeit haben.*

On Wednesday it **will** be sunny.

> *I will* heißt im Deutschen „ich werde" und nicht „ich will".
> Anders als im Englischen kann man im Deutschen mit der Zukunft oder der Gegenwart über Zukünftiges sprechen:
> *I'll phone you.* – Ich werde dich anrufen. / Ich rufe dich an.

b) *Will-future*: Verneinung

Für die Verneinung fügst du ein ***not*** hinter *will* ein.
Die Kurzform von ***will not*** heißt ***won't***. *Won't* ist für alle Personen gleich.

will-future: **Verneinung**	
It **won't** be cold tomorrow.	*Es wird morgen nicht kalt sein.*
I hope they **won't** forget us.	*Ich hoffe, sie werden uns nicht vergessen.*
I'm sure I **won't** live in Berlin.	*Ich bin mir sicher, dass ich nicht in Berlin leben werde.*

c) *Will-future*: Fragen

Bei **Entscheidungsfragen** stellst du *will* an den Satzanfang.
In den Kurzantworten verwendest du *will* und *won't*.
Bei **Fragen mit Fragewörtern** steht das Fragewort am Satzanfang.

will-future: **Fragen**	
Will I **be** a mechanic?	**Yes, you will.** / **No, you won't.**
Will you **live** in New York?	**Yes, I will.** / **No, I won't.**
Who will win the match?	I think our class will win it.
When will I **see** you again?	Maybe next week.

9 Adverbien der Art und Weise (Adverbs of manner) 21 , WEB 19

Wenn du eine Person, ein Tier oder eine Sache beschreibst, benutzt du ein Adjektiv.

*The kids are **loud**.* *The cat is **cute**.* *The garden is **big**.*

Wenn du beschreiben möchtest, wie jemand etwas tut oder wie etwas geschieht, benutzt du ein Adverb der Art und Weise.
Adverbien der Art und Weise bildest du, indem du an das Adjektiv ***-ly*** anhängst:

Adjektiv	Adverb	
loud	loud**ly**	The kids speak very **loudly**.
bad	bad**ly**	Tom sings **badly**.
slow	slow**ly**	Sina walks **slowly**.

He sings **badly**.

Bei manchen Adverbien ändert sich die Schreibweise, wenn ***-ly*** angehängt wird:
-y wird zu ***-ily***
-le wird zu ***-ly***

Adjektiv	Adverb	
happ**y**	happ**ily**	Meera laughed **happily**.
eas**y**	eas**ily**	Simon did it **easily**.
terrib**le**	terrib**ly**	The man dances **terribly**.

Einige Adverbien haben Sonderformen, die du wie Vokabeln lernen musst.
Manche Adjektive und Adverbien sind gleich.

Adjektiv	Adverb	
good	**well**	Sandeep is a good guitar player. He plays the guitar **well**.
fast	**fast**	Jack is a fast runner. He runs **fast**.
hard	**hard**	Emma is a hard worker. She works **hard**.

10 Die Zukunft mit *going to* (The *going to*-future) 22, WEB 20

Mit dem *going to-future* kannst du sagen, was jemand für die Zukunft plant oder vorhat.
Auch bei Ereignissen, die wahrscheinlich eintreten werden, verwendet man das *going to-future*.

Signalwörter
tomorrow
at the weekend
next week
soon
...

a) *Going to-future*: Aussagen

So bildest du das ***going to-future***:
am, **are**, **is** + **going to** + **Verb**
*We **are going to watch** a film.*

Das *going to-future* wird oft mit den Kurzformen (*I'm, you're, he's, ...*) gebildet.

	***going to-future:* Aussagen**		
Singular	I**'m**	**going to**	watch a film.
	You**'re**		
	He/She/It **is**		
Plural	We**'re**		
	You**'re**		
	They**'re**		

Im Deutschen gibt es verschiedene Möglichkeiten, das *going to-future* zu übersetzen:

I'm going to watch a film.	*Ich werde/will mir einen Film anschauen.* *Ich plane/habe vor, mir einen Film anzuschauen.*

b) *Going to-future*: Verneinung

Für die Verneinung stellst du ***not*** hinter die Form von *be*.

***going to-future:* Verneinung**		
I**'m not**	**going to**	eat sweets tomorrow.
She **isn't**		
They **aren't**		

Is he **going to** buy an ice cream?

c) *Going to-future*: Fragen

Entscheidungsfragen und ihre Kurzantworten sowie **Fragen mit Fragewörtern** bildest du so:

***going to-future:* Verneinung**	
Are you **going to** go to the party at the weekend?	**Yes, I am.** / **No, I'm not.**
Is he **going to** wear his new shirt?	**Yes, he is.** / **No, he isn't.**
What are you **going to** do?	I'm going to make pizza.
When is she **going to** play hockey?	I think on Friday.

11 Steigerung und Vergleich von Adjektiven (Comparison of adjectives)

23, WEB 21

Mit Adjektiven lassen sich Personen oder Sachen näher beschreiben.
Wenn du Personen oder Sachen miteinander vergleichen möchtest, kannst du ein Adjektiv steigern.
Die Steigerungsformen heißen ***comparative*** (Komparativ) und ***superlative*** (Superlativ).

a) Steigerung von Adjektiven mit *-er* und *-est*

Einsilbige Adjektive (z. B. *cheap*, *old*, *young*) werden durch das Anhängen von ***-er*** und ***-est*** gesteigert.

Adjektiv	Komparativ	Superlativ
cheap	cheap**er**	(the) cheap**est**
old	old**er**	(the) old**est**
young	young**er**	(the) young**est**

Bei zweisilbigen Adjektiven, die auf ***-y*** enden, wird aus dem *-y* ein ***-i***.

Adjektiv	Komparativ	Superlativ
pretty	prett**ier**	(the) prett**iest**
easy	eas**ier**	(the) eas**iest**
friendly	friendl**ier**	(the) friendl**iest**

Bei manchen Adjektiven ändert sich die Schreibweise.

Adjektiv	Komparativ	Superlativ
nice	nic**er**	(the) nic**est**
hot	hot**ter**	(the) hot**test**
big	big**ger**	(the) big**gest**

Einige Adjektive haben unregelmäßige Steigerungsformen. Diese Formen musst du wie Vokabeln lernen.

Adjektiv	Komparativ	Superlativ
good	**better**	(the) **best**
bad	**worse**	(the) **worst**
much/many	**more**	(the) **most**

b) Steigerung von Adjektiven mit *more* und *most*

Mehrsilbige Adjektive werden mit ***more*** und ***most*** gesteigert.
Du stellst dabei ***more*** oder ***most*** vor das Adjektiv. Das Adjektiv bleibt unverändert.

Adjektiv	Komparativ	Superlativ
interesting	**more** interesting	(the) **most** interesting
beautiful	**more** beautiful	(the) **most** beautiful

c) Vergleichssätze

Willst du ungleiche Dinge miteinander vergleichen, benutzt du den Komparativ mit ***than***.

Vergleichssätze	
The blue cap is **cheaper than** the green cap.	*Die blaue Kappe ist billiger als die grüne.*
The jacket is **more expensive than** the white T-shirt.	*Die Jacke ist teurer als das weiße T-Shirt.*

Today it's **windier than** yesterday.

I think the London Eye is **more beautiful than** Big Ben.

Sind die Eigenschaften von zwei Dingen oder Personen gleich, benutzt du ***as … as***.

Vergleichssätze	
Mike's brother is **as old as** Finn's brother.	*Mikes Bruder ist genauso alt wie Finns Bruder.*
Sarah is **as tall as** Anne.	*Sarah ist so groß wie Anne.*

12 Mengenangaben (Quantifiers) 24, WEB 22

a) Die Mengenangaben *some* und *any*

Mit ***some*** und ***any*** werden Mengen bezeichnet wie „etwas“, „einige“ oder „ein paar“.
Die Mengenangabe ***not ... any*** bedeutet „kein“ oder „keine“.

In bejahten Aussagesätzen benutzt du ***some***.

Bejahte Aussagesätze mit *some*

There are **some** apples in the kitchen.
In der Küche sind (ein paar) Äpfel.
I need **some** milk for my cornflakes.
Ich brauche (etwas) Milch für meine Cornflakes.

In verneinten Aussagesätzen und in den meisten Fragen verwendest du ***any***.

Fragen mit *any*	Verneinte Aussagesätze mit *any*
Are there **any** apples?	We have**n't** got **any** apples.
Gibt es Äpfel?	*Wir haben keine Äpfel.*
Have you got **any** milk?	There is**n't any** milk.
Hast du (etwas) Milch?	*Es gibt keine Milch.*

Have we got **any** toast?
And have we got **any** eggs?

Yes, there is **some** toast on the table.
But we have**n't** got **any** eggs.

Wenn du jemanden höflich um etwas bittest oder ihm etwas anbietest, benutzt du ***some*** auch in Fragen:
*Can I have **some** milk, please?*
Kann ich bitte (etwas/ein bisschen) Milch haben?
*Would you like **some** tea?*
Möchtest du etwas Tee?

b) Die Mengenangaben *much, many* und *a lot of*

Much (viel), ***many*** (viele) und ***a lot of*** (viel, viele) sind ebenfalls Mengenangaben.

In bejahten Aussagesätzen benutzt du ***a lot of*** oder ***lots of***.

Bejahte Aussagesätze mit *a lot of / lots of*
We need **lots of** sweets for the party. *Wir brauchen viele Süßigkeiten für die Party.* Jasmine made **a lot of** muffins. *Jasmine hat viele Muffins gemacht.*

In verneinten Aussagesätzen und in Fragen verwendest du ***much*** und ***many***.
Much wird dabei mit Nomen verwendet, die in der Einzahl stehen und nicht zählbar sind (z. B. *water, oil, salt, time, money, …*).
Many wird dagegen mit Nomen verwendet, die in der Mehrzahl stehen und zählbar sind (z. B. *eggs, tomatoes, books, phones, …*).

Verneinte Aussagesätze mit *much* und *many*	**Fragen mit *much* und *many***
I do**n't** have **much** time now. *Ich habe jetzt nicht viel Zeit.* There are**n't many** girls in my class. *In meiner Klasse gibt es nicht viele Mädchen.*	**How much** money have we got? *Wie viel Geld haben wir?* **How many** eggs would you like? *Wie viele Eier möchtest du?*

13 Modalverben (Modal verbs) 25 , WEB 23

Mit Modalverben kannst du ausdrücken, was jemand tun kann, darf oder muss.
Auf Modalverben folgt immer ein anderes Verb im Infinitiv.

can **can't**

Mit ***can*** kannst du sagen, was jemand tun kann oder tun darf.
Mit ***can't*** drückst du aus, was jemand nicht tun kann oder nicht tun darf.

He **can**/**can't** swim.	*Er kann / kann nicht schwimmen.*
She **can**/**can't** go to the party.	*Sie darf / darf nicht zu der Party gehen.*

Statt ***can*** kannst du auch ***may*** benutzen, wenn du um Erlaubnis bitten möchtest:

May I go to the cinema tomorrow?	*Darf ich morgen ins Kino gehen?*

mustn't

Must not oder die Kurzform ***mustn't*** klingt wie im Deutschen „muss nicht", heißt aber „nicht dürfen".

I **mustn't** eat my brother's sandwiches.	*Ich darf nicht die Brote von meinem Bruder essen.*

must
have to / has to

Must heißt „müssen". In der Regel kannst du es auch durch ***have to*** / ***has to*** ersetzen.

Megan **must** tidy her room. *oder* Megan **has to** tidy her room.	*Megan muss ihr Zimmer aufräumen.*

don't/doesn't have to

Wenn du sagen willst, was jemand nicht tun muss, benutzt du ***don't/doesn't have to***.

My sister **doesn't have to** make her bed. *Meine Schwester muss ihr Bett nicht machen.*

14 Das Perfekt (The present perfect) 26 , WEB 24

Das *present perfect* verwendest du,

- wenn etwas irgendwann, noch nie oder noch nicht geschehen ist:
  *Holly **has** never **eaten** fish.*
  (Holly hat noch nie Fisch gegessen.)
- wenn eine Handlung in der Vergangenheit Auswirkungen auf die Gegenwart hat:
  *David **has cleaned** the kitchen.*
  (David hat die Küche geputzt. → Sie ist jetzt sauber.)

She **has bought** new clothes.

a) *Present perfect*: Aussagen und Verneinung

Das *present perfect* bildest du mit **have/has** + **Partizip Perfekt (*past participle*)**.
Die Verneinung bildest du mit **haven't/hasn't** + **Partizip Perfekt**.

***present perfect*: Aussagen und Verneinung**

I	**have**	**brushed**	my teeth.
He	**has**	**gone**	to London.
We	**have**	**seen**	a tiger.
You	**haven't**	**helped**	your sister.
She	**hasn't**	**been**	to Scotland.
They	**haven't**	**made**	pizza.

Das *present perfect* kannst du mit folgenden Signalwörtern verwenden. Sie alle geben keinen genauen Zeitpunkt an.

Signalwörter
already, just, never, ever, not ... yet, ...

I have **already** done my homework.	*Ich habe meine Hausaufgaben schon gemacht.*
Lisa has **just** seen a crocodile.	*Lisa hat eben/gerade ein Krokodil gesehen.*
We've **never** done a backflip.	*Wir haben noch nie einen Rückwärtssalto gemacht.*
He hasn't tidied his room **yet**.	*Er hat sein Zimmer noch nicht aufgeräumt.*

Stop playing! You haven't finished your homework **yet**.

Die Signalwörter für das *present perfect* stehen direkt vor dem Partizip Perfekt. Nur ***yet*** steht am Satzende.

b) *Present perfect*: Fragen

Entscheidungsfragen im *present perfect* bildest du, indem du *have* oder *has* an den Satzanfang stellst.
Bei **Fragen mit Fragewörtern** steht das Fragewort am Satzanfang:

***present perfect*: Fragen**

Have you **finished** your homework?	**Yes, I have.** / **No, I haven't.**
Has Adam **bought** a new game?	**Yes, he has.** / **No, he hasn't.**
Have they ever **been** to New York?	**Yes, they have.** / **No, they haven't.**
What have you **done**?	Nothing.
Why hasn't she **come**?	I don't know.

c) Das Partizip Perfekt

Bei regelmäßigen Verben bildest du das Partizip Perfekt (*past participle*) mit dem **Infinitiv** + ***-ed***.

Infinitiv	*simple past*	*past participle*
clean	cleaned	clean**ed**
help	helped	help**ed**
play	played	play**ed**

Unregelmäßige Verben haben unregelmäßige Formen. Lerne sie wie Vokabeln. Auf Seite 334 – 335 findest du eine Liste der unregelmäßigen Verben.

Infinitiv	*simple past*	*past participle*
be	was/were	**been**
do	did	**done**
have	had	**had**
buy	bought	**bought**

15 Indirekte Rede ohne Zeitverschiebung (▶ 27, WEB 25)
(Reported speech without backshift of tenses)

Wenn du berichten willst, was jemand gesagt hat, benutzt du indirekte Rede.

Direkte Rede (*direct speech*)	**Indirekte Rede (*reported speech*)**	
	Begleitsatz	Wiedergegebene Aussage
Sandeep: "I play football."	Sandeep says (that)	he plays football.
Megan and Ben: "We like Camden."	Megan and Ben say (that)	they like Camden.

Indirekte Rede besteht aus einem Begleitsatz und der wiedergegebenen Aussage. Beide Satzteile können durch *that* verbunden werden, man kann es aber auch weglassen.

Wenn das Verb im Begleitsatz in der Gegenwart steht (z. B. *say*, *says*), verändern sich die Zeiten in der wiedergegebenen Aussage nicht.

Oft musst du Teile der indirekten Rede anpassen, damit dein Gesprächspartner versteht, was du meinst. Das betrifft z.B. die Pronomen und die Verbform.

Jasmine: "**My** pets are cute." → Jasmine says (that) **her** pets are cute.
Jason: "**I** like Baloo a lot." → Jason says (that) **he** like**s** Baloo a lot.

16 Stützwörter: *one/ones* (Prop words)

Du benutzt ***one***, um ein Nomen nicht zu wiederholen:

I'll also buy a scarf. This long **one** is really cool.	*Ich werde auch einen Schal kaufen. Der lange hier ist richtig cool.*

Wenn das Bezugswort im Plural steht, musst du ***ones*** benutzen:

Here are some apples. I think I'll take the small ones.	*Hier sind Äpfel. Ich glaube, ich nehme die kleinen.*

Im Deutschen kannst du das Nomen einfach weglassen, wenn du es nicht wiederholen möchtest. Im Englischen ist das nicht möglich. Du musst die Stützwörter ***one*** oder ***ones*** benutzen.

Which <u>T-shirt</u> should I take? The <u>yellow</u> **one** or the <u>blue</u> **one**?	*Welches <u>T-Shirt</u> soll ich nehmen? Das <u>gelbe</u> oder das <u>blaue</u>?*

17 Bedingungssätze Typ I (Conditional clauses type I) 28, WEB 26

Wenn du sagen möchtest, was unter bestimmten Bedingungen geschehen wird oder geschehen kann, benutzt du einen Bedingungssatz.

Ein Bedingungssatz besteht aus einem *if*-Satz und einem Hauptsatz. Der *if*-Satz nennt eine Bedingung. Der Hauptsatz drückt aus, was passiert, wenn die Bedingung erfüllt ist.
Im *if*-Satz steht das *simple present*, im Hauptsatz das *will-future*.

***if*-Satz** (Bedingung: Wenn …)	**Hauptsatz** (Folge: dann …)	
If you **miss** the bus,	you **will be** late.	*Wenn du den Bus verpasst, kommst du zu spät.*
If it **rains**,	they **won't go** outside.	*Wenn es regnet, werden sie nicht rausgehen.*

Bedingungssätze können entweder mit dem *if*-Satz oder mit dem Hauptsatz beginnen.
Wenn sie mit dem *if*-Satz beginnen, werden sie mit einem Komma getrennt.
Wenn sie mit dem Hauptsatz beginnen, verwendest du kein Komma:

***If** you go to the cinema, I'll come with you.*
*I'll come with you **if** you go to the cinema.*

18 Die Verlaufsform der Vergangenheit (The past progressive) 29, WEB 27

a) *Past progressive*: Aussagen und Verneinung

Das *present progressive* kennst du bereits (Grammar 3R). Es gibt auch für die Vergangenheit eine *progressive form*: das *past progressive*.
Es drückt aus,
- was jemand gerade tat oder was gerade passierte.
- was gerade vor sich ging, als etwas anderes geschah.

So bildest du das ***past progressive***:
***Simple past*-Form von *be* (*was/were*)** + **Verb** + **-ing**
*Sandeep **was playing** the guitar.*
Sandeep spielte (gerade) Gitarre.

*The friends **were singing**.*
Die Freunde sangen (gerade).

past progressive	*simple past*
Megan **was cooking** spaghetti	when the phone rang.
Megan kochte gerade Spaghetti,	*als das Telefon klingelte.*
David **was playing** video games	when his mum came in.
David spielte gerade Videospiele,	*als seine Mutter hereinkam.*

was gerade passierte:
past progressive

neues Ereignis:
simple past

Für die **Verneinung** fügst du ***not*** hinter *was/were* ein. Hier wird oft die Kurzform verwendet.

*I was**n't** watching a film.*
*They were**n't** reading a book.*

b) ***Past progressive*: Fragen**

Entscheidungsfragen bildest du, indem du *was/were* an den Satzanfang stellst.
Bei **Fragen mit Fragewörtern** stellst du das Fragewort an den Satzanfang.

Was Jasmine **laughing**?	**Yes, she was.** / **No, she wasn't.**
Were the children **running** around?	**Yes, they were.** / **No, they weren't.**
What was the teacher **doing**?	He was talking to a student.
Where were they **going**?	They were going to the cinema.

So funktionieren die Wortlisten

Es gibt alphabetische Wortlisten (*Dictionaries*) und Wortlisten nach *Themes*.

Alphabetische Wortlisten (*Dictionaries*)

Camden Market hat zwei *Dictionaries*:
Im *English-German dictionary* ab Seite 289 kannst du nachschlagen, wenn du die Bedeutung von einem englischen Wort aus dem Buch wissen möchtest.
Im *German-English dictionary* ab Seite 316 kannst du nachschlagen, wenn dir mal ein englisches Wort nicht einfällt.

Wortlisten nach *Themes*

In den Wortlisten nach *Themes* ab Seite 263 findest du alle neuen Lernwörter in der Reihenfolge, in der sie in den *Themes* vorkommen.
Hier siehst du, wie du die Wortlisten benutzen kannst:

(informal) bedeutet: Dieses Wort ist umgangssprachlich.

(no pl) bedeutet: Dieses Wort hat keinen Plural (Mehrzahl).

Die Lautschrift zeigt dir, wie man ein Wort ausspricht.

(irr) bedeutet: Dieses Verb ist unregelmäßig.

(only pl) bedeutet: Dieses Wort wird nur oder gewöhnlich im Plural (Mehrzahl) benutzt.

(pl wives) bedeutet: Dieses Wort hat einen unregelmäßigen Plural *(wives)*.

Wenn du den *Challenge*-Teil bearbeitest, solltest du dir die **grün** gedruckten Wörter merken.

amazing *(informal)* [əˈmeɪzɪŋ]	toll, unglaublich	
ship [ʃɪp]	das Schiff	 ship
clock [klɒk]	die Uhr	
money *(no pl)* [ˈmʌni]	das Geld	
metre [ˈmiːtə]	der Meter	
time [taɪm]	*hier*: das Mal	When was the last time you went to the gym?
like [laɪk]	wie	This cat looks like a small tiger.
after that [ˌɑːftə ˈðæt]	anschließend, danach	
weekend [ˌwiːkˈend]	das Wochenende	
to **show** *(irr)* [ʃəʊ]	zeigen	show – showed – shown
kind [kaɪnd]	nett, freundlich	kind = friendly

(BE) bedeutet: *British English*
(AE) bedeutet: *American English*

Kleine Bilder und Beispielsätze helfen dir dabei, dir Wörter besser einzuprägen.

surprise [səˈpraɪz]	die Überraschung	
to **guess** [ges]	*hier*: schätzen, vermuten, denken	Guess how old I am.
crisps *(only pl)* *(BE)* [krɪsps]	die Chips	 crisps ≠ chips 
at least [ət ˈliːst]	mindestens, wenigstens	
packet [ˈpækɪt]	die Packung, die Schachtel	
wife *(pl* **wives***)* [waɪf, waɪvz]	die Ehefrau	
to **be a mess** [ˌbi_ə ˈmes]	chaotisch/unordentlich sein; *hier*: ein einziges Durcheinander sein	My room is always a total mess.

Folgende Abkürzungen werden noch verwendet: *sb* = somebody, *etw* = etwas, *jmd* = jemand, *sth* = something, *jdm/jdn* = jemandem/jemanden

English sounds

Im Englischen spricht man Wörter oft anders aus, als man sie schreibt.
Deshalb ist die Lautschrift sehr nützlich: Sie gibt an, wie ein Wort ausgesprochen wird.
Hier ist eine Liste mit Lautschriftzeichen zusammen mit Beispielwörtern, in denen der entsprechende Laut vorkommt.

Vokale

[ɑː]	**a**rm
[ʌ]	b**u**t
[e]	d**e**sk
[ə]	**a**, **a**n
[ɜː]	g**i**rl, b**ir**d
[æ]	**a**pple
[ɪ]	**i**n, **i**t
[i]	ever**y**
[iː]	**ea**sy, **ea**t
[ɒ]	**o**range
[ɔː]	**a**ll, st**o**ry
[ʊ]	l**oo**k
[u]	Febr**u**ary
[uː]	f**oo**d

Doppellaute

[aɪ]	**eye**, b**uy**
[aʊ]	**ou**r
[eə]	th**ere**
[eɪ]	t**a**ke, th**ey**
[ɪə]	h**ere**
[ɔɪ]	b**oy**
[əʊ]	g**o**, **o**ld
[ʊə]	**you're**

Konsonanten

[b]	**b**ag, clu**b**
[d]	**d**uck, car**d**
[f]	**f**ish, lau**gh**
[g]	**g**et, do**g**
[h]	**h**ot
[j]	**y**ou
[k]	**c**an, du**ck**
[l]	**l**ot, sma**ll**
[m]	**m**ore, **m**u**m**
[n]	**n**ow, su**n**
[ŋ]	so**ng**, lo**ng**
[p]	**p**resent, to**p**
[r]	**r**ed, **r**ight
[s]	**s**i**s**ter, cla**ss** (scharfes **s**)
[t]	**t**ime, ca**t**
[z]	no**s**e, dog**s** (weiches **s**)
[ʒ]	televi**si**on
[dʒ]	oran**ge**
[ʃ]	**s**ure, Engli**sh**
[tʃ]	**ch**ild, **ch**eese
[ð]	**th**ese, mo**th**er (weicher Laut)
[θ]	mou**th**, **th**ink (harter Laut)
[v]	**v**ery, ha**v**e
[w]	**wh**at, **w**ord

Betonungszeichen für die folgende Silbe

[ˈ]	Hauptbetonung
[ˌ]	Nebenbetonung

The English alphabet

a	[eɪ]	**h**	[eɪtʃ]	**o**	[əʊ]	**v**	[viː]
b	[biː]	**i**	[aɪ]	**p**	[piː]	**w**	[ˈdʌbljuː]
c	[siː]	**j**	[dʒeɪ]	**q**	[kjuː]	**x**	[eks]
d	[diː]	**k**	[keɪ]	**r**	[ɑː]	**y**	[waɪ]
e	[iː]	**l**	[el]	**s**	[es]	**z**	[zed]
f	[ef]	**m**	[em]	**t**	[tiː]		
g	[dʒiː]	**n**	[en]	**u**	[juː]		

Ähnliche Wörter im Deutschen und Englischen

Es gibt viele Wörter, die im Englischen und im Deutschen gleich sind. Sie unterscheiden sich oft nur dadurch, dass die meisten von ihnen im Deutschen groß geschrieben werden. Diese Wörter stehen nicht in den Wortlisten, weil du sie ja kennst. Viele dieser Wörter sprechen wir gleich aus. Bei denen, die ein bisschen anders ausgesprochen werden als im Deutschen, ist die Lautschrift farbig hervorgehoben.

action [ˈækʃn]
adverb [ˈædvɜːb]
ah [ɑː]
anti- [ˈænti]
app [æp]
aquarium [əˈkweəriəm]
argument [ˈɑːgjʊmənt]
arm [ɑːm]
badminton [ˈbædmɪntən]
band [bænd]
basketball [ˈbɑːskɪtˌbɔːl]
beach volleyball [ˌbiːtʃ ˈvɒliˌbɔːl]
blog [blɒg]
blond [blɒnd]
board [bɔːd]
bodyboard [ˈbɒdiˌbɔːd]
box [bɒks]
bus [bʌs]
butter [ˈbʌtə]
café [ˈkæfeɪ]
cafeteria [ˌkæfəˈtɪəriə]
camp [kæmp]
camping [ˈkæmpɪŋ]
caravan [ˈkærəvæn]
cartoon [kɑːˈtuːn]
Celsius [ˈselsiəs]
chance [tʃɑːns]
chat [tʃæt]
chat room [ˈtʃæt ˌruːm]
clip [klɪp]
cocktail [ˈkɒkˌteɪl]
collage [ˈkɒlɑːʒ]
comic [ˈkɒmɪk]
computer [kəmˈpjuːtə]
cool [kuːl]
cornflakes [ˈkɔːnˌfleɪks]
cricket [ˈkrɪkɪt]
darts [dɑːts]
design [dɪˈzaɪn]
digital [ˈdɪdʒɪtl]
disco [ˈdɪskəʊ]
drama [ˈdrɑːmə]
DVD [ˌdiː viː ˈdiː]
email [ˈiːmeɪl]
euro [ˈjʊərəʊ]
event [ɪˈvent]
extra [ˈekstrə]
fair [feə]
fan [fæn]
feedback [ˈfiːdbæk]
film [fɪlm]
finger [ˈfɪŋgə]
flamingo [fləˈmɪŋgəʊ]
form [fɔːm]
fusilli [fuːˈzɪli]
gel [dʒel]
giraffe [dʒəˈrɑːf]
golden [ˈgəʊldn]
gorilla [gəˈrɪlə]
hamburger [ˈhæmˌbɜːgə]
hand [hænd]
hit [hɪt]
hobby [ˈhɒbi]
hockey [ˈhɒki]
home page [ˈhəʊm ˌpeɪdʒ]
horror [ˈhɒrə]
hotel [həʊˈtel]
intelligent [ɪnˈtelɪdʒənt]
international [ˌɪntəˈnæʃnəl]
Internet [ˈɪntənet]
interview [ˈɪntəˌvjuː]
interviewer [ˈɪntəˌvjuːə]
jeans [dʒiːnz]
job [dʒɒb]
judo [ˈdʒuːdəʊ]
karaoke [ˌkæriˈəʊki]
kilt [kɪlt]
laptop [ˈlæpˌtɒp]
link [lɪŋk]
live [laɪv]
Londoner [ˈlʌndənə]
magnet [ˈmægnɪt]
make-up [ˈmeɪkˌʌp]
manager [ˈmænɪdʒə]
marathon [ˈmærəθn]
marshmallow [ˌmɑːʃˈmæləʊ]
material [məˈtɪəriəl]
million [ˈmɪljən]
mini [mɪni]
minigolf [ˈminiˌgɒlf]
minute [ˈmɪnɪt]
moment [ˈməʊmənt]
muffin [ˈmʌfɪn]
museum [mjuːˈziːəm]
name [neɪm]
national [ˈnæʃnəl]
normal [ˈnɔːml]
oh [əʊ]
OK (= okay) [ˌəʊˈkeɪ]
olive [ˈɒlɪv]
online [ˈɒnlaɪn]
park [pɑːk]
partner [ˈpɑːtnə]

party ['pɑ:ti]
patient ['peɪʃnt]
penne ['peneɪ]
person ['pɜ:sn]
pilot ['paɪlət]
piñata [pin'jɑ:tə]
ping-pong ['pɪŋpɒŋ]
pizza ['pi:tsə]
plan [plæn]
planet ['plænɪt]
polo shirt ['pəʊləʊ ʃɜ:t]
pool [pu:l]
pop (music) [(')pɒp (ˌmju:zɪk)]
poster ['pəʊstə]
problem ['prɒbləm]
pullover ['pʊləʊvə]
quiz [kwɪz]
quiz show ['kwɪz ʃəʊ]
radio ['reɪdiəʊ]
Ramadan [ˌræmə'dɑ:n]
rap [ræp]
reporter [rɪ'pɔ:tə]
rest [rest]
restaurant ['restrɒnt]
rock (music) [(')rɒk (ˌmju:zɪk)]
sandwich ['sænwɪdʒ]
shopping ['ʃɒpɪŋ]
show [ʃəʊ]
sightseeing ['saɪtˌsi:ɪŋ]
skate park ['skeɪt pɑ:k]
skateboard ['skeɪtˌbɔ:d]
smiley ['smaɪli]
snack [snæk]
snooker ['snu:kə]
so [səʊ]
song [sɒŋ]
sound check ['saʊnd tʃek]
souvenir [ˌsu:və'nɪə]
sport [spɔ:t]
star [stɑ:]
studio ['stju:diəʊ]
stunt man ['stʌnt mæn]
surfing ['sɜ:fɪŋ]
sushi ['su:ʃi]
sweatshirt ['swetˌʃɜ:t]
symbol ['sɪmbl]
T-shirt ['ti:ʃɜ:t]
talk show ['tɔ:k ʃəʊ]
team [ti:m]
teen [ti:n]
teenager ['ti:nˌeɪdʒə]
tennis ['tenɪs]
text [tekst]
ticket ['tɪkɪt]
tiger ['taɪgə]
timing ['taɪmɪŋ]
toast [təʊst]
tour [tʊə]
tour bus ['tʊə bʌs]
tourist ['tʊərɪst]
tradition [trə'dɪʃn]
trick [trɪk]
tunnel ['tʌnl]
uniform ['ju:nɪˌfɔ:m]
verb [vɜ:b]
video ['vɪdiəʊ]
vlog [vlɒg]
warm [wɔ:m]
website ['webˌsaɪt]
wild [waɪld]
wind [wɪnd]
wow [waʊ]
zebra ['zebrə]
zoo [zu:]
zucchini [zʊ'ki:ni]

Theme 1 – After the holidays

Arbeitsanweisungen, die häufig im Buch vorkommen, kannst du in der Liste auf S. 222–223 nachschlagen.

p. 10

1	**holiday** ['hɒlɪdeɪ]	der Urlaub, die Ferien	
	first [fɜ:st]	zuerst, als Erstes	First we went to England.
	sunny ['sʌni]	sonnig	
	to **visit** ['vɪzɪt]	besuchen	
	famous ['feɪməs]	berühmt	
	castle ['kɑ:sl]	die Burg; das Schloss	castle 
	half brother ['hɑ:f ˌbrʌðə]	der Halbbruder	
	again [ə'gen]	wieder, noch (ein)mal	
	back [bæk]	zurück	
	weather ['weðə]	das Wetter	The weather was good. It was sunny.
	to **be lucky** [bi: 'lʌki]	Glück haben	I was really lucky.
	Spain [speɪn]	Spanien	
	to **stay** [steɪ]	*hier*: übernachten, wohnen	We stayed in a hotel.
	beach [bi:tʃ]	der Strand	
	German ['dʒɜ:mən]	Deutsch; deutsch	Are you German?
	cold [kəʊld]	kalt	
	rainy ['reɪni]	regnerisch	

p. 12

3	**How are you?** [haʊ‿'ɑ: ju:]	Wie geht es dir/Ihnen/euch?	
	I'm fine. [aɪm 'faɪn]	Es geht mir gut.	
	beautiful ['bju:təfl]	schön	
	tower ['taʊə]	der Turm	
	way [weɪ]	der Weg	
	top [tɒp]	das obere Ende, die Spitze	
	view [vju:]	die Sicht; der (Aus)blick, die Aussicht	We had a great view of the city.
	coast [kəʊst]	die Küste	
	to **look** [lʊk]	*hier*: aussehen	You look beautiful today.
	windy ['wɪndi]	windig	
	cloudy ['klaʊdi]	bewölkt, bedeckt	When it's cloudy, you can't see the sun.
	You're welcome. [ˌjɔ: 'welkəm]	Gern geschehen., Bitte.	Thank you. – You're welcome.
	them [ðem]	sie, ihnen	
	yesterday ['jestədeɪ]	gestern	yesterday ↔ today
	to **be free** [bi: 'fri:]	Zeit haben	Are you free this afternoon?
	fridge (*informal*) [frɪdʒ]	der Kühlschrank	

p. 14

6	**campsite** ['kæmpˌsaɪt]	der Campingplatz, der Zeltplatz	
	dolphin ['dɒlfɪn]	der Delfin	

p. 15			
7	**for (one week)** [fɔː]	(eine Woche) lang	We stayed in Berlin for one week.
	week [wiːk]	die Woche	 campfire
	campfire [ˈkæmpˌfaɪə]	das Lagerfeuer	
8	**postcard** [ˈpəʊstˌkɑːd]	die Postkarte	
	to **walk** [wɔːk]	gehen, laufen	
	hour [ˈaʊə]	die Stunde	1 hour = 60 minutes
	cloud [klaʊd]	die Wolke	
	sky [skaɪ]	der Himmel	There are no clouds in the sky.
	bye for now [ˈbaɪ fə naʊ]	bis bald	
p. 16			
9	**summer** [ˈsʌmə]	der Sommer	
	ice cream [ˌaɪs ˈkriːm]	die Eiscreme	
	outside [ˌaʊtˈsaɪd]	im Freien, draußen	Let's play outside.
	ride [raɪd]	die Fahrt; die Tour	We can go on a bike ride.
p. 17			
11	**diary** [ˈdaɪəri]	das Tagebuch	I write in my diary every day.
	bored [bɔːd]	gelangweilt	
	to **stay with sb** [ˈsteɪ wɪð ˌsʌmbədi]	bei jmd übernachten, wohnen	I sometimes stay with my grandparents.
	to **go for a walk** [ˌgəʊ fər‿ə ˈwɔːk]	spazieren gehen	
	night [naɪt]	die Nacht	night ↔ day
	to **rain** [reɪn]	regnen	
	inside [ɪnˈsaɪd]	drinnen; innen; (in ...) hinein	inside ↔ outside
	already [ɔːlˈredi]	schon	
	sad [sæd]	traurig	 happy ↔ sad 
	lonely [ˈləʊnli]	einsam	
	to **hire** [ˈhaɪə]	mieten, (aus)leihen	We hired bikes and went on a ride. 
	us [ʌs]	uns	
	sauce [sɔːs]	die Soße	
	wonderful [ˈwʌndəfl]	wunderbar, wundervoll	
	end [end]	das Ende	end ↔ start
p. 19			
15	**time** [taɪm]	die (Uhr)zeit	
	to **get** (*irr*) [get]	*hier*: gelangen	get – got – got/gotten
	by (bus) [baɪ]	mit (dem Bus)	I go to school by bus.
	train [treɪn]	der Zug, die Eisenbahn	train 
	plane [pleɪn]	das Flugzeug	 plane
	apartment [əˈpɑːtmənt]	die Wohnung	
	What's ... like? [wɒts ˈlaɪk]	Wie ist ...?	What's the weather like? – It's very rainy.

p. 20

1	**people** (*no pl*) [ˈpiːpl]	die Leute, die Menschen	
2	**poem** [ˈpəʊɪm]	das Gedicht	
	classmate [ˈklɑːsˌmeɪt]	der/die Klassenkamerad/in, der/die Mitschüler/in	
	crazy [ˈkreɪzi]	verrückt	
	biology (*no pl*) [baɪˈɒlədʒi]	Biologie	
	full [fʊl]	voll	

Teamwork
Zu zweit macht das Vokabellernen mehr Spaß. Fragt euch gegenseitig ab. Tauscht euch auch darüber aus, wie ihr am besten Wörter lernt. Wenn ihr Lust habt, könnt ihr selbst Lückentexte, Kreuzwort- oder Buchstabenrätsel erstellen.

p. 21

3	**large** [lɑːdʒ]	groß	large ↔ small
	open [ˈəʊpən]	offen, geöffnet	
	until [ənˈtɪl]	bis	The shop is open until 6 p.m.
	lunchtime [ˈlʌntʃˌtaɪm]	die Mittagszeit; die Mittagspause	It's lunchtime! I'm so hungry.
	healthy [ˈhelθi]	gesund	
	meal [miːl]	die Mahlzeit, das Essen	Fish with lots of vegetables is a healthy meal.
	fresh [freʃ]	frisch	
	to **offer** [ˈɒfə]	(an)bieten	They offer fresh orange juice.
	for example [fər‿ɪɡˈzɑːmpl]	zum Beispiel	
	to **wear** (*irr*) [weə]	tragen	wear – wore – worn
	shirt [ʃɜːt]	das Hemd; die Bluse	
	logo [ˈləʊɡəʊ]	das Abzeichen, das Logo	
	dark [dɑːk]	dunkel	
	blazer [ˈbleɪzə]	der Blazer, die Jacke	
	tie [taɪ]	die Krawatte	
	trousers (*only pl*) [ˈtraʊzəz]	die Hose	
	skirt [skɜːt]	der Rock	
	shoe [ʃuː]	der Schuh	
	to **use** [juːz]	benutzen	

p. 22

6	**sound** [saʊnd]	das Geräusch, der Klang; der Ton	
	dialogue [ˈdaɪəlɒɡ]	das Gespräch, der Dialog	
	to **take place** [ˌteɪk ˈpleɪs]	stattfinden	PE takes place in the gym.
	drama [ˈdrɑːmə]	Theater	

Unregelmäßig Verben (*irregular verbs*)
Unregelmäßige Verben erkennst du im Wörterverzeichnis an der Kennzeichnung (*irr*). Sie haben eine unregelmäßig Form für die einfache Vergangenheit (*simple past*), die du dir gut einprägen musst. Eine Liste der unregelmäßigen Verben findest du auf Seite 334–335.

be (*irr*) – was/were   do (*irr*) – did   go (*irr*) – went   have (*irr*) – had   …

p. 34			
3.1	**abroad** [əˈbrɔːd]	im/ins Ausland	Did you go abroad this summer?
	bar chart [ˈbɑː ˌtʃɑːt]	das Säulendiagramm, das Balkendiagramm	
	to **show** (*irr*) [ʃəʊ]	zeigen	show – showed – shown
4.1	**north** [nɔːθ]	der Norden	
	west [west]	der Westen	
	temperature [ˈtemprɪtʃə]	die Temperatur	
	between [bɪˈtwiːn]	zwischen	
	degree [dɪˈɡriː]	der Grad	It's 12 degrees Celsius.
p. 36			
11	**while** (*no pl*) [waɪl]	die Weile	Let's sit down for a while.
	I wish I could … [aɪ ˈwɪʃ‿aɪ kʊd]	Ich wünschte, ich könnte …	I wish I could fly.
	dry [draɪ]	trocken	
	skyscraper [ˈskaɪˌskreɪpə]	der Wolkenkratzer	
	to **call** [kɔːl]	(an)rufen, nennen	
	just [dʒʌst]	gleich; nur; einfach	
	all day [ˌɔːl ˈdeɪ]	den ganzen Tag	I want to play games all day.
p. 37			
5.1	**primary school** [ˈpraɪməri ˌskuːl]	die Grundschule	
	secondary school [ˈsekəndri ˌskuːl]	*die weiterführende Schule für Kinder zwischen 11 und 16/18*	I go to a secondary school.
	after that [ˌɑːftə ˈðæt]	anschließend, danach	
	A levels [ˈeɪ ˌlevlz]	das Abitur	
	during [ˈdjʊərɪŋ]	während	During the break I play football with my friends.
	Mexican [ˈmeksɪkən]	der/die Mexikaner/in; mexikanisch	
	verse [vɜːs]	die Strophe	
	to **prefer** [prɪˈfɜː]	vorziehen, bevorzugen, lieber mögen	I prefer chocolate to apples.
	half (*pl* **halves**) [hɑːf, hɑːvz]	die Hälfte	
	to **practise** [ˈpræktɪs]	üben	Let's practise the dialogue.
	mark [mɑːk]	die (Schul)note	
	worst [wɜːst]	schlechteste(r, s), schlimmste(r, s)	worst ↔ best
	report [rɪˈpɔːt]	der Bericht; das Zeugnis	
	Christmas [ˈkrɪsməs]	Weihnachten	
	Easter [ˈiːstə]	Ostern, das Osterfest	
p. 38			
8.1	**information** (*no pl*) [ˌɪnfəˈmeɪʃn]	die Information	Here's some information for you.
9.1	to **close** [kləʊz]	schließen, zumachen	close ↔ open
	to **sell** (*irr*) [sel]	verkaufen	sell – sold – sold

skyscraper

Theme 2 – Around London

p. 40

2	**sight** [saɪt]	die Sehenswürdigkeit	There are many famous sights in London.
	to **enjoy** [ɪnˈdʒɔɪ]	mögen; genießen	I enjoy reading.
	airport [ˈeəˌpɔːt]	der Flughafen	
	stadium [ˈsteɪdiəm]	das Stadion	
	bridge [brɪdʒ]	die Brücke	 bridge
	acrobat [ˈækrəˌbæt]	der/die Akrobat/in	
	musician [mjʊˈzɪʃn]	der/die Musiker/in	
	platform [ˈplætˌfɔːm]	der Bahnsteig, die Plattform	The train to Hogwarts leaves from Platform 9 ¾.
	railway station [ˈreɪlweɪ ˌsteɪʃn]	der Bahnhof	
	queen [kwiːn]	die Königin	
	even [ˈiːvn]	selbst; sogar	
	palace [ˈpæləs]	der Palast	Buckingham Palace 
	to **relax** [rɪˈlæks]	sich entspannen	
	grass (*no pl*) [ɡrɑːs]	das Gras; die Wiese, der Rasen	
	sun [sʌn]	die Sonne	Let's go out and enjoy the sun.
	boat [bəʊt]	das Boot; das Schiff	
	lake [leɪk]	der See	There is a boat on the lake.
	in the middle [ɪn ðə ˈmɪdl]	in der Mitte; mitten in/auf	
	dinosaur [ˈdaɪnəˌsɔː]	der Dinosaurier	
	to **find out** [ˌfaɪnd‿ˈaʊt]	herausfinden	
	free [friː]	*hier*: gratis, umsonst	How much is this book? – Nothing. It's free.
	amazing (*informal*) [əˈmeɪzɪŋ]	toll, unglaublich	
	ship [ʃɪp]	das Schiff	 ship
	clock [klɒk]	die Uhr	

p. 42

5	**money** (*no pl*) [ˈmʌni]	das Geld	
6	**metre** [ˈmiːtə]	der Meter	
	time [taɪm]	*hier*: das Mal	When was the last time you went to the gym?
	like [laɪk]	wie	This cat looks like a small tiger.

p. 43

9	**after that** [ˌɑːftə ˈðæt]	anschließend, danach	

p. 45

11	**weekend** [ˌwiːkˈend]	das Wochenende	
	to **show** (*irr*) [ʃəʊ]	zeigen	show – showed – shown
	kind [kaɪnd]	nett, freundlich	kind = friendly
	to **look forward to** [ˌlʊk ˈfɔːwəd tə]	sich freuen auf	I'm really looking forward to the holidays.

	to **let** (*irr*) [let]	lassen	let – let – let
	as soon as possible [əz‿ˌsuːn‿əz ˈpɒsəbəl]	so bald wie möglich	When do you want to go? – As soon as possible.
	forever [fərˈevə]	ewig	
	at the moment [æt ðə ˈməʊmənt]	im Moment	

Nur zehn Minuten
Übe die Vokabeln immer nur fünf bis zehn Minuten, aber dafür regelmäßig. Das ist viel wirkungsvoller als eine ganze Stunde oder nur zweimal im Monat.

p. 47

15	**tour guide** [ˈtʊə gaɪd]	der/die Reiseführer/in, der/die Reiseleiter/in	
	fact [fækt]	der Fakt	
	visit [ˈvɪzɪt]	der Besuch	

p. 48

1	**on the/your left** [ˌɒn ðə/jɔː ˈleft]	links, auf der linken Seite	
	on the/your right [ˌɒn ðə/jɔː ˈraɪt]	rechts, auf der rechten Seite	
	at the top [æt ðə ˈtɒp]	oben, am oberen Ende (von), an der Spitze (von)	
	at the bottom (of) [æt ðə ˈbɒtəm]	unten, am unteren Ende (von)	

p. 49

2	**worried** [ˈwʌrid]	beunruhigt, besorgt	I'm worried about my sister.
	to **follow** [ˈfɒləʊ]	folgen	
	directions (*only pl*) [dɪˈrekʃnz]	Wegbeschreibung	Follow the directions.
	strange [streɪndʒ]	sonderbar, komisch	
	to **reach** [riːtʃ]	(er)reichen	I can't reach my mum. She doesn't answer the phone.
	to **text** [tekst]	eine SMS/Kurznachricht schicken	I can text you.
	(three years) ago [əˈgəʊ]	vor (drei Jahren)	
	dead [ded]	tot; *hier*: leer	My phone is dead. I can't use it at the moment.
	someone [ˈsʌmwʌn]	jemand	
	Excuse me! [ɪkˈskjuːz mi]	Entschuldigen Sie bitte!, Entschuldigung!	Excuse me, can you tell me the way to Kings Cross, please?
	I'm sorry. [aɪm ˈsɒri]	Das tut mir leid.	I'm sorry, I don't know.

p. 50

3	to **turn** [tɜːn]	sich drehen; *hier*: abbiegen	
	left [left]	(nach) links	Turn left into Kent Road.
	right [raɪt]	(nach) rechts	
	straight (on) [streɪt]	gerade(aus)	Go straight on.
	past [pɑːst]	vorbei/vorüber an	
	to **cross** [krɒs]	überqueren	cross the street

p. 51			
5	**cap** [kæp]	die Mütze, die Kappe	
	to **charge** [tʃɑːdʒ]	(auf)laden	My phone is dead. I have to charge it.
p. 52			
6	**hippo** (= **hippopotamus**) [ˈhɪpəʊ, ˌhɪpəˈpɒtəməs]	das Nilpferd	 hippo
	plant [plɑːnt]	die Pflanze	
	frog [frɒg]	der Frosch	frog 
	world [wɜːld]	die Welt, die Erde	
	insect [ˈɪnsekt]	das Insekt	
	leaf (*pl* **leaves**) [liːf, liːvz]	das Blatt	 leaf
	tortoise [ˈtɔːtəs]	die (Land)schildkröte	
7	**penguin** [ˈpeŋgwɪn]	der Pinguin	
	fish (*pl* - *or* **-es**) [fɪʃ, fɪʃ, fɪʃɪz]	der Fisch	Penguins eat fish.
	carrot [ˈkærət]	die Möhre, die Karotte, die Mohrrübe	
	sure [ʃɔː]	sicher	Are you sure?
	I don't think so. [aɪ ˌdəʊnt ˈθɪŋk səʊ]	Das glaube ich nicht.	
p. 53			
8	**fur** [fɜː]	das Fell; der Pelz	My cat has black and white fur. 
	tail [teɪl]	der Schwanz	
	sharp [ʃɑːp]	scharf	
	mane [meɪn]	die Mähne	
	paw [pɔː]	die Pfote, die Tatze	
	clever [ˈklevə]	klug, gescheit, schlau	
	strong [strɒŋ]	stark	
	dangerous [ˈdeɪndʒərəs]	gefährlich	Lions are dangerous.
	to **jump** [dʒʌmp]	springen	

Schwierige Wörter

Wenn du merkst, dass du bei der Schreibweise einiger englischer Wörter Schwierigkeiten hast, kannst du Folgendes tun: Schreibe das Wort auf ein großes Blatt und markiere die Stelle, die dir Probleme macht. Hänge das Blatt in deinem Zimmer auf. Bald kannst du das Wort richtig schreiben!

p. 54			
10	**normally** [ˈnɔːmli]	normalerweise	I normally go to bed early.
11	**last** [lɑːst]	letzte(r, s)	
	quick [kwɪk]	schnell	quick = fast
	to **leave** (*irr*) [liːv]	verlassen	leave – left – left
	to **scream** [skriːm]	schreien; kreischen	

to **get off** [ˌget‿ˈɒf]	aussteigen	We have to get off the bus at the next stop.
to **be scared (of sth/sb)** [biː ˈskeəd]	(vor etw/jdm) Angst haben	Some people are scared of dogs.
high [haɪ]	hoch	
to **smile** [smaɪl]	lächeln	She smiled at me.
banana [bəˈnɑːnə]	die Banane	
to **pay** (*irr*) [peɪ]	(be)zahlen	pay – paid – paid
glad [glæd]	glücklich, froh	glad = happy

Probier's mal mit Gemütlichkeit
Nicht nur für das Vokabellernen gilt: Du solltest dich an dem Ort, an dem du arbeitest, wohlfühlen und durch nichts abgelenkt sein! Eine gewisse Ordnung erleichtert das Arbeiten. Mache regelmäßig Pausen, in denen du z. B. das Fenster öffnest, etwas trinkst und dich bewegst. So kannst du dich besser konzentrieren.

p. 64			
4.1	**church** [tʃɜːtʃ]	die Kirche	 church
	to **get married** [ˌget ˈmærid]	heiraten	I don't want to get married in a church.
	king [kɪŋ]	der König	
	department store [dɪˈpɑːtmənt ˌstɔː]	das Kaufhaus	Harrods is the largest and most famous department store in London.
	Europe [ˈjʊərəp]	Europa	
	everything [ˈevriθɪŋ]	alles	everything ↔ nothing
	medal [ˈmedl]	die Medaille	
p. 66			
14.1	**building** [ˈbɪldɪŋ]	das Gebäude	
	a bit [ə ˈbɪt]	ein bisschen	
	pyramid [ˈpɪrəmɪd]	die Pyramide	pyramid 
	reason [ˈriːzn]	der Grund	
	shard [ʃɑːd]	die Scherbe	
	star [stɑː]	der Stern	
	spectacular [spekˈtækjʊlə]	atemberaubend, spektakulär	The view is spectacular.
p. 68			
6.1	**lovely** [ˈlʌvli]	schön, hübsch; *hier*: wunderbar; nett	What a lovely day!
	than [ðæn]	als	A tiger is bigger than a cat.
	colleague [ˈkɒliːg]	der/die Kollege/Kollegin, der/die Mitarbeiter/in	

	seller ['selə]	der/die Verkäufer/in	
	vet (= **veterinarian**) [vet, ˌvetrɪ'neəriən]	der/die Tierarzt/-ärztin	I go to the vet with my pet.
	gardener ['gɑ:dnə]	der/die Gärtner/in	
	director [də'rektə]	der/die Direktor/in, der/die Leiter/in	
6.2	to **begin** (*irr*) [bɪ'gɪn]	anfangen, beginnen	begin – began – begun
	work [wɜ:k]	die Arbeit	
p. 69			
9.1	**thin** [θɪn]	dünn	
	spot [spɒt]	Fleck	There is a spot on my shirt.
	neck [nek]	der Hals; der Nacken	
11	to **leave** (*irr*) [li:v]	verlassen, *hier*: lassen	leave – left – left He left the door open.
	to **feel like doing sth** [ˌfi:l‿laɪk 'du:ɪŋ ˌsʌmθɪŋ]	Lust haben, etw zu tun	
	to **decide** [dɪ'saɪd]	(sich) entscheiden; beschließen	I can't decide what to do.
	to **wonder** ['wʌndə]	sich fragen	
	to **have a look (at sth)** [ˌhæv‿ə 'lʊk]	(sich) (etw) (an)schauen	Let's have a look.
	next [nekst]	dann, als Nächstes	
	across [ə'krɒs]	über	
	to **go for a ride** [ˌgəʊ fər‿ə 'raɪd]	eine Fahrt machen	We went for a ride on the London Eye.
	up [ʌp]	(nach) oben; hinauf	
	guard [gɑ:d]	die Wache	
	to **taste** [teɪst]	schmecken, probieren	Bananas taste great.
	still [stɪl]	(immer) noch, noch immer	
	salad ['sæləd]	der Salat	
	waiter/waitress ['weɪtə, 'weɪtrəs]	die Bedienung, der/die Kellner/in	waiter  waitress
	to **get** (*irr*) [get]	*hier*: werden	get – got – got/gotten
	angry ['æŋgri]	verärgert; zornig; wütend	He got really angry.
	what a ... ['wɒt‿ə]	was für ein(e) ...	What an exciting day!

Vergiss es einfach!

Hast du Probleme, dir bestimmte Wörter zu merken? Sind es immer dieselben Vokabeln, die dir nicht einfallen? Dann probiere es doch mal mit Vergessen! Das geht so: Suche fünf oder sechs schwierige Wörter aus, die du unbedingt vergessen willst. Schreibe sie auf Zettel und hänge sie neben dein Bett, über deinen Schreibtisch oder an den Badezimmerspiegel. Lies sie dir bei jeder Gelegenheit durch, damit du dich daran erinnerst, welche Wörter du unbedingt vergessen willst.

Theme 3 – Dreams

p. 72			
1	**star** [stɑː]	der Stern	The sky is full of stars.
	sign [saɪn]	das Zeichen; das (Straßen-/Verkehrs)schild	
	horoscope [ˈhɒrəˌskəʊp]	das Horoskop	
	next [nekst]	nächste(r, s)	Next stop: Buckingham Palace.
	to **believe (in)** [bɪˈliːv]	glauben (an)	Do you believe in horoscopes?
	to **trust** [trʌst]	vertrauen	Trust me!
p. 73			
2	**stupid** [ˈstjuːpɪd]	dumm, blöd	stupid ↔ clever
p. 74			
3	**lucky** [ˈlʌki]	glücklich; Glück bringend; *hier*: Glücks-	What's your lucky number? – Six.
	magazine [ˌmægəˈziːn]	die Zeitschrift, das Magazin	
	will [wɪl]	werden	
	to **happen** [ˈhæpən]	geschehen, passieren	Something wonderful will happen this month.
	won't [wəʊnt]	nicht werden	I won't have four kids.
	just [dʒʌst]	gleich; nur; einfach	
	to **worry** [ˈwʌri]	sich Sorgen machen	Don't worry!
	future [ˈfjuːtʃə]	die Zukunft	Do you often worry about your future?
	heart [hɑːt]	das Herz	
	to **get** (*irr*) [get]	erhalten, bekommen	I'll get a good job.
	vet (= **veterinarian**) [vet, ˌvetrɪˈneəriən]	der/die Tierarzt/-ärztin	I go to the vet with my pet.
	to **marry** [ˈmæri]	heiraten	Will you marry me?
p. 77			
10	to **take care of** [ˌteɪk‿ˈkeər‿əv]	sich kümmern um	A vet takes care of ill animals.
	ill [ɪl]	krank	
	driver [ˈdraɪvə]	der/die Fahrer/in	
	bricklayer [ˈbrɪkˌleɪə]	der/die Maurer/in	
	shop assistant [ˈʃɒp‿əˌsɪstənt]	der/die Verkäufer/in	shop assistant
	police officer [pəˈliːs‿ˌɒfɪsə]	der/die Polizeibeamte/-beamtin	
	hairdresser [ˈheəˌdresə]	der/die Friseur/in	
	video game designer [ˈvɪdiəʊ geɪm dɪˌzaɪnə]	der/die Videospielentwickler/in	
	mechanic [mɪˈkænɪk]	der/die Mechaniker/in	
	nurse [nɜːs]	die (Kranken)schwester, der (Kranken)pfleger	
	to **design** [dɪˈzaɪn]	entwerfen	I want to design computer games.

	to **build** (*irr*) [bɪld]	bauen	build – built – built
	to **drive** (*irr*) [draɪv]	fahren	drive – drove – driven
	to **sell** (*irr*) [sel]	verkaufen	sell – sold – sold
	to **cut** (*irr*) [kʌt]	schneiden	cut – cut – cut
	to **repair** [rɪˈpeə]	reparieren	
	to **grow up** [ˌgrəʊ‿ˈʌp]	erwachsen sein/werden	I will be a nurse when I grow up.
	perhaps [pəˈhæps]	vielleicht	perhaps = maybe
p. 78			
13	to **try** (*irr*) [traɪ]	versuchen, (aus)probieren	try – tried – tried
p. 79			
14	**as** [əz]	als	
	if [ɪf]	wenn, falls	If you're lucky, you can see a rainbow.

Mache sie zu deinen Wörtern!
Am besten kannst du dir Wörter merken, die du selbst verwendet hast.
Darum: Bilde Sätze mit den Wörtern, die du dir merken willst.
Sie können auch lustig sein oder sich reimen:
My mum can make a yummy cake.
I tried to sell my dog to the hairdresser.

p. 80			
1	**hero** (*pl* **-es**) [ˈhɪərəʊ, ˈhɪərəʊz]	der/die Held/in	Who is your hero?
	storm [stɔːm]	der Sturm	
	north [nɔːθ]	der Norden	
	the sea (*no pl*) [ðə ˈsiː]	das Meer, die See	
	to **rescue** [ˈreskjuː]	retten	
	shipwreck [ˈʃɪpˌrek]	das Schiffswrack, der Schiffbruch	shipwreck 
	brave [breɪv]	mutig, unerschrocken	Grace Darling was so brave. She's my hero.
	to **risk** [rɪsk]	riskieren, aufs Spiel setzen	They always risk their lives.
	real [rɪəl]	wirklich; echt	
	better [ˈbetə]	besser; lieber, mehr	
	player [ˈpleɪə]	der/die Spieler/in	play – player
	to **score a goal** [skɔːr‿ə ˈgəʊl]	ein Tor schießen	
	Africa [ˈæfrɪkə]	Afrika	
	to **study** [ˈstʌdi]	erforschen	
	chimpanzee [ˌtʃɪmpænˈziː]	Schimpanse	
	to **protect** [prəˈtekt]	(be)schützen	Jane Goodall protects animals and our planet.
p. 81			
2	**well** [wel]	gut	He plays the guitar really well.
3	to **laugh** [lɑːf]	lachen	

p. 82

4	**lighthouse** [ˈlaɪtˌhaʊs]	der Leuchtturm	
	keeper [ˈkiːpə]	*hier*: der/die Wärter/in	 island
	island [ˈaɪlənd]	die Insel	
	to **need to** [ˈniːd‿tə]	müssen	
	survivor [səˈvaɪvə]	der/die Überlebende	
	to **row** [rəʊ]	rudern	He rowed the boat quickly.
	those (*pl of* **that**) [ðəʊz]	diese; jene	
	poor [pɔː]	arm	
	careful [ˈkeəfl]	vorsichtig; sorgfältig	Be careful!
	safe [seɪf]	sicher	
	soup [suːp]	die Suppe	Eat some soup and get warm again.
	to **get** (*irr*) [get]	*hier*: werden	
	to **save** [seɪv]	retten	
	to **bring** (*irr*) [brɪŋ]	(mit)bringen	bring – brought – brought

p. 85

8	to **speak** (*irr*) [spiːk]	sprechen, reden	speak – spoke – spoken
	loud [laʊd]	laut	She speaks loudly.

p. 86

12	**young** [jʌŋ]	jung	young ↔ old
	stormy [ˈstɔːmi]	stürmisch	

Falsche Freunde

Im Englischen gibt es viele Wörter, die deutschen Wörtern zwar sehr ähnlich sehen, aber eine ganz andere Bedeutung haben. Man nennt sie deshalb *false friends* (falsche Freunde).
Für diese Wörter kannst du dir ein Merkblatt „Vorsicht Falle“ anlegen.

also = auch (nicht: also)
map = Karte (nicht: Mappe)
will = werden (nicht: wollen)
brave = mutig (nicht: brav)

p. 97

12	**actress** [ˈæktrəs]	die Schauspielerin	She wants to be an actress.
	photographer [fəˈtɒgrəfə]	der/die Fotograf/in	
	zoologist [zuˈɒlədʒɪst]	der/die Zoologe/-in	
	singer [ˈsɪŋə]	der/die Sänger/in	
	chef [ʃef]	der Koch/die Köchin	chef 
	baker [ˈbeɪkə]	der/die Bäcker/in	
14.1	**tool** [tuːl]	das Werkzeug	

p. 98

15.1	**trip** [trɪp]	der Ausflug; die Reise, die Fahrt	Tell me about your trip to England.
	out of [ˈaʊt‿əv]	(her)aus	
	gone [gɒn]	weg	Where is she? – She is gone.
	huge [hjuːdʒ]	riesig, riesengroß	huge = very, very big

	made of [ˈmeɪd‿əv]	(gemacht) aus	
	metal [ˈmetl]	das Metall	This tool is made of metal.
	to **get dressed** [ˌget‿ˈdrest]	sich anziehen	
	outside [ˌaʊtˈsaɪd]	*hier*: nach draußen, raus	Let's go outside.
	completely [kəmˈpliːtli]	völlig, ganz	
	empty [ˈempti]	leer	empty ↔ full
	suddenly [ˈsʌdnli]	plötzlich, auf einmal	
	spaceship [ˈspeɪsˌʃɪp]	das Raumschiff	 spaceship
	slow [sləʊ]	langsam	
	to **pull** [pʊl]	ziehen	
	to **hold** (*irr*) [həʊld]	(fest)halten	hold – held – held
	shut [ʃʌt]	geschlossen	It's not open. It's shut.
	into [ˈɪntʊ]	in	
	weapon [ˈwepən]	die Waffe	Weapons kill people.
	robot [ˈrəʊbɒt]	der Roboter	
	war [wɔː]	der Krieg	They are at war with the robots.
	to **rule** [ruːl]	regieren	
	most (of) [məʊst]	das meiste (von), ein Großteil	
	to **trip** [trɪp]	stolpern	
	to **fall** (*irr*) [fɔːl]	fallen	fall – fell – fallen 
	to **grab sth** [ˈgræb ˌsʌmθɪŋ]	(sich) etw schnappen	
	to **wake up** [weɪk‿ˈʌp]	aufwecken; aufwachen	
p. 99			
1	**out** [aʊt]	nach draußen, (he)raus	
	on one's own [ɒn wʌnz‿ˈəʊn]	allein(e)	I did it on my own.
	all over the world [ˌɔːl‿ˌəʊvə ðə ˈwɜːld]	auf der ganzen Welt	
	to **complain** [kəmˈpleɪn]	klagen, sich beschweren	She often complains about the weather.
	right [raɪt]	Recht	
	ape [eɪp]	(Menschen)affe	A gorilla is an ape. 
p. 101			
6	**finally** [ˈfaɪnli]	schließlich, endlich; zum Schluss	I finally went to bed.
12.1	**clear** [klɪə]	klar, verständlich, eindeutig	

Wortbilder

Vielleicht kannst du dir Vokabeln besser merken, wenn du daraus Wortbilder machst. Wenn du nicht gerne selbst zeichnest, kannst du auch Bilder aus Zeitschriften und Katalogen ausschneiden und auf ein Blatt Papier kleben. Schreibe die dazugehörigen Vokabeln direkt zum Bild. So kannst du englische Begriffe richtig "sehen".

Theme 4 – Celebrations

p. 106			
1	**celebration** [ˌseləˈbreɪʃn]	die Feier, das Fest	
	festival [ˈfestɪvl]	das Fest; das Festival	
	Christmas [ˈkrɪsməs]	Weihnachten	My favourite festival is Christmas.
	Mother's Day [ˈmʌðəz deɪ]	der Muttertag	
	Chinese [ˌtʃaɪˈniːz]	Chinesisch; chinesisch	I love eating Chinese food.
	New Year [ˌnjuː ˈjɪə]	Neujahr	
	Easter [ˈiːstə]	Ostern, das Osterfest	
	New Year's Eve [ˌnjuː jɪəz‿ˈiːv]	Silvester	New Year's Eve = 31st December
p. 108			
2	**during** [ˈdjʊərɪŋ]	während	During the party I ate cake.
	to **have a party** [ˌhæv‿ə ˈpɑːti]	eine Party machen, eine Party feiern	
	to **set off** [set‿ˈɒf]	(an)zünden	
	fireworks (*only pl*) [ˈfaɪəˌwɜːks]	das Feuerwerk	On New Year's Eve some people set off fireworks.
	Jew [dʒuː]	der Jude/die Jüdin	
	to **light** (*irr*) [laɪt]	erhellen; *hier:* anzünden	light – lit – lit We light candles. 
	evening [ˈiːvnɪŋ]	der Abend	
	pumpkin [ˈpʌmpkɪn]	der Kürbis	
	scary [ˈskeəri]	Furcht erregend; unheimlich	
	costume [ˈkɒstjuːm]	die Tracht, das Kostüm	costume 
	Muslim [ˈmʊzləm]	der/die Muslim/in; muslimisch	
	to **thank** [θæŋk]	danken	
	envelope [ˈenvələʊp]	der Briefumschlag, das Kuvert	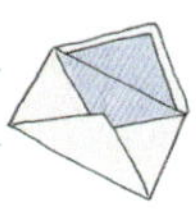 envelope
3	**church** [tʃɜːtʃ]	die Kirche	
	clothes (*only pl*) [kləʊðz]	die Kleider, die Kleidung	I like my new clothes.
p. 110			
5	to **guess** [ges]	(er)raten	Can you guess what it is?
	exactly [ɪgˈzæktli]	genau	
	to **be going to do sth** [ˌbiː ˌgəʊɪŋ tə ˈduː ˌsʌmθɪŋ]	etw tun werden	Neela is going to wear her most beautiful clothes.
	flower [ˈflaʊə]	die Blume	
	I'd like (to) [aɪd ˈlaɪk]	ich würde gern ...	I'd like to go to the cinema today.
	traditional [trəˈdɪʃnəl]	traditionell	
	Indian [ˈɪndiən]	indisch; indianisch	
	brilliant [ˈbrɪljənt]	toll, hervorragend, klasse	That's a brilliant idea!
	building [ˈbɪldɪŋ]	das Gebäude	A house is a building.
	to **shine** (*irr*) [ʃaɪn]	scheinen, leuchten	shine – shone – shone

> **Hosentaschenzettel**
> Schreibe dir kleine Zettel für unterwegs mit den wichtigsten oder schwierigsten Vokabeln. So hast du sie immer bei dir.

	different [ˈdɪfrənt]	anders, andere(r, s); *hier*: verschieden, unterschiedlich	
	to **call** [kɔːl]	(an)rufen, nennen	
p. 111			
6	**light** [laɪt]	das Licht	
p. 113			
11	**Jewish** [ˈdʒuːɪʃ]	jüdisch	
	beginning [bɪˈɡɪnɪŋ]	der Anfang	beginning ↔ end
	to **last** [lɑːst]	(an)dauern	The concert lasts three hours.
	god [ɡɒd]	der Gott	
	coin [kɔɪn]	die Münze, das Geldstück	
	pancake [ˈpæŋkeɪk]	der Pfannkuchen	
	potato (*pl* **-es**) [pəˈteɪtəʊ, pəˈteɪtəʊz]	die Kartoffel	 three potatoes
	to **fry** [fraɪ]	braten	I can fry eggs.
	oil [ɔɪl]	das Öl	
	delicious [dɪˈlɪʃəs]	köstlich, lecker	delicious = yummy
	garland [ˈɡɑːlənd]	die Girlande	garland 
p. 114			
2	**surprise** [səˈpraɪz]	die Überraschung	
	to **guess** [ɡes]	*hier*: schätzen, vermuten, denken	Guess how old I am.
	crisps (*only pl*) (*BE*) [krɪsps]	die Chips	 crisps ≠ chips 
	at least [ət ˈliːst]	mindestens, wenigstens	
	packet [ˈpækɪt]	die Packung, die Schachtel	
	second [ˈsekənd]	die Sekunde	60 seconds = 1 minute
	to **write down** [ˌraɪt ˈdaʊn]	aufschreiben	
	should [ʃʊd]	sollte/müsste	I should go now.
	a few [ə ˈfjuː]	einige, ein paar	
	cucumber [ˈkjuːˌkʌmbə]	die (Salat)gurke	 cucumber
	pepper [ˈpepə]	die Paprika	
	salad [ˈsæləd]	der Salat	salad 
	any [ˈeni]	irgendwelche, irgendein(e)	
	bottle [ˈbɒtl]	die Flasche	
	to **have a look (at sth)** [ˌhæv‿ə ˈlʊk]	(sich) (etw) (an)schauen	Let's have a look at the books.

> **Kim's game**
> Schreibe zehn Wörter auf ein Blatt Papier. Nimm dir drei Minuten Zeit, um sie dir einzuprägen. Dann drehe das Blatt um. Versuche nun, alle Wörter auswendig auf die Rückseite zu schreiben. Wie viele hast du dir gemerkt?

p. 115

3	**not any** [nɒt‿ˈeni]	kein(e)	There isn't any milk in the fridge.
	coffee [ˈkɒfi]	der Kaffee	
4	**hat** [hæt]	der Hut; die Mütze	I wear a hat when it's cold.

p. 116

6	**recipe** [ˈresəpi]	das Rezept	
	pasta (*no pl*) [ˈpæstə]	die Nudeln	
	onion [ˈʌnjən]	die Zwiebel	 onion
	tomato (*pl* **-es**) [təˈmɑːtəʊ, təˈmɑːtəʊz]	die Tomate	I love pasta with tomato sauce.
	tablespoon [ˈteɪbl,spuːn]	der Esslöffel	You eat soup with a tablespoon.
	vinegar (*no pl*) [ˈvɪnɪgə]	der Essig	
	teaspoon [ˈtiː,spuːn]	der Teelöffel	a teaspoon of salt and pepper
	pepper (*no pl*) [ˈpepə]	der Pfeffer	
	salt (*no pl*) [sɔːlt]	das Salz	

p. 117

8	**definitely** [ˈdefnətli]	eindeutig, definitiv	I'll definitely find a good present.
	to **smell (of)** [smel]	riechen (nach)	It smells of flowers.
	if [ɪf]	wenn, falls; *hier*: ob	
	than [ðæn]	als	The cap is nicer than the hat.
	voucher [ˈvaʊtʃə]	der Gutschein	I've got a voucher for the cinema.
	cheap [tʃiːp]	billig, preiswert	
	as ... as [əz əz]	(genau)so ... wie ...	Tea is as good as water.

p. 118

10	**sunglasses** (*only pl*) [ˈsʌn,glɑːsɪz]	die Sonnenbrille	sunglasses 
	scarf (*pl* **-s** *or* **scarves**) [skɑːf, skɑːvz]	der Schal	 scarf

p. 119

12	**a little** [ə ˈlɪtl]	ein bisschen	I can speak a little French.

Für gute Zuhörer

Du kannst dir Vokabeln auch merken, indem du sie dir immer wieder anhörst. Nimm das englische Wort auf, das du lernen willst – aber vergiss die deutsche Übersetzung nicht. Höre dir die Wörter regelmäßig an, und du wirst bald feststellen, dass du sie gelernt hast.

p. 130

2.2	**relative** [ˈrelətɪv]	die/der Verwandte, die/der Angehörige	My parents, grandparents, aunts and uncles are my relatives.
	to **hang** (*irr*) [hæŋ]	(auf)hängen	hang – hung – hung
	Christmas Eve [,krɪsməs‿ˈiːv]	Heiligabend	
	Father Christmas [,fɑːðə ˈkrɪsməs]	der Weihnachtsmann	Father Christmas brings presents for the children. 

	chimney ['tʃɪmni]	der Kamin; der Schornstein	
	down [daʊn]	(nach) unten; hinunter, hinab	He comes down the chimney.
	at night [æt 'naɪt]	nachts	
	Christmas Day [ˌkrɪsməs 'deɪ]	der erste Weihnachtsfeiertag	
	turkey ['tɜːki]	der/die Truthahn/-henne, der/die Pute/r	 On Christmas Day we often have turkey for lunch.
	neighbour ['neɪbə]	der/die Nachbar/in	
	plastic ['plæstɪk]	das Plastik, der Kunststoff	
	crown [kraʊn]	die Krone	
	silly ['sɪli]	dumm; albern	Don't be silly!
	rich [rɪtʃ]	reich	
	similar ['sɪmɪlə]	ähnlich	similar ↔ different
p. 132			
11	**sunset** ['sʌnˌset]	der Sonnenuntergang	
	to **place** [pleɪs]	stellen, legen	She places the vase on the table.
	silver ['sɪlvə]	silbern	
	I can't wait … [aɪ ˌkɑːnt 'weɪt]	Ich kann es kaum erwarten …	I can't wait to celebrate my birthday.
p. 134			
17.1	**aim** [eɪm]	das Ziel, die Absicht	The aim is to win the match.
	side [saɪd]	die Seite	
	to **score** [skɔː]	einen Punkt machen, punkten	
	point [pɔɪnt]	der Punkt	
	winner ['wɪnə]	der/die Gewinner/in, der/die Sieger/in	She is the winner. 
	South Africa [saʊθ‿'æfrɪkə]	Südafrika	
	circle ['sɜːkl]	der Kreis	
	to **roar** [rɔː]	(an)brüllen	Lions roar loudly.
	to **squeak** [skwiːk]	quieken; *hier*: piepsen	
	to **become** (*irr*) [bɪ'kʌm]	werden	become – became – become
p. 135			
17.2	**country** ['kʌntri]	das Land	What country are you from?
	Russia ['rʌʃə]	Russland	
	India ['ɪndiə]	Indien	
	temple ['templ]	der Tempel	
	colourful ['kʌləfl]	farbenfroh, farbenprächtig	
	fun [fʌn]	lustig, witzig, spaßig	This is a lot of fun!
	hundred ['hʌndrəd]	Hundert	one hundred = 100
	without [wɪð'aʊt]	ohne	I'm not going without you.
	prize [praɪz]	der Preis, der Gewinn	
	rope [rəʊp]	das Seil	
	guest [gest]	der Gast	

Theme 5 – Dos and don'ts

p. 136			
1	to **go with** [ˈgəʊ wɪð]	gehören zu, passen zu	The green T-shirt really goes with your eyes.
	angry [ˈæŋgri]	verärgert; zornig; wütend	Jason is angry. 
	frustrated [frʌˈstreɪtɪd]	frustriert; enttäuscht	
p. 138			
2	**grandma** (*informal*) [ˈgræn,mɑː]	die Oma, die Omi	My mother's mother is my grandma.
	hole [həʊl]	das Loch	There's a hole in your jeans.
	may [meɪ]	können; *hier*: dürfen	May I go to the park with my friends?
	to **study** [ˈstʌdi]	studieren; lernen	
	test [test]	die Prüfung, der Test; die Klassenarbeit	I have to study for my maths test.
	trainer (*BE*) [ˈtreɪnə]	der Turnschuh	 trainers
	youth club [ˈjuːθ ˌklʌb]	das Jugendzentrum	
	before [bɪˈfɔː]	bevor	
	by (eight o'clock) [baɪ]	(spätestens) bis (acht Uhr)	You have to be home by nine o'clock.
	expensive [ɪkˈspensɪv]	teuer	expensive ↔ cheap
3	to **go out** [gəʊ‿ˈaʊt]	(hinaus)gehen; *hier*: ausgehen	
	to **want sb to do sth** [ˌwɒnt ˌsʌmbədi tə ˈduː ˌsʌmθɪŋ]	wollen, dass jmd etw tut	My father wants me to clean the kitchen.
p. 139			
4	**How are things?** [ˌhaʊ‿ɑː ˈθɪŋz]	Wie geht's?	
	annoying [əˈnɔɪɪŋ]	nervig, lästig	My sister is so annoying.
	must not [mʌst ˈnɒt]	nicht dürfen	
	worst [wɜːst]	schlechteste(r, s), schlimmste(r, s)	This is the worst day of my life.
5	to **solve** [sɒlv]	lösen, klären	Let's solve the problem together.
p. 140			
6	**must** [mʌst]	müssen	must = have to
	mealtime [ˈmiːltaɪm]	die Essenszeit	
	dinner [ˈdɪnə]	das Abendessen; das Mittagessen	What's for dinner today?
7	**enough** [ɪˈnʌf]	genügend, ausreichend, genug	Do we have enough pasta at home?
p. 141			
9	**boyfriend** [ˈbɔɪ,frend]	der (feste) Freund	
	huge [hjuːdʒ]	riesig, riesengroß	huge = very, very big

	important [ɪmˈpɔ:tnt]	wichtig	It's really important to brush your teeth every day.
	to **send** (*irr*) [send]	(zu)schicken	send – sent – sent
p. 142			
10	**opinion** [əˈpɪnjən]	die Meinung, die Ansicht	What's your opinion?
	singer [ˈsɪŋə]	der/die Sänger/in	
	series (*only pl*) [ˈsɪəri:z]	die Serie, die Reihe	My favourite series is Game of Thrones.
	to **agree** [əˈgri:]	zustimmen, übereinstimmen	I don't agree with you.
p. 144			
1	to **break** (*irr*) [breɪk]	(zer)brechen	break – broke – broken
	polite [pəˈlaɪt]	höflich	
	respect (*no pl*) [rɪˈspekt]	der Respekt, die Achtung	Be polite and show respect for others.
	correct [kəˈrekt]	richtig, korrekt	
	to **chew** [tʃu:]	kauen	
	chewing gum (*no pl*) [ˈtʃu:ɪŋ ˌgʌm]	der/das Kaugummi	We must not chew chewing gum in class.
	to **separate** [ˈsepəreɪt]	trennen	
	litter (*no pl*) [ˈlɪtə]	der Müll, der Abfall	Please put the litter in the bin.
	plastic [ˈplæstɪk]	das Plastik, der Kunststoff	
	alarm clock [əˈlɑ:m ˌklɒk]	der Wecker	alarm clock 
	miniskirt [ˈmɪniˌskɜ:t]	der Minirock	
	to **throw** (*irr*) [θrəʊ]	werfen	throw – threw – thrown
p. 146			
6	**dress** [dres]	das Kleid	 boots
	boot [bu:t]	der Stiefel	
	jacket [ˈdʒækɪt]	die Jacke	
	worse [wɜ:s]	schlimmer, schlechter	bad – worse – worst
p. 148			
8	**against** [əˈgenst]	gegen	Are you for or against school uniforms?
	ugly [ˈʌgli]	hässlich	ugly ↔ beautiful
	horrible [ˈhɒrəbl]	schrecklich	
	sb would love (to) [ˌsʌmbədi wʊd ˈlʌv]	jmd möchte sehr gern	I would love to go on holiday.
	proud [praʊd]	stolz	I'm so proud of you.
p. 149			
10	to **attack** [əˈtæk]	angreifen	Don't attack others.
	text message [ˈtekst ˌmesɪdʒ]	die SMS, die Kurznachricht	
	to **call sb names** [ˌkɔ:l sʌmbədi ˈneɪmz]	jdn beschimpfen	The other students call him horrible names.
	another [əˈnʌðə]	noch ein(e, r, s); ein anderer/anderes, eine andere	

	to **ignore** [ɪɡˈnɔː]	ignorieren	
	bullying (*no pl*) [ˈbʊliɪŋ]	das Mobbing	
p. 150			
11	to **make fun of sb** [meɪk ˈfʌn‿əv ˌsʌmbədi]	sich über jdn lustig machen	Don't make fun of others.
	one day [ˈwʌn deɪ]	eines Tages	
	to **hold** (*irr*) [həʊld]	(fest)halten	hold – held – held
	embarrassed [ɪmˈbærəst]	verlegen, peinlich berührt	
	to **stink** (*irr*) [stɪŋk]	stinken	stink – stank – stunk
	to **post sth** [ˈpəʊst ˌsʌmθɪŋ]	etw schicken; *hier*: etw ins Internet stellen	They posted a picture of her online.
	comment [ˈkɒment]	der Kommentar, die Bemerkung	
	not anymore [ˌnɒt eniˈmɔː]	nicht mehr	I don't love you anymore.
	to **spend** (*irr*) [spend]	ausgeben (Geld); verbringen (Zeit)	spend – spent – spent
	to **be afraid (of sth/sb)** [ˌbi‿əˈfreɪd]	(vor etw/jdm) Angst haben	He isn't afraid anymore.
	alone [əˈləʊn]	allein	
	to **cry** (*irr*) [kraɪ]	weinen, schreien	cry – cried – cried
	to **get into trouble** [ɡet‿ɪntə ˈtrʌbl]	Schwierigkeiten bekommen	
	slow [sləʊ]	langsam	slow ↔ quick
	tip [tɪp]	der Tipp	
	still [stɪl]	(immer) noch, noch immer	I'm still here.
	bully [ˈbʊli]	*Person, die andere mobbt*	
p. 151			
12	to **beat** (*irr*) [biːt]	schlagen; *hier*: besiegen	beat – beat – beaten
	fault [fɔːlt]	die Schuld; der Fehler	It's my fault, I'm sorry.

Reimwörter

Damit du dir besser merken kannst, wie bestimmte Wörter ausgesprochen werden, suche Reimwörter für sie. Dir wird auffallen, dass die Reimwörter nicht immer dieselbe Schreibweise haben.

cry – fly slow – go beat – meet

p. 160			
4.1	**fashion** [ˈfæʃn]	die Mode	Jasmine loves fashion.
	relaxed [rɪˈlækst]	entspannt; locker, gelassen	
	to **understand** (*irr*) [ˌʌndəˈstænd]	verstehen	understand – understood – understood
	to **concentrate** [ˈkɒnsnˌtreɪt]	sich konzentrieren	
	to **stay up** [ˌsteɪ‿ˈʌp]	aufbleiben, wach bleiben	I usually stay up late.
	till (= **until**) [tɪl]	bis	My mother works till 6 p.m.

	free [friː]	frei	You're free to go.
	to **earn** [ɜːn]	verdienen	I will earn enough money.
	loudspeaker [ˌlaʊdˈspiːkə]	der Lautsprecher	
p. 161			
4.2	**wife** (*pl* **wives**) [waɪf, waɪvz]	die Ehefrau	
6.1	to **be a mess** [ˌbi‿ə ˈmes]	chaotisch/unordentlich sein; *hier*: ein einziges Durcheinander sein	My room is always a total mess.
p. 162			
9	**juicy** [ˈdʒuːsi]	saftig	Juicy apples are delicious.
	beef [biːf]	das Rindfleisch	
	stuff (*informal*) [stʌf]	das Zeug, die Sachen	He has so much stuff in his room.
	language [ˈlæŋgwɪdʒ]	die Sprache	
	to **improve** [ɪmˈpruːv]	verbessern	I want to improve my English.
	I'd rather … [aɪd ˈrɑːðə]	ich würde lieber …	I'd rather stay at home.
	nonsense [ˈnɒnsns]	der Unsinn, der Quatsch	What nonsense!
	such [sʌtʃ]	solche(r,s)	
p. 163			
4	to **skate** [skeɪt]	skaten, Skateboard fahren	
	to **be allowed to do sth** [bi‿əˌlaʊd tə ˈduː ˌsʌmθɪŋ]	etw tun dürfen	Students are not allowed to eat in class.
p. 164			
4.2	**thanks so much** [ˌθæŋks‿səʊ ˈmʌtʃ]	vielen Dank	
	first of all [ˌfɜːst‿əv‿ˈɔːl]	erstens, als Erstes	
	bag [bæg]	die Tasche	 bags 
	warning [ˈwɔːnɪŋ]	die Warnung	
	social worker [ˈsəʊʃl ˌwɜːkə]	der/die Sozialarbeiter/in	
	the same [ðə ˈseɪm]	der-/die-/dasselbe	It's the same at our school.
	nearly [ˈnɪəli]	fast, beinahe	I nearly forgot.
	all the best [ˌɔːl ðə ˈbest]	alles Gute	All the best to you.
p. 165			
8.1	**difference** [ˈdɪfrəns]	der Unterschied	
	to **belong to sb/sth** [biˈlɒŋ tə ˌsʌmbədi/ˌsʌmθɪŋ]	jdm/zu etw gehören	The ruler belongs to me.

Verknüpfungen herstellen

Bei Wörtern, die überhaupt nicht in deinen Kopf wollen, kannst du:

- dir das Wort bildlich vorstellen,
- ein kleines Bild dazu zeichnen,
- an ein Ereignis denken, das du selbst erlebt hast,
- einen Satz auswendig lernen, in dem das Wort vorkommt,
- dir eine Eselsbrücke (z. B. einen Reim) ausdenken.

Theme 6 – Let's go!

p. 166			
1	to **sleep over** [sli:p‿'əʊvə]	übernachten, über Nacht bleiben	I'm going to a sleep over at my friend's house.
	to **hurt** (*irr*) [hɜ:t]	wehtun, schmerzen	hurt – hurt – hurt
	to **have a temperature** [ˌhæv‿ə 'temprɪtʃə]	Fieber haben	
	tissue ['tɪʃu:]	das Taschentuch	I need a new tissue.
	concert ['kɒnsət]	das Konzert	
	not yet [nɒt 'jet]	noch nicht	I haven't had breakfast yet.
	to **cycle** ['saɪkl]	Rad fahren	cycle = ride one's bike
	instead (of) [ɪn'sted (‿əv)]	stattdessen; (an)statt	I wanted to go to the gym but I watched TV instead.
p. 167			
2	**bad** [bæd]	schlecht; *hier*: schlimm, stark	 She has a bad cold.
	to **have a cold** [ˌhæv‿ə 'kəʊld]	eine Erkältung haben, erkältet sein	
	cold [kəʊld]	die Kälte; *hier*: die Erkältung, der Schnupfen	
p. 168			
3	**doctor** ['dɒktə]	der Arzt/die Ärztin	
	to **cheer sb up** [tʃɪə ˌsʌmbədi‿'ʌp]	jdn aufmuntern	His friends tried to cheer him up.
	to **get well** [get 'wel]	gesund werden	Get well soon!
	to **miss** [mɪs]	*hier*: verpassen	Have I missed much at school?
	Cheer up! [tʃɪər‿'ʌp]	Lass (doch) den Kopf nicht hängen!, Kopf hoch!	
	love [lʌv]	die Liebe; *hier*: herzliche Grüße, alles Liebe	
p. 169			
5	**medicine** (*no pl*) ['medsn]	die Medizin, die Medikamente	Have you taken your medicine?
p. 170			
7	**headache** ['hedeɪk]	die Kopfschmerzen, das Kopfweh	He has a headache. 
	sore throat [ˌsɔ: 'θrəʊt]	die Halsschmerzen	
	throat [θrəʊt]	der Rachen, der Hals	My throat hurts.
	sore [sɔ:]	wund, entzündet	
	Oh dear! [əʊ 'dɪə]	Du meine Güte!	
	to **gargle** ['gɑ:gl]	gurgeln	You can gargle with salt water.
	goodbye [ˌgʊd'baɪ]	auf Wiedersehen	
	tablet ['tæblət]	*hier*: die Tablette	I take tablets for my sore throat.
	to **fall** (*irr*) [fɔ:l]	fallen	fall – fell – fallen

p. 172

12	**programme** [ˈprəʊgræm]	das Programm; *hier*: die Sendung	
	soap (opera) [ˈsəʊp (ˌɒprə)]	die Seifenoper, die Soap	
	talent show [ˈtælənt ˌʃəʊ]	der Talentwettbewerb	The X Factor is a talent show.
	news (*no pl*) [njuːz]	die Neuigkeit; die Nachrichten	Do you watch the news every day?

p. 174

1	**ever** [ˈevə]	jemals	
	Have you ever been to ...? [ˌhæv jəˌˌevə ˈbiːn tə]	Warst du jemals/schon einmal in ...?	Have you ever been to London?

Spell check
Buchstabiere ein Wort für einen Partner / eine Partnerin. Wechselt euch ab und kontrolliert anschließend gegenseitig, ob alles richtig geschrieben ist. Für jedes richtige Wort gibt es einen Punkt. Wer ist der *spelling king* oder die *spelling queen*?

p. 175

4	**trip** [trɪp]	der Ausflug; die Reise, die Fahrt	
	Scotland [ˈskɒtlənd]	Schottland	

p. 176

6	**UK** (= **United Kingdom**) [ˌjuːˈkeɪ, juːˌnaɪtɪd ˈkɪŋdəm]	das Vereinigte Königreich	
	fun [fʌn]	lustig, witzig, spaßig	
	to **explore** [ɪkˈsplɔː]	erforschen, erkunden	
	lovely [ˈlʌvli]	schön, hübsch	
	Britain [ˈbrɪtn]	Großbritannien	
	between [bɪˈtwiːn]	zwischen	Are you between 10 and 16 years old?
	age [eɪdʒ]	das Alter	What's your age?
	anything [ˈeniˌθɪŋ]	(irgend)(et)was	Do you know anything about Cornwall?

p. 177

8	**toothbrush** [ˈtuːθˌbrʌʃ]	die Zahnbürste	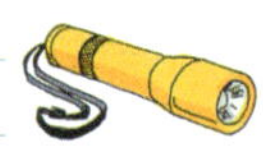
	torch [tɔːtʃ]	die Taschenlampe, die Fackel	torch
	to **pack** [pæk]	packen	
	dark (*no pl*) [dɑːk]	die Dunkelheit	With a torch you can see in the dark.
	made of [ˈmeɪdˌəv]	(gemacht) aus	Toothbrushes are made of plastic or wood.
	metal [ˈmetl]	das Metall	

p. 178

9	to **teach** (*irr*) [tiːtʃ]	unterrichten; *hier*: beibringen	teach – taught – taught
	movement [ˈmuːvmənt]	die Bewegung	
	land [lænd]	das (Fest)land	
	to the left [ˌtʊ ðə ˈleft]	nach links	You have to move to the left.
	a bit [ə ˈbɪt]	ein bisschen	It's a bit windy today.
	to **move** [muːv]	sich bewegen	
	up [ʌp]	(nach) oben; hinauf	up and down

to **lift** [lɪft]	(hoch)heben	
step [step]	die Stufe; der Schritt	
unhappy [ʌnˈhæpi]	unglücklich	happy ↔ unhappy
wave [weɪv]	die Welle	
unsure [ʌnˈʃʊə]	unsicher	
to **notice** [ˈnəʊtɪs]	bemerken	Ben is missing.
to **be missing** [bi ˈmɪsɪŋ]	fehlen	Let's look for him.
to **look for** [ˈlʊk fɔː]	suchen (nach)	
no one [ˈnəʊ wʌn]	keiner, niemand	
while (*no pl*) [waɪl]	die Weile	I haven't seen him for a while.
cliff [klɪf]	die Klippe, das Kliff	
surprised [səˈpraɪzd]	überrascht	
to **decide** [dɪˈsaɪd]	(sich) entscheiden; beschließen	I decided to go home.
lazy [ˈleɪzi]	faul, träge	

p. 180

10 to **put on** [ˌpʊt‿ˈɒn]	anziehen	I'll put on my new cap.
to **be right back** [biː ˌraɪt ˈbæk]	gleich zurück sein	I'll be right back.
see you [ˈsiː juː]	bis dann, bis bald	

Unregelmäßige Verben (*irregular verbs*)

Unregelmäßige Verben haben eine unregelmäßige Form für das *simple past* und auch für das *past participle* (Partizip Perfekt). Die Formen solltest du wie Vokabeln lernen. Du findest die Formen in der Liste der unregelmäßigen Verben auf Seite 334–335.

Infinitiv	***simple past***	***past participle***
be	was/were	been
have	had	had
hurt	hurt	hurt
fall	fell	fallen
teach	taught	taught

p. 190

2.1 **probably** [ˈprɒbəbli]	wahrscheinlich	Everyone has probably heard of Greta Thunberg.
few [fjuː]	wenige	
to **win** (*irr*) [wɪn]	gewinnen	win – won – won
hall [hɔːl]	die Halle; der Saal	
crowd [kraʊd]	die (Menschen)menge, die Zuschauermenge	There was a large crowd of people in front of the shop.
at first [ət ˈfɜːst]	anfangs, zuerst	
excited [ɪkˈsaɪtɪd]	aufgeregt	I'm so excited.
autograph [ˈɔːtəˌgrɑːf]	das Autogramm	
whole [həʊl]	ganz, gesamt	I ate the whole pizza.
to **answer** [ˈɑːnsə]	(be)antworten	answer ↔ ask
to **explain** [ɪkˈspleɪn]	erklären	Can you explain that again, please?

	to **ask questions** [ˌɑ:sk‿ˈkwestʃnz]	Fragen stellen	The reporters were asking questions.
	to **shout** [ʃaʊt]	schreien, rufen	
	screen [skri:n]	die Leinwand; der Bildschirm	Our TV has a big screen.
	sound system [ˈsaʊnd ˌsɪstəm]	die Stereoanlage, die Hi-Fi-Anlage	
	stage [steɪdʒ]	die Bühne	
	incredible [ɪnˈkredəbl]	unglaublich	
	feeling [ˈfi:lɪŋ]	das Gefühl	It's an incredible feeling to be on stage.
	to **cheer** [tʃɪə]	jubeln	The crowd is cheering loudly.
p. 191			
2.2	to **ring** (*irr*) [rɪŋ]	klingeln, läuten	ring – rang – rung My alarm clock rings at seven o'clock.
	puzzle [ˈpʌzl]	das Puzzle; das Rätsel	
p. 192			
7.1	**toothache** [ˈtu:θeɪk]	die Zahnschmerzen	
	stomach ache [ˈstʌmək ‿ˌeɪk]	die Magenschmerzen, die Bauchschmerzen	The woman has a stomach ache.
	broken [ˈbrəʊkən]	zerbrochen, kaputt; *hier*: gebrochen	He has a broken leg.
p. 193			
6	**village** [ˈvɪlɪdʒ]	das Dorf	Jim lives in a small village.
	summer camp [ˈsʌmə ˌkæmp]	das Ferienlager	
	harbour [ˈhɑ:bə]	der Hafen	You can see lots of ships and boats in a harbour.
	bay [beɪ]	die Bucht	There are so many beautiful bays on this island where you can swim in the sea.
	over [ˈəʊvə]	über	
	interested (in sth) [ˈɪntrəstɪd]	interessiert (an etw)	What are you interested in?
	exotic [ɪgˈzɒtɪk]	exotisch	
	outdoor(s) [ˌaʊtˈdɔ:]	draußen; im Freien; Outdoor-	I love being outdoors.
	that's why [ˈðæts waɪ]	deshalb; das ist der Grund, warum	That's why I often go for long bike rides.
p. 195			
10	**by the way** [ˌbaɪ ðə ˈweɪ]	übrigens	By the way, your English is really good.

DICTIONARY English-German

Hier findest du die Wörter, die in deinem Buch vorkommen.
- Die **fett gedruckten** Wörter solltest du dir merken.
- Wenn du den *Challenge*-Teil bearbeitest, solltest du dir auch die **grün gedruckten** Wörter merken.
- 1/16, 9 bedeutet: Dieses Wort kommt in *Theme* 1 auf Seite 16 in Aufgabe 9 vor.
- V bedeutet: Dieses Wort kommt in Band 5 (5. Klasse) vor.
- Folgende Abkürzungen werden noch verwendet:
  LL = Land & Leute CC = *Camden Chronicle* Op = *Optional – Writing Stories*

A

a [ə, eɪ] pro 2/CC
a/an [ə, ən] ein(e) V
A levels ['eɪ ˌlevlz] Abitur 1/37, 5.1
a lot (of) [ə 'lɒt] viel(e); sehr V
about [ə'baʊt] über V
about [ə'baʊt] ungefähr V
to be about [ˌbi‿ə'baʊt] handeln von Op/102, 1
What about ...? *(informal)* ['wɒt‿əˌbaʊt] Was ist mit ...?, Wie wäre es mit ...? V
above [ə'bʌv] oben 4/134, 17.1
abroad [ə'brɔːd] im/ins Ausland 1/34, 3.1
to go abroad [ˌgəʊ‿ə'brɔːd] ins Ausland gehen/reisen 1/16, 9
access *(no pl)* ['ækses] Zugang; Zugriff 1/23, 9
to accompany [ə'kʌmpni] begleiten 2/65, 10.1
stomach ache ['stʌmək ‿ˌeɪk] Magenschmerzen, Bauchschmerzen 6/192, 7.1
acrobat ['ækrəˌbæt] Akrobat/in 2/40, 2
across [ə'krɒs] über 2/69, 11
to act out [ˌækt‿'aʊt] nachspielen 1/16, 9
to get into action [ˌget‿ˌɪntʊ‿'ækʃn] aktiv werden, sich bewegen 3/76, 8
to take action [teɪk‿'ækʃn] handeln, etw unternehmen 5/150, 11
activity [æk'tɪvəti] Aktivität V
actress ['æktrəs] Schauspielerin 3/97, 12
to add [æd] hinzufügen 1/19, 16
address [ə'dres] Adresse 1/15, 8
adjective ['ædʒɪktɪv] Adjektiv 1/22, 4
adult ['ædʌlt] Erwachsene/r 2/65, 10.1
adventure [əd'ventʃə] Abenteuer, Erlebnis V
to **be afraid (of sth/sb)** [ˌbi‿ə'freɪd] (vor etw/jdm) Angst haben 5/150, 11
Africa ['æfrɪkə] Afrika 3/80, 1
after ['ɑːftə] nach V
after dark [ˌɑːftə 'dɑːk] nach Einbruch der Dunkelheit 2/CC
after that [ˌɑːftə 'ðæt] anschließend, danach 2/43, 9
afternoon [ˌɑːftə'nuːn] Nachmittag V
in the afternoon [ɪn ði‿ˌɑːftə'nuːn] am Nachmittag, nachmittags V
this afternoon [ˌðɪs‿ˌɑːftə'nuːn] heute Nachmittag V
afterwards ['ɑːftəwədz] danach, anschließend; später V
again [ə'gen] wieder, noch (ein)mal 1/10, 1
against [ə'genst] gegen 5/148, 8
age [eɪdʒ] Alter 6/176, 6
aged [eɪdʒd] im Alter (von) 6/194, 6.1
travel agency ['trævl‿ˌeɪdʒnsi] Reisebüro 6/181, 12
(three years) ago [ə'gəʊ] vor (drei Jahren) 2/49, 2
to **agree** [ə'griː] zustimmen; übereinstimmen 5/142, 10
to go ahead [ˌgəʊ‿ə'hed] loslegen 3/74, 3
aim [eɪm] Ziel, Absicht 4/134, 17.1
airport ['eəˌpɔːt] Flughafen 2/40, 2
alarm clock [ə'lɑːm ˌklɒk] Wecker 5/144, 1
all [ɔːl] alle(s) V
all [ɔːl] ganz, völlig 1/12, 3
all day [ˌɔːl 'deɪ] den ganzen Tag 1/36, 11
all over the world [ˌɔːl‿ˌəʊvə ðə 'wɜːld] auf der ganzen Welt 3/99, 1
all the best [ˌɔːl ðə 'best] alles Gute 5/164, 4.2
alley ['æli] Gasse 3/98, 15.1
allowed [ə'laʊd] erlaubt 5/164, 4.2
to **be allowed to do sth** [bi‿əˌlaʊd tə 'duː ˌsʌmθɪŋ] etw tun dürfen 5/163, 4
almost ['ɔːlməʊst] fast, beinahe 3/98, 15.1
alone [ə'ləʊn] allein 5/150, 11
along [ə'lɒŋ] entlang 1/17, 11
alphabetical [ˌælfə'betɪkl] alphabetisch 1/22, 4
already [ɔːl'redi] schon 1/17, 11
also ['ɔːlsəʊ] auch V
always ['ɔːlweɪz] immer V
am [æm] bin V
a.m. (= ante meridiem) [ˌeɪ'em, ˌænti mə'rɪdiəm] morgens, vormittags *(nur hinter Uhrzeit zwischen Mitternacht und 12 Uhr mittags)* V
amazing *(informal)* [ə'meɪzɪŋ] toll, unglaublich 2/40, 2
and [ænd] und V
angry ['æŋgri] verärgert; zornig; wütend 5/136, 1

animal ['ænɪml] Tier v
annoying [ə'nɔɪɪŋ] nervig, lästig 5/139, 4
another [ə'nʌðə] noch ein(e, r, s); ein anderer/anderes, eine andere 5/149, 10
answer ['ɑ:nsə] Antwort 1/19, 15
to **answer** ['ɑ:nsə] (be)antworten 6/190, 2.1
anthem ['ænθəm] Hymne 1/37, 5.1
any ['eni] irgendwelche, irgendein(e) 4/114, 2
not any [nɒt‿'eni] kein(e) 4/115, 3
not anymore [ˌnɒt eni'mɔ:] nicht mehr 5/150, 11
anyone ['eniˌwʌn] jede/r; (irgend)jemand 5/150, 11
not anyone [nɒt‿'eniwʌn] niemand 3/74, 3
anything ['eniˌθɪŋ] (irgend)(et)was 6/176, 6
Anything else? [ˌeniθɪŋ‿'els] Darf es noch etwas sein? v
anyway ['eniˌweɪ] sowieso, jedenfalls; trotzdem 6/180, 11
anywhere ['eniˌweə] überall(hin); irgendwo(hin) 1/16, 9
not anywhere [nɒt‿'eniˌweə] nirgendwo(hin) Op/102, 1
apartment [ə'pɑ:tmənt] Wohnung 1/19, 15
ape [eɪp] (Menschen)affe 3/99, 1
apple ['æpl] Apfel v
apricot ['eɪprɪˌkɒt] Aprikose v
April ['eɪprəl] April v
Aquarius [ə'kweəriəs] Wassermann *(Sternzeichen)* 3/76, 8
are [ɑ:] bist, sind, seid v
there are ['ðeər‿ə] da sind; es gibt v
area ['eəriə] Gebiet, Region 5/146, 5
to argue ['ɑ:gju] streiten 5/160, 4.1
Aries ['eəri:z] Widder *(Sternzeichen)* 3/96, 8.1
around [ə'raʊnd] herum, umher v
to turn around [ˌtɜ:n‿ə'raʊnd] (sich) umdrehen Op/102, 1
around the world [əˌraʊnd ðə 'wɜ:ld] weltweit, auf der ganzen Welt 3/90, 13
to **arrive** [ə'raɪv] ankommen v
art [ɑ:t] Kunst v
article ['ɑ:tɪkl] Artikel 5/150, 11
as [əz] als 3/79, 14
as [əz] während 2/46, 14; wie 2/47, 15
as … as [əz əz] (genau)so … wie … 4/117, 8
as soon as possible [əz‿ˌsu:n‿əz 'pɒsəbəl] so bald wie möglich 2/45, 11
Asia ['eɪʒə] Asien 2/52, 6
to **ask** [ɑ:sk] fragen; bitten v
to ask for sth ['ɑ:sk fə ˌsʌmθɪŋ] um etw bitten 1/25, 13
to **ask questions** [ˌɑ:sk‿'kwestʃnz] Fragen stellen 6/190, 2.1
to ask sb to do sth [ˌɑ:sk ˌsʌmbədi tə 'du: ˌsʌmθɪŋ] jdn bitten, etw zu tun 2/47, 15
assembly [ə'sembli] (Schüler)versammlung 1/25, 12
at [æt] auf, an, in, bei; um v
at a time [ət‿ə 'taɪm] auf einmal; je 1/23, 9
at first [ət 'fɜ:st] anfangs, zuerst 6/190, 2.1
at least [ət 'li:st] mindestens, wenigstens 4/114, 2
ate [eɪt] *Vergangenheitsform von „eat“*
Atlantic [ət'læntɪk] Atlantik; Atlantik- 1/12, 3
the Atlantic (Ocean) [ði‿ətˌlæntɪk(‿'əʊʃn)] Atlantischer Ozean 6/194, 6.1
to **attack** [ə'tæk] angreifen 5/149, 10
attraction [ə'trækʃn] Attraktion 2/65, 10.1
audio guide ['ɔ:diəʊ ˌgaɪd] Audioguide, Audioführer 2/47, 15
audio play ['ɔ:diəʊ ˌgaɪd] Hörstück, Hörspiel 3/87, 14
August ['ɔ:gəst] August v
aunt [ɑ:nt] Tante v
Australia [ɒ'streɪliə] Australien v
autograph ['ɔ:təˌgrɑ:f] Autogramm 6/190, 2.1
autumn ['ɔ:təm] Herbst Op/102, 1
away [ə'weɪ] weg v
awful ['ɔ:fl] furchtbar, schrecklich 6/CC
aww [ɔ:] ach, ah, oh 1/12, 3

B

back [bæk] Rücken; Rückseite v
back [bæk] zurück 1/10, 1
in the back [ˌɪn ðə 'bæk] hinten 1/36, 11
back door [ˌbæk 'dɔ:] Hintertür Op/102, 1
backflip ['bækflɪp] Rückwärtssalto, Rolle rückwärts 6/174, 1
backstage [ˌbæk'steɪdʒ] hinter der Bühne; backstage 6/190, 2.1
bad [bæd] schlecht v; schlimm, stark 6/167, 2
bag [bæg] Tasche 5/164, 4.2
baker ['beɪkə] Bäcker/in 3/97, 12
balcony ['bælkəni] Balkon v
balloon [bə'lu:n] (Luft)ballon v
banana [bə'nɑ:nə] Banane 2/54, 11
bar chart ['bɑ: ˌtʃɑ:t] Säulendiagramm, Balkendiagramm 1/34, 3.1
barbecue ['bɑ:bɪˌkju:] Grillparty; Grill v
to **have a barbecue** [ˌhæv‿ə 'bɑ:bɪˌkju:] grillen, eine Grillparty feiern v
to **bark** [bɑ:k] bellen v
basket ['bɑ:skɪt] Korb v
bathroom ['bɑ:θˌru:m] Bad(ezimmer) v
bay [beɪ] Bucht 6/193, 6

to be about [ˌbiˌəˈbaʊt] handeln von Op/102, 1
to **be going to do sth** [ˌbi: ˌgəʊɪŋ tə ˈdu: ˌsʌmθɪŋ] etw tun werden 4/110, 5
to **be good at sth** [ˌbi: ˈgʊdˌət ˌsʌmθɪŋ] gut in etw sein v
to **be** *(irr)* [bi:] sein v
to be like sth [ˌbi: ˌlaɪk ˈsʌmθɪŋ] wie etw sein 3/79, 14
Be right back! [bi: ˌraɪt ˈbæk] Bin gleich zurück! 2/45, 11
to be welcome to do sth [bi: ˌwelkəm tə ˈdu: ˌsʌmθɪŋ] etw gern tun können 2/65, 10.1
beach [bi:tʃ] Strand 1/10, 1
bean [bi:n] Bohne v
jelly bean [ˈdʒeli bi:n] *(bohnenförmiges) Geleebonbon* 4/117, 8
to **beat** *(irr)* [bi:t] schlagen; besiegen 5/151, 12
beautiful [ˈbju:təfl] schön 1/12, 3
because [bɪˈkɒz] weil v
to **become** *(irr)* [bɪˈkʌm] werden 4/134, 17.1
bed [bed] Bett v
bed sheet [ˈbed ʃi:t] Bettlaken 4/134, 17.1
bedroom [ˈbedru:m] Schlafzimmer v
beef [bi:f] Rindfleisch 5/162, 9
been [bi:n] *siehe „be“*
before [bɪˈfɔ:] vor v; bevor 5/138, 2
to **begin** *(irr)* [bɪˈgɪn] anfangen; beginnen 2/68, 6.2
beginning [bɪˈgɪnɪŋ] Anfang 4/113, 11
behaviour *(no pl)* [bɪˈheɪvjə] Verhalten, Benehmen 5/164, 4.2
behind [bɪˈhaɪnd] hinter v
to **believe (in)** [bɪˈli:v] glauben (an) 3/72, 1
to **belong to sb/sth** [biˈlɒŋ tə ˌsʌmbədi/ˌsʌmθɪŋ] jdm/zu etw gehören 5/165, 8.1
below [bɪˈləʊ] unten; unter(halb) 2/64, 4.1
bench [bentʃ] Bank 2/61, 1.1

best [best] beste(r, s) v
best [best] am meisten/liebsten/besten 4/120, 17
all the best [ˌɔ:l ðə ˈbest] alles Gute 5/164, 4.2
best wishes [ˌbest ˈwɪʃɪz] viele Grüße v
better [ˈbetə] besser; lieber, mehr 3/80, 1
better [ˈbetə] gesund 6/171, 9
between [bɪˈtwi:n] zwischen 6/176, 6
big [bɪg] groß v
biggest [ˈbɪgəst] größte(r, s) v
bike [baɪk] (Fahr)rad v
bin [bɪn] Mülleimer, Mülltonne v
biology *(no pl)* [baɪˈɒlədʒi] Biologie 1/20, 2
birthday [ˈbɜ:θdeɪ] Geburtstag v
birthplace [ˈbɜ:θˌpleɪs] Geburtsort 6/176, 6
a bit [ə ˈbɪt] ein bisschen 6/178, 9
to **bite** *(irr)* [baɪt] beißen v
black [blæk] schwarz v
blazer [ˈbleɪzə] Blazer, Jacke 1/21, 3
blessing [ˈblesɪŋ] Segen, Segensspruch 4/113, 11
blew [blu:] *Vergangenheitsform von „blow“*
blindfold [ˈblaɪnˌfəʊld] Augenbinde 4/134, 17.1
to blow *(irr)* [bləʊ] blasen, wehen Op/102, 1
to **blow out (a candle)** [ˌbləʊˌˈaʊt] (eine Kerze) ausblasen v
blue [blu:] blau v
board game [ˈbɔ:d geɪm] Brettspiel v
boarding school [ˈbɔ:dɪŋ ˌsku:l] Internat 1/20, LL
boat [bəʊt] Boot; Schiff 2/40, 2
rowing boat [ˈrəʊɪŋ bəʊt] Ruderboot 3/99, 1
body [ˈbɒdi] Körper v
upper body [ˌʌpə ˈbɒdi] Oberkörper 6/178, 9

bodyboarding *(no pl)* [ˈbɒdiˌbɔ:dɪŋ] Bodyboarden 6/176, 6
to bodyboard [ˈbɒdi ˌbɔ:d] Bodyboard fahren, bodyboarden 6/178, 9
boiling [ˈbɔɪlɪŋ] kochend 4/116, 6
book [bʊk] Buch v
bookcase [ˈbʊkˌkeɪs] Bücherregal, Bücherschrank v
boot [bu:t] Stiefel 5/146, 6
bored [bɔ:d] gelangweilt 1/17, 11
boring [ˈbɔ:rɪŋ] langweilig v
to borrow [ˈbɒrəʊ] leihen 1/23, 9
boss [bɒs] Chef/in 3/91, 14.1
both [bəʊθ] beide(s) v
bottle [ˈbɒtl] Flasche 4/114, 2
at the bottom (of) [æt ðə ˈbɒtəm] unten, am unteren Ende (von) 2/48, 1
bought [bɔ:t] *Vergangenheitsform von „buy“*
bowl [bəʊl] Schüssel 4/116, 6
Boxing Day [ˈbɒksɪŋ deɪ] zweiter Weihnachtsfeiertag 4/130, 2.2
boy [bɔɪ] Junge v
boyfriend [ˈbɔɪˌfrend] (fester) Freund 5/141, 9
branch [brɑ:ntʃ] Zweig; Ast Op/102, 1
brave [breɪv] mutig, unerschrocken 3/80, 1
bread *(no pl)* [bred] Brot v
bread roll [ˈbred rəʊl] Brötchen v
break [breɪk] Pause v
to **break** *(irr)* [breɪk] (zer)brechen 5/144, 1
breakfast [ˈbrekfəst] Frühstück v
to breathe [bri:ð] atmen Op/102, 1
breathtaking [ˈbreθˌteɪkɪŋ] atemberaubend 6/194, 6.1
bricklayer [ˈbrɪkˌleɪə] Maurer/in 3/77, 10
bridge [brɪdʒ] Brücke 2/40, 2
bright [braɪt] hell; leuchtend Op/104, 2
brilliant [ˈbrɪljənt] toll, hervorragend, klasse 4/110, 5
to **bring** *(irr)* [brɪŋ] (mit)bringen 3/82, 4

Britain ['brɪtn] Großbritannien 6/176, 6
British ['brɪtɪʃ] britische(r, s) 2/65, 10.1
brochure ['brəʊʃə] Broschüre 6/176, 6
broken ['brəʊkən] zerbrochen, kaputt; gebrochen 6/192, 7.1
brother ['brʌðə] Bruder V
half brother ['hɑ:f ˌbrʌðə] Halbbruder 1/10, 1
brought [brɔ:t] *Vergangenheitsform von „bring"*
brown [braʊn] braun V
bruise [bru:z] Bluterguss, blauer Fleck Op/102, 1
to **brush** [brʌʃ] bürsten; putzen V
budgie (= **budgerigar**) ['bʌdʒi, 'bʌdʒəriˌgɑ:] Wellensittich V
to **build** *(irr)* [bɪld] bauen 3/77, 10
building ['bɪldɪŋ] Gebäude 4/110, 5
bully ['bʊli] *Person, die andere mobbt* 5/150, 11
to bully ['bʊli] mobben 5/151, 12
bullying *(no pl)* ['bʊliɪŋ] Mobbing 5/149, 10
to bury ['beri] begraben 2/64, 4.1
bush [bʊʃ] Busch, Gebüsch Op/102, 1
busy ['bɪzi] beschäftigt; belebt, verkehrsreich V
but [bʌt] aber V
but [bʌt] außer 6/178, 9
butterfly ['bʌtəˌflaɪ] Schmetterling V
to **buy** *(irr)* [baɪ] kaufen V
buzz group ['bʌz gru:p] *Form der Gruppenarbeit* 2/49, 2
by [baɪ] bei, in der Nähe; mit, durch 1/17, 11; von 3/99, 1; indem 4/134, 17.1
by (bus) [baɪ] mit (dem Bus) 1/19, 15
by (eight o'clock) [baɪ] (spätestens) bis (acht Uhr) 5/138, 2
by the way [ˌbaɪ ðə 'weɪ] übrigens 6/195, 10
bye *(informal)* [baɪ] tschüss V
bye for now ['baɪ fə naʊ] bis bald 1/15, 8

C

cab [kæb] Taxi 2/44, LL
cage [keɪdʒ] Käfig V
cake [keɪk] Kuchen V
calculator ['kælkjʊˌleɪtə] (Taschen)rechner V
calendar ['kælɪndə] Kalender V
(phone) call ['fəʊn kɔ:l] (Telefon)anruf V
to **call** [kɔ:l] (an)rufen; nennen 4/110, 5
to **call sb names** [ˌkɔ:l sʌmbədi 'neɪmz] jdn beschimpfen 5/149, 10
to **be called** [bi: 'kɔ:ld] heißen V
came [keɪm] *Vergangenheitsform von „come"*
camera ['kæmrə] Kamera, Fotoapparat V
summer camp ['sʌmə ˌkæmp] Ferienlager 6/193, 6
camper ['kæmpc] Camper/in 6/178, 9
campfire ['kæmpˌfaɪə] Lagerfeuer 1/15, 7
campsite ['kæmpˌsaɪt] Campingplatz, Zeltplatz 1/14, 6
can [kæn] können V
can't (= **cannot**) [kɑ:nt, 'kænɒt] nicht können V
Cancer ['kænsə] Krebs *(Sternzeichen)* 3/96, 8.1
candle ['kændl] Kerze V
cap [kæp] Mütze, Kappe 2/51, 5
Capricorn ['kæprɪˌkɔ:n] Steinbock *(Sternzeichen)* 3/96, 8.1
car [kɑ:] Auto V
card [kɑ:d] Karte V
get well card [get 'wel kɑ:d] Genesungskarte 6/171, 11
to take care [teɪk 'keə] aufpassen 2/44, 10
to **take care of** [ˌteɪk‿'keər‿əv] sich kümmern um 3/77, 10
careful ['keəfl] vorsichtig; sorgfältig 3/82, 4

caretaker ['keəˌteɪkə] Hausmeister/in Op/102, 1
carnival ['kɑ:nɪvl] Karneval 4/131, 3.2
carrot ['kærət] Möhre, Karotte, Mohrrübe 2/52, 7
to carry ['kæri] tragen 2/44, 10
phone case ['fəʊn keɪs] Handyhülle 4/119, 12
castle ['kɑ:sl] Burg; Schloss 1/10, 1
cat [kæt] Katze V
to **catch** *(irr)* [kætʃ] fangen V
to catch a train [ˌkætʃ‿ə 'treɪn] einen Zug nehmen 2/40, 2
caught [kɔ:t] *Vergangenheitsform von „catch"*
celebration [ˌselə'breɪʃn] Feier, Fest 4/106, 1
to **celebrate** ['seləˌbreɪt] feiern V
central ['sentrəl] zentral, Zentral-, Mittel-; Haupt- 1/21, 3
centre ['sentə] Zentrum, Center V
shopping centre ['ʃɒpɪŋ ˌsentə] Einkaufszentrum V
century ['sentʃəri] Jahrhundert 6/194, 6.1
chair [tʃeə] Stuhl V
change [tʃeɪndʒ] (Ver)änderung; Wechselgeld V
to change [tʃeɪndʒ] (sich) (ver)ändern 2/68, 6.2
Changing of the Guard [ˌtʃeɪndʒɪŋ‿əv ðə 'gɑ:d] Wachablösung 2/40, 2
channel ['tʃænl] Kanal, Programm 6/173, 14
the Channel Islands [ðə 'tʃænl‿ˌaɪləndz] Kanalinseln 3/100, 4.1
character ['kærɪktə] Charakter; Figur 3/87, 14
to **charge** [tʃɑ:dʒ] (auf)laden 2/51, 5
charity ['tʃærəti] Wohltätigkeitsorganisation 2/CC
to **chase** [tʃeɪs] verfolgen, jagen V

to **chat** [tʃæt] chatten, sich unterhalten v
cheap [tʃi:p] billig, preiswert 4/117, 8
to check [tʃek] überprüfen, kontrollieren 1/19, 16
checklist ['tʃek,lɪst] Checkliste, Kontrollliste 4/133, 4.1
to **cheer** [tʃɪə] jubeln 6/190, 2.1
to **cheer sb up** [tʃɪə ˌsʌmbədi‿'ʌp] jdn aufmuntern 6/168, 3
Cheer up! [tʃɪər‿'ʌp] Lass (doch) den Kopf nicht hängen!, Kopf hoch! 6/168, 3
cheese *(no pl)* [tʃi:z] Käse v
chef [ʃef] Koch/Köchin 3/97, 12
cherry ['tʃeri] Kirsche v
cherry tomato *(pl -es)* [ˌtʃeri tə'ma:təʊ, ˌtʃeri tə'ma:təʊz] Kirschtomate 4/116, 6
chess *(no pl)* [tʃes] Schach(spiel) 1/21, 3
to **chew** [tʃu:] kauen 5/144, 1
chewing gum *(no pl)* ['tʃu:ɪŋ ˌgʌm] Kaugummi 5/144, 1
chicken ['tʃɪkɪn] Huhn; Hähnchen v
child *(pl* **children***)* [tʃaɪld, 'tʃɪldrən] Kind v
chime [tʃaɪm] Geläute, Glockenschlag 2/40, 2
chimney ['tʃɪmni] Kamin; Schornstein 4/130, 2.2
chimpanzee [ˌtʃɪmpæn'zi:] Schimpanse 3/80, 1
chimp (*informal*) [tʃɪmp] Schimpanse 3/80, 1
Chinese [ˌtʃaɪ'ni:z] Chinesisch; chinesisch 4/106, 1
chocolate *(no pl)* ['tʃɒklət] Schokolade v
to choose *(irr)* [tʃu:z] auswählen 1/18, 14
Christmas ['krɪsməs] Weihnachten 4/106, 1
Christmas Day [ˌkrɪsməs 'deɪ] erster Weihnachtsfeiertag 4/130, 2.2
Christmas Eve [ˌkrɪsməs‿'i:v] Heiligabend 4/130, 2.2
chunk [tʃʌŋk] Stück; Brocken; Phrase 2/46, 13
church [tʃɜ:tʃ] Kirche 4/108, 3
cinema ['sɪnəmə] Kino v
circle ['sɜ:kl] Kreis 4/134, 17.1
double circle [ˌdʌbl 'sɜ:kl] Doppelkreis 4/108, 3
to circle sth ['sɜ:kl ˌsʌmθɪŋ] um etw einen Kringel machen, etw umkringeln 3/84, 7
city ['sɪti] (Groß)stadt v
class [kla:s] (Schul)klasse v
class [kla:s] Kurs 1/21, 3
classmate ['kla:s,meɪt] Klassenkamerad/in, Mitschüler/in 1/20, 2
classroom ['kla:s,ru:m] Klassenzimmer v
to **clean** [kli:n] sauber machen, reinigen, putzen v
clean [kli:n] sauber 5/146, 5
clear [klɪə] klar, verständlich, eindeutig 3/101, 12.1
clever ['klevə] klug, gescheit, schlau 2/53, 8
cliff [klɪf] Klippe, Kliff 6/178, 9
clifftop ['klɪf,tɒp] Klippenrand, Felsspitze 6/193, 6
alarm clock [ə'la:m ˌklɒk] Wecker 5/144, 1
clock [klɒk] Uhr 2/40, 2
to **close** [kləʊz] schließen, zumachen 1/38, 9.1
closed [kləʊzd] geschlossen, zu 2/CC
clothes *(only pl)* [kləʊðz] Kleider, Kleidung 4/108, 3
cloud [klaʊd] Wolke 1/15, 8
cloudy ['klaʊdi] bewölkt, bedeckt 1/12, 3
club [klʌb] Klub, Verein; AG v
youth club ['ju:θ ˌklʌb] Jugendzentrum 5/138, 2
coast [kəʊst] Küste 1/12, 3
coastline ['kəʊst,laɪn] Küste(nlinie) 6/194, 6.1
coffee ['kɒfi] Kaffee 4/115, 3
coin [kɔɪn] Münze, Geldstück 4/113, 11
cold [kəʊld] Kälte; Erkältung, Schnupfen 6/167, 2
cold [kəʊld] kalt 1/10, 1
to **have a cold** [ˌhæv‿ə 'kəʊld] eine Erkältung haben, erkältet sein 6/167, 2
colleague ['kɒli:g] Kollege/Kollegin, Mitarbeiter/in 2/68, 6.1
to **collect** [kə'lekt] sammeln v
colour ['kʌlə] Farbe v
colourful ['kʌləfl] farbenfroh, farbenprächtig 4/135, 17.2
to **come** *(irr)* [kʌm] kommen v
to **come in** [ˌkʌm‿'ɪn] hereinkommen v
Come on! [ˌkʌm‿'ɒn] Auf geht's!, Na los! 6/178, 9
to come to sb's mind [ˌkʌm tə ˌsʌmbədiz 'maɪnd] jdm einfallen 2/40, 1
to come up [ˌkʌm‿'ʌp] bevorstehen, kommen 4/110, 5
comfortable ['kʌmftəbl] bequem 4/133, 8.1
comment ['kɒment] Kommentar, Bemerkung 5/150, 11
comparative (form) [kəm'pærətɪv] Komparativ 4/119, 13
to compare [kəm'peə] vergleichen 1/20, 1
comparison [kəm'pærɪsn] Vergleich 4/119, 14
to **complain** [kəm'pleɪn] klagen, sich beschweren 3/99, 1
to complete [kəm'pli:t] vervollständigen 1/14, 6
complete [kəm'pli:t] vollständig, komplett 2/67, 2

completely [kəm'pli:tli] völlig, ganz 3/98, 15.1
comprehensive school [ˌkɒmprɪ'hensɪv ˌsku:l] Gesamtschule 1/20, LL
to **concentrate** ['kɒnsnˌtreɪt] sich konzentrieren 5/160, 4.1
concert ['kɒnsət] Konzert 6/166, 1
to connect [kə'nekt] verbinden Op/105, 4
construction [kən'strʌkʃn] Bau, Gebäude 2/66, 14.1
to contact sb ['kɒntækt ˌsʌmbədi] jdn kontaktieren, sich mit jdm in Verbindung setzen 5/151, 12
contest ['kɒntest] Wettbewerb 6/190, 2.1
to continue [kən'tɪnju:] weitergehen 4/134, 17.1
to convince [kən'vɪns] überzeugen 5/160, 4.1
to **cook** [kʊk] kochen v
to **do the cooking** [ˌdu: ðə 'kʊkɪŋ] kochen v
to copy ['kɒpi] abschreiben 1/22, 5
corner ['kɔ:nə] Ecke 1/19, 16
Cornish ['kɔ:nɪʃ] kornisch, aus Cornwall 6/176, 6
to correct [kə'rekt] korrigieren 1/12, 3
correct [kə'rekt] richtig, korrekt 5/144, 1
costume ['kɒstju:m] Tracht, Kostüm 4/108, 2
could [kʊd] könnte(st, n, t) v
could [kʊd] *Vergangenheitsform von „can“*
counsellor ['kaʊnslə] Betreuer/in 5/150, 11
country ['kʌntri] Land 4/135, 17.2
course [kɔ:s] Kurs v
court [kɔ:t] Platz, Court 1/21, 3
cousin ['kʌzn] Cousin/e v
to cover ['kʌvə] bedecken 2/66, 14.1
cow [kaʊ] Kuh v
cracker ['krækə] Knallbonbon 4/109, LL
crazy ['kreɪzi] verrückt 1/20, 2
to creak [kri:k] knarren, quietschen, knirschen Op/102, 1
sour cream [ˌsaʊə 'kri:m] Sauerrahm, saure Sahne 4/113, 11
cream *(no pl)* [kri:m] Sahne v
cream *(no pl)* [kri:m] Creme 6/184, 7.2
to create [kri'eɪt] erstellen; entwerfen 3/78, 11
crew [kru:] Besatzung, Crew 3/100, 4.1
criminal ['krɪmɪnl] Verbrecher/in 3/77, 10
crisps *(only pl) (BE)* [krɪsps] Chips 4/114, 2
to **cross** [krɒs] überqueren 2/50, 3
crossword ['krɒsˌwɜ:d] Kreuzworträtsel 2/46, 14
crowd [kraʊd] (Menschen)menge, Zuschauermenge 6/190, 2.1
crown [kraʊn] Krone 4/130, 2.2
Crown Jewels *(only pl)* [ˌkraʊn 'dʒu:əlz] Kronjuwelen 2/42, 6
to **cry** *(irr)* [kraɪ] weinen; schreien 5/150, 11
cucumber ['kju:ˌkʌmbə] (Salat)gurke 4/114, 2
cup [kʌp] Tasse v
curry ['kʌri] Curry(gericht) 4/135, 17.2
to **cut** *(irr)* [kʌt] schneiden 3/77, 10
cute [kju:t] süß, niedlich v
to **cycle** ['saɪkl] Rad fahren 6/166, 1
cycling *(no pl)* ['saɪklɪŋ] Radfahren, Radeln 6/189, 12

D

dad *(informal)* [dæd] Papa, Vati v
daily ['deɪli] täglich 2/65, 10.1
damn *(informal)* [dæm] verdammt 2/49, 2
dance [dɑ:ns] Tanz v
to **dance** [dɑ:ns] tanzen v
dancing *(no pl)* ['dɑ:nsɪŋ] Tanzen v
danger ['deɪndʒə] Gefahr 3/100, 4.1
dangerous ['deɪndʒərəs] gefährlich 2/53, 8
dark *(no pl)* [dɑ:k] Dunkelheit 6/177, 8
after dark [ˌɑ:ftə 'dɑ:k] nach Einbruch der Dunkelheit 2/CC
dark [dɑ:k] dunkel 1/21, 3
date [deɪt] Datum v
daughter ['dɔ:tə] Tochter v
day [deɪ] Tag v
day out [deɪ‿'aʊt] Ausflug 2/54, 11
all day [ˌɔ:l 'deɪ] den ganzen Tag 1/36, 11
one day ['wʌn deɪ] eines Tages 5/150, 11
the next day [ðə ˌnekst‿'deɪ] am nächsten Tag v
dead [ded] tot; leer 2/49, 2
dear [dɪə] liebe(r) *(Anrede)* v
Oh dear! [əʊ 'dɪə] Du meine Güte! 6/170, 7
December [dɪ'sembə] Dezember v
to **decide** [dɪ'saɪd] (sich) entscheiden; beschließen 6/178, 9
to **decorate** ['dekəreɪt] schmücken; dekorieren v
decoration [ˌdekə'reɪʃn] Dekoration, Schmuck v
definitely ['defnətli] eindeutig, definitiv 4/117, 8
degree [dɪ'gri:] Grad 1/34, 4.1
delicious [dɪ'lɪʃəs] köstlich, lecker 4/113, 11
department store [dɪ'pɑ:tmənt ˌstɔ:] Kaufhaus 2/64, 4.1
deputy head ['depjʊti ˌhed] stellvertretende/r Schulleiter/in, Konrektor/in 5/144, 1
to describe [dɪ'skraɪb] beschreiben 1/17, 11
description [dɪ'skrɪpʃn] Beschreibung 6/177, 8
design [dɪ'zaɪn] Entwurf; Design 5/148, 9

to **design** [dɪ'zaɪn] entwerfen 3/77, 10
desk [desk] Schreibtisch v
detail ['di:teɪl] Detail, Einzelheit 2/65, 10.1
detective [dɪ'tektɪv] (Privat)detektiv/in 1/13, 5
dialogue ['daɪəlɒg] Gespräch, Dialog 1/22, 6
diary ['daɪəri] Tagebuch 1/17, 11
dictionary ['dɪkʃənri] Wörterbuch v
did [dɪd] *Vergangenheitsform von „do“*
difference ['dɪfrəns] Unterschied 5/165, 8.1
different ['dɪfrənt] anders, andere(r, s); verschieden, unterschiedlich 4/110, 5
difficult ['dɪfɪklt] schwierig, schwer v
dinner ['dɪnə] Abendessen; Mittagessen 5/140, 6
dinosaur ['daɪnəˌsɔ:] Dinosaurier 2/40, 2
direct speech [dɪˌrekt 'spi:tʃ] direkte Rede 2/68, 6.2
direction [dɪ'rekʃn] Richtung 3/98, 15.1
to give directions [ˌgɪv dɪ'rekʃnz] den Weg beschreiben 2/51, 4
directions *(only pl)* [dɪ'rekʃnz] Wegbeschreibung 2/49, 2
director [də'rektə] Direktor/in, Leiter/in 2/68, 6.1
dirty ['dɜ:ti] dreckig, schmutzig v
to discover [dɪ'skʌvə] entdecken 2/65, 10.1
to discuss [dɪ'skʌs] besprechen; diskutieren 5/142, 10
discussion [dɪ'skʌʃn] Diskussion, Besprechung 5/165, 8.1
dishwasher ['dɪʃˌwɒʃə] Geschirrspülmaschine v
firework display ['faɪəˌwɜ:k dɪˌspleɪ] Feuerwerk 4/110, 5
divorced [dɪ'vɔ:st] geschieden v
Diwali [dɪ'wɑ:li] *hinduistisches Lichterfest* 4/110, 5
to **do** *(irr)* [du:] machen, tun v
to do well [du: 'wel] gut abschneiden, erfolgreich sein 5/159, 11.1
doctor ['dɒktə] Arzt/Ärztin 6/168, 3
dog [dɒg] Hund v
to **walk the dog** [ˌwɔ:k ðə 'dɒg] den Hund ausführen v
dolphin ['dɒlfɪn] Delfin 1/14, 6
done [dʌn] gemacht; fertig, erledigt 6/169, 5; *siehe „do“*
door [dɔ:] Tür v
back door [ˌbæk 'dɔ:] Hintertür Op/102, 1
dos and don’ts [ˌdu:z‿ən 'dəʊnts] was man tun und was man nicht tun sollte 5/136, 1
double circle [ˌdʌbl 'sɜ:kl] Doppelkreis 1/16, 9
double-decker [ˌdʌbl 'dekə] Doppeldecker(bus) 2/44, LL
doughnut ['dəʊˌnʌt] Donut, Doughnut *(süßes Gebäck)* 4/113, 11
down [daʊn] (nach) unten; hinunter, hinab 4/130, 2.2
drama ['drɑ:mə] Theater 1/22, 6
dramatic [drə'mætɪk] dramatisch 3/85, 8
drank [dræŋk] *Vergangenheitsform von „drink“*
to **draw** *(irr)* [drɔ:] zeichnen v
dream [dri:m] Traum v
dress [dres] Kleid 5/146, 6
dressing ['dresɪŋ] Dressing, Salatsoße 4/116, 6
drew [dru:] *Vergangenheitsform von „draw“*
drink [drɪŋk] Getränk v
to **drink** *(irr)* [drɪŋk] trinken v
to **drive** *(irr)* [draɪv] fahren 3/77, 10
driver ['draɪvə] Fahrer/in 3/77, 10
to drop [drɒp] fallen lassen Op/102, 1
drummer ['drʌmə] Trommler/in; Schlagzeuger/in 1/16, 9
drunk [drʌŋk] *siehe „drink“*
dry [draɪ] trocken 1/36, 11
during ['djʊərɪŋ] während 4/108, 2

E

each [i:tʃ] jede(r, s) v
each other [ˌi:tʃ‿'ʌðə] einander 1/24, 10
ear [ɪə] Ohr v
early ['ɜ:li] früh, zeitig v
to **earn** [ɜ:n] verdienen 5/160, 4.1
earthquake ['ɜ:θˌkweɪk] Erdbeben 2/40, 2
Easter ['i:stə] Ostern, Osterfest 4/106, 1
easy ['i:zi] einfach; leicht v
to **eat** *(irr)* [i:t] essen v
eaten ['i:tn] *siehe „eat“*
edge [edʒ] Rand; Ufer 6/178, 9
to keep clear of the edges [ki:p ˌklɪər‿əv ði‿'edʒɪz] sich von den Rändern fernhalten 2/44, 10
to edit ['edɪt] bearbeiten, redigieren Op/105, 4
egg [eg] Ei v
Eid [i:d] *islamisches Fest zum Abschluss des Fastenmonats Ramadan* 4/106, 1
electric [ɪ'lektrɪk] elektrisch 3/79, 16
elephant ['elɪfənt] Elefant v
else [els] sonst, anders 1/36, 11
something else [ˌsʌmθɪŋ‿'els] (noch) etwas anderes 6/168, 3
what else [wɒt‿'els] was noch, was sonst 1/10, 1
embarrassed [ɪm'bærəst] verlegen, peinlich berührt 5/150, 11
to **empty** ['empti] ausräumen, (ent)leeren v
empty ['empti] leer 3/98, 15.1
end [end] Ende 1/17, 11
to **end** [end] enden v
ending ['endɪŋ] Ende, Schluss 2/42, 6
English ['ɪŋglɪʃ] Englisch; englisch v

in English [ˌɪn_ˈɪŋglɪʃ] auf Englisch v
English-speaking [ˈɪŋglɪʃ_ˌspiːkɪŋ] englischsprachig 4/113, 12
to **enjoy** [ɪnˈdʒɔɪ] mögen; genießen 2/40, 2
enough [ɪˈnʌf] genügend, ausreichend, genug 5/140, 7
sure enough [ˌʃɔ_ɪˈnʌf] tatsächlich 6/178, 9
to enter [ˈentə] betreten 5/146, 5
entire [ɪnˈtaɪə] gesamt, ganz 2/66, 14.1
entry [ˈentri] Eintrag 1/36, 11
envelope [ˈenvələʊp] Briefumschlag, Kuvert 4/108, 2
environmentally friendly [ɪnˌvaɪrənˌmentli ˈfrendli] umweltfreundlich 2/66, 14.1
especially [ɪˈspeʃli] besonders v
eTwinning [ˈiːˌtwɪnɪŋ] *Partnerschaftsprogramm für Schulen* 1/37, 5.1
Europe [ˈjʊərəp] Europa 2/64, 4.1
even [ˈiːvn] selbst; sogar 2/40, 2
even [ˈiːvn] noch 4/119, 12
not even [ˌnɒt_ˈiːvn] (noch) nicht (ein)mal 6/178, 9
evening [ˈiːvnɪŋ] Abend 4/108, 2
in the evening [ˌɪn ðiˈ_iːvnɪŋ] am Abend, abends v
ever [ˈevə] jemals 6/174, 1
every [ˈevri] jede(r, s) v
everyone [ˈevriwʌn] jede(r); alle v
everything [ˈevriθɪŋ] alles 2/64, 4.1
exactly [ɪgˈzæktli] genau 4/110, 5
example [ɪgˈzɑːmpl] Beispiel 1/20, 2
for example [fər_ɪgˈzɑːmpl] zum Beispiel 1/21, 3
excited [ɪkˈsaɪtɪd] aufgeregt 6/190, 2.1
exciting [ɪkˈsaɪtɪŋ] aufregend; spannend v
exclusive [ɪkˈskluːsɪv] exklusiv 2/CC
Excuse me! [ɪkˈskjuːz mi] Entschuldigen Sie bitte!, Entschuldigung! 2/49, 2
exercise book [ˈeksəsaɪz ˌbʊk] Heft v
exhibit [ɪgˈzɪbɪt] Ausstellungsstück; Ausstellung 2/CC
to exit [ˈeksɪt] verlassen 5/146, 5
exotic [ɪgˈzɒtɪk] exotisch 6/193, 6
expensive [ɪkˈspensɪv] teuer 5/138, 2
to experience [ɪkˈspɪəriəns] erleben, erfahren 3/98, 15.1
to **explain** [ɪkˈspleɪn] erklären 6/190, 2.1
to **explore** [ɪkˈsplɔː] erforschen, erkunden 6/176, 6
to express [ɪkˈspres] ausdrücken 5/143, 13
eye [aɪ] Auge v

F

face [feɪs] Gesicht v
face to face [ˌfeɪs tə ˈfeɪs] einander gegenüber, Auge in Auge 2/65, 10.1
in the face of [ˌɪn ðə ˈfeɪs_əv] angesichts 3/100, 4.1
fact [fækt] Fakt 2/47, 15
fact file [ˈfækt ˌfaɪl] Steckbrief 2/66, 14.1
fairy bread *(no pl)* [ˈfeəri bred] *Brot mit bunten Zuckerstreuseln* 4/135, 17.2
to **fall** *(irr)* [fɔːl] fallen 6/170, 7
family [ˈfæmli] Familie v
famous [ˈfeɪməs] berühmt 1/10, 1
fancy [ˈfænsi] schick, ausgefallen 4/119, 12
fantastic (informal) [fænˈtæstɪk] fantastisch, wunderbar v
fantasy [ˈfæntəsi] Fantasie; Fantasy 6/185, 14
far [fɑː] weit 3/78, 11
farm [fɑːm] Bauernhof v
Farne Islands [ˈfɑːn_ˌaɪləndz] Farne-Inseln 3/82, 4
fashion [ˈfæʃn] Mode 5/160, 4.1
fast [fɑːst] schnell v
fat [fæt] dick, fett 2/CC
father [ˈfɑːðə] Vater v
Father Christmas [ˌfɑːðə ˈkrɪsməs] Weihnachtsmann 4/130, 2.2
fault [fɔːlt] Schuld; Fehler 5/151, 12
favourite [ˈfeɪvrət] Lieblings- v
February [ˈfebruəri] Februar v
to **feed** *(irr)* [fiːd] füttern, zu Essen geben v
to **feel** *(irr)* [fiːl] (sich) fühlen v
to **feel like doing sth** [ˌfiːl_laɪk ˈduːɪŋ ˌsʌmθɪŋ] Lust haben, etw zu tun 2/69, 11
feeling [ˈfiːlɪŋ] Gefühl 6/190, 2.1
fell [fel] *Vergangenheitsform von „fall“*
felt [felt] *Vergangenheitsform von „feel“*
felt tip [ˈfelt_tɪp] Filzstift v
festival [ˈfestɪvl] Fest; Festival 4/106, 1
a few [ə ˈfjuː] einige, ein paar 4/114, 2
few [fjuː] wenige 6/190, 2.1
field [fiːld] Wiese, Weide, Feld 5/145, 3
fifth [fɪfθ] fünfte(r, s) v
to **fight** *(irr)* [faɪt] (be)kämpfen; streiten v
figure [ˈfɪgə] Gestalt; Persönlichkeit 2/65, 10.1
to fill in [ˌfɪl_ˈɪn] ausfüllen; einsetzen 3/81, 2
to filter [ˈfɪltə] filtern 1/23, 9
finally [ˈfaɪnli] schließlich, endlich; zum Schluss 3/101, 6
to **find** *(irr)* [faɪnd] finden v
to **find out** [ˌfaɪnd_ˈaʊt] herausfinden 2/40, 2
I'm fine. [aɪm ˈfaɪn] Es geht mir gut. 1/12, 3
to **finish** [ˈfɪnɪʃ] beenden, aufhören v
fire [faɪə] Feuer Op/104, 2
firework display [ˈfaɪəˌwɜːk dɪˌspleɪ] Feuerwerk 4/110, 5
fireworks *(only pl)* [ˈfaɪəˌwɜːks] Feuerwerk 4/108, 2
first [fɜːst] erste(r, s) v; zuerst, als Erstes 1/10, 1
at first [ət ˈfɜːst] anfangs, zuerst 6/190, 2.1

first of all [ˌfɜ:st‿əv‿ˈɔ:l] erstens, als Erstes 5/164, 4.2
fish *(pl - or* **-es***)* [fɪʃ, fɪʃ, fɪʃɪz] Fisch 2/52, 7
to keep fit [ˌki:p ˈfɪt] sich fit halten 3/90, 13
to fit *(irr)* [fɪt] passen (zu) 5/159, 11.1
flat [flæt] Wohnung v
floor [flɔ:] Boden; Stockwerk v
flower [ˈflaʊə] Blume 4/110, 5
to **fly** *(irr)* [flaɪ] fliegen v
folder [ˈfəʊldə] Mappe, Schnellhefter v
to **follow** [ˈfɒləʊ] folgen 2/49, 2
following [ˈfɒləʊɪŋ] folgende(r, s) 5/164, 4.2
food *(no pl)* [fu:d] Essen; Futter v
foot *(pl* **feet***)* [fʊt, fi:t] Fuß v
football [ˈfʊtbɔ:l] Fußball v
footprint [ˈfʊtˌprɪnt] Fußabdruck Op/102, 1
for [fɔ:] für v
for [fɔ:] als 4/135, 17.2; zu 5/138, 2; auf 6/193, 6
for example [fər‿ɪgˈzɑ:mpl] zum Beispiel 1/21, 3
for free [fɔ: ˈfri:] gratis, umsonst 5/151, 12
for he's a jolly good fellow [fə hiz‿ə ˌdʒɒli gʊd ˈfeləʊ] weil er so ein prima Kerl ist 4/120, 16
for (one week) [fɔ:] (eine Woche) lang 1/15, 7
forecast [ˈfɔ:kɑ:st] Vorhersage, Prognose 1/34, 4.1
forest [ˈfɒrɪst] Wald Op/102, 1
forever [fərˈevə] ewig 2/45, 11
to **forget** *(irr)* [fəˈget] vergessen v
forgot [fəˈgɒt] *Vergangenheitsform von „forget"*
fork [fɔ:k] Gabel v
to form [fɔ:m] bilden, formen 4/108, 3
former [ˈfɔ:mə] ehemalige(r, s), frühere(r, s) 2/64, 4.1

fortune [ˈfɔ:tʃən] Schicksal 3/76, 7
fortune-teller [ˈfɔ:tʃən ˌtelə] Wahrsager/in 3/76, 7
fortune-telling *(no pl)* [ˈfɔ:tʃən ˌtelɪŋ] Wahrsagen, Wahrsagerei 3/76, 7
to found [faʊnd] gründen 3/100, 4.1
fourth [fɔ:θ] vierte(r, s) v
France [frɑ:nts] Frankreich v
freckle [ˈfrekl] Sommersprosse v
free [fri:] gratis, umsonst 2/40, 2
to **be free** [bi: ˈfri:] Zeit haben 1/12, 3
free [fri:] frei 5/160, 4.1
for free [fɔ: ˈfri:] gratis, umsonst 5/151, 12
free time [ˈfri: taɪm] Freizeit v
French [frentʃ] Französisch; französisch v
in French [ɪn ˈfrentʃ] auf Französisch v
fresh [freʃ] frisch 1/21, 3
Fri (= Friday) *(informal)* [fraɪ] *Abkürzung für:* Freitag 1/23, 9
Friday [ˈfraɪdeɪ] Freitag v
fridge *(informal)* [frɪdʒ] Kühlschrank 1/12, 3
friend [frend] Freund/in v
friendly [ˈfrendli] freundlich v
friendship [ˈfrendʃɪp] Freundschaft 6/172, 13
frog [frɒg] Frosch 2/52, 6
from [frəm] von, aus v
Where are you from? [ˌweər‿ɑ: jə ˈfrɒm] Wo kommst du her? v
at the front [æt ðə ˈfrʌnt] vorn(e) 6/190, 2.1
fruit [fru:t] Frucht; Obst v
frustrated [frʌˈstreɪtɪd] frustriert; enttäuscht 5/136, 1
to **fry** [fraɪ] braten 4/113, 11
full [fʊl] voll 1/20, 2
full [fʊl] komplett v
full moon [ˌfʊl ˈmu:n] Vollmond Op/102, 1
fun [fʌn] lustig, witzig, spaßig 6/176, 6

to **be fun** [ˌbi: ˈfʌn] Spaß machen v
to **make fun of sb** [meɪk ˈfʌn‿əv ˌsʌmbədi] sich über jdn lustig machen 5/150, 11
fun *(no pl)* [fʌn] Spaß v
funny [ˈfʌni] lustig, witzig, komisch v
fur [fɜ:] Fell; Pelz 2/53, 8
future [ˈfju:tʃə] Zukunft 3/74, 3
future [ˈfju:tʃə] zukünftig, später 3/77, 10

G

Galapagos Islands [gəˈlæpəgəs‿ˌaɪləndz] Galapagosinseln 2/52, 6
gallery [ˈgæləri] Galerie 2/46, 14
board game [ˈbɔ:d geɪm] Brettspiel v
game [geɪm] Spiel v
garden [ˈgɑ:dn] Garten v
gardener [ˈgɑ:dnə] Gärtner/in 2/68, 6.1
to **gargle** [ˈgɑ:gl] gurgeln 6/170, 7
garland [ˈgɑ:lənd] Girlande 4/113, 11
gave [geɪv] *Vergangenheitsform von „give"*
Gemini [ˈdʒemɪnaɪ] Zwilling *(Sternzeichen)* 3/74, 3
geography [dʒi:ˈɒgrəfi] Erdkunde v
German [ˈdʒɜ:mən] Deutsch; deutsch 1/10, 1
in German [ɪn ˈdʒɜ:mən] auf Deutsch 3/78, 12
Germany [ˈdʒɜ:məni] Deutschland v
to **get** *(irr)* [get] gelangen 1/19, 15; erhalten, bekommen 3/74, 3; werden 3/82, 4
to get *(irr)* [get] bringen; holen Op/102, 1; besorgen 4/117, 8; kommen 6/CC
to **get dressed** [ˌget‿ˈdrest] sich anziehen 3/98, 15.1
to get into action [ˌget‿ˌɪntʊ‿ˈækʃn] aktiv werden, sich bewegen 3/76, 8
to get in(to) trouble [get‿ɪn(tə) ˈtrʌbl] Schwierigkeiten bekommen 5/150, 11

to get to know (sb/sth) [ˌget‿tə ˈnəʊ] (jdn/etw) kennenlernen 6/180, 11
to get lost [get ˈlɒst] sich verirren, sich verlaufen Op/105, 4
to **get married** [ˌget ˈmærid] heiraten 2/64, 4.1
to **get off** [ˌget‿ˈɒf] aussteigen 2/54, 11
to get ready (for sth) [get ˈredi] sich (für etw) bereit machen 6/190, 2.1
to get sb/sth to do sth [ˌget ˌsʌmbədi/ˌsʌmθɪŋ tə ˈduː ˌsʌmθɪŋ] jmd/etw dazu bringen, etw zu tun 4/134, 17.1
to get started (on sth) [ˌget ˈstɑːtɪd] (mit etw) beginnen/anfangen 4/114, 2
to **get up** [ˌget‿ˈʌp] aufstehen v
to **get well** [get ˈwel] gesund werden 6/168, 3
get well card [get ˈwel kɑːd] Genesungskarte 6/171, 11
Get well soon! [get wel ˈsuːn] Gute Besserung! 6/171, 11
ghost [gəʊst] Geist, Gespenst v
girl [gɜːl] Mädchen v
to **give** *(irr)* [gɪv] geben v
to give a talk [ˌgɪv‿ə ˈtɔːk] einen Vortrag halten 1/25, 13
to give directions [ˌgɪv dɪˈrekʃnz] den Weg beschreiben 2/51, 4
glad [glæd] glücklich, froh 2/54, 11
glass [glɑːs] Glas v
glasses *(only pl)* [ˈglɑːsɪz] Brille 6/CC
to **go** *(irr)* [gəʊ] gehen v
to **go** *(irr)* [gəʊ] fahren v
to go abroad [ˌgəʊ‿əˈbrɔːd] ins Ausland gehen/reisen 1/16, 9
to go ahead [ˌgəʊ‿əˈhed] loslegen 3/74, 3
to **go for a ride** [ˌgəʊ fər‿ə ˈraɪd] eine Fahrt machen 2/69, 11
to **go for a walk** [ˌgəʊ fər‿ə ˈwɔːk] spazieren gehen 1/17, 11
to **go out** [gəʊ‿ˈaʊt] (hinaus)gehen; ausgehen 5/138, 3
to **go shopping** [ˌgəʊ ˈʃɒpɪŋ] einkaufen gehen v
to go together [gəʊ təˈgeðə] zusammenpassen 6/169, 5
to **go with** [ˈgəʊ wɪð] gehören zu, passen zu 5/136, 1
goal [gəʊl] Tor v
goal [gəʊl] Ziel 1/21, 3
to **score a goal** [skɔːr‿ə ˈgəʊl] ein Tor schießen 3/80, 1
goalkeeper [ˈgəʊlˌkiːpə] Torfrau/Tormann v
god [gɒd] Gott 4/113, 11
goddess [ˈgɒdes] Göttin 4/111, 6
goggle-box *(BE)* [ˈgɒglbɒks] Glotze 6/CC
gone [gɒn] weg 3/98, 15.1
gone [gɒn] *siehe „go“*
good [gʊd] gut v
to **be good at sth** [ˌbiː ˈgʊd‿ət ˌsʌmθɪŋ] gut in etw sein v
good luck [gʊd ˈlʌk] Glück 4/123, 6
good-luck [ˌgʊd ˈlʌk] Glücks- 4/108, 2
good-looking [ˌgʊdˈlʊkɪŋ] gut aussehend v
goodbye [ˌgʊdˈbaɪ] auf Wiedersehen 6/170, 7
got [gɒt] *Vergangenheitsform von „get“*
to **grab sth** [ˈgræb ˌsʌmθɪŋ] (sich) etw schnappen 3/98, 15.1
grammar [ˈgræmə] Grammatik 1/11, 2
granddaughter [ˈgrænˌdɔːtə] Enkelin, Enkeltochter v
grandfather [ˈgrænˌfɑːðə] Großvater v
grandma *(informal)* [ˈgrænˌmɑː] Oma, Omi 5/138, 2
grandmother [ˈgrænˌmʌðə] Großmutter v
grandparents *(only pl)* [ˈgrænˌpeərənts] Großeltern v
grandson [ˈgrænˌsʌn] Enkel(sohn) v
grass *(no pl)* [grɑːs] Gras; Wiese, Rasen 2/40, 2
great [greɪt] großartig, toll v
Great Britain [ˌgreɪt ˈbrɪtn] Großbritannien 1/14, LL
Greece [griːs] Griechenland 6/CC
green [griːn] grün v
greetings *(only pl)* [ˈgriːtɪŋz] Grüße 6/CC
grey [greɪ] grau v
to **grill** [grɪl] grillen v
ground [graʊnd] (Erd)boden, Erde Op/102, 1
sports ground [ˈspɔːts ˌgraʊnd] Sportplatz v
school grounds [ˈskuːl ˌgraʊndz] Schulgelände 5/144, 1
group [gruːp] Gruppe v
to **grow up** [ˌgrəʊ‿ˈʌp] erwachsen sein/werden 3/77, 10
guard [gɑːd] Wache 2/69, 11
Changing of the Guard [ˌtʃeɪndʒɪŋ‿əv ðə ˈgɑːd] Wachablösung 2/40, 2
to **guess** [ges] (er)raten 4/110, 5; schätzen, vermuten, denken 4/114, 2
guessing game [ˈgesɪŋ ˌgeɪm] Ratespiel 3/89, 10.1
guest [gest] Gast 4/135, 17.2
tour guide [ˈtʊə gaɪd] Reiseführer/in, Reiseleiter/in 2/47, 15
audio guide [ˈɔːdiəʊ ˌgaɪd] Audioguide, Audioführer 2/47, 15
guinea pig [ˈgɪni pɪg] Meerschweinchen v
guitar [gɪˈtɑː] Gitarre v
to gulp [gʌlp] schlucken Op/102, 1
chewing gum *(no pl)* [ˈtʃuːɪŋ ˌgʌm] Kaugummi 5/144, 1
guys *(only pl) (informal)* [gaɪz] Leute 6/178, 9

gym (= **gymnasium**) [dʒɪm, dʒɪm'neɪziəm] Turnhalle, Fitnessstudio v

gymnastics *(only pl)* [dʒɪm'næstɪks] Turnen v

H

had [hæd] *Vergangenheitsform von „have"*

hair *(no pl)* [heə] Haar; Haare v

hairdresser ['heəˌdresə] Friseur/in 3/77, 10

half *(pl* **halves***)* [hɑ:f, hɑ:vz] Hälfte 1/37, 5.1

half an hour [ˌhɑ:f‿ən‿'aʊə] (eine) halbe Stunde v

half brother ['hɑ:f ˌbrʌðə] Halbbruder 1/10, 1

half past (eight) ['hɑ:f ˌpɑ:st] halb (neun) v

hall [hɔ:l] Halle; Saal 6/190, 2.1

to put one's hand up [ˌpʊt wʌnz 'hænd‿ʌp] sich melden 5/164, 4.2

handrail ['hændˌreɪl] Geländer 2/44, 10

to **hang** *(irr)* [hæŋ] (auf)hängen 4/130, 2.2

Hanukkah ['hɑ:nəkə] *jüdisches Lichterfest* 4/106, 1

to **happen** ['hæpən] geschehen, passieren 3/74, 3

happy ['hæpi] glücklich; zufrieden; fröhlich v

Happy Birthday! [ˌhæpi 'bɜ:θdeɪ] Alles Gute zum Geburtstag! v

harbour ['hɑ:bə] Hafen 6/193, 6

hard [hɑ:d] hart; schwer v

hat [hæt] Hut; Mütze 4/115, 4

to **hate** [heɪt] hassen, nicht ausstehen können v

to **have** *(irr)* [hæv] haben; essen v

to **have a barbecue** [ˌhæv‿ə 'bɑ:bɪˌkju:] grillen, eine Grillparty feiern v

to **have a cold** [ˌhæv‿ə 'kəʊld] eine Erkältung haben, erkältet sein 6/167, 2

to **have a look (at sth)** [ˌhæv‿ə 'lʊk] (sich) (etw) (an)schauen 4/114, 2

to **have a party** [ˌhæv‿ə 'pɑ:ti] eine Party machen/feiern 4/108, 2

to **have a picnic** [ˌhæv‿ə 'pɪknɪk] ein Picknick machen; picknicken v

to **have a temperature** [ˌhæv‿ə 'temprɪtʃə] Fieber haben 6/166, 1

to have a vote [ˌhæv‿ə 'vəʊt] abstimmen 5/148, 8

Have you ever been to ...? [ˌhæv jə‿ˌevə 'bi:n tə] Warst du jemals/schon einmal in ...? 6/174, 1

to **have got** [hæv 'gɒt] haben v

to have sb over [ˌhæv ˌsʌmbədi‿'əʊvə] jdn zu sich einladen, jdn zu Besuch haben 2/CC

to **have to** ['hæv tə] müssen v

he [hi] er v

head [hed] Kopf v

headache ['hedeɪk] Kopfschmerzen, Kopfweh 6/170, 7

heading ['hedɪŋ] Überschrift, Titel Op/102, 1

headteacher [ˌhed'ti:tʃə] Schulleiter/in, Rektor/in 1/25, 13

health *(no pl)* [helθ] Gesundheit 6/170, 7

healthy ['helθi] gesund 1/21, 3

to **hear** *(irr)* [hɪə] hören v

heard [hɜ:d] *Vergangenheitsform von „hear"*

heart [hɑ:t] Herz 3/74, 3

to learn sth by heart [ˌlɜ:n ˌsʌmθɪŋ baɪ 'hɑ:t] etw auswendig lernen 2/46, 14

held [held] *Vergangenheitsform von „hold"*

hello [hə'ləʊ] hallo v

help [help] Hilfe v

to **help** [help] helfen v

to help out [ˌhelp‿'aʊt] (aus)helfen, unterstützen 1/38, 9.1

her [hɜ:] ihr(e, n); sie v

here [hɪə] hier(her) v

Here you are. [ˌhɪə ju‿'ɑ:] Hier, bitte!, Bitte schön! v

hero *(pl* **-es***)* ['hɪərəʊ, 'hɪərəʊz] Held/in 3/80, 1

herself [hə'self] sich (selbst); selbst 5/160, 4.1

hi [haɪ] hallo, hi v

high [haɪ] hoch 2/54, 11

high school ['haɪ ˌsku:l] *weiterführende Schule in den USA (Klasse 9-12)* 1/37, 5.1

hiking trip ['haɪkɪŋ trɪp] Wanderung Op/105, 4

him [hɪm] ihm, ihn v

himself [hɪm'self] sich (selbst); selbst 4/117, 8

Hindu [ˌhɪn'du:] Hindu; hinduistisch 4/110, 5

hippo (= **hippopotamus**) ['hɪpəʊ, ˌhɪpə'pɒtəməs] Nilpferd 2/52, 6

to **hire** ['haɪə] mieten, (aus)leihen 1/17, 11

his [hɪz] sein(e, r) v

history ['hɪstri] Geschichte v

to hit *(irr)* [hɪt] schlagen; treffen Op/102, 1

to **hold** *(irr)* [həʊld] (fest)halten 5/150, 11

hole [həʊl] Loch 5/138, 2

holiday ['hɒlɪdeɪ] Urlaub, Ferien 1/10, 1

holiday ['hɒlɪdeɪ] Feiertag 4/130, 2.2

home [həʊm] Zuhause, Heim 2/46, 14

home [həʊm] zu Hause; nach Hause v

at home [ət 'həʊm] zu Hause v

home town [ˌhəʊm 'taʊn] Heimatort 2/65, 9.1

homework *(no pl)* ['həʊmˌwɜ:k] Hausaufgaben v

honey *(no pl)* ['hʌni] Honig 4/126, 4.1

to hop [hɒp] hüpfen 2/45, 11
to **hope** [həʊp] hoffen v
horoscope ['hɒrəˌskəʊp] Horoskop 3/72, 1
horrible ['hɒrəbl] schrecklich 5/148, 8
horse [hɔ:s] Pferd v
horse riding *(no pl)* ['hɔ:ʃ ˌraɪdɪŋ] Reiten 6/176, 6
hospital ['hɒspɪtl] Krankenhaus 3/78, 11
hot [hɒt] heiß v
hour ['aʊə] Stunde 1/15, 8
half an hour [ˌhɑ:f‿ən‿'aʊə] (eine) halbe Stunde v
house [haʊs] Haus v
how [haʊ] wie v
How are things? [ˌhaʊ‿ɑ: 'θɪŋz] Wie geht's? 5/139, 4
How are you? [haʊ‿'ɑ: ju:] Wie geht es dir/Ihnen/euch? 1/12, 3
How much is/are ... ? [ˌhaʊ 'mʌtʃ‿ɪz/ɑ:] Was kostet/kosten ...? v
How old are you? [haʊ‿'əʊld‿ə jʊ] Wie alt bist du? v
how to [haʊ tə] wie man v
however [haʊ'evə] aber, jedoch 2/CC
huge [hju:dʒ] riesig, riesengroß 5/141, 9
human ['hju:mən] Mensch 3/98, 15.1
hundred ['hʌndrəd] Hundert 4/135, 17.2
hungry ['hʌŋgri] hungrig v
treasure hunt ['treʒə hʌnt] Schatzsuche; Schnitzeljagd 6/176, 6
to **hurry up** [ˌhʌri‿'ʌp] sich beeilen v
to **hurt** *(irr)* [hɜ:t] wehtun, schmerzen 6/166, 1

I

I [aɪ] ich v
I can't wait ... [aɪ ˌkɑ:nt 'weɪt] Ich kann es kaum erwarten ... 4/132, 11
I don't think so. [aɪ ˌdəʊnt 'θɪŋk səʊ] Das glaube ich nicht. 2/52, 7
I wish I could ... [aɪ 'wɪʃ‿aɪ kʊd] Ich wünschte, ich könnte ... 1/36, 11
I'd like ... [aɪd 'laɪk] ich hätte gern ... v
I'd like (to) [aɪd 'laɪk] ich würde gern ... 4/110, 5
I'd rather ... [aɪd 'rɑ:ðə] Ich würde lieber ... 5/162, 9
I'm fine. [aɪm 'faɪn] Es geht mir gut. 1/12, 3
I'm sorry. [aɪm 'sɒri] Das tut mir leid. 2/49, 2
ice cream [ˌaɪs 'kri:m] Eiscreme 1/16, 9
ICT (= **information and communication technology**) [ˌaɪ si: 'ti:, ˌɪnfəˌmeɪʃn‿ən kəˌmju:nɪˌkeɪʃn tek'nɒlədʒi] Informatik v
idea [aɪ'dɪə] Idee v
identity card [aɪ'dentɪti kɑ:d] Ausweis v
if [ɪf] wenn, falls 3/79, 14; ob 4/117, 8
what if [wɒt‿ɪf] was ist/wäre, wenn 5/161, 4.2
to **ignore** [ɪg'nɔ:] ignorieren 5/149, 10
ill [ɪl] krank 3/77, 10
to imagine [ɪ'mædʒɪn] sich vorstellen 2/41, 3
important [ɪm'pɔ:tnt] wichtig 5/141, 9
to **improve** [ɪm'pru:v] verbessern 5/162, 9
in [ɪn] in v
in [ɪn] herein Op/102, 1
in English [ˌɪn‿'ɪŋglɪʃ] auf Englisch v
in fact [ɪn 'fækt] tatsächlich, in Wirklichkeit; sogar 4/135, 17.2
in French [ɪn 'frentʃ] auf Französisch v
in front of [ɪn 'frʌnt‿əv] vor v
in the back [ˌɪn ðə 'bæk] hinten 1/36, 11
in the face of [ˌɪn ðə 'feɪs‿əv] angesichts 3/100, 4.1
to include [ɪn'klu:d] einfügen, aufnehmen 2/67, 5
incredible [ɪn'kredəbl] unglaublich 6/190, 2.1
India ['ɪndiə] Indien 4/135, 17.2
Indian ['ɪndiən] indisch; indianisch 4/110, 5
individual [ˌɪndɪ'vɪdʒuəl] Individuum, (selbstständige) Persönlichkeit 4/134, 17.1
individual [ˌɪndɪ'vɪdʒuəl] individuell; eigen 5/165, 8.1
information *(no pl)* [ˌɪnfə'meɪʃn] Information 1/38, 8.1
tourist information [ˌtʊərɪst‿ˌɪnfə'meɪʃn] Touristeninfo(rmation) 2/47, 15
inline skating *(no pl)* [ˌɪnlaɪn 'skeɪtɪŋ] Inlineskaten 1/24, 11
insect ['ɪnsekt] Insekt 2/52, 6
inside [ɪn'saɪd] drinnen; innen; (in ...) hinein 1/17, 11
instead (of) [ɪn'sted (‿əv)] stattdessen; (an)statt 6/166, 1
interested (in sth) ['ɪntrəstɪd] interessiert (an etw) 6/193, 6
interesting ['ɪntrəstɪŋ] interessant v
to interview ['ɪntəˌvju:] befragen; interviewen 1/25, 13
into ['ɪntʊ] in 3/98, 15.1
invitation [ˌɪnvɪ'teɪʃn] Einladung v
to **invite** [ɪn'vaɪt] einladen v
Ireland ['aɪələnd] Irland 1/14, LL
Irish ['aɪrɪʃ] Irisch; irisch 4/130, 2.1
is [ɪz] ist v
island ['aɪlənd] Insel 3/82, 4
it [ɪt] es v
it says ... [ɪt 'sez] darauf steht ... 6/168, 3
its [ɪts] sein(e), ihr(e) v

J

jacket ['dʒækɪt] Jacke 5/146, 6
jam [dʒæm] Marmelade v
January ['dʒænjuəri] Januar v
jelly bean ['dʒeli bi:n] *(bohnenförmiges) Geleebonbon* 4/117, 8
Jew [dʒu:] Jude/Jüdin 4/108, 2

Crown Jewels *(only pl)* [ˌkraʊn ˈdʒuːəlz] Kronjuwelen 2/42, 6
Jewish [ˈdʒuːɪʃ] jüdisch 4/113, 11
to **join** [dʒɔɪn] mitmachen bei; beitreten v
joke [dʒəʊk] Witz 6/CC
to joke [dʒəʊk] scherzen; Spaß machen 3/98, 15.1
orange juice [ˈɒrɪndʒ ˌdʒuːs] Orangensaft v
juice [dʒuːs] Saft v
juicy [ˈdʒuːsi] saftig 5/162, 9
July [dʒʊˈlaɪ] Juli v
to **jump** [dʒʌmp] springen 2/53, 8
June [dʒuːn] Juni v
jungle [ˈdʒʌŋgl] Dschungel, Urwald 6/193, 6
just [dʒʌst] gleich; nur; einfach 3/74, 3
just [dʒʌst] genau 3/76, 8

K

kangaroo [ˌkæŋgəˈruː] Känguru v
kayaking *(no pl)* [ˈkaɪækɪŋ] Kajakfahren, Kajaken 6/176, 6
to **keep** *(irr)* [kiːp] (be)halten; aufbewahren v
to keep clear of the edges [kiːp ˌklɪər‿əv ðiˈedʒɪz] sich von den Rändern fernhalten 2/44, 10
to keep doing sth [ˌkiːp ˈduːɪŋ ˌsʌmθɪŋ] etw weiter tun 3/98, 15.1
to keep fit [ˌkiːp ˈfɪt] sich fit halten 3/90, 13
keeper [ˈkiːpə] Wärter/in 3/82, 4
keyword [ˈkiːˌwɜːd] Schlüsselwort 3/101, 6
kid [kɪd] Kind v
kilometre [ˈkɪləˌmiːtə] Kilometer v
kind [kaɪnd] Art, Sorte v; nett, freundlich 2/45, 11
king [kɪŋ] König 2/64, 4.1
kit [kɪt] Ausrüstung 5/144, 1
kitchen [ˈkɪtʃən] Küche v
knee [niː] Knie 1/21, 3
knew [njuː] *Vergangenheitsform von „know“*
knife *(pl **knives**)* [naɪf, naɪvz] Messer v
to knock over sb [ˌnɒk‿ˈəʊvə ˌsʌmbədi] jdn umstoßen 6/178, 9
to **know** *(irr)* [nəʊ] wissen; kennen v
to get to know (sb/sth) [ˌget‿tə ˈnəʊ] (jdn/etw) kennenlernen 6/180, 11

L

to label [ˈleɪbl] beschriften 2/62, 8.1
lake [leɪk] See 2/40, 2
lamp [læmp] Lampe v
land [lænd] (Fest)land 6/178, 9
landmark [ˈlænˌmɑːk] Erkennungszeichen, Wahrzeichen 2/66, 14.1
language [ˈlæŋgwɪdʒ] Sprache 5/162, 9
large [lɑːdʒ] groß 1/21, 3
to **last** [lɑːst] (an)dauern 4/113, 11
last [lɑːst] letzte(r, s) 2/54, 11
last but not least [ˌlɑːst bət nɒt ˈliːst] nicht zuletzt 6/176, 6
to **be late** [ˌbiː ˈleɪt] (zu) spät kommen, sich verspäten v
late [leɪt] (zu) spät v
later [ˈleɪtə] später v
latke [ˈlætkə] Kartoffelpuffer 4/113, 11
to **laugh** [lɑːf] lachen 3/81, 3
to **lay the table** [ˌleɪ ðə ˈteɪbl] den Tisch decken v
lazy [ˈleɪzi] faul, träge 6/178, 9
lead singer [liːd ˈsɪŋə] Leadsänger/in 6/190, 2.1
leader [ˈliːdə] Leiter/in, Führer/in 2/55, 12
leaf *(pl **leaves**)* [liːf, liːvz] Blatt 2/52, 6
to lean *(irr)* [liːn] (sich) lehnen 6/178, 9
to **learn** *(irr)* [lɜːn] lernen v
to learn *(irr)* [lɜːn] erfahren 6/166, 1
to learn about [ˈlɜːn‿əˌbaʊt] erfahren von/über 1/10, 1
to learn sth by heart [ˌlɜːn ˌsʌmθɪŋ baɪ ˈhɑːt] etw auswendig lernen 2/46, 14
last but not least [ˌlɑːst bət nɒt ˈliːst] nicht zuletzt 6/176, 6
to **leave** *(irr)* [liːv] verlassen 2/54, 11
to **leave** *(irr)* [liːv] lassen 2/69, 11
to leave *(irr)* [liːv] gehen 5/138, 2
left [left] (nach) links 2/50, 3
on the/your left [ˌɒn ðə/jɔː ˈleft] links, auf der linken Seite 2/48, 1
to the left [ˌtʊ ðə ˈleft] nach links 6/178, 9
left [left] *Vergangenheitsform von „leave“*
leftovers *(only pl)* [ˈleftˌəʊvəz] Reste 4/130, 2.2
leg [leg] Bein v
legend [ˈledʒnd] Legende, Sage 2/65, 10.1
lemon [ˈlemən] Zitrone v
lemonade [ˌleməˈneɪd] Limonade v
length [leŋθ] Länge 1/21, 3
Leo [ˈliːəʊ] Löwe *(Sternzeichen)* 3/96, 8.1
lesson [ˈlesn] Stunde v
to **let** *(irr)* [let] lassen 2/45, 11
to let sb down [ˌlet sʌmbədi ˈdaʊn] jdn enttäuschen, jdn im Stich lassen 3/81, 3
let's (= **let us**) [lets, ˈlet‿əs] lass(t) uns v
letter [ˈletə] Brief; Buchstabe 3/84, 7
Libra [ˈliːbrə] Waage *(Sternzeichen)* 3/96, 8.1
librarian [laɪˈbreəriən] Bibliothekar/in 1/21, 3
library [ˈlaɪbrəri] Bibliothek, Bücherei v
to lie *(irr)* [laɪ] liegen Op/102, 1
life *(pl **lives**)* [laɪf, laɪvz] Leben v
lifeboat [ˈlaɪfˌbəʊt] Rettungsboot 3/100, 4.1

lifeguard ['laɪf,ga:d] Rettungsschwimmer/in; Bademeister/in 3/100, 4.1
lifelike ['laɪf,laɪk] lebensecht, naturgetreu 2/65, 10.1
to **lift** [lɪft] (hoch)heben 6/178, 9
light [laɪt] Licht 4/111, 6
to **light** *(irr)* [laɪt] erhellen; anzünden 4/108, 2
lighthouse ['laɪt,haʊs] Leuchtturm 3/82, 4
to **like** [laɪk] mögen v
like [laɪk] wie 2/42, 6
like [laɪk] nach 4/123, 6
What's ... like? [wɒts 'laɪk] Wie ist ...? 1/19, 15
to be like sth [,bi: ,laɪk 'sʌmθɪŋ] wie etw sein 3/79, 14
like that [laɪk 'ðæt] so; solche(r, s) 5/136, 1
like this [laɪk 'ðɪs] so 5/150, 11; so; solche(r, s) 5/158, 11
limerick ['lɪmərɪk] *lustiges Gedicht mit fünf Zeilen* 2/CC
to limit ['lɪmɪt] einschränken, reduzieren 5/155, 13
line [laɪn] Linie; Zeile 4/119, 12
linking word ['lɪŋkɪŋ wɜ:d] Bindewort Op/105, 4
lion ['laɪən] Löwe v
list [lɪst] Liste v
shopping list ['ʃɒpɪŋ lɪst] Einkaufszettel, Einkaufsliste 4/114, 2
to **listen (to)** ['lɪsn] (zu)hören v
litter *(no pl)* ['lɪtə] Müll, Abfall 5/144, 1
little ['lɪtl] klein v
a little [ə 'lɪtl] ein bisschen 4/119, 12
to **live** [lɪv] leben, wohnen v
living room ['lɪvɪŋ ru:m] Wohnzimmer v
loads (of) *(informal)* [ləʊds] jede Menge, massenhaft 4/114, 2

to be located [bi: ləʊ'keɪtɪd] sich befinden, liegen, gelegen sein 6/194, 6.1
locker ['lɒkə] Schließfach, Spind v
lodge [lɒdʒ] Hütte, Lodge 2/CC
logo ['ləʊgəʊ] Abzeichen, Logo 1/21, 3
lonely ['ləʊnli] einsam 1/17, 11
long [lɒŋ] lang v
to **have a look (at sth)** [,hæv‿ə 'lʊk] (sich) (etw) (an)schauen 4/114, 2
to take a look (at) [teɪk‿ə 'lʊk] einen Blick werfen (auf) 3/98, 15.1
to look after [,lʊk‿'a:ftə] sich kümmern um; aufpassen auf 3/78, 11
to **look (at)** ['lʊk‿ət] (an)sehen, (an)schauen v
to **look** [lʊk] aussehen 1/12, 3
to **look for** ['lʊk fɔ:] suchen (nach) 6/178, 9
to **look forward to** [,lʊk 'fɔ:wəd tə] sich freuen auf 2/45, 11
to look up [,lʊk‿'ʌp] nachschlagen 1/21, 3; nach oben sehen; hinaufsehen 3/98, 15.1
lost [lɒst] verloren Op/102, 1
to get lost [get 'lɒst] sich verirren, sich verlaufen Op/105, 4
lots (= a lot) *(informal)* [lɒts] viel, jede Menge 1/24, 10
lots of ['lɒts‿əv] viel, jede Menge v
loud [laʊd] laut 3/85, 8
loudspeaker [,laʊd'spi:kə] Lautsprecher 5/160, 4.1
love [lʌv] Liebe; herzliche Grüße, alles Liebe 6/168, 3
to **love** [lʌv] lieben; sehr gern mögen v
lovely ['lʌvli] schön, hübsch 6/176, 6
lovely ['lʌvli] wunderbar; nett 2/68, 6.1
to lower ['ləʊə] senken 4/134, 17.1
good luck [gʊd 'lʌk] Glück 4/123, 6
lucky ['lʌki] glücklich; Glück bringend; Glücks- 3/74, 3

to **be lucky** [bi: 'lʌki] Glück haben 1/10, 1
lunch [lʌntʃ] Mittagessen v
lunchtime ['lʌntʃ,taɪm] Mittagszeit; Mittagspause 1/21, 3
luxury *(no pl)* ['lʌkʃəri] Luxus 2/66, 14.1

M

machine [mə'ʃi:n] Maschine 2/46, 14
made [meɪd] *Vergangenheitsform von „make"*
made of ['meɪd‿əv] (gemacht) aus 6/177, 8
magazine [,mægə'zi:n] Zeitschrift, Magazin 3/74, 3
magical ['mædʒɪkl] magisch 6/176, 6
magically ['mædʒɪkli] wie durch ein Wunder 6/CC
to **make** *(irr)* [meɪk] machen v
to **make a wish** [,meɪk‿ə 'wɪʃ] sich etwas wünschen v
to **make fun of sb** [meɪk 'fʌn‿əv ,sʌmbədi] sich über jdn lustig machen 5/150, 11
to make notes [,meɪk 'nəʊts] (sich) Notizen machen 1/37, 5.1
to make one's way [,meɪk wʌnz 'weɪ] gehen 6/190, 2.1
to make sb do sth [,meɪk sʌmbədi 'du: sʌmθɪŋ] jdn dazu bringen/veranlassen, etw zu tun 5/150, 11
to make sure [,meɪk 'ʃɔ:] sichergehen 5/150, 11
to make up sth [,meɪk‿'ʌp ,sʌmθɪŋ] (sich) etw ausdenken, etw erfinden 1/24, 10
male [meɪl] männlich 2/55, 12
man *(pl* **men***)* [mæn, men] Mann v
mane [meɪn] Mähne 2/53, 8
mantelpiece ['mæntl,pi:s] Kaminsims 4/130, 2.2
many ['meni] viele v
map [mæp] (Land)karte v

March [mɑ:tʃ] März v
mark [mɑ:k] (Schul)note 1/37, 5.1
to mark [mɑ:k] markieren, kennzeichnen 4/133, 8.1; benoten, korrigieren 6/CC
market ['mɑ:kɪt] Markt v
to **marry** ['mæri] heiraten 3/74, 3
match [mætʃ] Spiel v
to match (with) [mætʃ] zuordnen 1/13, 4
mate *(informal)* [meɪt] Kumpel, Freund/in 6/168, 3
maths [mæθs] Mathe v
May [meɪ] Mai v
may [meɪ] können; dürfen 5/138, 2
maybe ['meɪbi] vielleicht, möglicherweise v
me [mi:] mir, mich v
me [mi:] ich 1/12, 3
meal [mi:l] Mahlzeit, Essen 1/21, 3
mealtime ['mi:ltaɪm] Essenszeit 5/140, 6
to **mean** *(irr)* [mi:n] bedeuten; meinen v
meaning ['mi:nɪŋ] Bedeutung 1/21, 3
meat *(no pl)* [mi:t] Fleisch v
mechanic [mɪ'kænɪk] Mechaniker/in 3/77, 10
medal ['medl] Medaille 2/64, 4.1
medicine *(no pl)* ['medsn] Medizin, Medikamente 6/169, 5
to **meet** *(irr)* [mi:t] (sich) treffen; kennenlernen v
member ['membə] Mitglied v
Menorah [mə'nɔ:rə] Menora *(siebenarmiger Kerzenleuchter)* 4/108, 2
to mention ['menʃn] erwähnen 2/65, 9.1
to **be a mess** [ˌbi‿ə 'mes] chaotisch/unordentlich sein; ein einziges Durcheinander sein 5/161, 6.1
message ['mesɪdʒ] Nachricht v
text message ['tekst ˌmesɪdʒ] SMS, Kurznachricht 5/149, 10
messy ['mesi] unordentlich; chaotisch 4/135, 17.2
met [met] *Vergangenheitsform von „meet“*
metal ['metl] Metall 6/177, 8
metre ['mi:tə] Meter 2/42, 6
Mexican ['meksɪkən] Mexikaner/in; mexikanisch 1/37, 5.1
Mexico ['meksɪˌkəʊ] Mexiko v
Mexico City [ˌmeksɪkəʊ 'sɪti] Mexiko-Stadt v
in the middle [ɪn ðə 'mɪdl] in der Mitte; mitten in/auf 2/40, 2
midfielder ['mɪdˌfi:ldə] Mittelfeldspieler/in 3/99, 1
midnight *(no pl)* ['mɪdˌnaɪt] Mitternacht 5/143, 12
might [maɪt] könnte 1/34, 4.1
milk *(no pl)* [mɪlk] Milch v
milkshake ['mɪlkˌʃeɪk] Milchshake v
to mill around [ˌmɪl‿ə'raʊnd] umherlaufen 1/11, 2
to mime [maɪm] mimen, pantomimisch darstellen 3/89, 10.1
mince pie ['mɪns paɪ] *Kuchen gefüllt mit Dörrobst und Sirup* 4/130, 2.2
miniskirt ['mɪniˌskɜ:t] Minirock 5/144, 1
to **miss** [mɪs] vermissen v; verpassen 6/168, 3
to miss out sth [ˌmɪs‿'aʊt ˌsʌmθɪŋ] etw vergessen; sich etw entgehen lassen 6/176, 6
to **be missing** [bi 'mɪsɪŋ] fehlen 6/178, 9
missing ['mɪsɪŋ] fehlend 3/94, 10.1
to **mix** [mɪks] (ver)mischen v
(mobile) phone [ˌməʊbaɪl 'fəʊn] Mobiltelefon, Handy v
at the moment [æt ðə 'məʊmənt] im Moment 2/45, 11
Mon (= Monday) *(informal)* [mʌn] *Abkürzung für:* Montag 1/23, 9
Monday ['mʌndeɪ] Montag v
money *(no pl)* ['mʌni] Geld 2/42, 5
monkey ['mʌŋki] Affe v
month [mʌnθ] Monat v
moon [mu:n] Mond Op/104, 2
full moon [ˌfʊl 'mu:n] Vollmond Op/102, 1
more [mɔ:] (noch) mehr v
morning ['mɔ:nɪŋ] Morgen v
in the morning [ˌɪn ðə 'mɔ:nɪŋ] morgens, am Morgen, vormittags v
most [məʊst] die meisten 2/CC; am meisten 5/148, 9
most (of) [məʊst] das meiste (von), ein Großteil 3/98, 15.1
most beautiful [ˌməʊst 'bju:təfl] schönste(r, s) 4/110, 5
mother ['mʌðə] Mutter v
Mother's Day ['mʌðəz deɪ] Muttertag 4/106, 1
mountain biking *(no pl)* ['maʊntɪn ˌbaɪkɪŋ] Mountainbiken, Mountainbikefahren 6/176, 6
mouse *(pl* **mice***)* [maʊs, maɪs] Maus v
mouth [maʊθ] Mund v
to **move** [mu:v] sich bewegen 6/178, 9
movement ['mu:vmənt] Bewegung 6/178, 9
Mr ['mɪstə] Herr *(Anrede)* v
Mrs ['mɪsɪz] Frau *(Anrede)* v
much [mʌtʃ] viel; sehr v
muesli *(no pl)* ['mju:zli] Müsli v
mum *(informal)* [mʌm] Mama, Mutti v
mushroom ['mʌʃru:m] Pilz v
music *(no pl)* ['mju:zɪk] Musik v
musician [mjʊ'zɪʃn] Musiker/in 2/40, 2
Muslim ['mʊzləm] Muslim/in; muslimisch 4/108, 2
must [mʌst] müssen 5/140, 6
must not [mʌst 'nɒt] nicht dürfen 5/139, 4
must-see [ˌmʌst'si:] *etwas, das man gesehen haben muss* 2/40, 2
my [maɪ] mein(e) v

N

What's your name? [ˌwɒts jə ˈneɪm] Wie heißt du? V
to **call sb names** [ˌkɔ:l sʌmbədi ˈneɪmz] jdn beschimpfen 5/149, 10
to name [neɪm] (be)nennen 3/78, 11
narrator [nəˈreɪtə] Erzähler/in 3/85, 8
the Natural History Museum [ðə ˌnætʃərəl ˈhɪstəri mju:ˌzi:əm] Naturkundemuseum 2/40, 2
naughty [ˈnɔ:ti] ungezogen, frech V
near [nɪə] nah(e); in der Nähe V
nearly [ˈnɪəli] fast, beinahe 5/164, 4.2
neck [nek] Hals; Nacken 2/69, 9.1
to **need** [ni:d] brauchen V
to **need to** [ˈni:d‿tə] müssen 3/82, 4
neighbour [ˈneɪbə] Nachbar/in 4/130, 2.2
neighbourhood [ˈneɪbəˌhʊd] Viertel; Nachbarschaft V
nervous [ˈnɜ:vəs] nervös; aufgeregt V
never [ˈnevə] nie(mals) V
new [nju:] neu V
New Year [ˌnju: ˈjɪə] Neujahr 4/106, 1
New Year's Eve [ˌnju: jɪəz‿ˈi:v] Silvester 4/106, 1
news *(no pl)* [nju:z] Neuigkeit; Nachrichten 6/172, 12
next [nekst] nächste(r, s) 3/72, 1
next [nekst] dann, als Nächstes 2/69, 11
the next day [ðə ˌnekst‿ˈdeɪ] am nächsten Tag V
next door [ˌnekst ˈdɔ:] neben(an) V
next to [ˈnekst‿tə] neben V
nice [naɪs] nett; schön V
night [naɪt] Nacht 1/17, 11
at night [æt ˈnaɪt] nachts 4/130, 2.2
no [nəʊ] nein; kein(e) V
no one [ˈnəʊ wʌn] keiner, niemand 6/178, 9
noise [nɔɪz] Lärm, Krach; Geräusch V
non- [nɒn] nicht- 2/CC
nonsense [ˈnɒnsns] Unsinn, Quatsch 5/162, 9
noodle [ˈnu:dl] Nudel 4/135, 17.2
normally [ˈnɔ:mli] normalerweise 2/54, 10
north [nɔ:θ] Norden 3/80, 1
Northern Ireland [ˌnɔ:ðn‿ˈaɪələnd] Nordirland 1/14, LL
nose [nəʊz] Nase V
not [nɒt] nicht V
must not [mʌst ˈnɒt] nicht dürfen 5/139, 4
not a [nɒt‿ə] kein(e) V
not any [nɒt‿ə] kein(e) 3/79, 16
not anywhere [nɒt‿ˈeniˌweə] nirgendwo(hin) Op/102, 1
not even [ˌnɒt‿ˈi:vn] (noch) nicht (ein)mal 6/178, 9
not yet [nɒt ˈjet] noch nicht 6/166, 1
note [nəʊt] Notiz V
to make notes [ˌmeɪk ˈnəʊts] (sich) Notizen machen 1/37, 5.1
to take notes [ˌteɪk ˈnəʊts] (sich) Notizen machen 2/65, 9.1
to note down [nəʊt ˈdaʊn] (sich) notieren 1/21, 3
nothing [ˈnʌθɪŋ] nichts V
nothing else [ˌnʌθɪŋ‿ˈels] sonst nichts, nichts anderes 6/172, 13
to **notice** [ˈnəʊtɪs] bemerken 6/178, 9
noun [naʊn] Substantiv 2/46, 13
November [nəʊˈvembə] November V
now [naʊ] jetzt V
number [ˈnʌmbə] Zahl; Ziffer, Nummer V
nurse [nɜ:s] (Kranken)schwester, (Kranken)pfleger 3/77, 10
nut [nʌt] Nuss V

O

(eight) o'clock [əˈklɒk] (acht) Uhr V
October [ɒkˈtəʊbə] Oktober V
the odd one out [ði‿ɒd wʌn‿ˈaʊt] *fünftes Rad am Wagen* 2/43, 7
of [əv] von V
of course [əv ˈkɔ:s] natürlich V
off [ɒf] herunter, hinunter 4/134, 17.1
to **offer** [ˈɒfə] (an)bieten 1/21, 3
office [ˈɒfɪs] Büro V
official [əˈfɪʃl] offiziell, amtlich 2/40, 2
often [ˈɒfn] oft, häufig V
Oh dear! [əʊ ˈdɪə] Du meine Güte! 6/170, 7
oil [ɔɪl] Öl 4/113, 11
old [əʊld] alt V
How old are you? [haʊ‿ˈəʊld‿ə jʊ] Wie alt bist du? V
on [ɒn] auf, an; in; am V
on [ɒn] über, zu 1/25, 13; weiter 2/50, 3
on one's own [ɒn wʌnz‿ˈəʊn] allein(e) 3/99, 1
on-call [ˌɒnˈkɔ:l] dienstbereit, auf Abruf 3/100, 4.1
once [wʌns] einmal 2/CC
one [wʌn] eins; ein(e) V
one day [ˈwʌn deɪ] eines Tages 5/150, 11
one hundred [ˌwʌn ˈhʌndrəd] einhundert V
onion [ˈʌnjən] Zwiebel 4/116, 6
only [ˈəʊnli] nur V
only [ˈəʊnli] einzige(r, s) Op/102, 1
onto [ˈɒntə] auf; in 3/98, 15.1
to **open** [ˈəʊpən] (sich) öffnen V
to open up [ˌəʊpən‿ˈʌp] sich öffnen 2/40, 2
open [ˈəʊpən] offen, geöffnet 1/21, 3
opening times *(only pl)* [ˈəʊpnɪŋ ˌtaɪmz] Öffnungszeiten 1/23, 9
to operate [ˈɒpəreɪt] betreiben 3/100, 4.1
opinion [əˈpɪnjən] Meinung, Ansicht 5/142, 10
opposite [ˈɒpəzɪt] Gegenteil 5/153, 7.1; gegenüberliegend 4/134, 17.1
or [ɔ:] oder V

orange ['ɒrɪndʒ] Orange, Apfelsine 3/76, 9
orange ['ɒrɪndʒ] orange(farben) v
orange juice ['ɒrɪndʒ ˌdʒuːs] Orangensaft v
order ['ɔːdə] Ordnung, Reihenfolge 1/17, 11
to organise ['ɔːgənaɪz] organisieren 4/126, 1
other ['ʌðər] andere(r, s) v
ouch [aʊtʃ] aua, autsch 6/166, 1
our [aʊə] unser(e) v
out [aʊt] nach draußen, (he)raus 3/99, 1
out [aʊt] im Freien, draußen 3/98, 15.1
to go out [gəʊ‿'aʊt] (hinaus)gehen; ausgehen Op/104, 2
out of ['aʊt‿əv] (her)aus 3/98, 15.1
outdoor(s) [ˌaʊt'dɔː] draußen; im Freien; Outdoor- 6/193, 6
outside [ˌaʊt'saɪd] im Freien, draußen 1/16, 9
outside [ˌaʊt'saɪd] nach draußen, raus 3/98, 15.1
to **sleep over** [sliːp‿'əʊvə] übernachten, über Nacht bleiben 6/166, 1
over ['əʊvə] über 6/193, 6
over ['əʊvə] hinüber, herüber Op/102, 1; vorbei 6/CC
to have sb over [ˌhæv ˌsʌmbədi‿'əʊvə] jdn zu sich einladen, jdn zu Besuch haben 2/CC
over there [ˌəʊvə 'ðeə] dort (drüben) v
own [əʊn] eigene(r, s) v
on one's own [ɒn wʌnz‿'əʊn] allein(e) 3/99, 1

P

to **pack** [pæk] packen 6/177, 8
packet ['pækɪt] Packung, Schachtel 4/114, 2
page [peɪdʒ] Seite 1/21, 3
paid [peɪd] *Vergangenheitsform von „pay“*
pain [peɪn] Schmerz, Leid Op/102, 1
pair [peə] Paar 1/20, 1
rhyming pair ['raɪmɪŋ peə] Reimpaar 2/62, 8.2
Pakistani [ˌpɑːkɪ'stɑːni] pakistanisch 6/172, 13
palace ['pæləs] Palast 2/40, 2
pancake ['pæŋkeɪk] Pfannkuchen 4/113, 11
panic ['pænɪk] Panik Op/102, 1
paper *(no pl)* ['peɪpə] Papier v
parents *(only pl)* ['peərənts] Eltern v
parrot ['pærət] Papagei 2/CC
part [pɑːt] Teil 2/42, 6
to **have a party** [ˌhæv‿ə 'pɑːti] eine Party machen/feiern 4/108, 2
pass [pɑːs] Pass 6/190, 2.1
to pass by [pɑːs baɪ] vorbeifahren, vorbeigehen 4/132, 11
to pass through [ˌpɑːs 'θruː] durchreisen, durchlaufen 2/40, 2
past [pɑːst] Vergangenheit 1/15, 8
past [pɑːst] nach *(bei Uhrzeitangaben)* v; vorbei/vorüber an 2/50, 3
half past (eight) ['hɑːf ˌpɑːst] halb (neun) v
past participle [ˌpɑːst 'pɑːtɪsɪpl] Partizip Perfekt 6/186, 5
past progressive [ˌpɑːst prəʊ'gresɪv] Verlaufsform der Vergangenheit 6/191, 2.2
pasta *(no pl)* ['pæstə] Nudeln 4/116, 6
path [pɑːθ] Weg, Pfad 3/98, 15.1
paw [pɔː] Pfote, Tatze 2/53, 8
to **pay** *(irr)* [peɪ] (be)zahlen 2/54, 11
to pay respect [ˌpeɪ‿rɪ'spekt] Respekt zollen 4/113, 11
PE (= **physical education**) [ˌpiː‿'iː, ˌfɪzɪkl‿ˌedjʊ'keɪʃn] Sport(unterricht) v
to peel [piːl] schälen 4/116, 6
pen [pen] Stift v
pencil ['pensl] Bleistift v
pencil case ['pensl keɪs] (Feder)mäppchen v
pencil sharpener ['pensl ˌʃɑːpnə] (Bleistift)spitzer v
penguin ['peŋgwɪn] Pinguin 2/52, 7
people *(no pl)* ['piːpl] Leute, Menschen 1/20, 1
pepper ['pepə] Paprika 4/114, 2
pepper *(no pl)* ['pepə] Pfeffer 4/116, 6
per [pɜː] pro v
perfect ['pɜːfɪkt] perfekt v
perhaps [pə'hæps] vielleicht 3/77, 10
personal ['pɜːsnəl] persönlich; privat 1/21, 3
pet [pet] Haustier v
(tele)phone [fəʊn] Telefon v
(mobile) phone [ˌməʊbaɪl 'fəʊn] Mobiltelefon, Handy v
(phone) call ['fəʊn kɔːl] (Telefon)anruf v
phone case ['fəʊn keɪs] Handyhülle 4/119, 12
to **phone** [fəʊn] anrufen v
photo ['fəʊtəʊ] Foto v
to **take photos** [ˌteɪk 'fəʊtəʊz] Bilder machen, fotografieren v
photographer [fə'tɒgrəfə] Fotograf/in 3/97, 12
phrase [freɪz] Satz; Ausdruck, (Rede)wendung 2/50, 3
to pick [pɪk] aussuchen, auswählen 1/32, 11
to pick up [ˌpɪk‿'ʌp] aufheben Op/102, 1
to **have a picnic** [ˌhæv‿ə 'pɪknɪk] ein Picknick machen; picknicken v
picture ['pɪktʃə] Bild, Foto v
piece [piːs] Stück 4/116, 6
pig [pɪg] Schwein v
pineapple ['paɪnˌæpl] Ananas v
pink [pɪŋk] rosa, pink v
Pisces ['paɪsiːz] Fische *(Sternzeichen)* 3/96, 8.1

place [pleɪs] Ort; Platz v
to **place** [pleɪs] stellen, legen 4/132, 11
placemat ['pleɪs,mæt] Set, Platzdeckchen 5/151, 12
to plan [plæn] planen Op/105, 4
plane [pleɪn] Flugzeug 1/19, 15
planner ['plænə] Planer/in; Kalender zur Arbeitsplanung 1/21, 3
plant [plɑ:nt] Pflanze 2/52, 6
plastic ['plæstɪk] Plastik, Kunststoff 5/144, 1
plate [pleɪt] Teller v
platform ['plæt,fɔ:m] Bahnsteig, Plattform 2/40, 2
play [pleɪ] Spiel; (Theater)stück 3/87, 14
to **play** [pleɪ] spielen v
to play sth for/to sb ['pleɪ ,sʌmθɪŋ fə/tə ,sʌmbədi] jmd etw vorspielen, etw für jmd abspielen 3/87, 13
player ['pleɪə] Spieler/in 3/80, 1
playground ['pleɪ,graʊnd] Spielplatz v
please [pli:z] bitte v
plus [plʌs] plus, zuzüglich 6/176, 6
p.m. (= **post meridiem**) [,pi:'em, ,pəʊst mə'rɪdiəm] nachmittags, abends *(nur hinter Uhrzeit zwischen 12 Uhr mittags und Mitternacht)* v
poem ['pəʊɪm] Gedicht 1/20, 2
point [pɔɪnt] Punkt 4/134, 17.1
point of view [,pɔɪnt‿əv‿'vju:] Standpunkt; Perspektive 5/150, 11
Poland ['pəʊlənd] Polen v
police officer [pə'li:s‿,ɒfɪsə] Polizeibeamter/-beamtin 3/77, 10
polite [pə'laɪt] höflich 5/144, 1
poor [pɔ:] arm 3/82, 4
possible ['pɒsəbəl] möglich 1/24, 10
to **post sth** ['pəʊst ,sʌmθɪŋ] etw schicken; etw ins Internet stellen 5/150, 11
postcard ['pəʊst,kɑ:d] Postkarte 1/15, 8
potato *(pl* **-es***)* [pə'teɪtəʊ, pə'teɪtəʊz] Kartoffel 4/113, 11
pound [paʊnd] Pfund (brit. Währung) v
to pour [pɔ:] gießen, schütten 4/116, 6
to **practise** ['præktɪs] üben 1/37, 5.1
predator ['predətə] Raubtier 2/53, 8
to **prefer** [prɪ'fɜ:] vorziehen, bevorzugen, lieber mögen 1/37, 5.1
to **prepare** [prɪ'peə] (sich) vorbereiten; zubereiten v
present ['preznt] Geschenk v
to present [prɪ'zent] präsentieren 1/19, 16
present perfect [,preznt 'pɜ:fɪkt] Perfekt 6/169, 5
presentation [,prezn'teɪʃn] Präsentation 1/25, 13
to press [pres] drücken 6/CC
pretty ['prɪti] hübsch v
pretty *(informal)* ['prɪti] ziemlich 4/110, 5
price [praɪs] Preis v
primary school ['praɪməri ,sku:l] Grundschule 1/37, 5.1
private ['praɪvət] privat 2/CC
prize [praɪz] Preis, Gewinn 4/135, 17.2
probably ['prɒbəbli] wahrscheinlich 6/190, 2.1
professional [prə'feʃnəl] professionell, Profi- 3/88, 5
program ['prəʊgræm] (Computer)programm 1/19, 16
programme ['prəʊgræm] Programm; Sendung 6/172, 12
project ['prɒdʒekt] Projekt 1/37, 5.1
to **protect** [prə'tekt] (be)schützen 3/80, 1
proud [praʊd] stolz 5/148, 8
to provide [prə'vaɪd] zur Verfügung stellen, sorgen für; bieten, liefern 3/100, 4.1
public school ['pʌblɪk ,sku:l] Privatschule 1/20, LL
pudding ['pʊdɪŋ] Süßspeise, Nachspeise; Pudding 4/135, 17.2
to **pull** [pʊl] ziehen 3/98, 15.1
pumpkin ['pʌmpkɪn] Kürbis 4/108, 2
punch [pʌntʃ] Punsch, Bowle 4/133, 4.1
purple ['pɜ:pl] violett, lila(farben) v
to **put** *(irr)* [pʊt] setzen, legen, stellen v
to **put on** [,pʊt‿'ɒn] anziehen 6/180, 10
to put on [,pʊt‿'ɒn] auftragen 2/CC
to put one's hand up [,pʊt wʌnz 'hænd‿ʌp] sich melden 5/164, 4.2
to put up [,pʊt‿'ʌp] aufhängen 1/19, 16; aufstellen 4/130, 2.2
puzzle ['pʌzl] Puzzle; Rätsel 6/191, 2.2
pyramid ['pɪrəmɪd] Pyramide 2/66, 14.1

Q

quarter (to/past) ['kwɔ:tə] Viertel (vor/nach) v
queen [kwi:n] Königin 2/40, 2
question ['kwestʃn] Frage v
to **ask questions** [,ɑ:sk‿'kwestʃnz] Fragen stellen 6/190, 2.1
queue [kju:] Schlange, Reihe 6/CC
quick [kwɪk] schnell 2/54, 11
quiet ['kwaɪət] leise, ruhig v
to quiz sb ['kwɪz‿,sʌmbədi] jdn befragen/prüfen 5/157, 6.2

R

racing *(no pl)* ['reɪsɪŋ] Rennen 3/78, 12
raffle ['ræfl] Tombola, Verlosung 2/CC
railway station ['reɪlweɪ ,steɪʃn] Bahnhof 2/40, 2
to **rain** [reɪn] regnen 1/17, 11
rainy ['reɪni] regnerisch 1/10, 1
to raise [reɪz] heben 4/134, 17.1
ran [ræn] *Vergangenheitsform von „run“*

rang [ræŋ] *Vergangenheitsform von „ring“*
to rank [ræŋk] einstufen; anordnen 5/151, 13
rather ['rɑːðə] ziemlich; lieber 6/178, 9
I'd rather … [aɪd 'rɑːðə] ich würde lieber … 5/162, 9
raven ['reɪvn] Rabe 2/58, 12
RE (= **religious education**) [ˌɑːr‿'iː, rəˌlɪdʒəs‿ˌedjʊ'keɪʃn] Religion(sunterricht) v
to **reach** [riːtʃ] (er)reichen 2/49, 2
to **read** *(irr)* [riːd] lesen v
to read along [ˌriːd‿ə'lɒŋ] mitlesen 1/12, 3
to read sth to sb ['riːd ˌsʌmθɪŋ tə ˌsʌmbədi] jdm etw vorlesen Op/104, 3
reader ['riːdə] Leser/in 4/135, 17.2
reading ['riːdɪŋ] Lesen; Lesung 3/85, 8
ready ['redi] fertig, bereit v
to get ready (for sth) [get 'redi] sich (für etw) bereit machen 6/190, 2.1
real [rɪəl] wirklich; echt 3/80, 1
really ['rɪəli] wirklich v
reason ['riːzn] Grund 2/66, 14.1
recipe ['resəpi] Rezept 4/116, 6
to record [rɪ'kɔːd] aufnehmen, aufzeichnen 1/19, 16
recording [rɪ'kɔːdɪŋ] Aufnahme 2/47, 15
to recycle [riː'saɪkl] wiederverwerten, recyceln 2/66, 14.1
red [red] rot v
red-haired [ˌred'heəd] rothaarig 3/98, 15.1
registration [ˌredʒɪ'streɪʃn] Anmeldung; Überprüfung der Anwesenheit 1/38, 8.1
regular ['regjʊlə] regelmäßig; normal 5/164, 4.2
reindeer ['reɪnˌdɪə] Rentier 4/130, 2.2
relative ['relətɪv] Verwandte/r, Angehörige/r 4/130, 2.2
to **relax** [rɪ'læks] sich entspannen 2/40, 2
relaxed [rɪ'lækst] entspannt; locker, gelassen 5/160, 4.1
relieved [rɪ'liːvd] erleichtert Op/102, 1
to remember [rɪ'membə] sich erinnern (an) 1/20, 1; (an etw) denken 2/47, 15
to **repair** [rɪ'peə] reparieren 3/77, 10
to repeat [rɪ'piːt] wiederholen 4/109, 4
to replace [rɪ'pleɪs] ersetzen 4/133, 8.1
report [rɪ'pɔːt] Bericht; Zeugnis 1/37, 5.1
to report [rɪ'pɔːt] berichten, (sich) melden 5/144, 1
reported speech [rɪˌpɔːtɪd 'spiːtʃ] indirekte Rede 2/68, 6.2
the Republic of Ireland [ðə rɪˌpʌblɪk‿əv‿'aɪələnd] Republik Irland 3/100, 4.1
rescue ['reskjuː] Rettung 3/100, 4.1
to **rescue** ['reskjuː] retten 3/80, 1
respect *(no pl)* [rɪ'spekt] Respekt, Achtung 5/144, 1
to pay respect [ˌpeɪ‿rɪ'spekt] Respekt zollen 4/113, 11
result [rɪ'zʌlt] Ergebnis 1/34, 3.1
rhyming pair ['raɪmɪŋ peə] Reimpaar 2/62, 8.2
rice *(no pl)* [raɪs] Reis v
rich [rɪtʃ] reich 4/130, 2.2
ride [raɪd] Fahrt; Tour 1/16, 9
ride [raɪd] (Aus)ritt 2/CC
to **go for a ride** [ˌgəʊ fər‿ə 'raɪd] eine Fahrt machen 2/69, 11
to **ride** *(irr)* [raɪd] fahren; reiten v
right [raɪt] richtig v; (nach) rechts 2/50, 3
right [raɪt] genau, direkt 2/49, 2
on the/your right [ˌɒn ðə/jɔː 'raɪt] rechts, auf der rechten Seite 2/48, 1
right [raɪt] Recht 3/99, 1
to **be right** [ˌbiː 'raɪt] Recht haben v
to **be right back** [biː ˌraɪt 'bæk] gleich zurück sein 6/180, 10
right now [raɪt 'naʊ] gerade, jetzt, im Augenblick v
to **ring** *(irr)* [rɪŋ] klingeln; läuten 6/191, 2.2
to **risk** [rɪsk] riskieren, aufs Spiel setzen 3/80, 1
to **roar** [rɔː] (an)brüllen 4/134, 17.1
robot ['rəʊbɒt] Roboter 3/98, 15.1
role [rəʊl] Rolle 5/143, 13
role play ['rəʊlˌpleɪ] Rollenspiel 5/143, 13
Rome [rəʊm] Rom 6/174, 1
room [ruːm] Zimmer v
living room ['lɪvɪŋ ruːm] Wohnzimmer v
root [ruːt] Wurzel 2/52, 6
rope [rəʊp] Seil 4/135, 17.2
rough [rʌf] rau 3/101, 12.1
to **row** [rəʊ] rudern 3/82, 4
rowing boat ['rəʊɪŋ bəʊt] Ruderboot 3/99, 1
rubber *(BE)* ['rʌbə] Radiergummi v
rubbish *(no pl)* ['rʌbɪʃ] Müll v
ruin ['ruːɪn] Ruine 6/194, 6.1
rule [ruːl] Regel v
to **rule** [ruːl] regieren 3/98, 15.1
ruler ['ruːlə] Lineal v
to **run** *(irr)* [rʌn] laufen, rennen v
Russia ['rʌʃə] Russland 4/135, 17.2

S

sad [sæd] traurig 1/17, 11
safe [seɪf] sicher 3/82, 4
Sagittarius [ˌsædʒɪ'teəriəs] Schütze *(Sternzeichen)* 3/96, 8.1
said [sed] *Vergangenheitsform von „say“*
sailing *(no pl)* ['seɪlɪŋ] Segeln 6/176, 6
salad ['sæləd] Salat 4/114, 2
salt *(no pl)* [sɔːlt] Salz 4/116, 6
salted ['sɔːltɪd] gesalzen 4/116, 6

the same [ðə 'seɪm] der-/die-/dasselbe 5/164, 4.2
sandy ['sændi] sandig 6/193, 6
sang [sæŋ] *Vergangenheitsform von „sing"*
sari ['sɑ:ri] Sari *(gewickeltes Gewand indischer Frauen)* 4/110, 5
sat [sæt] *Vergangenheitsform von „sit"*
Saturday ['sætədeɪ] Samstag v
sauce [sɔ:s] Soße 1/17, 11
sausage ['sɒsɪdʒ] Wurst, Würstchen v
to **save** [seɪv] retten 3/82, 4
saw [sɔ:] *Vergangenheitsform von „see"*
to **say** *(irr)* [seɪ] sagen v
scared [skeəd] verängstigt Op/102, 1
to **be scared (of sth/sb)** [bi: 'skeəd] (vor etw/jdm) Angst haben 2/54, 11
scarf *(pl* **-s** *or* **scarves***)* [skɑ:f, skɑ:vz] Schal 4/118, 10
scary ['skeəri] Furcht erregend; unheimlich 4/108, 2
school [sku:l] Schule v
schoolbag ['sku:lbæg] Schultasche v
school grounds ['sku:l ˌgraʊndz] Schulgelände 5/144, 1
boarding school ['bɔ:dɪŋ ˌsku:l] Internat 1/20, LL
comprehensive school [ˌkɒmprɪ'hensɪv ˌsku:l] Gesamtschule 1/20, LL
high school ['haɪ ˌsku:l] *weiterführende Schule (Klasse 9-12)* 1/37, 5.1
primary school ['praɪməri ˌsku:l] Grundschule 1/37, 5.1
public school ['pʌblɪk ˌsku:l] Privatschule 1/20, LL
science ['saɪəns] Naturwissenschaft v
(pair of) scissors *(only pl)* ['sɪzəz] Schere v
scooter ['sku:tə] (Tret)roller 3/79, 16
to **score** [skɔ:] einen Punkt machen, punkten 4/134, 17.1
to **score a goal** [skɔ:r‿ə 'gəʊl] ein Tor schießen 3/80, 1
Scorpio ['skɔ:piəʊ] Skorpion *(Sternzeichen)* 3/72, 1
Scotland ['skɒtlənd] Schottland 6/175, 4
scrambled ['skræmbld] verrührt; durcheinander 1/27, 6.1
scrambled egg [ˌskræmbld‿'eg] Rührei v
to **scream** [skri:m] schreien; kreischen 2/54, 11
screen [skri:n] Leinwand; Bildschirm 6/190, 2.1
the sea *(no pl)* [ðə 'si:] Meer, See 3/80, 1
search [sɜ:tʃ] Suche 3/100, 4.1
to search [sɜ:tʃ] (durch)suchen 2/46, 14
seat [si:t] (Sitz)platz 5/146, 5
second ['sekənd] Sekunde 4/114, 2
second ['sekənd] zweite(r, s) v
second-hand [ˌsekənd'hænd] gebraucht, secondhand 5/150, 11
secondary school ['sekəndri ˌsku:l] *weiterführende Schule für Kinder zwischen 11 und 16/18* 1/37, 5.1
secret ['si:krət] geheim 3/98, 15.1
secretary ['sekrətri] Sekretär/in v
to **see** *(irr)* [si:] sehen v
to see *(irr)* [si:] besuchen 5/159, 11.2
see you ['si: ju:] bis dann, bis bald 6/180, 10
seed [si:d] Same(n), Korn v
seen [si:n] *siehe „see"*
selection [sɪ'lekʃn] Auswahl 1/21, 3
to **sell** *(irr)* [sel] verkaufen 3/77, 10
seller ['selə] Verkäufer/in 2/68, 6.1
to **send** *(irr)* [send] (zu)schicken 5/141, 9
sentence ['sentəns] Satz 1/12, 3
to **separate** ['sepəreɪt] trennen 5/144, 1
September [sep'tembə] September v
series *(only pl)* ['sɪəri:z] Serie, Reihe 5/142, 10
serious ['sɪəriəs] ernst(haft) 6/172, 13
to serve [sɜ:v] (be)dienen; servieren 1/21, 3
service ['sɜ:vɪs] Service; Bedienung 3/100, 4.1
to set *(irr)* [set] (fest)setzen, vereinbaren 1/21, 3; (ein)stellen 4/132, 11
to **set off** [set‿'ɒf] (an)zünden 4/108, 2
several ['sevrəl] einige 2/CC
shall [ʃæl] sollen 4/134, 8.2
shape [ʃeɪp] Form; Art 3/98, 15.1
shard [ʃɑ:d] Scherbe 2/66, 14.1
to **share** [ʃeə] teilen v
sharp [ʃɑ:p] scharf 2/53, 8
she [ʃi:] sie v
bed sheet ['bed ʃi:t] Bettlaken 4/134, 17.1
shelf *(pl* **shelves***)* [ʃelf, ʃelvz] Regal v
to **shine** *(irr)* [ʃaɪn] scheinen, leuchten 4/110, 5
shiny ['ʃaɪni] glänzend 3/98, 15.1
ship [ʃɪp] Schiff 2/40, 2
shipwreck ['ʃɪpˌrek] Schiffswrack, Schiffbruch 3/80, 1
shirt [ʃɜ:t] Hemd; Bluse 1/21, 3
shoe [ʃu:] Schuh 1/21, 3
to **shoot** *(irr)* [ʃu:t] (er)schießen v
shop [ʃɒp] Geschäft, Laden v
shop assistant ['ʃɒp‿əˌsɪstənt] Verkäufer/in 3/77, 10
to **do the shopping** [ˌdu: ðə 'ʃɒpɪŋ] einkaufen (gehen) v
to **go shopping** [ˌgəʊ 'ʃɒpɪŋ] einkaufen gehen v
shopping centre ['ʃɒpɪŋ ˌsentə] Einkaufszentrum v
shopping list ['ʃɒpɪŋ lɪst] Einkaufszettel, Einkaufsliste 4/114, 2
short [ʃɔ:t] kurz v
short form ['ʃɔ:t fɔ:m] Abkürzung 2/45, 11
should [ʃʊd] sollte/müsste 4/114, 2

to **shout** [ʃaʊt] schreien, rufen 6/190, 2.1
talent show ['tælənt ˌʃəʊ] Talentwettbewerb 6/172, 12
to **show** *(irr)* [ʃəʊ] zeigen 2/45, 11
shut [ʃʌt] geschlossen 3/98, 15.1
side [saɪd] Seite 4/134, 17.1
sight [saɪt] Sehenswürdigkeit 2/40, 2
sign [saɪn] Zeichen; (Straßen-/Verkehrs)schild 3/72, 1
silly ['sɪli] dumm; albern 4/130, 2.2
silver ['sɪlvə] silbern 4/132, 11
silverback ['sɪlvəˌbæk] Silberrücken 2/55, 12
similar ['sɪmɪlə] ähnlich 4/130, 2.2
simple ['sɪmpl] einfach 3/98, 15.1
simple past [ˌsɪmpl 'pɑ:st] einfache Vergangenheit 1/18, 13
since [sɪns] seit 3/100, 4.1
to **sing** *(irr)* [sɪŋ] singen v
to sing along [ˌsɪŋ‿ə'lɒŋ] mitsingen 3/81, 3
singer ['sɪŋə] Sänger/in 5/142, 10
lead singer [li:d 'sɪŋə] Leadsänger/in 6/190, 2.1
sister ['sɪstə] Schwester v
to **sit** *(irr)* [sɪt] sitzen v
to **sit down** [ˌsɪt 'daʊn] sich (hin)setzen v
situation [ˌsɪtʃu'eɪʃn] Situation, Lage 5/159, 11.1
to **skate** [skeɪt] skaten, Skateboard fahren 5/163, 4
skateboarding *(no pl)* ['skeɪtˌbɔ:dɪŋ] Skateboardfahren v
sketchbook ['sketʃˌbʊk] Skizzenbuch 6/178, 9
skill [skɪl] Fähigkeit, Fertigkeit 1/11, 2
skirt [skɜ:t] Rock 1/21, 3
sky [skaɪ] Himmel 1/15, 8
skyscraper ['skaɪˌskreɪpə] Wolkenkratzer 1/36, 11
slave [sleɪv] Sklave/Sklavin 3/98, 15.1
to **sleep** *(irr)* [sli:p] schlafen v
to sleep in [ˌsli:p‿'ɪn] ausschlafen 2/cc
to **sleep over** [sli:p‿'əʊvə] übernachten, über Nacht bleiben 6/166, 1
sleepover ['sli:pˌəʊvə] Übernachtung; Übernachtungsparty v
slice [slaɪs] Scheibe 4/127, 6
slim [slɪm] schlank, schmal, dünn v
slow [sləʊ] langsam 5/150, 11
small [smɔ:l] klein v
smart [smɑ:t] schlau; schick 5/148, 8
to **smell (of)** [smel] riechen (nach) 4/117, 8
smile [smaɪl] Lächeln 2/cc
to **smile** [smaɪl] lächeln 2/54, 11
to smoke [sməʊk] rauchen 2/44, 10
snail [sneɪl] Schnecke 6/174, 1
snake [sneɪk] Schlange v
sneaker ['sni:kə] Sneaker, Turnschuh 4/133, 8.1
so [səʊ] deshalb; also v
so that ['səʊ ðæt] sodass, damit v
soap [səʊp] Seife v
soap (opera) ['səʊp (‿ˌɒprə)] Seifenoper, Soap 6/172, 12
social worker ['səʊʃl ˌwɜ:kə] Sozialarbeiter/in 5/164, 4.2
soft [sɒft] weich Op/102, 1
solution [sə'lu:ʃn] Lösung 5/143, 13
to **solve** [sɒlv] lösen, klären 5/139, 5
some [sʌm] einige; etwas v
someone ['sʌmwʌn] jemand 2/49, 2
something ['sʌmθɪŋ] etwas v
something else [ˌsʌmθɪŋ‿'els] (noch) etwas anderes 6/168, 3
sometimes ['sʌmtaɪmz] manchmal v
son [sʌn] Sohn v
soon [su:n] bald v
sore [sɔ:] wund, entzündet 6/170, 7
sore throat [ˌsɔ: 'θrəʊt] Halsschmerzen 6/170, 7
sorry ['sɒri] Verzeihung!, Entschuldigung!; Wie bitte? v
I'm sorry. [aɪm 'sɒri] Das tut mir leid. 2/49, 2
to sort [sɔ:t] sortieren 5/165, 8.1
to sort out [ˌsɔ:t‿'aʊt] aussortieren 5/155, 13
sound [saʊnd] Geräusch, Klang; Ton 1/22, 6
to **sound** [saʊnd] klingen, sich anhören v
sound system ['saʊnd ˌsɪstəm] Stereoanlage, Hi-Fi-Anlage 6/190, 2.1
soup [su:p] Suppe 3/82, 4
sour cream [ˌsaʊə 'kri:m] Sauerrahm, saure Sahne 4/113, 11
South Africa [saʊθ‿'æfrɪkə] Südafrika 4/134, 17.1
South America [ˌsaʊθ‿ə'merɪkə] Südamerika 2/52, 6
south-westerly [ˌsaʊθ'westəli] südwestlich 6/176, 6
spaceship ['speɪsˌʃɪp] Raumschiff 3/98, 15.1
Spain [speɪn] Spanien 1/10, 1
Spanish ['spænɪʃ] Spanisch; spanisch v
to **speak** *(irr)* [spi:k] sprechen, reden 3/85, 8
special ['speʃl] besondere(r, s), speziell v
spectacular [spek'tækjʊlə] atemberaubend, spektakulär 2/66, 14.1
to **spell** *(irr)* [spel] buchstabieren v
to **spend** *(irr)* [spend] ausgeben *(Geld)*; verbringen *(Zeit)* 5/150, 11
spent [spent] *Vergangenheitsform von „spend"*
to split *(irr)* [splɪt] teilen; spalten 4/134, 17.1
spooky *(informal)* ['spu:ki] unheimlich; schaurig Op/102, 1
spoon [spu:n] Löffel v

sports *(only pl)* [spɔːts] Sport; Sportart 6/172, 12
sports ground ['spɔːts ˌgraʊnd] Sportplatz v
sports hall ['spɔːts hɔːl] Sporthalle v
sportsperson ['spɔːtsˌpɜːsn] Sportler/in 3/100, 1.1
spot [spɒt] Fleck; Stelle 2/69, 9.1
sprinkles *(only pl)* ['sprɪŋkls] Streusel 4/135, 17.2
to **squeak** [skwiːk] quieken; piepsen 4/134, 17.1
stadium ['steɪdiəm] Stadion 2/40, 2
staff *(no pl)* [stɑːf] Mitarbeiter, Personal 1/21, 3
stage [steɪdʒ] Bühne 6/190, 2.1
stall [stɔːl] (Verkaufs)stand 2/40, 2
to **stand** *(irr)* [stænd] stehen; ertragen, ausstehen, aushalten v
to stand up [ˌstænd‿'ʌp] aufstehen 6/CC
stand up paddleboarding *(no pl)* [ˌstænd‿ʌp 'pædlbɔːdɪŋ] Stehpaddeln 6/193, 6
star [stɑː] Stern 3/72, 1
to **start** [stɑːt] anfangen, beginnen v
statement ['steɪtmənt] Aussage; Äußerung 5/149, 10
station ['steɪʃn] Bahnhof; Station 3/100, 4.1
to **stay** [steɪ] bleiben v; übernachten, wohnen 1/10, 1
to **stay up** [ˌsteɪ‿'ʌp] aufbleiben; wach bleiben 5/160, 4.1
to **stay with sb** ['steɪ wɪð ˌsʌmbədi] bei jmd übernachten, wohnen 1/17, 11
to **steal** *(irr)* [stiːl] stehlen, klauen v
step [step] Stufe; Schritt 6/178, 9
to step [step] treten 3/98, 15.1
stick [stɪk] Stift, Stück 4/114, 2
still [stɪl] (immer) noch, noch immer 5/150, 11
to **stink** *(irr)* [stɪŋk] stinken 5/150, 11
stocking ['stɒkɪŋ] (Weihnachts)strumpf 4/109, LL
stomach ache ['stʌmək ‿ˌeɪk] Magenschmerzen, Bauchschmerzen 6/192, 7.1
stood [stʊd] *Vergangenheitsform von „stand"*
to **stop** [stɒp] aufhören; beenden v
to stop [stɒp] anhalten Op/102, 1
Stop it! ['stɒp‿ɪt] Hör(t) auf (damit)! v
department store [dɪ'pɑːtmənt ˌstɔː] Kaufhaus 2/64, 4.1
storm [stɔːm] Sturm 3/80, 1
stormy ['stɔːmi] stürmisch 3/86, 12
story ['stɔːri] Geschichte, Erzählung v
straight [streɪt] direkt Op/102, 1
straight (on) [streɪt] gerade(aus) 2/50, 3
strange [streɪndʒ] sonderbar, komisch 2/49, 2
straw [strɔː] Strohhalm, Trinkhalm v
street [striːt] Straße v
stretch [stretʃ] Wegstrecke, Streckenabschnitt 6/194, 6.1
strong [strɒŋ] stark 2/53, 8
student ['stjuːdnt] Schüler/in; Student/in v
study ['stʌdi] Lernen 1/23, 9
to **study** ['stʌdi] erforschen 3/80, 1; studieren; lernen 5/138, 2
stuff *(informal)* [stʌf] Zeug, Sachen 5/162, 9
stupid ['stjuːpɪd] dumm, blöd 3/73, 2
to style [staɪl] frisieren 3/77, 10
subject ['sʌbdʒɪkt] (Schul)fach v
such [sʌtʃ] solche(r,s) 5/162, 9
suddenly ['sʌdnli] plötzlich, auf einmal 3/98, 15.1
sugar *(no pl)* ['ʃʊgə] Zucker v
to suggest [sə'dʒest] vorschlagen 5/160, 3
summer ['sʌmə] Sommer 1/16, 9
summer camp ['sʌmə ˌkæmp] Ferienlager 6/193, 6
sun [sʌn] Sonne 2/40, 2
Sunday ['sʌndeɪ] Sonntag v
sunglasses *(only pl)* ['sʌnˌglɑːsɪz] Sonnenbrille 4/118, 10
sunny ['sʌni] sonnig 1/10, 1
sunset ['sʌnˌset] Sonnenuntergang 4/132, 11
superhero ['suːpəˌhɪərəʊ] Superheld/in 2/65, 10.1
superlative (form) [sʊ'pɜːlətɪv] Superlativ 4/119, 13
supervisor ['suːpəˌvaɪzə] Betreuer/in 6/178, 9
sure [ʃɔː] sicher 2/52, 7
to make sure [ˌmeɪk 'ʃɔː] sichergehen 5/150, 11
sure enough [ˌʃɔ‿ɪ'nʌf] tatsächlich 6/178, 9
surprise [sə'praɪz] Überraschung 4/114, 2
to surprise [sə'praɪz] überraschen 4/121, 18
surprised [sə'praɪzd] überrascht 6/178, 9
survey ['sɜːveɪ] Untersuchung, Umfrage 1/34, 3.1
survivor [sə'vaɪvə] Überlebende/r 3/82, 4
to swap [swɒp] tauschen Op/105, 4
swearword ['sweəˌwɜːd] Schimpfwort 5/164, 4.2
sweet [swiːt] Süßigkeit v; süß v
to have a sweet tooth [hæv‿ə swiːt 'tuːθ] gerne Süßigkeiten essen, eine Naschkatze sein 4/117, 8
sweetheart ['swiːtˌhɑːt] Liebling, Schatz v
to **swim** *(irr)* [swɪm] schwimmen v
swimmer ['swɪmə] Schwimmer/in v
swimming ['swɪmɪŋ] Schwimmen v

swimming pool ['swɪmɪŋ pu:l] Schwimmbecken, -bad v
swimwear *(no pl)* ['swɪm,weə] Badebekleidung 6/177, 8
sound system ['saʊnd ,sɪstəm] Stereoanlage, Hi-Fi-Anlage 6/190, 2.1

T

T. Rex (= tyrannosaurus rex) ['ti: reks, tɪ,rænəsɔ:rəs 'reks] Tyrannosaurus Rex 6/174, 1
table ['teɪbl] Tisch v
table ['teɪbl] Tabelle 1/22, 5
to **lay the table** [,leɪ ðə 'teɪbl] den Tisch decken v
table tennis *(no pl)* ['teɪbl ,tenɪs] Tischtennis v
tablespoon ['teɪbl,spu:n] Esslöffel 4/116, 6
tablet ['tæblət] Tablette 6/170, 7
tag *(no pl)* [tæg] Fangen (Spiel) 4/134, 17.1
tail [teɪl] Schwanz 2/53, 8
to **take** *(irr)* [teɪk] (mit)nehmen; bringen v
to take a look (at) [teɪk‿ə 'lʊk] einen Blick werfen (auf) 3/98, 15.1
to take action [teɪk‿'ækʃn] handeln, etw unternehmen 5/150, 11
to take care [teɪk 'keə] aufpassen 2/44, 10
to **take care of** [,teɪk‿'keər‿əv] sich kümmern um 3/77, 10
to take notes [,teɪk 'nəʊts] (sich) Notizen machen 2/65, 9.1
to **take out** [,teɪk‿'aʊt] hinausbringen v
to take part (in) [,teɪk 'pɑ:t] teilnehmen (an) 1/21, 3
to **take photos** [,teɪk 'fəʊtəʊz] Bilder machen, fotografieren v
to **take place** [,teɪk 'pleɪs] stattfinden 1/22, 6
to take turns [,teɪk 'tɜ:nz] sich abwechseln 1/28, 9.1
taken ['teɪkən] *siehe „take“*
talent show ['tælənt ,ʃəʊ] Talentwettbewerb 6/172, 12
talk [tɔ:k] Vortrag 2/65, 9.1; Gespräch; Unterhaltung 3/72, 1
to **talk (to)** [tɔ:k] sprechen/reden/ sich unterhalten (mit) v
to give a talk [,gɪv‿ə 'tɔ:k] einen Vortrag halten 2/46, 14
tall [tɔ:l] hoch; groß v
target task ['tɑ:gɪt‿tɑ:sk] Zielaufgabe 1/19, 16
to **taste** [teɪst] schmecken; probieren 2/69, 11
taught [tɔ:t] *Vergangenheitsform von „teach“*
Taurus ['tɔ:rəs] Stier *(Sternzeichen)* 3/96, 8.1
tea [ti:] Tee v
to **teach** *(irr)* [ti:tʃ] unterrichten; beibringen 6/178, 9
teacher ['ti:tʃə] Lehrer/in v
teammate ['ti:m,meɪt] Mannschaftskamerad/in, Mitspieler/in v
teaspoon ['ti:,spu:n] Teelöffel 4/116, 6
television ['telɪ,vɪʒn] Fernseher; Fernsehen 6/CC
to **tell** *(irr)* [tel] erzählen; sagen v
to tell sb to do sth [,tel ,sʌmbədi tə 'du: ,sʌmθɪŋ] jdm etw vorschreiben/ befehlen 2/49, 2
telly *(informal)* ['teli] Fernseher 6/172, 13
temperature ['temprɪtʃə] Temperatur 1/34, 4.1
to **have a temperature** [,hæv‿ə 'temprɪtʃə] Fieber haben 6/166, 1
temple ['templ] Tempel 4/135, 17.2
terrible ['terəbl] schrecklich, furchtbar v
test [test] Prüfung, Test; Klassenarbeit 5/138, 2
to test [test] prüfen, testen 1/25, 13
to **text** [tekst] eine SMS/ Kurznachricht schicken 2/49, 2
text message ['tekst ,mesɪdʒ] SMS, Kurznachricht 5/149, 10
text messaging *(no pl)* ['tekst ,mesɪdʒɪŋ] Versenden von SMS/Kurznachrichten 2/45, 11
the (River) Thames [ðə 'temz] Themse 2/40, 2
than [ðæn] als 4/117, 8
to **thank** [θæŋk] danken 4/108, 2
thank you ['θæŋk ju] danke v
thanks [θæŋks] danke v
thanks a lot [,θæŋks‿ə 'lɒt] vielen Dank v
thanks so much [,θæŋks‿səʊ 'mʌtʃ] vielen Dank 5/164, 4.2
that [ðæt] das; der/die/das v
that [ðæt] dass v
that [ðæt] wo 1/16, 9; diese(r, s) 2/CC; so 6/178, 9
like that [laɪk 'ðæt] so; solche(r, s) 5/136, 1
that's why ['ðæts waɪ] deshalb; das ist der Grund, warum 6/193, 6
the [ðə] der/die/das v
the … way [ðə 'weɪ] auf die … Art 2/CC
to the left [,tʊ ðə 'left] nach links 6/178, 9
their [ðeə] ihr(e) v
them [ðem] sie, ihnen 1/12, 3
theme [θi:m] Thema; Lektion, Kapitel 1/10, 1
then [ðen] dann, danach v
there [ðeə] dort, da v
there are ['ðeər‿ə] da sind; es gibt v
there is ['ðeər‿ɪz] da ist; es gibt v
these *(pl of* **this***)* [ði:z] diese v

they [ðeɪ] sie v
thin [θɪn] dünn 2/69, 9.1
thing [θɪŋ] Ding, Gegenstand, Sache v
How are things? [ˌhaʊ‿ɑː 'θɪŋz] Wie geht's? 5/139, 4
to **think** *(irr)* [θɪŋk] denken, glauben, meinen v
to think about (sb/sth) ['θɪŋk‿əˌbaʊt] an (jdn/etw) denken; sich (etw) überlegen 1/25, 13
to think of ['θɪŋk‿əv] denken an; sich ausdenken 1/24, 10
third [θɜːd] dritte(r, s) v
this [ðɪs] diese(r, s); das v
like this [laɪk 'ðɪs] so 5/150, 11; solche(r, s) 5/158, 11
this afternoon [ˌðɪs‿ˌɑːftə'nuːn] heute Nachmittag v
those *(pl of* **that***)* [ðəʊz] diese; jene 3/82, 4
though [ðəʊ] trotzdem, dennoch; aber 6/178, 9
thought [θɔːt] Gedanke 4/133, 4.1
thought [θɔːt] *Vergangenheitsform von „think"*
threatening ['θretnɪŋ] drohend, Droh-; bedrohlich 5/149, 10
throat [θrəʊt] Rachen, Hals 6/170, 7
sore throat [ˌsɔː 'θrəʊt] Halsschmerzen 6/170, 7
through [θruː] durch 5/151, 13
to **throw** *(irr)* [θrəʊ] werfen 5/144, 1
Thursday ['θɜːzdeɪ] Donnerstag v
to **tidy** ['taɪdi] aufräumen v
tidy ['taɪdi] ordentlich v
tie [taɪ] Krawatte 1/21, 3
till (= **until**) [tɪl] bis 5/160, 4.1
time [taɪm] (Uhr)zeit 1/19, 15; Mal 2/42, 6
free time ['friː taɪm] Freizeit v
What time is it? [ˌwɒt‿'taɪm‿ɪz‿ɪt] Wie viel Uhr ist es? v
Time's up! *(informal)* [ˌtaɪmz‿'ʌp] Die Zeit ist vorüber! 6/190, 2.1

time-saving ['taɪmˌseɪvɪŋ] Zeit sparend 6/CC
timetable ['taɪmteɪbl] Stundenplan v
tiny ['taɪni] winzig 2/CC
tip [tɪp] Tipp 5/150, 11
tired ['taɪəd] müde v
tissue ['tɪʃuː] Taschentuch 6/166, 1
title ['taɪtl] Titel 1/12, 3
to [tə] vor *(bei Uhrzeitangaben)*; in, nach, zu, an v
to [tə] bis v
to [tə] um zu 1/16, 9; für 2/CC
today [tə'deɪ] heute v
together [tə'geðə] zusammen, gemeinsam v
to go together [gəʊ tə'geðə] zusammenpassen 6/169, 5
Tokyo ['təʊkiəʊ] Tokio 6/CC
told [təʊld] *Vergangenheitsform von „tell"*
tomato *(pl* **-es***)* [tə'mɑːtəʊ, tə'mɑːtəʊz] Tomate 4/116, 6
cherry ['tʃeri] Kirsche 4/128, 7
tomorrow [tə'mɒrəʊ] morgen v
tongue twister ['tʌŋ ˌtwɪstə] Zungenbrecher 2/CC
tonight [tə'naɪt] heute Abend 4/132, 9.1
too [tuː] auch v
too (small/big/...) [tuː] zu (klein/groß/...) v
took [tʊk] *Vergangenheitsform von „take"*
tool [tuːl] Werkzeug 3/97, 14.1
tooth *(pl* **teeth***)* [tuːθ, tiːθ] Zahn v
to have a sweet tooth [hæv‿ə swiːt 'tuːθ] gerne Süßigkeiten essen, eine Naschkatze sein 4/117, 8
toothache ['tuːθeɪk] Zahnschmerzen 6/192, 7.1
toothbrush ['tuːθˌbrʌʃ] Zahnbürste 6/177, 8
top [tɒp] oberes Ende, Spitze 1/12, 3

top [tɒp] Top-, Spitzen- 1/16, 9
top [tɒp] oberste (r, s); Top- 2/66, 14.1
at the top [æt ðə 'tɒp] oben, am oberen Ende (von), an der Spitze (von) 2/48, 1
torch [tɔːtʃ] Taschenlampe, Fackel 6/177, 8
tortoise ['tɔːtəs] (Land)schildkröte 2/52, 6
to **touch** [tʌtʃ] berühren, anfassen v
tough [tʌf] robust, zäh, tough; hart 5/164, 4.2
tour guide ['tʊə gaɪd] Reiseführer/in, Reiseleiter/in 2/47, 15
tourist information [ˌtʊərɪst‿ˌɪnfə'meɪʃn] Touristeninfo(rmation) 2/47, 15
toward(s) [tə'wɔːd(z)] in Richtung 3/98, 15.1
tower ['taʊə] Turm 1/12, 3
town [taʊn] Stadt v
home town [ˌhəʊm 'taʊn] Heimatort 2/65, 9.1
toy [tɔɪ] Spielzeug v
tracksuit ['trækˌsuːt] Trainingsanzug 1/21, 3
traditional [trə'dɪʃnəl] traditionell 4/110, 5
train [treɪn] Zug, Eisenbahn 1/19, 15
to catch a train [ˌkætʃ‿ə 'treɪn] einen Zug nehmen 2/40, 2
trainer *(BE)* ['treɪnə] Turnschuh 5/138, 2
transparency [træns'pærənsi] (Overhead)folie 1/25, 13
to travel ['trævl] reisen 1/11, 2
travel agency ['trævl‿ˌeɪdʒnsi] Reisebüro 6/181, 12
treasure hunt ['treʒə hʌnt] Schatzsuche; Schnitzeljagd 6/176, 6
tree [triː] Baum v
Trick or treat! [ˌtrɪk‿ɔː 'triːt] Süßes oder Saures! 4/109, LL

tried [traɪd] *Vergangenheitsform von „try"*
trip [trɪp] Ausflug; Reise, Fahrt 6/175, 4
to **trip** [trɪp] stolpern 3/98, 15.1
hiking trip ['haɪkɪŋ trɪp] Wanderung Op/105, 4
trouble *(no pl)* ['trʌbl] Schwierigkeiten 3/77, 10
to **get in(to) trouble** [get‿ɪn(tə) 'trʌbl] Schwierigkeiten bekommen 5/150, 11
trousers *(only pl)* ['traʊzəz] Hose 1/21, 3
true [tru:] wahr; richtig v
to **trust** [trʌst] vertrauen 3/72, 1
to **try** *(irr)* [traɪ] versuchen; (aus)probieren 3/78, 13
the Tube [ðə 'tju:b] (Londoner) U-Bahn 2/44, LL
Tuesday ['tju:zdeɪ] Dienstag v
Turkey ['tɜ:ki] Türkei v
turkey ['tɜ:ki] Truthahn/-henne, Pute/r 4/130, 2.2
Turkish ['tɜ:kɪʃ] Türkisch; türkisch v
to **turn** [tɜ:n] sich drehen; abbiegen 2/50, 3
to turn [tɜ:n] verwandeln 2/68, 6.2; werden 4/135, 17.2
to turn around [ˌtɜ:n‿ə'raʊnd] (sich) umdrehen Op/102, 1
to turn on [ˌtɜ:n‿'ɒn] einschalten 5/139, 5
to turn out [ˌtɜ:n‿'aʊt] sich herausstellen 6/190, 2.1
(it's) your turn ['jɔ: ˌtɜ:n] du bist dran v
tutor room ['tju:tə ru:m] *Klassenzimmer, in dem sich die Schüler am Anfang des Schultages versammeln* 1/25, 12
TV (= **television**) [ˌti:'vi:, 'telɪˌvɪʒn] Fernseher; Fernsehen v
type [taɪp] Art; Typ, Sorte 5/149, 10

U

ugh *(informal)* [ʊx] bäh, igitt 4/114, 2
ugly ['ʌgli] hässlich 5/148, 8
UK (= **United Kingdom**) [ˌju:'keɪ, ju:ˌnaɪtɪd 'kɪŋdəm] Vereinigtes Königreich 6/176, 6
uncle ['ʌŋkl] Onkel v
under ['ʌndə] unter v
underground ['ʌndəˌgraʊnd] U-Bahn 2/44, LL
to **understand** *(irr)* [ˌʌndə'stænd] verstehen 5/160, 4.1
underwater [ˌʌndə'wɔ:tə] Unterwasser- 6/176, 6
unfriendly [ʌn'frendli] unfreundlich 6/CC
unhappy [ʌn'hæpi] unglücklich 6/178, 9
the United Kingdom [ðə ju:ˌnaɪtɪd 'kɪŋdəm] Vereinigtes Königreich (Großbritannien und Nordirland) 1/14, LL
unsure [ʌn'ʃʊə] unsicher 6/178, 9
untidy [ʌn'taɪdi] unordentlich, ungepflegt v
until [ən'tɪl] bis 1/21, 3
up [ʌp] (nach) oben; hinauf 6/178, 9
up to ['ʌp tu:] bis (zu) 1/23, 9
upper body [ˌʌpə 'bɒdi] Oberkörper 6/178, 9
us [ʌs] uns 1/17, 11
to **use** [ju:z] benutzen 1/21, 3
usually ['ju:ʒʊəli] gewöhnlich, normalerweise v

V

to **vacuum** ['vækjʊəm] (staub)saugen v
Valentine's Day ['væləntaɪnz deɪ] Valentinstag 4/109, LL
to vary ['veəri] verschieden sein, schwanken 2/65, 10.1
vegetable ['vedʒtəbl] Gemüse v
verse [vɜ:s] Strophe 1/37, 5.1
very ['veri] sehr v
vet (= **veterinarian**) [vet, ˌvetrɪ'neəriən] Tierarzt/-ärztin 3/74, 3
video game designer ['vɪdiəʊ geɪm dɪˌzaɪnə] Videospielentwickler/in 3/77, 10
view [vju:] Sicht; (Aus)blick, Aussicht 1/12, 3
point of view [ˌpɔɪnt‿əv‿'vju:] Standpunkt; Perspektive 5/150, 11
village ['vɪlɪdʒ] Dorf 6/193, 6
vinegar *(no pl)* ['vɪnɪgə] Essig 4/116, 6
Virgo ['vɜ:gəʊ] Jungfrau *(Sternzeichen)* 3/96, 8.1
visit ['vɪzɪt] Besuch 2/47, 15
to **visit** ['vɪzɪt] besuchen 1/10, 1
voice [vɔɪs] Stimme Op/102, 1
to have a vote [ˌhæv‿ə 'vəʊt] abstimmen 5/148, 8
voucher ['vaʊtʃə] Gutschein 4/117, 8

W

to **wait** [weɪt] warten v
waiter/waitress ['weɪtə, 'weɪtrəs] Bedienung, Kellner/in 2/69, 11
to wake [weɪk] aufwachen 2/CC
to **wake up** [weɪk‿'ʌp] aufwecken; aufwachen 3/98, 15.1
to **walk** [wɔ:k] gehen; laufen 1/15, 8
to **go for a walk** [ˌgəʊ fər‿ə 'wɔ:k] spazieren gehen 1/17, 11
to **walk the dog** [ˌwɔ:k ðə 'dɒg] den Hund ausführen v
wall [wɔ:l] Wand v
wall climbing ['wɔ:l ˌklaɪmɪŋ] Klettern an der Kletterwand 1/21, 3
to **want to do sth** [ˌwɒnt‿tə 'du: ˌsʌmθɪŋ] etw tun wollen v
to **want sb to do sth** [ˌwɒnt ˌsʌmbədi tə 'du: ˌsʌmθɪŋ] wollen, dass jmd etw tut 5/138, 3

war [wɔː] Krieg 3/98, 15.1
wardrobe ['wɔːdrəʊb] Kleiderschrank v
warning ['wɔːnɪŋ] Warnung 5/164, 4.2
was [wɒz] *Vergangenheitsform von „be"*
to **wash** [wɒʃ] (sich) waschen v
to **watch** [wɒtʃ] beobachten; anschauen v
to **watch TV** [ˌwɒtʃ ˌtiː 'viː] fernsehen v
water *(no pl)* ['wɔːtə] Wasser v
wave [weɪv] Welle 6/178, 9
wax [wæks] Wachs 2/65, 10.1
way [weɪ] Weg 1/12, 3
way [weɪ] Art, Weise 3/85, 8
the … way [ðə 'weɪ] auf die … Art 2/CC
to make one's way [ˌmeɪk wʌnz 'weɪ] gehen 6/190, 2.1
we [wiː] wir v
weapon ['wepən] Waffe 3/98, 15.1
to **wear** *(irr)* [weə] tragen 1/21, 3
weather ['weðə] Wetter 1/10, 1
Wednesday ['wenzdeɪ] Mittwoch v
week [wiːk] Woche 1/15, 7
weekend [ˌwiːk'end] Wochenende 2/45, 11
at the weekend [æt ðə 'wiːkˌend] am Wochenende v
welcome (to) ['welkəm] willkommen (in) v
You're welcome. [ˌjɔː 'welkəm] Gern geschehen., Bitte. 1/12, 3
to be welcome to do sth [biː ˌwelkəm tə 'duː ˌsʌmθɪŋ] etw gern tun können 2/65, 10.1
well [wel] nun (ja), tja v; gut 3/81, 2
to **get well** [get 'wel] gesund werden 6/168, 3
to do well [duː 'wel] gut abschneiden, erfolgreich sein 5/159, 11.1

Welsh [welʃ] Walisisch; walisisch 1/14, LL
went [went] *Vergangenheitsform von „go"*
were [wɜː] *Vergangenheitsform von „be"*
werewolf *(pl* werewolves*)* ['weəˌwʊlf, 'weəˌwʊlvz] Werwolf Op/102, 1
west [west] Westen 1/34, 4.1
Western Europe [ˌwestən 'jʊərəp] Westeuropa 2/66, 14.1
wet [wet] nass 6/184, 7.2
what [wɒt] was v
what [wɒt] welche(r, s) 1/13, 4
what a … ['wɒt‿ə] was für ein(e) … 2/69, 11
What about …? *(informal)* ['wɒt‿əˌbaʊt] Was ist mit …?, Wie wäre es mit …? v
what else [wɒt‿'els] was noch, was sonst 1/10, 1
what if [wɒt‿ɪf] was ist/wäre, wenn 5/161, 4.2
What time is it? [ˌwɒt‿'taɪm‿ɪz‿ɪt] Wie viel Uhr ist es? v
What's … like? [wɒts 'laɪk] Wie ist …? 1/19, 15
what's more [ˌwɒts 'mɔː] außerdem 6/176, 6
What's on? *(informal)* [wɒts‿'ɒn] Was ist los?, Was steht an? 6/168, 3
What's your name? [ˌwɒts jə 'neɪm] Wie heißt du? v
wheelchair ['wiːlˌtʃeə] Rollstuhl v
when [wen] wann; wenn; als v
where [weə] wo(hin) v
Where are you from? [ˌweər‿ɑː jə 'frɒm] Wo kommst du her? v
which [wɪtʃ] welche(r, s) 1/18, 14; was 2/66, 14.1
while *(no pl)* [waɪl] Weile 6/178, 9
to whisper ['wɪspə] flüstern Op/102, 1

white [waɪt] weiß v
who [huː] wer v
who [huː] der/die/das 2/CC
whole [həʊl] ganz, gesamt 6/190, 2.1
whose [huːz] wessen 4/120, 17
why [waɪ] warum v
that's why ['ðæts waɪ] deshalb; das ist der Grund, warum 5/159, 11.2
wife *(pl* **wives***)* [waɪf, waɪvz] Ehefrau 5/161, 4.2
will [wɪl] werden 3/74, 3
to **win** *(irr)* [wɪn] gewinnen 6/190, 2.1
window ['wɪndəʊ] Fenster v
windy ['wɪndi] windig 1/12, 3
winner ['wɪnə] Gewinner/in, Sieger/in 4/134, 17.1
I wish I could … [aɪ 'wɪʃ‿aɪ kʊd] Ich wünschte, ich könnte … 1/36, 11
to **make a wish** [ˌmeɪk‿ə 'wɪʃ] sich etwas wünschen v
best wishes [ˌbest 'wɪʃɪz] viele Grüße v
with [wɪð] mit v
to **go with** ['gəʊ wɪð] gehören zu, passen zu 5/136, 1
without [wɪð'aʊt] ohne 4/135, 17.2
woke up [wəʊk‿'ʌp] *Vergangenheitsform von „wake up"*
wolf *(pl* wolves*)* [wʊlf, wʊlvz] Wolf Op/102, 1
woman *(pl* **women***)* ['wʊmən, 'wɪmɪn] Frau v
won [wʌn] *Vergangenheitsform von „win"*
won't [wəʊnt] nicht werden 3/74, 3
to **wonder** ['wʌndə] sich fragen 2/69, 11
wonderful ['wʌndəfl] wunderbar, wundervoll 1/17, 11
wooden ['wʊdn] hölzern, Holz- 6/194, 6.1
woods *(only pl)* [wʊdz] Wald Op/102, 1
woof [wʊf] wau 4/114, 2

word [wɜ:d] Wort v
linking word ['lɪŋkɪŋ wɜ:d] Bindewort Op/105, 4
word web ['wɜ:d web] Wortnetz 1/20, 1
wordbank ['wɜ:dbæŋk] Wortfeld 1/11, 2
wore [wɔ:] *Vergangenheitsform von „wear“*
work [wɜ:k] Arbeit 2/68, 6.2
to **work** [wɜ:k] arbeiten v
to work [wɜ:k] funktionieren 5/144, 1
working day ['wɜ:kɪŋ deɪ] Werktag 4/130, 2.2
world [wɜ:ld] Welt, Erde 2/52, 6
all over the world [ˌɔ:l‿ˌəʊvə ðə 'wɜ:ld] auf der ganzen Welt 3/99, 1
around the world [əˌraʊnd ðə 'wɜ:ld] weltweit, auf der ganzen Welt 3/90, 13
world-famous ['wɜ:ldˌfeɪməs] weltberühmt, weltbekannt 2/40, 2
worried ['wʌrid] beunruhigt, besorgt 2/49, 2
to **worry** ['wʌri] sich Sorgen machen 3/74, 3
worse [wɜ:s] schlimmer, schlechter 5/146, 6
worst [wɜ:st] schlechteste(r, s), schlimmste(r, s) 5/139, 4
would [wʊd] würde(st, n, t) v
sb would like (to) [wʊd 'laɪk] jmd möchte (gern) v
sb would love (to) [ˌsʌmbədi wʊd 'lʌv] jmd möchte sehr gern 5/148, 8
to wreck [rek] zerstören 3/101, 12.1
to **write** *(irr)* [raɪt] schreiben v
to **write down** [ˌraɪt 'daʊn] aufschreiben 4/114, 2
written ['rɪtn] *siehe „write“*
wrong [rɒŋ] falsch v
to be wrong [bi: 'rɒŋ] nicht stimmen 2/67, 2
wrote [rəʊt] *Vergangenheitsform von „write“*

Y

yeah *(informal)* [jeə] ja 1/12, 3
year [jɪə] Jahr v
year [jɪə] Jahrgang(sstufe) 1/37, 5.1
yech *(informal)* [jek] i, igitt 2/CC
yellow ['jeləʊ] gelb v
to yelp [jelp] kläffen, jaulen Op/102, 1
yes [jes] ja v
yesterday ['jestədeɪ] gestern 1/12, 3
not yet [nɒt 'jet] noch nicht 6/166, 1
yoghurt *(no pl)* ['jɒgət] Joghurt v
you [ju:] du, dich, dir, Sie, Ihnen; ihr, euch v
You're welcome. [ˌjɔ: 'welkəm] Gern geschehen., Bitte. 1/12, 3
young [jʌŋ] jung 3/86, 12
your [jɔ:] dein(e); euer/eure; Ihr(e) v
yourself *(pl yourselves)* [jə'self, jə'selvz] dich, dir; selbst/ihr, euch; selbst 1/23, 7
youth club ['ju:θ ˌklʌb] Jugendzentrum 5/138, 2
yummy *(informal)* ['jʌmi] lecker v

Z

zookeeper ['zu:ˌki:pə] Zoowärter/in v
zoologist [zu'ɒlədʒɪst] Zoologe/-in 3/97, 12

A

abbiegen to turn
Abend evening
Abendessen dinner
abends in the evening; p.m. (= post meridiem) *(nur hinter Uhrzeit)*
Abenteuer adventure
aber but
Abfall litter *(no pl)*
Abitur A levels
Absicht aim
Abzeichen logo
Achtung respect *(no pl)*
Affe monkey; ape
Afrika Africa
AG club
ähnlich similar
Akrobat/in acrobat
Aktivität activity
albern silly
alle everyone; all
allein(e) alone; on one's own
alles everything; all
alles Gute all the best
alles Liebe love
als when; than; as
als Erstes first; first of all
als Nächstes next
also so
alt old
Wie alt bist du? How old are you?
Alter age
am on
am Abend in the evening
am Morgen in the morning
am Nachmittag in the afternoon
am nächsten Tag the next day
am Wochenende at the weekend
an at; on; to
Ananas pineapple
anbieten to offer
anbrüllen to roar
andauern to last
andere(r, s) other; different
ein(e) andere(r, s) another
anders different
Änderung change
Anfang beginning
anfangen to begin *(irr)*; to start
anfangs at first
anfassen to touch
angreifen to attack
(vor etw/jdm) Angst haben to be scared (of sth/sb); to be afraid (of sth/sb)
ankommen to arrive
Anruf (phone) call
anrufen to call; to phone
anschauen to look (at); to have a look (at sth); to watch
anschließend after that; afterwards
ansehen to look (at)
anstatt instead (of)
antworten to answer
anziehen to put on
sich anziehen to get dressed
anzünden to set off; to light *(irr)*
Apfel apple
Aprikose apricot
April April
Arbeit work
arbeiten to work
arm poor
Art kind; shape
Arzt doctor
Ärztin doctor
atemberaubend spectacular
auch too; also
auf at; on
auf der ganzen Welt all over the world
auf der linken Seite on the/your left
auf der rechten Seite on the/your right
auf einmal suddenly
auf Englisch in English
auf Französisch in French
auf Wiedersehen goodbye
aufbewahren to keep *(irr)*
aufbleiben to stay up
aufgeregt excited; nervous
aufhängen to hang *(irr)*
aufhören to finish; to stop
aufladen to charge
jdn aufmuntern to cheer sb up
aufräumen to tidy
aufregend exciting
aufschreiben to write down
aufstehen to get up
aufwachen to wake up
aufwecken to wake up
Auge eye
im Augenblick right now
August August
aus out of; from; made of
(eine Kerze) ausblasen to blow out (a candle)
Ausblick view
Ausflug trip
ausgeben *(Geld)* to spend *(irr)*
ausgehen to go out
aushalten to stand *(irr)*
im Ausland abroad
ausleihen to hire
ausprobieren to try *(irr)*
ausräumen to empty
ausreichend enough
aussehen to look
Aussicht view
ausstehen to stand *(irr)*
nicht ausstehen können to hate
aussteigen to get off
Australien Australia
Ausweis identity card
Auto car
Autogramm autograph

B

Bäcker/in baker
Bad(ezimmer) bathroom
Bahnhof railway station
Bahnsteig platform
bald soon
Balkendiagramm bar chart
Balkon balcony
Ballon balloon
Banane banana
Bauchschmerzen stomach ache
bauen to build *(irr)*
Bauernhof farm
Baum tree
beantworten to answer
bedeckt cloudy
bedeuten to mean *(irr)*
Bedienung waiter/waitress
sich beeilen to hurry up
beenden to finish; to stop
beginnen to begin *(irr)*; to start
behalten to keep *(irr)*
bei at
beibringen to teach *(irr)*
beide(s) both
Bein leg
beinahe nearly
zum Beispiel for example
beißen to bite *(irr)*
beitreten to join
bekämpfen to fight *(irr)*
bekommen to get *(irr)*
belebt busy
bellen to bark
bemerken to notice
Bemerkung comment
benutzen to use
beobachten to watch
bereit ready
Bericht report
berühmt famous
berühren to touch
beschäftigt busy
jdn beschimpfen to call sb names
beschließen to decide
beschützen to protect
sich beschweren to complain
besiegen to beat *(irr)*
besondere(r, s) special
besonders especially
besorgt worried
besser better
beste(r, s) best
Besuch visit
besuchen to visit
Bett bed
beunruhigt worried
bevor before
bevorzugen to prefer
Bewegung movement
sich bewegen to move
bewölkt cloudy
bezahlen to pay *(irr)*
Bibliothek library
bieten to offer
Bild picture
Bilder machen to take photos
Bildschirm screen
billig cheap
bin am
Biologie biology *(no pl)*
bis to; until; till
bis (acht Uhr) by (eight o'clock)
bis bald/dann bye for now; see you
ein bisschen a bit; a little
bist are
bitte please
Bitte schön! Here you are.
bitten to ask
Blatt leaf *(pl* leaves*)*
blau blue
bleiben to stay
Bleistift pencil
Bleistiftspitzer pencil sharpener
Blick view
blöd stupid
Blume flower
Bluse shirt
Boden floor
Bohne bean
Boot boat
braten to fry
brauchen to need
braun brown
brechen to break *(irr)*
Brettspiel board game
Briefumschlag envelope
bringen to bring *(irr)*; to take *(irr)*
Brot bread *(no pl)*
Brötchen bread roll
Brücke bridge
Bruder brother
brüllen to roar
Buch book
Bücherei library
Bücherregal bookcase
buchstabieren to spell *(irr)*
Bucht bay
Bühne stage
Burg castle
Büro office
bürsten to brush

C

Campingplatz campsite
Center centre
chaotisch sein to be a mess
chatten to chat
Chinesisch; chinesisch Chinese
Chips crisps *(only pl) (BE)*
Cousin/e cousin

D

da there
da ist there is
da sind there are
damit so that

danach after that; afterwards; then
danke thank you; thanks
danken to thank
vielen Dank thanks a lot; thanks so much
dann next; then
das the; this; that
dass that
dasselbe the same
Datum date
dauern to last
definitiv definitely
dein(e) your
Dekoration decoration
dekorieren to decorate
Delfin dolphin
denken to think *(irr)*; to guess
der the; that
derselbe the same
deshalb so; that's why
Deutsch; deutsch German
Deutschland Germany
Dezember December
Dialog dialogue
dich you
die the; that
Dienstag Tuesday
diese these *(pl of* this*)*; those *(pl of* that*)*
diese(r, s) this
dieselbe the same
Ding thing
Dinosaurier dinosaur
dir you
Direktor/in director
Donnerstag Thursday
Dorf village
dort there; over there
dort drüben over there
draußen outdoor(s); outside
dreckig dirty
sich drehen to turn
drinnen inside
dritte(r, s) third
du you
dumm stupid; silly
dunkel dark
Dunkelheit dark *(no pl)*
dünn thin; slim
dürfen may
etw tun dürfen to be allowed to do sth
nicht dürfen must not

E

echt real
Ehefrau wife *(pl* wives*)*
Ei egg
eigene(r, s) own
ein paar a few
ein(e) a/an; one
eines Tages one day
eindeutig clear; definitely
einfach easy; just
einige a few; some
einkaufen (gehen) to do the shopping; to go shopping
Einkaufszentrum shopping centre
einladen to invite
Einladung invitation
einsam lonely
Eiscreme ice cream
Eisenbahn train
Elefant elephant
Eltern parents *(only pl)*
Ende end
enden to end
endlich finally
Englisch; englisch English
auf Englisch in English
Enkelsohn grandson
Enkeltochter granddaughter
(sich) entscheiden to decide
Entschuldigen Sie bitte! Excuse me!
Entschuldigung! Excuse me!; Sorry!
sich entspannen to relax
entspannt relaxed
enttäuscht frustrated
entwerfen to design
entzündet sore
er he
Erde world
Erdkunde geography
erforschen to explore; to study
erhalten to get *(irr)*
Erkältung cold
eine Erkältung haben to have a cold
erklären to explain
Erlebnis adventure
erraten to guess
erreichen to reach
erschießen to shoot *(irr)*
erste(r, s) first
erstens first of all
ertragen to stand *(irr)*
erwachsen sein/werden to grow up
erzählen to tell *(irr)*
Erzählung story
es it
Essen food *(no pl)*; meal
essen to eat *(irr)*; to have *(irr)*
Essenszeit mealtime
Essig vinegar *(no pl)*
Esslöffel tablespoon
etwas some; something
euch you
euer; eure your
Europa Europe
ewig forever
exotisch exotic

F

Fach subject
Fackel torch
fahren to go *(irr)*; to drive *(irr)*; to ride *(irr)*
Fahrer/in driver
Fahrrad bike
Fahrrad fahren to ride a bike; to cycle
Fahrt trip; ride
Fakt fact
fallen to fall *(irr)*
falls if
falsch wrong
Familie family
fangen to catch *(irr)*
fantastisch fantastic *(informal)*
Farbe colour
farbenfroh colourful
fast nearly
faul lazy
Februar February
Federmäppchen pencil case
fehlen to be missing
Feier celebration
feiern to celebrate
Fell fur
Fenster window
Ferien holiday
Ferienlager summer camp
Fernsehen TV (= television)
fernsehen to watch TV
Fernseher TV (= television)
fertig ready
Fest celebration; festival
fester Freund boyfriend
festhalten to hold *(irr)*
Festland land
Feuerwerk fireworks *(only pl)*
Fieber haben to have a temperature
Filzstift felt tip
finden to find *(irr)*
Fisch fish *(pl - or -es)*
Fitnessstudio gym (= gymnasium)
Flasche bottle
Fleck spot
Fleisch meat *(no pl)*
fliegen to fly *(irr)*
Flughafen airport
Flugzeug plane
folgen to follow
Form shape
Foto picture; photo
Fotoapparat camera
Fotograf/in photographer
fotografieren to take photos
Frage question
fragen to ask
Fragen stellen to ask questions
sich fragen to wonder
Frankreich France
Französisch; französisch French
auf Französisch in French
Frau woman *(pl women)*
Frau *(Anrede)* Mrs
frech naughty
frei free
im Freien outdoor(s); outside
Freitag Friday
Freizeit free time
sich freuen auf to look forward to
Freund/in friend
freundlich friendly; kind
frisch fresh
Friseur/in hairdresser
froh glad
fröhlich happy
Frosch frog
Frucht fruit
früh early
Frühstück breakfast
frustriert frustrated
(sich) fühlen to feel *(irr)*
fünfte(r, s) fifth
für for
Furcht erregend scary
furchtbar terrible
Fuß foot *(pl feet)*
Fußball football
Futter food *(no pl)*
füttern to feed *(irr)*

G

Gabel fork
ganz whole; completely
Garten garden
Gärtner/in gardener
Gast guest
Gebäude building
geben to give *(irr)*
gebrochen broken
Geburtstag birthday
Gedicht poem
gefährlich dangerous
Gefühl feeling
gegen against
Gegenstand thing
gehen to go *(irr)*; to walk
gehören zu to go with
jdm/zu etw gehören to belong to sb/sth
Geist ghost
gelangen to get *(irr)*
gelangweilt bored
gelassen relaxed
gelb yellow
Geld money *(no pl)*
Geldstück coin
gemacht aus made of
gemeinsam together
Gemüse vegetable
genau exactly
genauso ... wie ... as ... as
genießen to enjoy
genug enough
geöffnet open
gerade right now
geradeaus straight (on)
Geräusch sound; noise

Gern geschehen. You're welcome.
gesamt whole
Geschäft shop
geschehen to happen
gescheit clever
Geschenk present
Geschichte history; story
geschieden divorced
Geschirrspülmaschine dishwasher
geschlossen shut
Gesicht face
Gespenst ghost
Gespräch dialogue
gestern yesterday
gesund healthy
gesund werden to get well
Getränk drink
Gewinn prize
gewinnen to win *(irr)*
Gewinner/in winner
gewöhnlich usually
Girlande garland
Gitarre guitar
Glas glass
glauben to think *(irr)*
glauben (an) to believe (in)
gleich just
gleich zurück sein to be right back
Glück haben to be lucky
glücklich happy; glad; lucky
Glücks- lucky
Gott god
Grad degree
Gras grass *(no pl)*
gratis free
grau grey
Grill barbecue
grillen to grill; to have a barbecue
Grillparty barbecue
eine Grillparty feiern to have a barbecue
groß big; large; tall
größte(r, s) biggest
großartig great
Großbritannien Britain
Großeltern grandparents *(only pl)*
Großmutter grandmother
Großstadt city
Großvater grandfather
grün green
Grund reason
das ist der Grund, warum that's why
Grundschule primary school
Gruppe group
viele Grüße best wishes
gurgeln to gargle
Gurke cucumber
gut good; well
gut aussehend good-looking
gut in etw sein to be good at sth
Gutschein voucher

H

Haar(e) hair *(no pl)*
haben to have got; to have *(irr)*
Hafen harbour
Hähnchen chicken
halb (neun) half past (eight)
Halbbruder half brother
(eine) halbe Stunde half an hour
Hälfte half *(pl halves)*
Halle hall
hallo hello; hi
Hals throat; neck
Halsschmerzen sore throat
halten to hold *(irr)*; to keep *(irr)*
Handy (mobile) phone
hängen to hang *(irr)*
hart hard
hassen to hate
hässlich ugly
häufig often
Haus house
nach Hause home
Hausaufgaben homework *(no pl)*
Haustier pet
heben to lift
Heft exercise book
Heiligabend Christmas Eve
heiraten to get married; to marry
heiß hot
heißen to be called
Held/in hero *(pl -es)*
helfen to help
Hemd shirt
heraus out of; out
herausfinden to find out
hereinkommen to come in
Herr *(Anrede)* Mr
herum around
hervorragend brilliant
Herz heart
herzliche Grüße love
heute today
heute Nachmittag this afternoon
hier(her) here
Hier, bitte! Here you are.
Hi-Fi-Anlage sound system
Hilfe help
Himmel sky
hinab down
hinauf up
hinausbringen to take out
hinausgehen to go out
hinein inside
sich hinsetzen to sit down
hinter behind
hinunter down
hoch high; tall
hochheben to lift
hoffen to hope
höflich polite
hören to hear *(irr)*; to listen (to)
Horoskop horoscope
Hose trousers *(only pl)*
hübsch pretty; lovely
Hund dog

den Hund ausführen to walk the dog
Hundert hundred
hungrig hungry
Hut hat

I

ich I
Idee idea
ignorieren to ignore
ihm him
ihn him
Ihnen you
ihnen them
ihr you
Ihr(e) your
ihr(e, n) her; its; their
immer always
immer noch still
in in; into; at; on; to
indianisch Indian
Indien India
indisch Indian
Informatik ICT (= information and communication technology)
Information information *(no pl)*
innen inside
Insekt insect
Insel island
interessant interesting
interessiert (an etw) interested (in sth)
etw ins Internet stellen to post sth
irgend(et)was anything
irgendein(e) any
irgendwelche any
ist is

J

ja yes
Jacke jacket; blazer
jagen to chase
Jahr year
Januar January
jede(r) everyone
jede(r, s) every; each
jemals ever
jemand someone
jene those *(pl of* that*)*
jetzt now; right now
Joghurt yoghurt *(no pl)*
jubeln to cheer
Jude Jew
Jüdin Jew
jüdisch Jewish
Jugendzentrum youth club
Juli July
jung young
Junge boy
Juni June

K

Kaffee coffee
Käfig cage
Kalender calendar
kalt cold
Kälte cold
Kamera camera
Kamin chimney
kämpfen to fight *(irr)*
Känguru kangaroo
Kappe cap
kaputt broken
Karotte carrot
Karte card; map
Kartoffel potato *(pl -es)*
Käse cheese *(no pl)*
Katze cat
kauen to chew
kaufen to buy *(irr)*
Kaufhaus department store
Kaugummi chewing gum *(no pl)*
kein(e) no; not any
keiner no one
Kellner/in waiter/waitress
kennen to know *(irr)*
kennenlernen to meet *(irr)*
Kerze candle
Kilometer kilometre
Kind kid; child *(pl* children*)*
Kino cinema
Kirche church
Kirsche cherry
klagen to complain
Klang sound
klar clear
klären to solve
Klasse class
klasse brilliant
Klassenarbeit test
Klassenkamerad/in classmate
Klassenzimmer classroom
klauen to steal *(irr)*
Kleid dress
Kleiderschrank wardrobe
Kleidung clothes *(only pl)*
klein small; little
klingeln to ring *(irr)*
klingen to sound
Klippe cliff
Klub club
klug clever
Koch chef
kochen to cook; to do the cooking
Köchin chef
Kollege/Kollegin colleague
komisch funny; strange
kommen to come *(irr)*
Kommentar comment
komplett full
König king
Königin queen
können can; may
könnte(st, n, t) could
sich konzentrieren to concentrate
Konzert concert

Kopf head
Kopf hoch! Cheer up!
Kopfschmerzen headache
Kopfweh headache
Korb basket
Korn seed
Körper body
korrekt correct
köstlich delicious
Kostüm costume
Krach noise
krank ill
Krankenpfleger nurse
Krankenschwester nurse
Krawatte tie
Kreis circle
kreischen to scream
Krieg war
Krone crown
Küche kitchen
Kuchen cake
Kuh cow
Kühlschrank fridge *(informal)*
sich kümmern um to take care of
Kunst art
Kunststoff plastic
Kürbis pumpkin
Kurs course
kurz short
Kurznachricht text message
eine Kurznachricht schicken to text
Küste coast

L

lächeln to smile
lachen to laugh
laden to charge
Laden shop
Lagerfeuer campfire
Lampe lamp
Land country
Landkarte map
Landschildkröte tortoise
lang long
(eine Woche) lang for (one week)
langsam slow
langweilig boring
Lärm noise
lassen to let *(irr)*; to leave *(irr)*
lass(t) uns let's (= let us)
lästig annoying
laufen to walk; to run *(irr)*
laut loud
läuten to ring *(irr)*
Lautsprecher loudspeaker
Leben life *(pl* lives*)*
leben to live
lecker delicious; yummy *(informal)*
leer empty; dead
leeren to empty
legen to put *(irr)*; to place
Lehrer/in teacher
leicht easy
Das tut mir leid. I'm sorry.
leihen to hire
Leinwand screen
leise quiet
Leiter/in director
lernen to learn *(irr)*; to study
lesen to read *(irr)*
letzte(r, s) last
leuchten to shine *(irr)*
Leuchtturm lighthouse
Leute people *(no pl)*
Licht light
Liebe love
liebe(r) *(Anrede)* dear
lieben to love
lieber better
lieber mögen to prefer
ich würde lieber ... I'd rather ...
Liebling sweetheart
Lieblings- favourite
lila(farben) purple
Limonade lemonade
Lineal ruler
links left; on the/your left
nach links to the left
Liste list
Loch hole
locker relaxed
Löffel spoon
lösen to solve
Löwe lion
Luftballon balloon
Lust haben, etw zu tun to feel like doing sth
lustig funny; fun
sich über jdn lustig machen to make fun of sb

M

machen to make *(irr)*; to do *(irr)*
Mädchen girl
Magazin magazine
Magenschmerzen stomach ache
Mahlzeit meal
Mähne mane
Mai May
Mal time
Mama mum *(informal)*
manchmal sometimes
Mann man *(pl* men*)*
Mannschaftskamerad/in teammate
Mäppchen pencil case
Mappe folder
Markt market
Marmelade jam
März March
Mathe maths
Maurer/in bricklayer
Maus mouse *(pl* mice*)*
Mechaniker/in mechanic
Medaille medal
Medikamente medicine *(no pl)*
Medizin medicine *(no pl)*
Meer the sea *(no pl)*

Meerschweinchen guinea pig
mehr more; better
nicht mehr not anymore
noch mehr more
mein(e) my
meinen to mean *(irr)*; to think *(irr)*
Meinung opinion
das meiste (von) most (of)
Menge crowd
Menschen people *(no pl)*
Menschenmenge crowd
Messer knife *(pl* knives*)*
Metall metal
Meter metre
Mexikaner/in Mexican
mexikanisch Mexican
Mexiko Mexico
Mexiko-Stadt Mexico City
mich me
mieten to hire
Milch milk *(no pl)*
Milchshake milkshake
mindestens at least
Minirock miniskirt
mir me
mischen to mix
mit with
mit (dem Bus) by (bus)
Mitarbeiter/in colleague
mitbringen to bring *(irr)*
Mitglied member
mitmachen bei to join
mitnehmen to take *(irr)*
Mitschüler/in classmate
Mitspieler/in teammate
Mittagessen lunch; dinner
Mittagspause lunchtime
Mittagszeit lunchtime
mitten in/auf in the middle
in der Mitte in the middle
Mittwoch Wednesday
Mobbing bullying *(no pl)*
Mobiltelefon (mobile) phone
Mode fashion
mögen to like; to enjoy
möglicherweise maybe
Möhre carrot
Mohrrübe carrot
im Moment at the moment
Monat month
Montag Monday
Morgen morning
morgen tomorrow
morgens in the morning; a.m. (= ante meridiem) *(nur hinter Uhrzeit)*
müde tired
Müll rubbish *(no pl)*; litter *(no pl)*
Mülleimer bin
Mülltonne bin
Mund mouth
Münze coin
Musik music *(no pl)*
Musiker/in musician
Müsli muesli *(no pl)*
Muslim/in Muslim
muslimisch Muslim
müssen to have to; to need to; must
müsste should
mutig brave
Mutter mother
Mutti mum *(informal)*
Muttertag Mother's Day
Mütze cap; hat

N

nach after; to
nach *(bei Uhrzeitangaben)* past
nach draußen outside; out
nach Hause home
nach links to the left
nach oben up
nach rechts right
nach unten down
Nachbar/in neighbour
Nachbarschaft neighbourhood
Nachmittag afternoon
nachmittags in the afternoon; p.m. (= post meridiem) *(nur hinter Uhrzeit)*
heute Nachmittag this afternoon
Nachricht message
Nachrichten news *(no pl)*
nächste(r, s) next
am nächsten Tag the next day
Nacht night
nachts at night
Nacken neck
nah(e) near
in der Nähe near
Nase nose
natürlich of course
Naturwissenschaft science
neben next to
neben(an) next door
nehmen to take *(irr)*
nein no
nennen to call
nervig annoying
nervös nervous
nett nice; kind; lovely
neu new
Neuigkeit news *(no pl)*
Neujahr New Year
nicht not
nicht ausstehen können to hate
nicht dürfen must not
nicht können can't (= cannot)
nicht mehr not anymore
nicht werden won't
noch nicht not yet
nichts nothing
nie(mals) never
niedlich cute
niemand no one
Nilpferd hippo (= hippopotamus)
noch still
noch (ein)mal again
noch ein(e, r, s) another

noch immer still
noch mehr more
noch nicht not yet
Norden north
normalerweise normally; usually
Note mark
Notiz note
November November
Nudeln pasta *(no pl)*
Nummer number
nun (ja) well
nur just; only
Nuss nut

O

ob if
oben at the top; up
nach oben up
oberes Ende top
oberste top
Obst fruit
oder or
offen open
(sich) öffnen to open
oft often
ohne without
Ohr ear
Oktober October
Öl oil
Oma grandma *(informal)*
Onkel uncle
orange(farben) orange
Orangensaft orange juice
ordentlich tidy
Ort place
Ostern Easter

P

packen to pack
Packung packet
Palast palace
Papa dad *(informal)*
Papier paper *(no pl)*
Paprika pepper
eine Party feiern to have a party
passen zu to go with
passieren to happen
Pause break
peinlich berührt embarrassed
Pelz fur
perfekt perfect
Pfannkuchen pancake
Pfeffer pepper *(no pl)*
Pferd horse
Pflanze plant
Pfleger nurse
Pfote paw
Pfund *(brit. Währung)* pound
ein Picknick machen to have a picnic
piepsen to squeak
Pilz mushroom
Pinguin penguin
Plastik plastic
Plattform platform
Platz place
plötzlich suddenly
Polen Poland
Polizeibeamter/-beamtin police officer
Postkarte postcard
Preis price; prize
preiswert cheap
pro per
probieren to taste; to try *(irr)*
Programm programme
Prüfung test
Punkt point
Pute/r turkey
putzen to clean; to brush
Pyramide pyramid

Q

Quatsch nonsense
quieken to squeak

R

Rachen throat
Rad bike
Rad fahren to ride a bike; to cycle
Radiergummi rubber *(BE)*
Rasen grass *(no pl)*
raten to guess
Rätsel puzzle
Raumschiff spaceship
raus outside; out
Rechner calculator
Recht right
Recht haben to be right
rechts right; on the/your right
nach rechts right
reden to speak *(irr)*; to talk (to)
Regal shelf *(pl shelves)*
Regel rule
regieren to rule
regnen to rain
regnerisch rainy
reich rich
reichen to reach
reinigen to clean
Reis rice *(no pl)*
Reise trip
Reiseführer/in tour guide
reiten to ride *(irr)*
Religion(sunterricht) RE (= religious education)
rennen to run *(irr)*
reparieren to repair
Respekt respect *(no pl)*
retten to rescue; to save
Rezept recipe
richtig correct; right; true
Richtung direction
riechen (nach) to smell (of)
riesig huge
Rindfleisch beef
riskieren to risk
Roboter robot
Rock skirt

Rollstuhl wheelchair
rosa pink
rot red
Rücken back
Rückseite back
rudern to row
rufen to call; to shout
ruhig quiet
Rührei scrambled egg
Russland Russia

S

Saal hall
Sache thing
Sachen stuff *(informal)*
Saft juice
saftig juicy
sagen to say *(irr)*; to tell *(irr)*
Sahne cream *(no pl)*
Salat salad
Salatgurke cucumber
Salz salt (no pl)
Same(n) seed
sammeln to collect
Samstag Saturday
Sänger/in singer
sauber machen to clean
saugen to vacuum
Säulendiagramm bar chart
Schachtel packet
Schal scarf *(pl -s or scarves)*
scharf sharp
Schatz sweetheart
schätzen to guess
schauen to look (at); to have a look (at sth)
Schauspielerin actress
scheinen to shine *(irr)*
Scherbe shard
Schere (pair of) scissors *(only pl)*
schicken to send *(irr)*; to post sth
schießen to shoot *(irr)*
ein Tor schießen to score a goal
Schiff boat; ship
Schiffswrack shipwreck
Schildkröte tortoise
Schimpanse chimpanzee
schlafen to sleep *(irr)*
Schlafzimmer bedroom
schlagen to beat *(irr)*
Schlange snake
schlank slim
schlau clever
schlecht bad
schlechter worse
schlechteste(r, s) worst
schließen to close
Schließfach locker
schließlich finally
schlimm bad
schlimmer worse
schlimmste(r, s) worst
Schloss castle
zum Schluss finally
schmal slim
schmecken to taste
schmerzen to hurt *(irr)*
Schmetterling butterfly
Schmuck decoration
schmücken to decorate
schmutzig dirty
(sich) (etw) schnappen to grab sth
schneiden to cut *(irr)*
schnell fast; quick
Schnellhefter folder
Schnupfen cold
Schokolade chocolate *(no pl)*
schon already
schön beautiful; lovely; nice
Schornstein chimney
Schottland Scotland
schrecklich horrible; terrible
schreiben to write *(irr)*
Schreibtisch desk
schreien to cry *(irr)*; to shout; to scream
Schritt step
Schuh shoe
Schuld fault
Schule school
Schüler/in student
Schulfach subject
Schulklasse class
Schulnote mark
Schultasche schoolbag
schützen to protect
Schwanz tail
schwarz black
Schwein pig
schwer difficult; hard
Schwester sister; nurse
schwierig difficult
Schwierigkeiten bekommen to get in(to) trouble
Schwimmbad swimming pool
Schwimmen swimming
schwimmen to swim *(irr)*
Schwimmer/in swimmer
See lake
die See the sea *(no pl)*
sehen to see *(irr)*; to look
Sehenswürdigkeit sight
sehr very; a lot; much
seid are
Seife soap
Seifenoper soap (opera)
Seil rope
sein to be *(irr)*
sein(e, r) his; its
Seite side
auf der linken Seite on the/your left
auf der rechten Seite on the/your right
Sekretär/in secretary
Sekunde second
selbst even
Sendung programme
September September
Serie series *(only pl)*

setzen to put *(irr)*
sich setzen to sit down
sich über jdn lustig machen to make fun of sb
sicher sure; safe
Sicht view
Sie you
sie she; her; they; them
Sieger/in winner
silbern silver
Silvester New Year's Eve
sind are
singen to sing *(irr)*
sitzen to sit *(irr)*
Skateboard fahren to skate
Skateboardfahren skateboarding *(no pl)*
skaten to skate
SMS text message
eine SMS schicken to text
so ... wie ... as ... as
so bald wie möglich as soon as possible
sodass so that
sogar even
Sohn son
solche(r,s) such
sollte should
Sommer summer
Sommersprosse freckle
sonderbar strange
Sonne sun
Sonnenbrille sunglasses *(only pl)*
Sonnenuntergang sunset
sonnig sunny
Sonntag Sunday
sich Sorgen machen to worry
sorgfältig careful
Sorte kind
Soße sauce
Sozialarbeiter/in social worker
Spanien Spain
Spanisch; spanisch Spanish
spannend exciting
Spaß fun *(no pl)*
Spaß machen to be fun
spaßig fun
spät late
spät kommen to be late
später later; afterwards
spätestens bis (acht Uhr) by (eight o'clock)
spazieren gehen to go for a walk
spektakulär spectacular
speziell special
Spiel game; match
aufs Spiel setzen to risk
spielen to play
Spieler/in player
Spielplatz playground
Spielzeug toy
Spind locker
Spitze top
Sport(unterricht) PE (= physical education)
Sporthalle sports hall
Sportplatz sports ground
Sprache language
sprechen to speak *(irr)*; to talk (to)
springen to jump
Stadion stadium
Stadt city; town
stark strong; bad
(an)statt instead (of)
stattdessen instead (of)
stattfinden to take place
staubsaugen to vacuum
stehen to stand *(irr)*
stehlen to steal *(irr)*
stellen to put *(irr)*; to place
Stereoanlage sound system
Stern star
Stiefel boot
Stift pen
stinken to stink *(irr)*
Stockwerk floor
stolpern to trip
stolz proud
Strand beach
Straße street
Straßenschild sign
streiten to fight *(irr)*
Strohhalm straw
Strophe verse
studieren to study
Stufe step
Stuhl chair
Stunde lesson; hour
Stundenplan timetable
Sturm storm
stürmisch stormy
suchen (nach) to look for
Südafrika South Africa
Suppe soup
süß sweet; cute
Süßigkeit sweet

T

Tablette tablet
Tag day
am nächsten Tag the next day
den ganzen Tag all day
eines Tages one day
Tagebuch diary
Talentwettbewerb talent show
Tante aunt
Tanz dance
Tanzen dancing *(no pl)*
tanzen to dance
Tasche bag
Taschenlampe torch
Taschenrechner calculator
Taschentuch tissue
Tasse cup
Tatze paw
Tee tea
Teelöffel teaspoon
teilen to share
Telefon (tele)phone
Telefonanruf (phone) call

Teller plate
Tempel temple
Temperatur temperature
teuer expensive
Theater drama
Tier animal
Tierarzt/-ärztin vet (= veterinarian)
Tipp tip
Tisch table
den Tisch decken to lay the table
Tischtennis table tennis *(no pl)*
tja well
Tochter daughter
toll great; brilliant; amazing *(informal)*
Tomate tomato *(pl -es)*
Ton sound
Tor goal
ein Tor schießen to score a goal
Torfrau/Tormann goalkeeper
tot dead
Tracht costume
traditionell traditional
träge lazy
tragen *(Kleidung)* to wear *(irr)*
Traum dream
traurig sad
(sich) treffen to meet *(irr)*
trennen to separate
trinken to drink *(irr)*
Trinkhalm straw
trocken dry
Truthahn/Truthenne turkey
tschüss bye *(informal)*
tun to do *(irr)*
etw tun dürfen to be allowed to do sth
etw tun werden to be going to do sth
etw tun wollen to want to do sth
Tür door
Türkei Turkey
Türkisch; türkisch Turkish
Turm tower
Turnen gymnastics *(only pl)*
Turnhalle gym (= gymnasium)
Turnschuh trainer *(BE)*

U

üben to practise
über about; across; over
über Nacht bleiben to sleep over
übereinstimmen to agree
Überlebende/r survivor
übernachten to sleep over
Übernachtungsparty sleepover
überqueren to cross
überrascht surprised
Überraschung surprise
übrigens by the way
Uhr clock
(acht) Uhr (eight) o'clock
Wie viel Uhr ist es? What time is it?
Uhrzeit time
um at
umher around
umsonst free
und and
unerschrocken brave
ungefähr about
ungepflegt untidy
ungezogen naughty
unglaublich amazing *(informal)*; incredible
unglücklich unhappy
unheimlich scary
unordentlich untidy
uns us
unser(e) our
unsicher unsure
Unsinn nonsense
unten at the bottom (of); down
nach unten down
unter under
sich unterhalten (mit) to talk (to); to chat
unterrichten to teach *(irr)*
Unterschied difference
unterschiedlich different
Urlaub holiday

V

Vater father
Vati dad *(informal)*
Veränderung change
verärgert angry
verbessern to improve
verbringen *(Zeit)* to spend *(irr)*
verdienen to earn
Verein club
Vereinigtes Königreich UK (= United Kingdom)
verfolgen to chase
vergessen to forget *(irr)*
verkaufen to sell *(irr)*
Verkäufer/in shop assistant; seller
Verkehrsschild sign
verlassen to leave *(irr)*
verlegen embarrassed
vermischen to mix
vermissen to miss
vermuten to guess
verpassen to miss
verrückt crazy
verschieden different
sich verspäten to be late
verständlich clear
verstehen to understand *(irr)*
versuchen to try *(irr)*
vertrauen to trust
Verwandte/r relative
Verzeihung! sorry
Videospielentwickler/in video game designer
viel lots of; much
viele many; a lot (of)

viele Grüße best wishes
vielen Dank thanks a lot; thanks so much
vielleicht perhaps; maybe
vierte(r, s) fourth
Viertel neighbourhood
Viertel (vor/nach) quarter (to/past)
violett purple
voll full
völlig completely
von from; of
vor before; in front of
vor *(bei Uhrzeitangaben)* to
vor (drei Jahren) (three years) ago
vorbei an past
(sich) vorbereiten to prepare
vormittags in the morning; a.m. (= ante meridiem) *(nur hinter Uhrzeit)*
vorsichtig careful
vorüber an past
vorziehen to prefer

W

wach bleiben to stay up
Wache guard
Waffe weapon
wahr true
während during
wahrscheinlich probably
Wand wall
wann when
Warnung warning
warten to wait
Wärter/in keeper
warum why
was what
was für ein(e) ... what a ...
was ist what's (= what is)
Was ist mit ...? What about ...? *(informal)*
Was kostet/kosten ...? How much is/are ... ?
(sich) waschen to wash
Wasser water *(no pl)*
Wechselgeld change
Wecker alarm clock
Weg way
weg away; gone
Wegbeschreibung directions *(only pl)*
wehtun to hurt *(irr)*
Weihnachten Christmas
erster Weihnachtsfeiertag Christmas Day
Weihnachtsmann Father Christmas
weil because
Weile while *(no pl)*
weinen to cry *(irr)*
weiß white
Welle wave
Wellensittich budgie (= budgerigar)
Welt world
auf der ganzen Welt all over the world
wenige few
wenigstens at least
wenn when; if
wer who
werden to get *(irr)*; to become *(irr)*; will
etw tun werden to be going to do sth
werfen to throw *(irr)*
Werkzeug tool
Westen west
Wetter weather
wichtig important
wie how; like
Wie alt bist du? How old are you?
Wie bitte? sorry
Wie geht es dir/Ihnen/euch? How are you?
Wie geht's? How are things?
Wie heißt du? What's your name?
Wie ist ...? What's ... like?
Wie viel Uhr ist es? What time is it?
wieder again
auf Wiedersehen goodbye
Wiese grass *(no pl)*
willkommen (in) welcome (to)
windig windy
wir we
wirklich real; really
wissen to know (irr)
witzig funny; fun
Wo kommst du her? Where are you from?
wo(hin) where
Woche week
Wochenende weekend
am Wochenende at the weekend
wohnen to live; to stay (with sb)
Wohnung flat; apartment
Wohnzimmer living room
Wolke cloud
Wolkenkratzer skyscraper
etw tun wollen to want to do sth
Wort word
Wörterbuch dictionary
wund sore
wunderbar fantastic *(informal)*; lovely; wonderful
sich etw wünschen to make a wish
würde(st, n, t) would
Wurst sausage
Würstchen sausage
wütend angry

Z

Zahl number
zahlen to pay *(irr)*
Zahn tooth *(pl* teeth*)*
Zahnbürste toothbrush
Zahnschmerzen toothache
Zeichen sign
zeichnen to draw *(irr)*
zeigen to show *(irr)*
Zeit time
Zeit haben to be free
zeitig early
Zeitschrift magazine
Zeltplatz campsite
Zentrum centre
zerbrechen to break *(irr)*
zerbrochen broken
Zeug stuff *(informal)*
Zeugnis report
ziehen to pull
Ziel aim
Ziffer number
Zimmer room
Zitrone lemon
Zoologe/-in zoologist
Zoowärter/in zookeeper
zornig angry
zu to
zu (klein/groß/...) too (small/big/...)
zu Essen geben to feed *(irr)*
zu Hause at home; home
zu spät late
zu spät kommen to be late
zubereiten to prepare
Zucker sugar *(no pl)*
zuerst at first; first
zufrieden happy
Zug train
zuhören to listen (to)
Zukunft future
zum Beispiel for example
zum Schluss finally
zumachen to close
zünden to set off
zurück back
zusammen together
Zuschauermenge crowd
zuschicken to send *(irr)*
zustimmen to agree
zweite(r, s) second
Zwiebel onion
zwischen between

Names

Girls / Women

Abigail ['æbɪgeɪəl]
Alia ['æli,ə]
Alisha [ə'lɪʃə]
Amy ['eɪmi]
Annie ['æni]
Ellie ['eli]
Emily ['eməli]
Emma ['emə]
Grace [greɪs]
Hannah ['hænə]
Helen ['helən]
Hila ['haɪlə]
Jasmine ['dʒæzmɪn]
Jessica ['dʒesɪkə]
Judy ['dʒu:di]
Karla ['kɑ:lə]
Kate [keɪt]
Laura ['lɔ:rə]
Layla ['li:lə]
Lena ['li:nə]
Lynn [lɪn]
Maddie ['mædi]
Maria [mə'ri:ə]
Mary ['meəri]
Megan ['megən]
Nasaar [nə'sɑ:]
Neela ['ni:lə]
Rebecca [ri'bekə]
Rosa ['rəʊzə]
Rosie ['rəʊzi]
Sarah ['seərə]
Sonja ['sɒnjə]
Trisha ['trɪʃə]
Vicky ['vɪki]
Zadie ['zeɪdi]
Zoe ['zəʊi]

Boys / Men

Alex ['ælɪks]
Andrew ['ændru:]
Ben [ben]
Brian ['braɪən]
Callum ['kæləm]
Carlos ['kɑ:lɒs]
Charlie ['tʃɑ:li]
Chris [krɪs]
David ['deɪvɪd]
Dele ['di:li:]
Eran ['erən]
Fergus ['fɜ:gəs]
George [dʒɔ:dʒ]
Gernot ['geərnət]
Harry ['hæri]
Jack [dʒæk]
Jason ['dʒeɪsən]
Jasper ['dʒæspə]
Joe [dʒəʊ]
Joel ['dʒəʊəl]
John [dʒɒn]
Josh [dʒɒʃ]
Justin ['dʒʌstɪn]
Kaan [kɑ:n]
Ken [ken]
Lewis ['lu:ɪs]
Liam ['li:əm]
Luke [lu:k]
Mark [mɑ:k]
Morris ['mɒrɪs]
Oliver ['ɒlɪvə]
Ollie ['ɒli]
Onur ['əʊnʊə]
Paddy ['pædi]
Patrick ['pætrɪk]
Pete [pi:t]
Pradeep [præ'di:p]
Rémy ['reɪmi]
Rick [rɪk]
Sam [sæm]
Samuel ['sæmjuəl]
Sandeep [sæn'di:p]
Selim ['selɪm]
Simon ['saɪmən]
Steven ['sti:vən]
Tim [tɪm]
Tom [tɒm]
Victor ['vɪktə]
Vito ['vi:təʊ]
Will [wɪl]
William ['wɪljəm]

Families

Ahmed ['ɑ:med]
Alli ['æli]
Bolt [bəʊlt]
Chopra ['tʃɒprə]
Clarke [klɑ:k]
Darling ['dɑ:lɪŋ]
Davis ['deɪvɪs]
Flores ['flɔ:rɪz]
Fox [fɒks]
Gómez ['gəʊmez]
Hancock ['hænkɒk]
McClement [mə'klemənt]
McGregor [mə'gregə]
Miller ['mɪlə]
Muir [mjʊə]
Perkins ['pɜ:kɪnz]
Thompson ['tɒmpsən]
Walton ['wɔ:ltən]
White [waɪt]

Other names

Ackley Bridge [ˌækli ˈbrɪdʒ]
Arsenal [ˈɑːsnl]
Auld Lang Syne [ˌɔːld ˌlæŋ ˈzaɪn]
Bagheera [bæɡˈɪərə]
Baloo [bəˈluː]
BBC (= British Broadcasting Corporation) [ˌbiː biː ˈsiː, ˌbrɪtɪʃ ˈbrɔːdkɑːstɪŋ ˌkɔːpəˌreɪʃn]
BBC1 [ˌbiː biː ˌsiː ˈwʌn]
BBC2 [ˌbiː biː ˌsiː ˈtuː]
Big Ben [ˌbɪɡ ˈben]
Blue Mosque [ˌbluː ˈmɒsk]
Blue Reef Newquay [ˌbluː ˌriːf ˈnjuːkiː]
Buck House [ˈbʌk haʊs]
Buck Palace [ˌbʌk ˈpæləs]
Buckingham Palace [ˌbʌkɪŋəm ˈpæləs]
the Camden Chronicle [ðə ˌkæmdən ˈkrɒnɪkl]
Camden Market [ˌkæmdən ˈmɑːkɪt]
Channel 4 [ˌtʃænl ˈfɔː]
Childline [ˈtʃaɪldlaɪn]
Covent Garden [ˌkɒvənt ˈɡɑːdn]
Eiffel Tower [ˌaɪfəl ˈtaʊə]
Elizabeth Tower [iˌlɪzəbəθ ˈtaʊə]
the Empire State Building [ðiˌˌempaɪə ˈsteɪt ˌbɪldɪŋ]
the Gherkin [ðə ˈɡɜːkɪn]
Grace Darling [ˌɡreɪs ˈdɑːlɪŋ]
Halloween [ˌhæləʊˈiːn]
Harrods [ˈhærədz]
Harry Potter [ˌhæri ˈpɒtə]
Havafax [ˈhævəfæks]
Haverstock School [ˈhævəstɒk skuːl]
Hogwarts [ˈhɒɡwɔːts]
James Bond [ˌdʒeɪmz ˈbɒnd]
Jane Goodall [ˌdʒeɪn ˈɡʊdɔːl]
Jewel House [ˈdʒuːəl ˌhaʊs]
King Arthur [kɪŋ‿ˈɑːθə]
King's Cross Railway Station [ˌkɪŋz ˌkrɒs ˈreɪlweɪ ˌsteɪʃn]
Lakshmi [ˈlʌkʃmi]
the London Eye [ðə ˌlʌndən‿ˈaɪ]
London Zoo [ˌlʌndən ˈzuː]
Longstone [ˈlɒŋstən]
Lost Gardens of Heligan [ˌlɒst ˌɡɑːdənz‿əv ˈhelɪˌɡən]
Madame Tussauds [məˌdɑːm təˈsɔːdz]
Mainhattan [maɪnˈhætən]
Mickey Mouse [ˌmɪki ˈmaʊs]
Midhurst Rother College [ˌmɪdhɜːst ˌrɒðə ˈkɒlɪdʒ]
the Palace of Westminster [ðə ˌpæləs‿əv ˈwestmɪntstə]
the Queen [ðə ˈkwiːn]
Queen Victoria [ˌkwiːn vɪkˈtɔːriə]
Rama [ˈrɑːmə]
Robin Hood [ˌrɒbɪn ˈhʊd]
the Royal Family [ðə ˌrɔɪəl ˈfæmli]
Royal National Lifeboat Institution [ˌrɔɪəl ˌnæʃnəl‿ˈlaɪfˌbəʊt‿ˌɪnstɪˌtjuːʃn]
Shamash [ʃæˈmæʃ]
Shard [ðə ˈʃɑːd]
Sir Barks-A-Lot [ˌsɜː ˈbɑːks‿ə ˌlɒt]
Snowdon Mountain Railway [ˌsnəʊdən ˌmaʊntɪn ˈreɪlweɪ]
SS Forfarshire [ˌes‿ˌes ˈfɔːfəʃə]
St Michael's Mount [sənt ˌmaɪkəlz ˈmaʊnt]
St Patrick's Day [sənt ˈpætrɪks deɪ]
Sultan Ahmed Mosque [ˌsʌltən‿ˌɑːmed ˈmɒsk]
Tintagel Castle [tɪnˌtædʒəl ˈkɑːsl]
Topkapi Palace [ˌtɒpkæpɪ ˈpæləs]
Tower Bridge [ˌtaʊə ˈbrɪdʒ]
Tower of London [ðə ˌtaʊər‿əv ˈlʌndən]
Westminster Abbey [ˌwestmɪnstər‿ˈæbi]
Wild Gang [ˈwaɪld ɡæŋ]

Geographical names

Africa [æfrɪkə]
Albert Street [ˈælbət striːt]
Asia [ˈeɪʒə]
the Atlantic (Ocean) [ðiˌətˌlæntɪk(‿ˈəʊʃn)]
Australia [ɒˈstreɪliə]
Avenue Road [ˌævəˌnjuː ˈrəʊd]
Bamburgh [ˈbæmbərə]
Berlin [ˌbɜːˈlɪn]
the Black Sea [ðə ˌblæk ˈsiː]
Bosporus [ˈbɒspərəs]
Bristol [ˈbrɪstl]
Britain [ˈbrɪtn]
Camden [ˈkæmdən]
Camden High Street [ˌkæmdən ˈhaɪ striːt]
Canada [ˈkænədə]
Cardiff [ˈkɑːdɪf]
Castle Road [ˌkɑːsl ˈrəʊd]

the Channel Islands [ðə ˈtʃænl‿ˌaɪləndz]
China [ˈtʃaɪnə]
Church Street [ˈtʃɜ:tʃ stri:t]
Clarence Way [ˌklærənts ˈweɪ]
Cornwall [ˈkɔrnwəl]
Edinburgh [ˈedɪnbərə]
England [ˈɪŋglənd]
Eton Road [ˈi:tən rəʊd]
Europe [ˈjʊərəp]
the Farne Islands [ðə ˈfɑ:n‿ˌaɪləndz]
Florida [ˈflɒrɪdə]
France [frɑ:nts]
Frankfurt [ˈfræŋkfɜ:t]
the Galapagos Islands [ðə gəˈlæpəgəs‿ˌaɪləndz]
Germany [ˈdʒɜ:məni]
Great Britain [ˌgreɪt ˈbrɪtn]
Greece [gri:s]
Hamburg [ˈhæmbɜ:g]
Hartland Road [ˌhɑ:tlənd ˈrəʊd]
Hawaii [həˈwaii]
High Street [ˈhaɪ stri:t]
Hyde Park [ˌhaɪd ˈpɑ:k]
India [ˈɪndiə]
Inverness Street Market [ˌɪnvəˌnes‿ˌstri:t ˈmɑ:kɪt]
Ireland [ˈaɪələnd]
the Isle of Man [ðiˌ‿aɪl‿əv ˈmæn]
Istanbul [ˌɪstænˈbʊl]
Japan [dʒəˈpæn]
Land's End [ˌlændz‿ˈend]
Leeds [li:dz]
Loch Ness [ˌlɒk ˈnes]
London [ˈlʌndən]
Marylebone Road [ˈmærələbən rəʊd]
Mevagissey [ˌmevəˈgɪsi]
Mexico [ˈmeksɪˌkəʊ]
Mexico City [ˌmeksɪkəʊ ˈsɪti]
Milton Keynes [ˌmɪltən ˈki:nz]
Mount Snowdon [ˌmaʊnt ˈsnəʊdən]
New York [nju: ˈjɔ:k]
Newquay [ˈnju:ki:]
North London [ˌnɔ:θ ˈlʌndən]
Northern Ireland [ˌnɔ:ðn‿ˈaɪələnd]
Nottinghamshire [ˈnɒtɪŋəmʃə]
Outer Circle [ˌaʊtə ˈsɜ:kl]
Oxford Street [ˈɒksfəd stri:t]
Paris [ˈpærɪs]
Park Avenue [ˌpɑ:k‿ˈævəˌnju:]
Parkway [ˈpɑ:kweɪ]
Penzance [penˈzænts]
Poland [ˈpəʊlənd]
Prince Albert Road [ˌprɪns‿ˌælbət ˈrəʊd]
Regent's Canal [ˌri:dʒənts kəˈnæl]
the Republic of Ireland [ðə rɪˌpʌblɪk‿əv‿ˈaɪələnd]
Riga [ˈri:gə]
Rome [rəʊm]
Russia [ˈrʌʃə]
Scotland [ˈskɒtlənd]
Serpentine [ˈsɜ:pəntaɪn]
South Africa [saʊθ‿ˈæfrɪkə]
South America [ˌsaʊθ‿əˈmerɪkə]
Spain [speɪn]
Station Lane [ˌsteɪʃn ˈleɪn]
the Thames [ðə ˈtemz]
The Avenue [ði‿ˈævəˌnju:]
Tintagel [tɪnˈtædʒəl]
Tokyo [ˈtəʊkiəʊ]
Trafalgar Square [trəˌfælgə ˈskweə]
Turkey [ˈtɜ:ki]
UK (= United Kingdom) [ˌju:ˈkeɪ, ju:ˌnaɪtɪd ˈkɪŋdəm]
the United Kingdom [ðə ju:ˌnaɪtɪd ˈkɪŋdəm]
USA (= United States of America) [ˌju:esˈeɪ, ju:ˌnaɪtɪd ˌsteɪts‿əv‿əˈmerɪkə]
Victoria Road [vɪkˌtɔ:riə ˈrəʊd]
Wales [weɪlz]
Western Europe [ˌwestən ˈjʊərəp]
Wood Lane [ˌwʊd ˈleɪn]

Numbers

Cardinal numbers

0	zero ['zɪərəʊ]
1	one [wʌn]
2	two [tu:]
3	three [θri:]
4	four [fɔ:]
5	five [faɪv]
6	six [sɪks]
7	seven ['sevn]
8	eight [eɪt]
9	nine [naɪn]
10	ten [ten]
11	eleven [ɪ'levn]
12	twelve [twelv]
13	thirteen [ˌθɜ:'ti:n]
14	fourteen [ˌfɔ:'ti:n]
15	fifteen [ˌfɪf'ti:n]
16	sixteen [ˌsɪks'ti:n]
17	seventeen [ˌsevn'ti:n]
18	eighteen [ˌeɪ'ti:n]
19	nineteen [ˌnaɪn'ti:n]
20	twenty ['twenti]
21	twenty-one [ˌtwenti'wʌn]
...	
30	thirty ['θɜ:ti]
40	forty ['fɔ:ti]
50	fifty ['fɪfti]
...	
90	ninety ['naɪnti]
100	one hundred ['wʌn ˌhʌndrəd]
...	
900	nine hundred ['naɪn ˌhʌndrəd]
1,000	one thousand ['wʌn ˌθauznd]

Ordinal numbers

1st	first [fɜ:st]
2nd	second ['sekənd]
3rd	third [θɜ:d]
4th	fourth [fɔ:θ]
5th	fifth [fɪfθ]
6th	sixth [sɪksθ]
7th	seventh ['sevnθ]
8th	eighth [eɪtθ]
9th	ninth [naɪnθ]
10th	tenth [tenθ]
11th	eleventh [ɪ'levnθ]
12th	twelfth [twelfθ]
13th	thirteenth [ˌθɜ:'ti:nθ]
14th	fourteenth [ˌfɔ:'ti:nθ]
15th	fifteenth [ˌfɪf'ti:nθ]
16th	sixteenth [ˌsɪks'ti:nθ]
...	
20th	twentieth ['twentiəθ]
21st	twenty-first [ˌtwenti'fɜ:st]
22nd	twenty-second [ˌtwenti'sekənd]
23rd	twenty-third [ˌtwenti'θɜ:d]
24th	twenty-fourth [ˌtwenti'fɔ:θ]
...	
30th	thirtieth ['θɜ:tiəθ]
31st	thirty-first [ˌθɜ:ti'fɜ:st]
...	
40th	fortieth ['fɔ:tiəθ]
50th	fiftieth ['fɪftiəθ]
60th	sixtieth ['sɪkstiəθ]
70th	seventieth ['sevntiəθ]
80th	eightieth ['eɪtiəθ]
90th	ninetieth ['naɪntiəθ]
100th	hundredth ['hʌndrədθ]

infinitive	simple past	past participle	German
be [bi:]	was/were [wɒz/wɜ:]	been [bi:n]	sein
beat [bi:t]	beat [bi:t]	beaten ['bi:tn]	schlagen; besiegen
become [bɪ'kʌm]	became [bɪ'keɪm]	become [bɪ'kʌm]	werden
begin [bɪ'gɪn]	began [bɪ'gæn]	begun [bɪ'gʌn]	anfangen; beginnen
bite [baɪt]	bit [bɪt]	bitten ['bɪtn]	beißen
blow [bləʊ]	blew [blu:]	blown [bləʊn]	blasen, wehen
break [breɪk]	broke [brəʊk]	broken ['brəʊkən]	(zer)brechen
bring [brɪŋ]	brought [brɔ:t]	brought [brɔ:t]	(mit)bringen
build [bɪld]	built [bɪlt]	built [bɪlt]	bauen
buy [baɪ]	bought [bɔ:t]	bought [bɔ:t]	kaufen
catch [kætʃ]	caught [kɔ:t]	caught [kɔ:t]	fangen
choose [tʃu:z]	chose [tʃəʊz]	chosen ['tʃəʊzn]	auswählen
come [kʌm]	came [keɪm]	come [kʌm]	kommen
cry [kraɪ]	cried [kraɪd]	cried [kraɪd]	schreien; weinen
cut [kʌt]	cut [kʌt]	cut [kʌt]	schneiden
do [du:]	did [dɪd]	done [dʌn]	machen, tun
draw [drɔ:]	drew [dru:]	drawn [drɔ:n]	zeichnen
drink [drɪŋk]	drank [dræŋk]	drunk [drʌŋk]	trinken
drive [draɪv]	drove [drəʊv]	driven ['drɪvn]	fahren
eat [i:t]	ate [eɪt]	eaten ['i:tn]	essen
fall [fɔ:l]	fell [fel]	fallen ['fɔ:lən]	fallen
feed [fi:d]	fed [fed]	fed [fed]	füttern, zu Essen geben
feel [fi:l]	felt [felt]	felt [felt]	(sich) fühlen
fight [faɪt]	fought [fɔ:t]	fought [fɔ:t]	(be)kämpfen; streiten
find [faɪnd]	found [faʊnd]	found [faʊnd]	finden
fit [fɪt]	fit/fitted [fɪt/'fɪtɪd]	fit/fitted [fɪt/'fɪtɪd]	passen (zu)
fly [flaɪ]	flew [flu:]	flown [fləʊn]	fliegen
forget [fə'get]	forgot [fə'gɒt]	forgotten [fə'gɒtn]	vergessen
get [get]	got [gɒt]	got/gotten [gɒt/'gɒtn]	erhalten, bekommen; gelangen; werden
give [gɪv]	gave [geɪv]	given ['gɪvn]	geben
go [gəʊ]	went [went]	gone [gɒn]	gehen; fahren
hang [hæŋ]	hung [hʌŋ]	hung [hʌŋ]	(auf)hängen
have [hæv]	had [hæd]	had [hæd]	haben; essen
hear [hɪə]	heard [hɜ:d]	heard [hɜ:d]	hören
hit [hɪt]	hit [hɪt]	hit [hɪt]	schlagen; treffen
hold [həʊld]	held [held]	held [held]	(fest)halten
keep [ki:p]	kept [kept]	kept [kept]	(be)halten; aufbewahren
know [nəʊ]	knew [nju:]	known [nəʊn]	wissen; kennen
lean [li:n]	leant/leaned [lent/li:nd]	leant/leaned [lent/li:nd]	(sich) lehnen
learn [lɜ:n]	learnt/learned [lɜ:nt/lɜ:nd]	learnt/learned [lɜ:nt/lɜ:nd]	lernen; erfahren
leave [li:v]	left [left]	left [left]	verlassen; lassen; gehen
let [let]	let [let]	let [let]	lassen

infinitive	simple past	past participle	German
lie [laɪ]	lay [leɪ]	lain [leɪn]	liegen
light [laɪt]	lit [lɪt]	lit [lɪt]	erhellen; anzünden
make [meɪk]	made [meɪd]	made [meɪd]	machen
mean [mi:n]	meant [ment]	meant [ment]	bedeuten; meinen
meet [mi:t]	met [met]	met [met]	(sich) treffen; kennenlernen
pay [peɪ]	paid [peɪd]	paid [peɪd]	(be)zahlen
put [pʊt]	put [pʊt]	put [pʊt]	setzen, legen, stellen
read [ri:d]	read [red]	read [red]	lesen
ride [raɪd]	rode [rəʊd]	ridden ['rɪdn]	fahren; reiten
ring [rɪŋ]	rang [ræŋ]	rung [rʌŋ]	klingeln; läuten
run [rʌn]	ran [ræn]	run [rʌn]	laufen, rennen
say [seɪ]	said [sed]	said [sed]	sagen
see [si:]	saw [sɔ:]	seen [si:n]	sehen
sell [sel]	sold [səʊld]	sold [səʊld]	verkaufen
send [send]	sent [sent]	sent [sent]	(zu)schicken
set [set]	set [set]	set [set]	(ein)stellen; (fest)setzen, vereinbaren
shine [ʃaɪn]	shone [ʃɒn]	shone [ʃɒn]	scheinen, leuchten
shoot [ʃu:t]	shot [ʃɒt]	shot [ʃɒt]	(er)schießen
show [ʃəʊ]	showed [ʃəʊd]	shown [ʃəʊn]	zeigen
sing [sɪŋ]	sang [sæŋ]	sung [sʌŋ]	singen
sit [sɪt]	sat [sæt]	sat [sæt]	sitzen
sleep [sli:p]	slept [slept]	slept [slept]	schlafen
speak [spi:k]	spoke [spəʊk]	spoken ['spəʊkən]	sprechen, reden
spell [spel]	spelt/spelled [spelt/speld]	spelt/spelled [spelt/speld]	buchstabieren
spend [spend]	spent [spent]	spent [spent]	ausgeben *(Geld)*; verbringen *(Zeit)*
split [splɪt]	split [splɪt]	split [splɪt]	spalten; teilen
stand [stænd]	stood [stʊd]	stood [stʊd]	stehen; ertragen, aushalten
steal [sti:l]	stole [stəʊl]	stolen ['stəʊlən]	stehlen, klauen
stink [stɪŋk]	stank/stunk [stæŋk/stʌŋk]	stunk [stʌŋk]	stinken
swim [swɪm]	swam [swæm]	swum [swʌm]	schwimmen
take [teɪk]	took [tʊk]	taken ['teɪkən]	(mit)nehmen; bringen
teach [ti:tʃ]	taught [tɔ:t]	taught [tɔ:t]	unterrichten; beibringen
tell [tel]	told [təʊld]	told [təʊld]	erzählen; sagen
think [θɪŋk]	thought [θɔ:t]	thought [θɔ:t]	denken, glauben, meinen
throw [θrəʊ]	threw [θru:]	thrown [θrəʊn]	werfen
try [traɪ]	tried [traɪd]	tried [traɪd]	(aus)probieren; versuchen
understand [ˌʌndə'stænd]	understood [ˌʌndə'stʊd]	understood [ˌʌndə'stʊd]	verstehen
wear [weə]	wore [wɔ:]	worn [wɔ:n]	tragen *(Kleidung)*
win [wɪn]	won [wʌn]	won [wʌn]	gewinnen
write [raɪt]	wrote [rəʊt]	written ['rɪtn]	schreiben

Bildquellen

|123RF.com, Hong Kong: Scanrail 181.3. |Alamy Stock Photo, Abingdon/Oxfordshire: Bollo, Carlo 176.1; Bowling, John 83.5; Corrigan, Matthew 202.1; Eversley, Thomas 41.3; geogphotos 100.2; Hall, Adrian 83.4; Hall, Ben 203.3; Hotson, Helen 176.3; imageBROKER 173.2; Justin Kase zsixz 44.4; Kruse, Joana 193.3; Londonstills.com 40.3; Morgan, Jeff 70.2; R Handley, Richard 77.1; Rouse, Neil 42.3; Sherratt, Adrian 147.4; The Photolibrary Wales 83.3; Vibrant Pictures 71.2; WENN Rights Ltd 65.3; ZUMA Press, Inc. 194.3. |Alamy Stock Photo (RMB), Abingdon/Oxfordshire: 172.1, 172.3; Alan Jeffery 66.3; Holmes Garden Photos 42.4; Image Source 148.2; imageBROKER/Cuveland, Justus de 52.2; Implementar Films 80.1, 92.2, 99.2, 141.1, 154.2; Kelly Redinger / Design Pics Inc. 148.1; Michael Cullen 172.8; Novelli, Alan 15.2, 28.2, 35.2; one-image photography 64.4; Steve Vidler 20.3; True Images 147.3; © KAKIMAGE 109.2. |Amortegui, Miguel, Saltdean - Rottingdean: 14.4, 20.4, 25.1, 34.2, 120.1, 139.6, 147.5, 169.2. |Barker, Ruth, Plauen: 143.1, 143.2, 143.3. |CartoonStock.com, Bath: Loren Fishman 70.1. |Colourbox.com, Odense: Dmitry Naumov 202.3; Rubino, Marco 66.2. |Connor, Laurence, Braunschweig: 46.1, 62.2, 62.3, 79.5, 91.2. |ddp images GmbH, Hamburg: Lennart Preiss 172.4. |dreamstime.com, Brentwood: Arne9001 19.1. |Fischer, Knoblauch & Co. Medienproduktionsgesellschaft mbH, München: 21.6. |fotolia.com, New York: (c) picture-optimize 135.2; bertys30 52.4; Fotolia XIII 203.4; Geijer, K. 52.3; graphixmania 45.1, 45.2, 45.3, 45.4, 45.5; Ivo Brezina 181.7; JiSign 181.9, 181.10, 181.11, 181.12; joningall1 42.2; Monkey Business 109.3; moonrun 14.2, 20.2, 44.1, 83.2, 109.1, 147.2, 173.1; OHRAUGE 41.2; photolas 145.2, 156.2, 163.3; Sinayko, Ivan 53.1; Smileus 106.5; TravelPhotography 65.2; vektorisiert 145.1, 156.3, 163.2. |Getty Images, München: FatCamera 107.1. |Getty Images (RF), München: Leland Bobbe 107.2. |Hammersen-Schiffner, Bettina, Braunschweig: 61.2. |Interfoto, München: 197.1; Travel Library / Grant Pritchard 107.4. |iStockphoto.com, Calgary: _ultraforma_ 44.3; arsenisspyros 106.1; AYImages 52.5; Bakai 9.2, 12.1, 13.2, 16.2, 22.1, 23.1, 23.3, 41.7, 43.2, 43.3, 44.7, 47.1, 52.7, 53.3, 75.2, 76.2, 79.2, 79.4, 80.2, 83.1, 86.2, 108.2, 108.4, 111.3, 112.1, 115.3, 117.1, 120.2, 139.5, 140.2, 145.3, 148.3, 151.1, 167.1, 170.2, 172.10, 176.4, 179.2, 181.1; burakkarademir 173.3; littleny 44.2; mammuth 40.1; MATJAZ SLANIC 172.5; monkeybusinessimages Titel, 21.2; santypan 106.4; svetikd 107.3; taikrixel 64.2; Zolotov, Vladislav 203.1. |Klahold, Doreen, Braunschweig: 116.1, 127.2, 127.3, 127.4, 127.5, 127.6, 127.7, 127.8, 128.2, 181.2, 181.4. |Koerner, Amy, Frankfurt am Main: 78.2, 97.2. |Krause, Charlotte, Wolfenbüttel: 148.4, 148.5, 148.6, 148.7, 148.8, 148.9, 148.10, 151.2. |mauritius images GmbH, Mittenwald: Alamy 203.2; Alamy / Schneider, Daniele / Photononstop 106.3; TopFoto 202.2. |McBriarty, Connor, Heere: 42.1. |Melching, Daniel, Braunschweig: 109.4. |Mohm, Julia, Braunschweig: 21.1, 21.3, 21.4, 21.5, 23.2, 165.2. |Orion Publishing Group, London: Horrid Henry's Birthday Party Text © Francesca Simon 1995 and illustrator Tony Ross 2009 204.1. |PantherMedia GmbH (panthermedia.net), München: kapu 229.1. |Picture-Alliance GmbH, Frankfurt/M.: dpa 111.1, 123.2; dpa / ABC Television Network 172.9; dpa/Karl-Josef Hildenbrand 106.2; picture alliance / GEORG HOCHMUTH / APA / picturedesk.com 77.8. |Quandt, Susanne, Bremen: 76.1. |Schmidt-Brücken, Frank, Weiterstadt: 44.5. |Shutterstock.com, New York: 202.4, 202.5; ChameleonsEye 41.4; fim.design 164.2; FrameStockFootages 77.7; Ian_Stewart 77.5; urbanbuzz 100.3; VGstockstudio 77.3. |Shutterstock.com (RM), New York: Warner Bros/Kobal 172.6. |stock.adobe.com, Dublin: 55.1; 3D generator 14.3; ALEXANDRE ZVEIGER 199.2; Aufort, Jérome 52.1; bayu harsa 40.4; Bonn, Andre 171.1; Cervo, Diego 77.4; denisgorelkin 139.1, 139.2, 139.3, 139.4; elxeneize 181.5; fedorovekb 172.3; fotolupa 64.3; giemmephoto 41.1; Hotson, Helen 193.2; irisphoto1 176.2; JackF 77.6; JM Fotografie 181.8; Kadic, Bjanka 194.2; Kadmy 77.2; Kaulitzki, Sebastian 206.1; Maridav 40.2; Moravcik, Jaroslav 41.5; motortion 172.7; my pen 9.1, 13.1, 14.1, 15.1, 16.1, 20.1, 24.1, 41.6, 43.1, 44.6, 45.6, 48.1, 50.2, 53.2, 75.1, 77.11, 78.1, 79.1, 79.3, 86.1, 108.1, 108.3, 111.2, 113.1, 115.1, 115.2, 116.2, 119.1, 119.2, 140.1, 140.3, 142.1, 142.2, 144.1, 147.1, 149.1, 150.1, 169.1, 170.1, 174.1, 179.1; romaset 77.9; Tiplyashina, Evgenia 199.1; van Wijk, Fred 57.2; viyadafotolia 207.1, 207.2, 207.3, 207.4; WavebreakMediaMicro 77.10; ymoiseeva 57.3, 57.4; YUN_1 52.6. |Thinkstock, Sandyford/Dublin: QQ7 181.6. |vario images, Bonn: 130.2. |Wefringhaus, Klaus, Braunschweig: 89.2, 183.2. |ZSL London Zoo, London: 71.1. |Zwick, Joachim, Gießen: 1.1, 50.1.

Wir arbeiten sehr sorgfältig daran, für alle verwendeten Abbildungen die Rechteinhaberinnen und Rechteinhaber zu ermitteln. Sollte uns dies im Einzelfall nicht vollständig gelungen sein, werden berechtigte Ansprüche selbstverständlich im Rahmen der üblichen Vereinbarungen abgegolten.

Textquellen

202–203: „Horrid Henry's Birthday Party" © Francesca Simon 1995, Orion Children's Books, an imprint of the Orion Publishing Group London.